PELICAN BOOKS
A 657

KU-780-226

TYNAN ON THEATRE

Kenneth Tynan, who became Literary Manager of
the National Theatre in 1963, was born in 1927 and
educated at King Edward's School, Birmingham,
and Magdalen College, Oxford. He became dramatic
critic for the *Spectator* in 1950 and went in the same
capacity to the *Evening Standard* (1952–3) and the
Daily Sketch (1953–4). In 1954 he joined the
Observer, where he remained as Drama Critic until
1963. He was in New York for two theatre seasons
as the *New Yorker*'s highly controversial drama
critic in 1958–60.

He has been script editor for Ealing Films and
Editor of the TV programme *Tempo*. He is a
member of the Drama Panel of the British Council.
His publications are: *He that Plays the King* (1950);
Persona Grata (1953); *Alec Guinness* (1954); *Bull
Fever* (1955); and *Curtains* (1961), the original
version of this book.

Kenneth Tynan is married to the novelist Elaine
Dundy, and they have one daughter.

Kenneth Tynan

TYNAN
ON THEATRE

Penguin Books

Penguin Books Ltd, Harmondsworth, Middlesex

AUSTRALIA: Penguin Books Pty Ltd, 763 Whitehorse Road,
Mitcham, Victoria

Curtains first published by Longmans, Green 1961
This selection published in Pelican Books 1964

Copyright © Kenneth Tynan, 1961, 1964

Made and printed in Great Britain
by Richard Clay and Company, Ltd, Bungay, Suffolk
Set in Monotype Bembo

Contents

Acknowledgements

For permission to reprint most of what follows the author is
grateful to the editors of twelve publications, six of them
English – *The Observer, Evening Standard, Spectator, Encounter,
Sight and Sound*, and *Band Wagon* – and six American – *The New
Yorker, Holiday, Harper's Bazaar, Harper's Magazine, Mademoiselle*,
and *The Atlantic*.

Selections beginning on pp. 82, 160, 173, 180, and 216,
copyright © 1959 by the New Yorker Magazine, Inc;
on p. 102, copyright © 1951 by The Hearst Corporation;
on p. 288, copyright © 1956 by The Curtis Publishing Company;
on p. 54, copyright © 1958 by The Curtis Publishing Company;
on p. 152, copyright © 1956 by Street & Smith Publications, Inc.;
and on p. 263, copyright © 1956 by Harper & Brothers.

General Preface to the Pelican Edition

•

Since the winter of 1948, when I came floating down from Oxford, I have earned most of my living by writing about the theatre. Long before I became an undergraduate I enjoyed setting down my impressions of plays in performance; it seemed to me unfair that an art so potent should also be so transient, and I was deeply seduced by the challenge of perpetuating it in print. Both at school and at the university I reviewed plays; whenever it was possible, I acted in them and directed them as well. In the autumn of 1950 I brought out a book on the theatre. Its style was ornate, and many of its opinions were outrageous, but it launched me as a drama critic, in which capacity I have since worked for the *Spectator*, the *Evening Standard*, the *Daily Sketch*, *the Observer*, and – from 1958 to 1960 – the *New Yorker*. This volume is an anthology of theatre pieces I contributed during the 1950s to these and other newspapers and magazines on both sides of the Atlantic. I have also included a few studies of film people, and a handful of essays that, for one reason or another, never got into print.

To be a critic on nationally distributed newsprint is very different from being a critic who writes only for publication in learned magazines or between hard covers. People in the latter group often regard me as an opinionated imposter, a fairground barker disguised in the robes of prophecy; while to many of my journalistic colleagues I seem a pedantic intellectual. Caught in this crossfire, I sometimes sway, but try not to topple. My chief problem is to walk the hazardous tight-rope of my prose style, which is that of a provincial writer who fell out of love with the mandarin class too late to forswear his early love of mandarin prose. The result is a bizarrely quilted amalgam in which patches of exhortation and colloquial simplicity are joined together by embroidery remembered from Max Beerbohm. I wish it were more of a piece, but it is all I have – a refugee from Birmingham, an adopted son of Oxford, and a permanent stranger in London.

It is not easy to produce a homogeneous tone from a background of such rootless disunity; and if I manage to be both elegant and eloquent for more than a sentence at a time, I count myself extremely lucky. Only when I have finished a piece do I sit back and, rereading it, allow myself to meditate on those general topics that are always being proposed for lectures – 'The Critic's Function' and 'The Nature of Critical Responsibility'. The main task is over; and I can indulge in speculation. Nothing in the arts is harder than to write a first-rate play, and, because I believe this, I am a critic. It is infinitely simpler (though still hard) to write a first-rate review; but to write about the writing of reviews is easier than either.

I can only be personal. For me, a critic's last responsibility is to the people who read him first. He is neither a ticket salesman nor a weather-vane, though at times he may choose to reveal aspects of both. At his best, he is writing letters to posterity. His traffic is with those who may want to know, a few decades hence, exactly what it was like to be in a particular theatre on a particular night. His job is to record a unique experience as it impinged on his mind and sensibility, and the whole machinery of bias and preference contained therein. As George Jean Nathan said, there is no such thing as an impersonal critic because there is no such thing as an impersonal person. There are temperaments, and impacts; and good criticism is the aftermath of a fruitful collision.

Unlike many of my colleagues, I do not shun the theatrical profession outside office hours; on the contrary, I feel myself bound to it, since its *raison d'être* is also mine. If we take our work seriously, we are on the same side (if not of the footlights); and among my closest acquaintances there are many actors, playwrights, and directors. I have long since overcome my qualms about insulting them in print; in this respect I am entirely incorruptible and conceivably inhuman. Every year I lose two or three friends, and make a hundred un-admitted enemies. One of the losses was Oscar Hammerstein, a large, forgiving man whose last two shows I attacked; and I regret that we had no chance to be properly reconciled before his death. Only one actor has ever taken a swing at me – a right hook, mistimed through drink, that caught me a glancing blow on the shoulder – and he launched it not to avenge himself but his mistress, about whom I had written something faintly unchivalrous. Missiles through the post are more frequent than blows. 'Your vicious campaign to undermine my career . . .' begins one actor's letter; and when I was in New York, an American actress wrote to me: 'Go home and go to Hell. Or go to Hell and go home.' I admire actors; but I worship the theatre. Serving the end, I must occasionally injure the means.

Most critics, when they collect their work for publication, are astonished to find how consistent they have been; their reviews turn out to be held together by an unbroken thread of conviction that the years have not frayed. My own experience, as I went through my files, was very different. I found a great many inconsistencies, and was not in the least surprised. Since I set up shop as a taster of plays, my palate has undergone a process that some may call a development and others a degeneration; it is, anyway, a process of change. I still have the same hunger for theatre (which is, after all, the art that keeps me off the streets), but to assuage it I nowadays look for a different kind of dramatic cuisine.

At Oxford I adored the theatre of fantasy and shock. I wrote in a university magazine that 'this sad age needs to be dazzled, shaped, and spurred by the spectacle of heroism. . . . If heroic plays take the stage, life may produce, in honest emulation, its own poor heroes of flesh and fact.' I revered poetic plays about the deaths of kings, especially if they had not been performed since the seventeenth century; I suspected that all really first-rate drama was about great men and dying and mourning: beyond that, nothing. It rarely occurred to me that theatre could be more than a combination of technical brilliance (on the part of directors and designers) and personal extravagance (on the part of actors and actresses). For me, in short, drama was apart from life, not a part of it.

Since then, like many of my contemporaries, I have swung over to another viewpoint; or, to put it more accurately, I use a wider lens. Travel – in France, America, Russia, and Germany – did a lot to broaden my outlook; so did the threat and pressure, no longer escapable, of world events; and so, no doubt, did the mere fact of growing up. For whatever reasons, I became aware that art, ethics, politics, and economics were inseparable one from another; I realized that theatre was a branch of sociology as well as a means of self-expression. From people like Bertolt Brecht and Arthur Miller I learned that all drama was political, in the widest sense of a wide word; and that no theatre could sanely flourish unless there was an umbilical connexion between what was happening on the stage and what was happening in the world. That, roughly, is where I stand today, and this book may give some indication of how I got there.

The British Theatre

PREFACE

People say, with some truth, that a turning-point in the history of the British theatre was reached when John Osborne's *Look Back in Anger* opened at the Royal Court in the spring of 1956. The first part of this book deals with the events leading up to and away from that memorable upheaval; that is to say, with the splendours, miseries, and occasional acts of madness that confronted (or affronted) my critical sense as the British theatre jolted its way through the 1950s. This opening section is a mosaic, made up of reviews and essays I wrote during that invigorating period of high promise and vivacious, though patchy, achievement.

We begin in the dust-bowl of Shaftesbury Avenue, a waste-land owing its aridity to improvident speculators. Famine seems imminent, when suddenly, to everyone's amazement, life blossoms in the virgin lands of Sloane Square and the East End, respectively irrigated by the English Stage Company and Joan Littlewood's Theatre Workshop. Two beach-heads for a splashing new wave of drama were triumphantly established. Whether they constituted a break-through is less easy, in hindsight, to determine.

I am writing in the spring of 1963, and as I look at the list of productions available in the West End, my heart sinks a little. Old hat retains its ancient preponderance over new wave. In 1950, two out of three London theatres were occupied by detective stories, melodramas, quarter-witted farces, débutante comedies, overweight musicals, and unreviewable revues: much the same is true today. The theatre advertisements are packed with titles such as *Boeing Boeing*, *Miss Pell is Missing*, *One for the Pot*, and *Goodnight, Mrs Puffin*, and Agatha Christie's *The Mousetrap* is still with us, ten years old and cheesier than ever.

The modish new playwright twelve years ago was Christopher Fry; last autumn he was back in the West End with *Curtmantle*, a staunchly old-fashioned chronicle play about the reign of Henry II. Joan Littlewood's Theatre Workshop has ceased to exist, destroyed in a sense by its own success. To survive economically, it had to transfer its hits from the East End to the West End and Broadway; and every such transfer struck at the root of Miss Littlewood's endeavour, which was to build up a permanent company of actors working under one roof. Art, lacking a state subsidy, was divided and conquered by commerce. Theatrically, though not otherwise, Brendan Behan has been silent since *The Hostage*; and Shelagh Delaney has not yet fulfilled the high hopes raised by *A Taste of Honey*. Nothing by N. F. Simpson, Harold Pinter, or Alun Owen currently adorns our stages; and Keith Waterhouse and Willis Hall – two working-class playwrights who owe their London success to *Billy Liar*, a middle-class parlour farce – have lately flopped twice in quick succession. We can still expect an annual eruption from John Osborne, that dedicated volcano half in love with the Pompeii he professes to despise; but although Arnold Wesker has finally stormed the West End with *Chips with Everything*, a frankly subversive display of theatrical fireworks, he was sworn off writing plays for two years in order to direct the efforts of Centre 42, an organization designed to bring art and the art-starved closer together. I wish him well, but I cannot help thinking that he would be better employed creating art than spreading it. To borrow an image from Cyril Connolly, the cow should not serve in the milk-bar.

Dispassionately eyed, and judged by the size of the audience it has actually captured, the great proletarian upsurge of which we bragged so freely a few years ago (and of which so many foreign critics wrote in envy) has proved to be something of a frost. The same hands control the West End, as they control the other means of communication. Perhaps we expected too much, too soon; perhaps the breakthrough temporarily broke down because we lacked a sense of history. We might have remembered the *caveat* of that remarkable critic, Trotsky:

It is fundamentally wrong to oppose proletarian to bourgeois culture and art. Proletarian culture and art will never exist. The proletarian régime is temporary and transitory. Our revolution derives its historic significance and moral greatness from the fact that it lays the foundations for a classless society and for the first truly universal culture.

In other words, the worker's task is purely militant – to build a new society from which a new kind of art will emerge. Until then, we should not repine, we should even rejoice if working-class art shows signs of being influenced by the best of bourgeois culture. It was by publicly expressing sentiments like these that Trotsky hastened his expulsion from the Soviet Union. Too many of our younger playwrights have forgotten, in their drive towards novelty of content, the vital disciplines of style. Rightly determined to look beyond the drawing-room for their subject-matter, they have tended to sacrifice baby and bath-water alike. In the battle for content, form has been the loser.

What I look for in our new drama is the sort of play that is not ashamed to assimilate and acknowledge the bourgeois tradition, which includes a multiplicity of styles (*vide* Ibsen), not all of them despicable. Otherwise, the drift of writers towards television and the cinema will rise to a flood, since dialogue composed in snippets soldered together by dissolves and background music will always be easier to write than dialogue orchestrated into the longer cadences of set-pieces and acts. Nothing is more crucially stupid than to dismiss the artistic achievements of a social class because one deplores its historical record.

Those achievements (from Shakespeare to Pirandello) belong to the past; but between them and the work of people now living a link must be forged and maintained – between Strindberg and Osborne, Chekhov and Pinter, Galsworthy and Wesker, Büchner and John Arden, and other such pairings. But these connexions can rarely be made, since the opportunities for comparison so seldom arise. As yet, London has no playhouse in which the best of world drama is constantly on tap, accessible for immediate ingestion by spectators and authors of eclectic tastes. A primary function of such a theatre would be to bridge the gap between those elements of bourgeois drama that lean towards the future and those elements of the new drama that extend a hand towards the past. That is the ideal, and at present it is impracticable. As I write, the London theatre is to all intents and purposes cut off from history. Of forty playhouses, only three are staging plays that were written before 1950 – the Aldwych (*King Lear*), the Royal Court (with a stop-gap revival of Shaw's *Misalliance*), and the Old Vic. I am all for modernity, but this is ridiculous.

To make predictions is rash but unavoidable. My guess is that the

West End, long discredited as a spawning-ground for new British drama, may tend to dry up altogether, though it will survive as an outlet for revues, musicals, and imported straight plays that have already proved themselves commercially in New York or Paris. A similar process has been taking place on Broadway during the past decade; but Shaftesbury Avenue cannot plead the Broadway excuse that experiment has been stifled by exorbitant production costs. Tot up the number of good new playwrights, over the last ten years or so, who owe their theatrical débuts to the West End managers: you can count them on your thumbs.

Outside the money-making belt, there are grounds for rational hope. Chichester has its Festival Theatre; the Yvonne Arnaud Theatre will soon open at Guildford; and in many other provincial centres there are signs that, artistically speaking, civic pride is overcoming civic xenophobia. The Royal Shakespeare Company, with one foot in Stratford-upon-Avon and the other in the Aldwych, already bestrides the narrow world of Shaftesbury Avenue, and may well develop into a colossus. It has the right idea, which is to foster continuity by staging the best of the new drama alongside the best of the old, with a permanent company to back up its convictions. The Royal Court Theatre remains, and will doubtless prosper, as a pocket of *avant-garde* resistance on the genteel borders of sw1 and sw3. In an ideal world, this invaluable organization would participate in the running of the second, experimental house of our great impending newcomer, the National Theatre, whose director-elect is Laurence Olivier. We know from *The Entertainer* that an alliance between Sir Laurence and the Royal Court can bear exciting fruit.

One can predict, of course, objections on both sides. The Court might not wish to compromise its independence any more than Sir Laurence would want to commit himself to a company with a clear and unequivocal policy of its own; but however he decides to shape our official playhouse, and whether or not his methods work, the results will surely make playgoing in the coming years a uniquely exciting occupation. Instead of going to somebody else's theatre, we shall be going to *our* theatre, for the first time in our history; and if it fails to connect the legacy of the past with the immense potentialities of the present – when we are as rich in actors and writers as any country in Europe – we shall have no one but ourselves to blame.

THE DEEP BLUE SEA

BY TERENCE RATTIGAN, AT THE DUCHESS

Terence Rattigan's new play is a searing study of the destructive zeal of love. It has already been acclaimed as 'brilliant theatre', but there is a patronizing ring to the phrase which I must set about demolishing. It implies that for a play to suit the theatre is not quite enough; that it is somehow improper to write deliberately for the medium you have selected – not print, not pure sound, but for an up-turned host of credulous faces in a darkened hall. *The Deep Blue Sea*, for its first two acts, is a masterly piece of work, and I went out exulting into the second interval, persuaded that I was seeing the most striking new play I could remember, and delighted at having divined a heart-pricking strength of purpose with which I had never before credited Mr Rattigan.

The play opens with the discovery of a gassed woman whose intended suicide has been foiled by the expiry of the shilling in the meter. And it invites us to piece a jigsaw together, to explore why she wanted to die, to rebuild her past; and by withholding this information until it tells most – by, in fact, beginning his action where most plays of the sort would end – Mr Rattigan keys us up almost to exploding point. Piece by piece, with seeming idleness, he presents the facts to us. She had left her husband and taken a lover, a clumsy, graceless, but boyishly desirable oaf, of whom she has made possessive demands that he is incapable of meeting. Apprised of her suicide attempt, and appalled by it, he walks out on her; and we leave her, at the second-act curtain, pleading riotously and without shame for him to stay.

I shall never forgive Mr Rattigan for his last act. It is intolerable: his brilliance lays an ambush for itself, and walks straight into it. If his heroine kills herself, he will merely be repeating the pattern, so he decides to let her live. But he has stated the case of her death so pungently that he cannot argue her out of the impasse without forfeiting our respect. He ekes out ingeniously, lecturing her about the necessity of sublimating her impulses in painting and going to a good Art School. Dishonestly, he makes her insist that she does not *deserve* to live, thus hauling in all kinds of moral implications which are totally irrelevant, since her point was purely that she could not *bear* to live. When, finally, she chooses survival, it is for all the wrong reasons.

The Deep Blue Sea remains the most absorbing new English play for many seasons. And it contains something which no English playwright (save Shaw in *Saint Joan*) has provided since Pinero – a long, straight, emotional part for a young woman. Peggy Ashcroft plays it superbly, as she should, for it is analogous in shape to that of *The Heiress*: deserted by her lover at the end of Act II, she rejects love itself at the end of Act III. And in Kenneth More, who plays her fumbling bar-fly bedfellow, we have acquired an actor who may become our best retort to Marlon Brando, with the same doubting proviso: can he do anything else?

(1952)

THE LIVING ROOM

BY GRAHAM GREENE, AT WYNDHAM'S

The Living Room is Graham Greene's first play, and also the best first play of its (English) generation. Its subject-matter can be compressed into two texts. One from Shaw: 'You can't make a man a Christian unless you first make him believe he is a sinner'; and one from a nameless theatrical manager: 'The triangle isn't eternal, but it's good for six months at the box-office.' Greene attempts to weld these two propositions, one cosmic and one commercial, into a dramatic unity.

In *The Notorious Mrs Ebbsmith* Pinero scandalized a Victorian audience by making his heroine throw a Bible into the fire, and immediately comforted them by letting her pull it out again. Greene's heroine, so to speak, chucks it in and leaves it there. She is a young orphan, physically in love with a middle-aged lecturer in psychology who is burdened with a hysterical wife. That is the textbook triangle: Greene now sets about projecting it towards infinity. For the girl is a

Roman Catholic. She has come to live with a pair of ancient aunts and an uncle who is a crippled priest. They inhabit a dank suburban house in which strange rituals persist, among them a refusal on the part of the female inmates to admit that they ever go to the bathroom except to take a bath. Greene is a Roman Catholic, but he is also a born rebel; this sepulchral mansion symbolizes, I imagine, the obscurantist aspects of the Roman faith. Childishly scared of death, the two aunts have sealed off every room in which anyone has died. The younger of them, a great bulky zealot (fearsomely played by Violet Farebrother), learns of the girl's adultery and threatens her with mortal sin. The wheelchair priest seeks to intensify her feelings of guilt, while her psychiatrist lover seeks to remove them. She vacillates between her lover and her God – between an earthly and a heavenly father-substitute – and finally cries out to the priest, in a striking phrase, that she is one of God's 'happy failures'.

The play is rising to its climax. The wife, a ravaged neurotic, stages a suicide attempt, which restores to her husband a shamed sense of his responsibilities. And now, on the threshold of triumph, Greene slips and falls. His heroine takes poison. The whole elaborate itinerary of sin and salvation has led us nowhere: she behaves in the crisis like any discarded mistress in a Victorian melodrama. Having tied a modern Catholic knot, Greene cuts it with an old-fashioned theatrical axe. I felt profoundly cheated.

If he stumbles on the highest level, Greene is wonderfully sure-footed on the way up. He has given Dorothy Tutin a chance which has been withheld from young English actresses for nearly thirty years: the chance of playing a long, serious part in an important new play. She takes it superbly, as if it were her birthright. Her role is half of what must be the most fully documented love affair in dramatic literature; we are privy to all her secrets, sexual and spiritual alike. Miss Tutin's performance is masterly: the very nakedness of acting. In her greatest sorrow she blazes like a diamond in a mine.

Elsewhere in the cast Peter Glenville (who has directed the play with a midwife's care) is less lucky. John Robinson plays the lover, for instance, in a highly unlovable vein of unctuous rhetoric. And though I applaud Eric Portman's unselfishness in accepting the role of the priest, I must deplore the waste involved. His legs are cut off at the knees, and his temperament is cut off at the mains. Mr Portman is an active actor miscast in a passive part. His game struggle to repress his natural exuberance produces an effect which I can only describe as vocal costiveness.

To sum up, then: a potentially great dramatist has launched a potentially great actress. He has also transmitted a message, which I can most gracefully summarize in the words of a fellow first-nighter: 'Be it ever so lustful, there's no place like Rome.'

(1953)

THE CONFIDENTIAL CLERK

BY T. S. ELIOT, AT THE NEW THEATRE

Hamlet is easy meat, a welcome febrifuge, after Eliot's new play, which uses devices borrowed from Coward, Pirandello, Wilde, Euripides, and Gilbert and Sullivan to illustrate moral precepts borrowed from nobody. *The Cocktail Party*, which many thought obscure, I found almost painfully simple; but *The Confidential Clerk*, acclaimed in England for its simplicity, strikes me as being one of the most complex pieces of work Mr Eliot has ever attempted. The language, admittedly, is far from abstruse, and the characters are easy to grasp, but the narrative pattern is staggeringly intricate. It is bizarre; it is 'the wrong shape'; it has the weird whorls and inter-sections one might expect if one's eccentric uncle set about playing with a model railway set. Mr Eliot has coated a hard moral pill with a myriad layers of theatrical sugar, which cannot but irritate those who, like myself, feel that only children need sugar on their pills.

Although there is little direct action, the play is nearly all plot. The central character is Colby Simpkins, a young ex-organist appointed to replace old Eggerson, a kindly grey-beard, as confidential clerk to Sir Claude Mulhammer, a city financier who believes Colby to be his illegitimate son. The Mulhammer household is full of dynastic dis-crepancies, including the vivacious Lucasta Angel, another of Sir Claude's bastards, and a breezy stockbroker named Kaghan, who announces himself a foundling. (*Vide* Wilde: 'To lose one parent, Mr Worthing, may be regarded as a misfortune; to lose both looks like carelessness.') An incipient romance between Colby and Lucasta is blighted by Colby's knowledge that they share the same father; at which point, halfway through, the play shifts gear to farce. Sir Claude's wife, the lark-brained Lady Elizabeth, hears Colby's story of his upbringing at the hands of a Mrs Guzzard in Teddington, and instantly declares that he is *her* illegitimate son, and not her husband's. (*Vide* the *Ion* of Euripides, in which Xuthus and Creusa dispute Ion's parentage, neither of them knowing the truth.) In the third and last scene Mrs Guzzard herself is summoned to settle the argument: a solid middle-class matron, in whose speeches there are disturbingly oracular overtones, and who may conceivably be Pallas Athene. She is a part-time baby-farmer. (*Vide* Buttercup's song in *H.M.S. Pinafore*:

> A many years ago,
> When I was young and charming,
> As some of you may know,
> I practised baby-farming. . . .
> Two tender babes I nussed;
> One was of low condition,
> The other, upper crust,
> A regular patrician. . . .)

I am not giving away any vital secrets when I divulge that Colby proves to be neither Sir Claude's nor Lady Elizabeth's child, and that a parent is found for the mysterious Mr Kaghan. Eliot's message has to do with what Mrs Guzzard calls 'wishing wisely': we must all choose vocations that are commensurate with our capacities. What we want to be must tally with what we are. Three acts are spent in establishing *who* the characters are (*vide* Pirandello, *passim*), but more important, Eliot implies, is *what* they are. The conclusion is that geniuses may carve for themselves, reckless of heredity, but the rest, the sublunary lot, must follow their parents.

The dialogue, deliberately flat and explicit, often reminiscent of automatic writing, is much concerned with the difference between imposing terms on life and accepting life's terms, between rejection of routine (the rare, abnormal way) and compromise with it (the sane, usual way). The London critics have agreed that the play is a comedy: but if you subtract Lady Elizabeth, a Cowardesque creature whose first lover was 'run over by a rhinoceros', there are precious few laughs in the evening. Truer to say that Eliot invokes the comic spirit, with its attendant mechanism of coincidence and absurdity, to disguise a hard core of sombre theorizing.

The words are physically unexciting to listen to – verse in aspic, you might say. Eliot's gift as a playwright is not to raise the temperature, but to lower it, as spooks are said to do when they enter a room. By the use of an unexpected, hieratic word, he can induce a chill mystery. This is what gives his characters their solitude and remoteness; we are always, the style insists, isolated from one another; there can be no earthly fruition – and, the style being the man, one sympathizes profoundly with the author. In *The Confidential Clerk*, however, he has moved far enough towards mundane humanity to create one warm, complete, stock character: Eggerson, the old retainer, which Alan Webb plays to perfection, interlarding the lines with blinks, coughs, and chuckles enough to outface Mr Chips himself. The women, Margaret Leighton and Isabel Jeans, are both enslaved to the most potent influence on English actresses since the 1918 armistice – the soaring vocal style of Edith Evans, whose nonchalant music has led our comediennes to believe that to get good notices it is absolutely necessary to mimic Lady Bracknell.

If you look hard, you cannot help noticing that *The Confidential Clerk* nurses, close to its heart, a tiny fictional absurdity. It depends on an undelivered letter sent by Mrs Guzzard to Sir Claude (conveniently in Canada), informing him that his mistress has died and with her his unborn child. But then, as Mr Eliot is well aware, the *dénouement* of *Romeo and Juliet* is likewise dependent on postal bungling. No matter how logic may puncture it, *The Confidential Clerk* remains tantalizingly clever – a labyrinth all the more teasing because it leaves you, at curtain-fall, a day's trot away from the centre. It is fascinating in performance, puzzling in retrospect, and, at all times and from whatever angle, unique.

(*1953*)

RATTIGAN IN TWO VOLUMES

Reading Terence Rattigan's ten collected plays is an experience
not unlike reclining on the bank of a suavely trickling stream in hot
weather. One basks, stretches, is lulled by the swift, interminable
murmur; one's reflexes are neutralized, and life pauses. Except when,
at long intervals, the roar of a distant waterfall obtrudes, one's
pleasure is negative, derived wholly from that marketable quality
known to cynics as ingratiation and to romantics as charm.

It is a charm closely related to that of Bing Crosby, in that it looks
deceptively, guilelessly imitable; indeed, it would not be too unfair to
call Rattigan the bathtub baritone of the drama. So steadily does he
aim to please that in his whole *œuvre* there is but one 'unpleasant'
character – the rapacious Mrs Crocker-Harris in *The Browning Version*, which stands beside the first two acts of *The Deep Blue Sea* as
his most impressive work for the theatre. Elsewhere the negative
virtues predominate: tact, understatement, avoidance of cliché – the
hallmarks, in fact, of the 'gentleman code' which holds so much of
West End playwrighting in curious thrall.

The very title of Rattigan's play about Alexander of Macedon is
significant: *Adventure Story*. Is it a modest shrug, or a form of insurance
against the terrible charge of pretentiousness? After reading the play
one is forced to conclude that Alexander's real crime, in Rattigan's
eyes, was to have been guilty of conduct which would get him
expelled from any decent club. His pagan legionaries move like gods
and talk like prefects: 'Been cheeking Alexander again, I expect,'
says a general of his son; the language will not rise to the occasion.
Rather than risk the embarrassment of rhetoric, Rattigan, like many
other English playwrights, has developed a talent for drawing un-
dramatic people, and for deriding people who take life 'dramatically',
such as the actor-manager in *Harlequinade*, the sulky, Hamletesque
son in *Love in Idleness*, or the little Frenchman in *While the Sun
Shines*, with his talk of 'a white-hot burning of the heart'. There is
no question that if Cyrano de Bergerac were to turn up in a Rattigan
play, he would be laughed off the stage in two minutes.

The author's long preface to the two volumes must be one of the most articulate confessions of faith ever penned by a popular playwright. Much of it is an unexceptionable defence of 'good theatre'. What demands refutation is the way in which Rattigan generalizes from his own example. It is a pity that he feels it necessary to ironize at the expense of dramatists whose plays fail to please the million – there is, after all, such a thing as a minority audience, and it is a matter of shame, not of self-congratulation, that there is less minority theatre here than in Paris. Nor is it true to assert that 'A play does not fail because it is too good; it fails because it is not good enough.' Thornton Wilder's *Our Town* failed in London seven years ago: for whom, one wonders, was it not good enough? The answer is that many plays fail because they are not bad enough.

I understand, though I cannot applaud, Rattigan's allegiance to a mythical, middle-class admirer called 'Aunt Edna', whom he holds to be the backbone of the theatre. Confusion arises when, blind to her failings, he credits Aunt Edna with having been the first to decide that *Hamlet* was a better play than *Timon of Athens*; the truth, of course, is that she goes to *Hamlet* because generations of highbrows have told her to. She follows, never leads, intelligent taste; nor does she abandon for an instant her inner conviction that *Hamlet* is a far less suitable play than *Quiet Weekend*. In his loyalty to the old lady, as in his subsequent declaration that the theatre is not the place in which to express 'ideas', Rattigan is rationalizing to the top of his bent. The fact that Aunt Edna is collectively flocking to see *The Sleeping Prince* (described by an American visitor as 'a breath of old caviare') will doubtless do much to comfort him.

Whatever his shortcomings as a theorist, nobody can deny Rattigan's supreme agility as a craftsman. His mastery of exposition is complete: give one of his characters a telephone, and within a minute, imperceptibly, the essentials of the situation will have been clearly sketched in. To the complaint that there is nothing quotable in his work, he has prepared an elaborate answer. He refers in the preface to an 'element of the pioneering and the experimental' in his comedies, by which he means their verbal economy; he believes that 'Yes', in context, can be more effective (i.e., funnier) than an ornately turned paragraph – which, if one judges comedies entirely on the number of sides they split, is indisputable. But in setting his face against what he calls 'the "gilded phrase" school' (Congreve and his contemporaries), Rattigan overlooks a vital point, which is that Congreve was writing about men and women of exceptional wit: and extraordinary people do tend to speak extraordinarily, even memorably.

The greatest plays are those which convince us that men can occasionally speak like angels. The rest, which conspire to imply that angels speak exactly like men, deserve and achieve respectable acclaim, but they must not repine if, finally, their passports to immortality are found invalid. The Grand Duchess in *The Sleeping Prince* is the first exceptional human being Rattigan has invented. We must now hope for more. He has already given us two striking tragedies of understatement, a vivid *drame à thèse*, and a clutch of likeable comedies, but I doubt whether he will long be content with a position, however secure and widely acknowledged, at the head of the second rank. Meanwhile, I commend to him Shaw's dictum: 'the drama's laws the drama's patrons do *not* give: that is the prerogative of the dramatist, and of the dramatist alone.'

(*1954*)

SEPARATE TABLES

BY TERENCE RATTIGAN, AT THE ST JAMES'S

(*The scene is the dining-room of a Kensington hotel, not unlike the Bournemouth hotel in which* Separate Tables, *Terence Rattigan's new double bill, takes place. A Young Perfectionist is dining; beside him, Aunt Edna, whom Mr Rattigan has described as the 'universal and immortal' middle-class playgoer.*)

AUNT EDNA: Excuse me, young man, but have you seen Mr Rattigan's latest?

YOUNG PERFECTIONIST: I have indeed.

A.E.: And what is it about?

Y.P.: It is two plays about four people who are driven by loneliness into a state of desperation.

A.E. (*sighing*): Is there not enough morbidity in the world . . .?

Y.P.: One of them is a drunken Left-wing journalist who has been imprisoned for wife-beating. Another is his ex-wife, who takes drugs to palliate the loss of her looks. She revives his masochistic love for her, and by curtain-fall they are gingerly reunited.

A.E. (*quailing*): Does Mr Rattigan analyse these creatures?

Y.P.: He does, in great detail.

A.E.: How very unwholesome! Pray go on.

Y.P.: In the second play the central character is a bogus major who has lately been convicted of assaulting women in a cinema.

A.E.: Ouf!

Y.P.: His fellow-guests hold conclave to decide whether he should be expelled from the hotel. Each contributes to a symposium on sexual deviation. . . .

A.E.: In pity's name, stop!

Y.P.: The major reveals that his foible is the result of fear, which has made him a hermit, a liar, and a pervert. This revelation kindles sympathy in the heart of the fourth misfit, a broken spinster, who befriends him in his despair.

A.E. (*aghast*): I *knew* I was wrong when I applauded *The Deep Blue Sea*. And what conclusion does Mr Rattigan draw from these squalid anecdotes?

Y.P.: From the first, that love unbridled is a destroyer. From the second, that love bridled is a destroyer. You will enjoy yourself.

A.E.: But I go to the theatre to be taken out of myself!

Y.P.: Mr Rattigan will take you into an intricately charted world of suspense. By withholding vital information, he will tantalize you; by disclosing it unexpectedly, he will astound you.

A.E.: But what information! Sex and frustration!

Y.P.: I agree that the principal characters, especially the journalist and the major, are original and disturbing creations. But there is also a tactful, omniscient *hôtelière*, beautifully played by Beryl Measor. And what do you say to a comic Cockney maid?

A.E.: Ah!

Y.P.: Or to Aubrey Mather as a whimsical dominie? Or to a pair of opinionated medical students? Or to a tyrannical matriarch – no less than Phyllis Neilson-Terry?

A.E.: *That* sounds more like it. You console me.

Y.P.: I thought you would feel at home. And Peter Glenville, the director, has craftily engaged for these parts actors subtle enough to disguise their flatness.

A.E. (*clouding over*): But what about those difficult leading roles?

Y.P.: Margaret Leighton plays two of them, rather externally. Her beauty annihilates the pathos of the ex-wife, who should be oppressed with crow's-feet. And her mousy spinster, dim and pink-knuckled, verges on caricature. It is Eric Portman who commands the stage, volcanic as the journalist, but even better as the major, speaking in nervous spasms and walking stiff-legged with his shoulders protectively hunched. He has the mask of the true mime, the *comédien* as opposed to the *acteur*.

A.E.: Yet you sound a trifle peaky. Is something biting you?

Y.P.: Since you ask, I regretted that the major's crime was not something more cathartic than mere cinema flirtation. Yet I suppose the play is as good a handling of sexual abnormality as English play-goers will tolerate.

A.E.: For my part, I am glad it is no better.

Y.P.: I guessed you would be; and so did Mr Rattigan. Will you accompany me on a second visit tomorrow?

A.E.: With great pleasure. Clearly, there is something here for both of us.

Y.P.: Yes. But not quite enough for either of us.

(*1954*)

WEST-END APATHY

'And how,' ask my friends, having debated the opera, the ballet, politics, and the Italian cinema, 'how is the theatre getting along?' The very set of their features, so patiently quizzical, tells me I am being indulged; after the serious business of conversation, they are permitting themselves a lapse into idleness. I shrug cheerily, like a martyr to rheumatism. A wan, tingling silence ensues. Then: 'De Sica's new film is superb,' says somebody, and talk begins again, happy and devout. I stew, meanwhile, in what Zelda Fitzgerald once called 'the boiling oil of sour grapes'.

The bare fact is that, apart from revivals and imports, there is nothing in the London theatre that one dares discuss with an intelligent man for more than five minutes. Since the great Ibsen challenge of the nineties, the English intellectuals have been drifting away from drama. Synge, Pirandello, and O'Casey briefly recaptured them, and they will still perk up at the mention of Giraudoux. But – cowards – they know Eliot and Fry only in the study; and of a native prose playwright who might set the boards smouldering they see no sign at all. Last week I welcomed a young Frenchwoman engaged in writing a thesis on contemporary English drama. We talked hopefully of John Whiting; but before long embarrassment moved me to ask why she had not chosen her own theatre as a subject for study. She smiled wryly. 'Paris is in decline,' she said. 'Apart from Sartre, Anouilh, Camus, Cocteau, Aymé, Claudel, Beckett, and Salacrou, we have almost nobody.'

If you seek a tombstone, look about you; survey the peculiar nullity of our drama's prevalent *genre*, the Loamshire play. Its setting is a country house in what used to be called Loamshire but is now, as a heroic tribute to realism, sometimes called Berkshire. Except when someone must sneeze, or be murdered, the sun invariably shines. The inhabitants belong to a social class derived partly from romantic novels and partly from the playwright's vision of the leisured life he will lead after the play is a success – this being the only effort of imagination he is called on to make. Joys and sorrows are giggles and whimpers: the crash of denunciation dwindles into 'Oh, stuff, Mummy!' and 'Oh, really, Daddy!' And so grim is the continuity of these things that the foregoing paragraph might have been written at any time during the last thirty years.

Loamshire is a glibly codified fairy-tale world, of no more use to the student of life than a doll's-house would be to a student of town planning. Its vice is to have engulfed the theatre, thereby expelling better minds. Never believe that there is a shortage of playwrights; there are more than we have ever known; but they are all writing the same play. Nor is there a dearth of English actors; the land is alive with them; but they are all playing the same part. Should they wish to test themselves beyond Loamshire's simple major thirds, they must find employment in revivals, foreign plays, or films. Perhaps Loamshire's greatest triumph is the crippling of creative talent in English directors and designers. After all, how many ways are there of directing a tea-party? And how may a designer spread his wings in a mews flat or 'The living-room at "Binsgate", Vyvyan Bulstrode's country house near Dymsdyke'? Assume the miracle: assume the advent of a masterpiece. There it crouches, a pink-eyed, many-muscled, salivating monster. Who shall harness it? We have a handful of directors fit to tame something less malleable than a mouse, and a few designers still capable of dressing something less submissive than a clothes-horse. But they are the end, not the beginning, of a tradition.

Some of us need no miracles to keep our faith; we feed it on memories and imaginings. But many more – people of passionate intellectual appetites – are losing heart, falling away, joining the queues outside the Curzon Cinema. To lure them home, the theatre must widen its scope, broaden its horizon so that Loamshire appears merely as the play-pen, not as the whole palace of drama. We need plays about cabmen and demi-gods, plays about warriors, politicians, and grocers – I care not, so Loamshire be invaded and subdued. I counsel aggression because, as a critic, I had rather be a war correspondent than a necrologist.

(1954)

THE LOST ART OF BAD DRAMA

Night-nurses at the bedside of good drama, we critics keep a holy vigil. Black circles rim our eyes as we pray for the survival of our pet patient, starved and racked, the theatre of passion and ideas. We pump in our printed transfusions – 'honest and forthright', 'rooted in a closely observed reality' – but so avidly do we seize on signs of relapse that we fail to observe that, for the moment at least, the cripple is out of bed and almost convalescent. He can claim, this season, three successes: *Hedda Gabler*, Anouilh's *Time Remembered*, and Pirandello's *Rules of the Game* – and he had a vestigial hand in *Separate Tables*. (Mr Rattigan is the Formosa of the contemporary theatre, occupied by the old guard, but geographically inclined towards the progressives.) Further tonics lie ahead, among them a Giraudoux and another Anouilh before spring is out. Implausible as it may sound, good drama may be able to walk unaided within a year or so.

But what of bad drama, the kind which repudiates art and scoffs at depth, which thrives on reviewers who state themselves 'shocked, but I rocked with laughter'? We assume that it is healthy; in fact, it looks extremely frail. Many a frankly 'commercial' play has come smiling to town in recent months and walked straight into an uppercut from both critics and public. Take *The Night of the Ball*, for instance – a knightly piece, glib and well-nourished, star-bright and silk-swathed, yet see how scarred and blunderbussed the critics left it! And is old *Happy Holiday* dead? As any doornail. Jesu, Jesu, the bad plays that I have seen! and to think how many of my old acquaintance are dead! How a good yoke of starlets at Cambridge Circus? Truly, cousin, I was not there.

It is now, in fact, a risky proposition to back plays that twenty years ago would have swept the boards unopposed. One imagines a box-office mogul bewailing his lot in Justice Shallow's vein: 'By the masses I was call'd everything.... There was I, and little Noël Coward of Teddington, and black Ben Travers, and Frederick Lonsdale, and Vernon Sylvaine, a Manchester man – you had not four such rib-crackers in all of Shaftesbury Avenue again; and, I may say to you, we knew where the bona-robas were, and had the best of them all under two weeks' notice.... Is old *double-entente* of your town living yet?' Dead, sir, dead.

One begins to suspect that the English have lost the art of writing a bad successful play. Perhaps some sort of competition should be organized; the rules, after all, are simple enough. At no point may the plot or characters make more than superficial contact with reality. Characters earning less than £1,000 a year should be restricted to small parts or exaggerated into types so patently farcical that no member of the audience could possibly identify himself with such absurd esurience. Rhythm in dialogue is achieved by means either of vocatives ('That, my dear Hilary, is a moot point') or qualifying clauses ('What, if you'll pardon the interruption, is going on here?'); and irony is confined to having an irate male character shout: 'I am perfectly calm!'

All plays should contain parts fit to be turned down by Gladys Cooper, Coral Browne, Hugh Williams, and Robert Flemyng. Apart from hysterical adolescents, nobody may weep; apart from triumphant protagonists, nobody may laugh; anyone, needless to say, may smile. European place-names (Positano and Ischia) are romantic; English place-names (Herne Bay and Bognor Regis) are comic. Women who help themselves unasked to cigarettes must be either frantic careerists or lustful opportunists. The latter should declare themselves by running the palm of one hand up their victim's lapel and saying, when it reaches the neck: 'Let's face it, Arthur, you're not exactly indifferent to me.' The use of 'Let's face it' in modern drama deserves in itself a special study. It means that something true is about to be uttered, and should strike the audience with the same shock as the blast of the whistle before the train plunges into a tunnel. . . .

But I falter. I cannot convince myself that these rules, archaic already, will assure success. For bad plays, dependent on what is topical and ephemeral in mankind, are much harder to write than good ones, for which the rules are permanent and unchanging. The commercial writer must blind himself to history, close his eyes, stop his ears, shutter his mind to the onslaught of reality; he must ignore all the promptings which instinct tells him to be valid, about unity of action and the necessity of reducing one or more of his characters to a logical crisis of desperation; he must live the life of a spiritual hermit. Such self-abnegation is seldom found. The great age of the thoroughly bad play seems to be over, and it behoves the critic to sing a requiem.

A thermometer, meanwhile, might be left in the mouth of good drama. Our season's tally is certainly encouraging, but it pales by comparison with last season's record in Sweden. There, according to the report in *World Theatre*, one might have seen four Strindbergs, four Shakespeares, three Chekhovs, three Pirandellos, two Molières, two Shaws, two Ibsens, two Giraudoux, and one each from Vanbrugh, Wycherley, Lorca, Kafka, Brecht, Ugo Betti, Arthur Miller, Anouilh, Eliot, Bernanos, and Samuel Beckett – not to mention the *Oresteia* of Aeschylus. Yet 'the season', mourns the compiler of the report, 'was not a milestone'. We have a long way to go.

(*1955*)

NOTES ON A DEAD LANGUAGE

When the London theatre takes to its bed, the habit of criticism is to scourge the invalid; the sick-room resounds with bullying cries of 'Who are the new English playwrights?' A more acute inquiry might be: 'Who were the old ones?' For the brute fact is that no Englishman since the third decade of the seventeenth century has written an acknowledged dramatic masterpiece. Note that I say 'acknowledged'; I might make claims for Otway or Dryden, you for Pinero or Maugham, but in the general censure we should be outvoted. The truth would out: that the legend of English drama springs partly from Shakespeare, our luminous accident, and mostly from an Irish conspiracy to make us ashamed of our weakness. English drama is a procession of glittering Irishmen: Farquhar, Goldsmith, Sheridan, Shaw, Wilde, Synge, and O'Casey are there; and even Congreve slips in on a quibble, since his Irish upbringing served to correct the fault of his English birth. We should not mourn that there are no great English playwrights; we should marvel that there are any English playwrights at all.

Come closer; observe how few fine plays have been written *about* the English in the last three hundred years. High drama presupposes high colloquial speech, which, since Cromwell, has been a rarity on English lips. We will accept eloquence from a Tartar emperor, a Dublin pickpocket, or a New York taxi-driver, but we would rightly baulk at verbal beauty in a Yarmouth policeman. When Shakespeare was born, our language was being pelted with imports, from France, from Italy, from classical translations; 'thought', as Virginia Woolf said, 'plunged into a sea of words and came up dripping.' A stock-pot was bubbling which everyone tasted and tried out in speech; and drama evolved out of an epidemic of logorrhoea.

For half a century we have watched a similar process in America, where a clash of immigrant tongues has produced the same experimental play of language. In England the riot is over. Lexicography has battened on the invaders, and our dictionaries swell with the slain; a memorable phrase flies sometimes from a typewriter into

print, but seldom from a larynx into a listening ear. Christopher Fry
has performed prodigies of artificial respiration; the words are there,
and richly he deploys them; but do they not resemble the bright, life-
simulating dyes which American morticians apply to the faces of the
dead? To gain admission to drama, words must be used; they must
put on flesh, throng the streets, and bellow through the buses. Dylan
Thomas's *Under Milk Wood* was one of the last outposts of the living
vernacular, a memory of a time when a phrase was as concrete a thing
as a brick: and Thomas, remember, was not English, but a Welshman
writing about Welshmen.

The sudden onslaught of a million immigrants of mixed nationali-
ties might help. Until then, I propose an agonizing reappraisal of our
theatrical status, which is now that of a showroom for foreign goods.
A swarm of Continental plays crowds our stage-door; our part, as
hosts, is to provide for them translators of genius. Mr Fry, who is now
adapting Anouilh's *L'Alouette* and Giraudoux' *La Guerre de Troie
n'aura pas lieu*, has set a noble, instructive, and realistic example.

(1955)

WAITING FOR GODOT

BY SAMUEL BECKETT, AT THE ARTS

A special virtue attaches to plays which remind the drama of how
much it can do without and still exist. By all the known criteria,
Samuel Beckett's *Waiting for Godot* is a dramatic vacuum. Pity the
critic who seeks a chink in its armour, for it is all chink. It has no plot,
no climax, no *dénouement*; no beginning, no middle, and no end.
Unavoidably, it has a situation, and it might be accused of having
suspense, since it deals with the impatience of two tramps, waiting
beneath a tree for a cryptic Mr Godot to keep his appointment with
them; but the situation is never developed, and a glance at the programme shows that Mr Godot is not going to arrive. *Waiting for
Godot* frankly jettisons everything by which we recognize theatre.
It arrives at the custom-house, as it were, with no luggage, no passport, and nothing to declare; yet it gets through, as might a pilgrim

from Mars. It does this, I believe, by appealing to a definition of drama much more fundamental than any in the books. A play, it asserts and proves, is basically a means of spending two hours in the dark without being bored.

Its author is an Irishman living in France, a fact which should prepare us for the extra, oddly serious joke he now plays on us. Passing the time in the dark, he suggests, is not only what drama is about but also what life is about. Existence depends on those metaphysical Micawbers who will go on waiting, against all rational argument, for something which may one day turn up to explain the purpose of living. Twenty years ago Mr Odets had us waiting for Lefty, the social messiah; less naïvely, Mr Beckett bids us wait for Godot, the spiritual signpost. His two tramps pass the time of day just as we, the audience, are passing the time of night. Were we not in the theatre, we should, like them, be clowning and quarrelling, aimlessly bickering and aimlessly making up – all, as one of them says, 'to give us the impression that we exist'.

Mr Beckett's tramps do not often talk like that. For the most part they converse in the double-talk of vaudeville: one of them has the ragged aplomb of Buster Keaton, while the other is Chaplin at his airiest and fairiest. Their exchanges are like those conversations at the next table which one can almost but not quite decipher – human speech half-heard and reproduced with all its *non-sequiturs* absurdly intact. From time to time other characters intrude. Fat Pozzo, Humpty Dumpty with a whip in his fist, puffs into sight with Lucky, his dumb slave. They are clearly going somewhere in a hurry: perhaps they know where Godot is? But the interview subsides into Lewis-Carrollian inanity. All that emerges is that the master needs the slave as much as the slave needs the master; it gives both a sense of spurious purpose; and one thinks of Laurel and Hardy, the ideal casting in these roles. Commanded to think, Lucky stammers out a ghostly, ghastly, interminable tirade, compounded of cliché and gibberish, whose general tenor is that, in spite of material progress and 'all kinds of tennis', man spiritually dwindles. The style hereabouts reminds us forcibly that Mr Beckett once worked for James Joyce. In the next act Pozzo and Lucky return, this time moving, just as purposefully, in the opposite direction. The tramps decide to stay where they are. A child arrives, presenting Mr Godot's compliments and regretting that he is unable to meet them today. It is the same message as yesterday; all the same, they wait. The hero of *Crime and Punishment* reflects that if a condemned man 'had to remain standing on a square yard of space all his life, a thousand years, eternity, it were better to live so than to die at once. . . . Man is a vile creature! and vile is he who calls him vile for that!' Something of this crossed my mind as the curtain fell on Mr Beckett's tatterdemalion stoics.

The play sees the human condition in terms of baggy pants and red noses. Hastily labelling their disquiet disgust, many of the first-night audience found it pretentious. But what, exactly, are its pretensions? To state that mankind is waiting for a sign that is late in coming is a platitude which none but an illiterate would interpret as making claims to profundity. What vexed the play's enemies was, I suspect, the opposite: it was not pretentious enough to enable them to deride it. I care little for its enormous success in Europe over the past three years, but much for the way in which it pricked and stimulated my own nervous system. It summoned the music-hall and the parable to present a view of life which banished the sentimentality of the music-hall and the parable's fulsome uplift. It forced me to re-examine the rules which have hitherto governed the drama; and, having done so, to pronounce them not elastic enough. It is validly new, and hence I declare myself, as the Spanish would say, *godotista*.

Peter Hall directs the play with a marvellous ear for its elusive rhythms, and Peter Woodthorpe and Paul Daneman give the tramps a compassionate lunacy which only professional clowns could excel. Physically, Peter Bull is Pozzo to the life; vocally, he overplays his hand. Timothy Bateson's Lucky is anguish made comic, a remarkable achievement, and perfectly in keeping with the spirit of the play.

(*1955*)

NOTES ON THE NATIONAL THEATRE

Since today begins a New Year, it is fitting that the English should be reminded of a resolution that was made in their name on 21 January 1949. That, as the fervent will remember, was the day of the Giant Step, when the drama received its greatest (and almost its only) official boost since Charles II created the patent theatres. It was the day on which the House of Commons unanimously approved the National Theatre Bill, empowering the Treasury to spend a million pounds on building a home for the nation's drama.

Seven years have passed, and what has become of that august and imaginative resolve? One stone has been regally laid; and that, by mischance, in the wrong place. Having expressed our will, we, the people, left things to them, the National Theatre Executive Committee, and shortly afterwards relapsed into what Matthew Arnold bitterly called 'our favourite doctrines of the mischief of State interference, of the blessedness of leaving every man to do as he likes, of the impertinence of presuming to check any man's natural taste for the bathos and pressing him to relish the sublime.'

Why? Has the theatre forgotten the long passion that brought its dream to the brink of fact? Surely the classic arguments, endorsed always by the few and seven years ago by the many, need no re-iteration. Must it again be urged that Britain is the only European country with a living theatrical tradition which lacks a national theatre; and that the public money which gave us a visual library, the National Gallery, is needed just as vitally to provide (in Benn Levy's phrase) a 'living library' of plays? But the points were all made in the Commons debate. The general impotence of our theatre, as opposed to the individual excellence of our actors, is the laughing-stock of the Continent; and it is unthinkable that anyone nowadays would sink to the crassness of saying, as a daily paper did in 1938: 'To have no National Theatre is a tribute to our liberty.' To whom, one wonders, is the following quotation still controversial? 'I consider it a pity, and even a folly, that we do not make some national effort to aid and assist dramatic representation. . . . Think with what excitement and interest this people witnesses the construction or launching of a Dreadnought! What a pity it is that some measure of that interest cannot be turned in the direction of the launching, say, of a National Theatre!' The speech from which these extracts are taken was delivered by Sir Winston Churchill in 1906.

Geoffrey Whitworth, the pioneer of the National Theatre, died in 1951; one regrets that he did not live to see and surmount the ironies with which time has festooned his vision. One recalls William Archer and Granville Barker, in the first flush of certainty, graciously smiling on the idea of a subsidized opera-house, but never doubting for an instant that the theatre would come first, since 'England possesses a national drama but does not as yet possess a national opera'. Well, that was in 1904. We now have a subsidized opera-house; we are soon to have a second concert-hall on the South Bank; and the L.C.C. has just agreed to spend seven million pounds on the 'rehabilitation' of the Crystal Palace. And still that lonely, misplaced stone is all we have of our theatre.

But what, the diehards may ask, will the National Theatre give us that Stratford and the Old Vic do not? Firstly, a really modern theatre, comparable with those abroad and capable of staging the widest variety of plays. Secondly, not a cast of underpaid second-stringers, like the Old Vic, nor yet a starry, short-term band, like Stratford, but a large, experienced, permanent company, drawn from our finest talent and paid accordingly. Of the several objects pre-scribed for the National Theatre, Stratford and the Old Vic fulfil but one – that of presenting Shakespeare. The others (those of reviving the rest of our classical drama, presenting new plays and the best of foreign drama, and preventing recent plays of merit from rusting in oblivion) have no roof at all over their heads. At the X Theatre the play is good; at the Y, the acting; and the decor at the Z is magni-ficent. But there is nowhere we can send our guests, confidently saying: 'This is our theatre's best. On this we stand.'

Our theatre has always been dogged by poverty; it is now dan-gerously close to being bitched by it. In 1880 Matthew Arnold con-cluded his great germinal essay with the words: 'The theatre is irresistible; organize the theatre!' To which one would add: 'The Act is irresistible; implement the Act!'

(1956)

LOOK BACK IN ANGER
BY JOHN OSBORNE, AT THE ROYAL COURT

'They are scum' was Mr Maugham's famous verdict on the class of State-aided university students to which Kingsley Amis's Lucky Jim belongs; and since Mr Maugham seldom says anything controversial or uncertain of wide acceptance, his opinion must clearly be that of many. Those who share it had better stay well away from John Osborne's Look Back in Anger, which is all scum and a mile wide.

Its hero, a provincial graduate who runs a sweet-stall, has already been summed up in print as 'a young pup', and it is not hard to see why. What with his flair for introspection, his gift for ribald parody, his excoriating candour, his contempt for 'phoneyness', his weakness for soliloquy, and his desperate conviction that the time is out of joint, Jimmy Porter is the completest young pup in our literature since Hamlet, Prince of Denmark. His wife, whose Anglo-Indian parents resent him, is persuaded by an actress friend to leave him; Jimmy's prompt response is to go to bed with the actress. Mr Osborne's picture of a certain kind of modern marriage is hilariously accurate: he shows us two attractive young animals engaged in competitive martyrdom, each with its teeth sunk deep in the other's neck, and each reluctant to break the clinch for fear of bleeding to death.

The fact that he writes with charity has led many critics into the trap of supposing that Mr Osborne's sympathies are wholly with Jimmy. Nothing could be more false. Jimmy is simply and abundantly alive; that rarest of dramatic phenomena, the act of original creation, has taken place; and those who carp were better silent. Is Jimmy's anger justified? Why doesn't he do something? These questions might be relevant if the character had failed to come to life; in the presence of such evident and blazing vitality, I marvel at the pedantry that could ask them. Why don't Chekhov's people do something? Is the sun justified in scorching us? There will be time enough to debate Mr Osborne's moral position when he has written a few more plays. In the present one he certainly goes off the deep end, but I cannot regard this as a vice in a theatre that seldom ventures more than a toe into the water.

Look Back in Anger presents post-war youth as it really is, with special emphasis on the non-U intelligentsia who live in bed-sitters and divide the Sunday papers into two groups, 'posh' and 'wet'. To have done this at all would be a signal achievement; to have done it in a first play is a minor miracle. All the qualities are there, qualities one had despaired of ever seeing on the stage – the drift towards anarchy, the instinctive leftishness, the automatic rejection of 'official' attitudes, the surrealist sense of humour (Jimmy describes a pansy friend as 'a female Emily Brontë'), the casual promiscuity, the sense of lacking a crusade worth fighting for, and, underlying all these, the determination that no one who dies shall go unmourned.

One cannot imagine Jimmy Porter listening with a straight face to speeches about our inalienable right to flog Cypriot schoolboys. You could never mobilize him and his kind into a lynching mob, since the art he lives for, jazz, was invented by Negroes; and if you gave him a razor, he would do nothing with it but shave. The Porters of our time deplore the tyranny of 'good taste' and refuse to accept 'emotional' as a term of abuse; they are classless, and they are also leaderless. Mr Osborne is their first spokesman in the London theatre. He has been lucky in his sponsors (the English Stage Company), his director (Tony Richardson), and his interpreters: Mary Ure, Helena Hughes, and Alan Bates give fresh and unforced performances, and in the taxing central role Kenneth Haigh never puts a foot wrong.

That the play needs changes I do not deny: it is twenty minutes too long, and not even Mr Haigh's bravura could blind me to the painful whimsey of the final reconciliation scene. I agree that *Look Back in Anger* is likely to remain a minority taste. What matters, however, is the size of the minority. I estimate it at roughly 6,733,000, which is the number of people in this country between the ages of twenty and thirty. And this figure will doubtless be swelled by refugees from other age-groups who are curious to know precisely what the contemporary young pup is thinking and feeling. I doubt if I could love anyone who did not wish to see *Look Back in Anger*. It is the best young play of its decade.

(*1956*)

THE FAMILY REUNION

BY T. S. ELIOT, AT THE PHOENIX

After *Hamlet* and *The Power and the Glory*, the Peter Brook–Paul Scofield season of sin and damnation has entered on its last anguished lap with Mr Eliot's *The Family Reunion*.

To Mr Scofield, who has hardly had a cheerful line to speak in the past six months, one's heart goes out; having worked like a Trojan, he is now called on to impersonate a tormented pseudo-Greek. He does it yeomanly. On Mr Eliot's Orestean hero he bestows a sleepless mien, gently haggard, and an anxious warmth of utterance that very nearly cures the character of its priggishness. As he is softened by Mr Scofield, we almost come to like Harry. Almost, we believe that he might exist.

This, of course, is just a trick of mimetic *trompe-l'œil*. Harry has no real blood in his veins. He is merely a projection of the obsessive guilt (often connected with the death of a woman) that constantly recurs in Mr Eliot's work. 'Sweeney Agonistes' gives the clue

> I knew a man once did a girl in
> Any man might do a girl in
> Any man has to, needs to, wants to
> Once in a lifetime, do a girl in.

Harry returns to his aunt-haunted ancestral home convinced that he has done his wife in. Through his sibylline Aunt Agatha he discovers that the true culprit was his father, who sought and failed to knock off his mother. Harry embarks, enlightened, on a pilgrimage of atonement; but the suddenness of his departure has the ironic effect of striking his mother dead. Now, if Mr Eliot had admitted that Harry was a rare and special case, all might have been well. Instead, he insists that we accept him as a timeless and universal symbol. We are to identify ourselves with Harry when he decides to embrace the Furies, saying that 'my business is not to run away but to pursue'. But at this point I could not help recalling a sentence from Manès Sperber's essay on Freud: 'In the circle of his actions the neurotic is as much in pursuit of the Furies as he is pursued.' Harry is an interesting upper-class neurotic (more New England than North Country, by the way), but he is nothing more, except to those who still retain an objective belief in fate. Mr Eliot has dressed him in borrowed classical robes, but he sinks beneath their weight.

To preserve Harry from disaster as he swings about on the metaphysical high trapeze, Mr Eliot has thoughtfully installed a safety net. He has given him two stupid aunts and two stupid uncles who cannot understand what he is driving at. In them the obtuseness of Philistia is incarnate; they suspect that Harry's spiritual garments have come from the Emperor's tailor; and if we agree with them, that makes us Philistines too.

The play contains two splendid jokes (in prose) and many passages of bony analytic precision. It also demonstrates Mr Eliot's gift for imposing a sudden chill, as ghosts are said to do when they enter a room. Images of vague nursery dread insistently recur – the attraction of the dark passage, the noxious smell untraceable in the drain, the evil in the dark closet (which was really, as Dylan Thomas used impiously to say, the school boot-cupboard), the cerebral acne in the monastery garden, the agony in the dark, the agony in the curtained bedroom, the chilly pretences in the silent bedroom. (One of these phrases is my own invention. Entries by Ash Wednesday.) But though Mr Eliot can always lower the dramatic temperature, he can never raise it; and this is why the theatre, an impure assembly that loves strong emotions, must ultimately reject him. He is glacial, a theatrical Jack Frost; at the first breath of warmth, he melts and vanishes.

This has-been, would-be masterpiece is magnificently revived by Peter Brook, who also designed the setting, an eerie upholstered vault. Apart from Mr Scofield, Sybil Thorndike as the doomed matriarch and Gwen Ffrangcon-Davies as Agatha the oracle perform magisterially, and fine work is done by Nora Nicholson and Patience Collier. The whole cast inhales Mr Eliot's thin air as if it were nourishing them; or as if it held some scent more refreshing than that of dry bones.

(1956)

THE QUARE FELLOW
BY BRENDAN BEHAN, AT STRATFORD-ATTE-BOWE

'Bloddy sparklin' dialogue,' said a pensive Irishman during the first interval of *The Quare Fellow* – and sparkle, by any standards, it amazingly did. The English hoard words like misers; the Irish spend them like sailors; and in Brendan Behan's tremendous new play language is out on a spree, ribald, dauntless, and spoiling for a fight. In itself, of course, this is scarcely amazing. It is Ireland's sacred duty to send over, every few years, a playwright to save the English theatre from inarticulate glumness. And Irish dialogue almost invariably sparkles. But now consider the context of Mr Behan's hilarity. His setting is an Ulster prison, and one of its inmates is shortly to drop, rope-necklaced, through the untender trap.

> To move wild laughter in the throat of death?
> It cannot be: it is impossible.

But Berowne was wrong. To a countryman of Swift many things are possible, and this among them; this, perhaps, especially.

In adversity the Irish always sparkle. 'If this is how Her Majesty treats her prisoners,' said one of them, handcuffed in the rain *en route* for gaol, 'she doesn't deserve to have any.' With this remark of Oscar Wilde's, Mr Behan, who has spent eight years of his life in prison for sundry acts of I.R.A. mischief, entirely agrees; and his protest is lodged in the same spirit of laconic detachment. The Irish are often sentimental about causes and crusades, but they are hardly ever sentimental about human beings. So far from trying to gain sympathy for the condemned man, an axe-murderer known as 'the quare fellow', Mr Behan keeps him off-stage throughout the action. All he shows us is the effect on the prison population of the knowledge that one of their number is about to be ritually strangled.

There are no tears in the story, no complaints, no visible agonies; nor is there even suspense, since we know from the outset that there will be no reprieve. Mr Behan's only weapon is a gay, fatalistic gallows-humour, and he wields it with the mastery of Ned Kelly, the

Australian bandit, whose last words, as the noose encircled his neck, were: 'Such is life.' Mr Behan's convicts behave with hair-raising jocularity, exchanging obscene insults even while they are digging the murderer's grave. An old lag feigns a bad leg in order to steal a swig of methylated spirits; a newcomer anxious to raise bail is blithely advised to 'get a bucket and bail yourself out'. Even the hangman is presented serio-comically as a bowler-hatted publican with a marked addiction to the wares he sells. The tension is intolerable, but it is we who feel it, not the people in the play. We are moved precisely in the degree that they are not. With superb dramatic tact, the tragedy is concealed beneath layer after layer of rough comedy.

Meanwhile, almost imperceptibly, the horror approaches. Two warders, chosen to share the murderer's last eight hours of life, thoughtfully discard their wrist-watches in anticipation of his in-evitable demand: What time is it? His last letters are thrown un-opened into his grave: better there than in the Sunday papers. Dawn breaks, accompanied by the ghastly, anguished clatter of tin cups and plates against iron bars that is the tribute traditionally paid by the thousand convicts who will see tomorrow to the one who will not. The empty exercise yard now falls silent. The hush is broken by a unique *coup de théâtre*, Mr Behan's supreme dramatic achievement. An unseen humorist, bawling from some lofty window, embarks on an imaginary description, phrased as racily as a Grand National commentary, of the hundred-yard dash from condemned cell to scaffold. They're coming into the straight now; the chaplain's leading by a short head. . . . A young warder, new to the ceremony, faints and is carried across the stage for treatment. A sad, bawdy ballad filters through from the punishment block. The curtain falls, but not before we have heard the swing and jerk of the drop. I left the theatre feeling overwhelmed and thanking all the powers that be for Sydney Silverman.

John Bury's two sets exactly capture the aridity of confinement. And Joan Littlewood's production is the best advertisement for Theatre Workshop that I have yet seen: a model of restraint, integrity, and disciplined naturalism. Glynn Edwards, Brian Murphy, and Maxwell Shaw, as three of Her Majesty's guests, and Dudley Foster, as one of the same lady's uniformed hosts, stand out from an inspired all-male company. Miss Littlewood's cast knows perfectly well what it is doing. She must now devote a few rehearsals to making sure that we can understand precisely what it is saying. That done, *The Quare Fellow* will belong not only in such transient records as this, but in theatrical history.

(1956)

CARDS OF IDENTITY
BY NIGEL DENNIS, AT THE ROYAL COURT

'I must know who I am, mustn't I?'

'Surely your own play isn't going to tell you?'

'Of course not, dear; it's the critics who'll tell me. At the moment I don't exist; I don't even know what to *become*. But once my play's done, I'll know. . . .'

NIGEL DENNIS, *Cards of Identity*

Vain hope. Having seen the play that Mr Dennis has excavated from his novel, I will be keel-hauled if I know what to tell him. At his true identity I cannot guess. I know him for a master satirist, and also for a stylist. To boot, he is a conjurer, a card-manipulator who has yet to learn that a straight flush in the hand may look somewhat repetitive when laid face upward, card by card, on the stage; may even, such is the waywardness of theatre, fail to vanquish a full house. But one thing is certain: for all his talents, Mr Dennis does not yet belong in the company of those writers the very tone of whose voices, urgent and hypnotic, at once sets our minds shaping the question: 'And then what happened?' The power to do this is not the highest of dramatic skills, but it is one of the hardest; and whenever he lays claim to it, whenever he assumes the identity of story-teller, Mr Dennis lets us down. I do not know what he essentially is; but I do know what he is not.

The novel was an extravagant *bal masqué* whose theme was: 'Come as you aren't.' Three formidable frauds, closely reminiscent of Subtle, Face, and Doll in *The Alchemist*, commandeer a derelict country house in the name of the Identity Club. Triumphantly they test the club's maxim, that modern man no longer knows exactly who he is and can easily be persuaded that he is someone else; a man in whom arrogance and servility alternate can, for example, be transformed overnight, to his entire satisfaction, into a butler. The idea is to cram the largest possible number of mutually exclusive qualities into the same new personality. (The Club's *chef d'œuvre* is a Catholic Communist who is also an alcoholic.) Perhaps by chance, Mr Dennis stumbled on the notion that the basic symbol of our time was not the atom scientist but the actor, the *histrio*, the man of multiple selfhood who had a brave new face for each sad new situation.

The idea that human personality is neither absolute nor immutable is no novelty: it was Pirandello's obsession, and we find it in the changeable masks used by the people in O'Neill's *The Great God Brown*. Nor is it a stranger to the novel: we are in its presence when Mr Amis's Lucky Jim puts on his 'Edith Sitwell face'. Mr Dennis's contribution was to elaborate it into a whole philosophy of life.

His book was a series of firework displays, each of which illuminated the same thesis. It had a plot, something to do with a conspiracy to assassinate the Club's President, but this was an appendage that wise readers skipped. We now approach the vital distinction between novel and play. A novel is a static thing that one moves through; a play is a dynamic thing that moves past one. Mr Dennis has made the mistake of supposing his plot robust enough to haul his parade of set-pieces across the stage. Observe, for instance, the gorgeous tableau in which two dandies, Edwardians born too late, find fulfilment in the twin sinecures of Co-Wardens of the Badgeries, where their only duty is to parade an imaginary badger on State occasions. Superb! But now poor Plot comes puffing back to drag the next float into view. This is Father Orfe's account, delivered by George Devine with the most squalid unctuousness, of how modern religion is not only reconcilable with but inseparable from the basest debauchery: 'I stink, therefore I am.' *Éclatant!* Then in plods Plot again, trudging and sweating and patently loathing the job.

The spectacle grows painful. In the novel, Plot works only a seven-hour day; but in the theatre it must work overtime, from dawn to dusk, nudging and sheep-dogging the action into its predestined fold. Mr Dennis's Plot is too frail to stand the strain; instead of being vigilant, it dozes, snores, and then awakens, quite unexpectedly, in alarming convulsions. If Mr Dennis were to cut the whole of Act Two, Scene Three, and most of the last act, he would ease the burden on Plot and allow us to concentrate on the set-pieces, which bristle with wit, style, perception, audacity, malice, and profundity.

Tony Richardson's production brings Mr Dennis's nightmare to pungent life. As the Machiavellian hero, Michael Gwynn excels himself; this is a display of caddishness at once rich and racy, genial and sinister, false-faced and multi-faceted. Joan Greenwood repeats her well-known impersonation of a baby theatrical Dame with 'strep throat'; and who should turn up, wearing false sabre-teeth and a hairless dome, but John Osborne, ruthlessly funny as the Custodian of Ancient Offices! The Royal Court's captive playwright stands out from an excellent supporting cast.

(*1956*)

THE ENTERTAINER
BY JOHN OSBORNE, AT THE ROYAL COURT

This has been one of the most varied, nourishing, and provocative weeks that the London theatre has known since the war. Let me but list its riches – Olivier working with John Osborne, Peter Hall directing Tennessee Williams,* and the West End début of the funniest one-man show on earth.† For once, I felt mine was an enviable *métier*.

To begin at the deep end: Mr Osborne has had the big and brilliant notion of putting the whole of contemporary England on to one and the same stage. *The Entertainer* is his diagnosis of the sickness that is currently afflicting our slaphappy breed. He chooses, as his national microcosm, a family of run-down vaudevillians. Grandad, stately and retired, represents Edwardian graciousness, for which Mr Osborne has a deeply submerged nostalgia. But the key figure is Dad: Archie Rice, a fiftyish song-and-dance man reduced to appearing in twice-nightly nude revue. This is the role that has tempted Sir Laurence to return to the Royal Court after twenty-nine years.

* *Camino Real.*   † Victor Borge.

Archie is a droll, lecherous fellow, comically corrupted. With his blue patter and jingo songs he is a licensed pedlar of emotional dope to every audience in Britain. The tragedy is that, being intelligent, he knows it. His talent for destructive self-analysis is as great as Jimmy Porter's. At times, indeed, when he rails in fuddled derision at 'our nasty sordid unlikely little problems', he comes too close to Jimmy Porter for comfort or verisimilitude. He also shares the Porter Pathological Pull towards bisexuality, which chimes with nothing else in his character, though it may be intended to imply that he has made a sexual as well as a moral compromise.

But I am carping too soon. To show the ironic disparity between Archie's mind and the use he makes of it, Mr Osborne has hit on a stunningly original device. He sets out the programme like a variety bill, and switches abruptly from Archie at home, insulated by gin, to Archie on stage, ogling and mincing, joshing the conductor, doing the chin-up bit and braying with false effusiveness such aptly named numbers as 'Why Should I Bother to Care?', 'We're All Out for Good Old Number One', and 'Thank God We're Normal'. In these passages, author, actor, and composer (John Addison) are all at peak form. A bitter hilarity fills the theatre, which becomes for a while England in little: 'Don't clap too hard, lady, it's an old building.'

Archie has abdicated from responsibility. He despises his wife, sleeps out nightly, and morally murders his father by coaxing him back into grease-paint: yet he can still button-hole us with songs and routines that enjoin us to share the very couldn't-care-less-ness that has degraded him. The death of his son, kidnapped and killed in Egypt, restores him for a while to real feeling. He has just been reminiscing, with drunken fervour, about a Negress he once heard singing in a night-club, making out of her oppression 'the most beautiful fuss in the world'. Now, shattered himself, he crumples, and out of his gaping mouth come disorganized moans that slowly reveal themselves as melody. Archie the untouchable is singing the blues.

With Sir Laurence in the saddle, miracles like this come often. At the end of the first act Archie is struggling to tell his daughter about the proudest encounter of his life, the one occasion when he was addressed with awe. 'Two nuns came towards me,' he says. 'Two nuns . . .' All at once he halts, strangled by self-disgust. The curtain falls on an unfinished sentence. Sir Laurence brings the same virtuosity to Archie's last story, about a little man who went to heaven and, when asked what he thought of the glory, jerked up two fingers, unequivocally parted. The crown, perhaps, of this great performance is Archie's jocular, venomous farewell to the audience: 'Let me know where you're working tomorrow night – and I'll come and see *you*.'

When Archie is offstage, the action droops. His father is a bore and his children are ciphers: the most disquieting thing about the play is the author's failure to state the case of youth. There is a pacifist son who sings a Brechtian elegy for his dead brother, but does little else of moment. And there is Jean, Archie's daughter, a Suez baby who came of age at the Trafalgar Square rally but seems to have lost her political ardour with the passing of that old adrenalin glow. She is vaguely anti-Queen and goes in for loose generalities like 'We've only got ourselves'; beyond that, *nada*. Rather than commit himself, Mr Osborne has watered the girl down to a nullity, and Dorothy Tutin can do nothing with her.

This character, coupled with Archie's wife (Brenda de Banzie, bedraggled-genteel), reinforces one's feeling that Mr Osborne cannot yet write convincing parts for women. He has bitten off, in this broad new subject, rather more than he can maul. Although the members of Archie's family incessantly harangue each other, they seldom make a human connexion, and you cannot persuade an audience that people are related simply by making them call each other bastards. Tony Richardson's direction is fairly lax throughout, but I cannot see how any director could disguise either the sloth of the first act or the over-compression of the third.

In short: Mr Osborne has planned a gigantic social mural and carried it out in a colour range too narrow for the job. Within that range he has written one of the great acting parts of our age. Archie is a truly desperate man, and to present desperation is a hard dramatic achievement. To explain and account for it, however, is harder still, and that is the task to which I would now direct this dazzling, self-bound writer.

(*1957*)

THE MAKING OF MOO
BY NIGEL DENNIS, AT THE ROYAL COURT

'As to that detestable religion, the Christian...' Thus would Shelley, speaking gently and uncontentiously, strike up conversation at the dinner-table, causing among his fellow-guests much the same affronted consternation that seems to have been felt last Tuesday by many of the critics who witnessed Nigel Dennis's *The Making of Moo*. Few of them, of course, admitted that they had been shocked, but whenever critics use words like 'old-fashioned' and 'tasteless' you may begin to suspect that they have been outraged to the core of their being; and if 'undergraduate joke' is the phrase qualified by 'tasteless', you can be absolutely sure.

Now I will not slander my colleagues by supposing that what shocked them was the play's intellectual content. Mr Dennis is a straightforward rationalist who regards organized religion as an insult to human intelligence. My own guess would be that he leans rather to atheism than agnosticism, that cloak under which atheists gain admission to the Royal Enclosure; but I cannot see how any of his ideas could really startle even the seventy-one per cent of our population who, according to a recent poll, believe that Jesus Christ was the Son of God. No: what shocked my colleagues was not the novelty of Mr Dennis's ideas, but the novelty of hearing them in a theatre. '*Pas devant les enfants!*' was the essence of their reaction to a play which, for all its faults, is a milestone in history: the first outright attack on religion ever to be presented on the English stage.

It is Mr Dennis's simple belief that God, as human beings envisage him, is a thoroughly bad influence on society. And he has had the audacity not only to state his belief in a theatre, but to state it *without reverence* – thereby offending against the rules of fair play. The militant sceptic, according to this curious code, is permitted to disbelieve only as long as he disbelieves reverently; as long as he shows respect for that which he is sworn to demolish. Mr Dennis violates this hypocrisy by showing no respect at all. He is by turns skittish and savage. His final advice to those contemplating religion is:

'Stop when you come to a pool of blood.' Stop, in fact, when you come to a ritual sacrifice, a massacre of heretics, a holy war, or a God-sanctioned nuclear weapon; in other words, don't start. To compare Mr Dennis with Shaw, as several critics have, is to miss the point completely. Even at his most iconoclastic, Shaw always made it clear that he was only kidding. Mr Dennis, by contrast, is in earnest: he means what he says, and expects us to act on it. If his play is crude, it is the forgivable crudity of all pioneer work.

The first act is mild enough. A pompous English dam-builder discovers that he has inadvertently flooded and destroyed the ancestral home of Ega, a native god. Deciding to replace what he has destroyed with (as Robert Ruark's novel has it) 'something of value', he invents a new deity, Moo. His wife takes on the job of writing suitable scriptures, and his secretary, an amateur musician, sets about composing appropriately intimidating hymns. In the second act the cult is really rolling, with a garish liturgy of its own and thousands of adherents blissfully shouting their affirmative answer to the solemn question: 'Have you taken leave of all your senses?' The curtain falls on a tableau at which Shaw would certainly have jibbed: the ritual murder of two casual visitors from the old country. The last scene whisks us into the future. The inventor of the myth has now become a senile patriarch, wheeled daily on to the balcony to receive homage, and his son, a new character, quickly discloses that passionate interest in pain and guilt that stamps the true Protestant.

Mr Dennis makes his points with reckless pungency and eldritch wit. He is more concerned, of course, with ideas than with character, and it takes all the efforts of George Devine, Joan Plowright, and John Osborne to persuade us that a dim trio of suburban expatriates would be capable of such bloody excesses. But my main criticism of the piece is that, for a *soi-disant* 'history of religion', it omits altogether too much. Is Christianity really what Remy de Gourmont called it, 'a machine for creating remorse'? Is a sense of sin a natural endowment or a conditioned reflex? These questions Mr Dennis does not discuss; nor does he investigate the political influence exerted by the Church in such matters as convincing the poor that poverty is a virtue.

But, in spite of these and other gaps, Mr Dennis deserves all our thanks for having introduced the full gaiety of blasphemy to the

English theatre, and our apologies for having welcomed him with reviews that paid no attention to whether his ideas were true or false but devoted themselves instead to the totally irrelevant question of whether or not they would 'give offence'. To 'give offence', it seems, is to be 'in bad taste'. A healthy state, I should judge, to be in. To a theatre that is perishing of decorum, a few more truly offensive, sincerely tasteless plays would come as a reviving boon.

(*1957*)

THE ANGRY YOUNG MOVEMENT

It all came to a head one May evening in 1956 at the Royal Court Theatre in Sloane Square. There had of course been plenty of preliminary rumbles. A group of young British writers had recently published a series of picaresque novels featuring a new sort of hero – a lower-class intellectual with a ribald sense of humour, a robust taste for beer and sex, and an attitude of villainous irreverence towards the established order. A butterfly-theorist named Colin Wilson had written an apocalyptic best-seller about the necessity of being an 'outsider'. An attack had just been launched by the younger movie critics and directors against the genteel vacuity of the British cinema: their new watchword was 'commitment', by which they meant commitment to reality and social truth. A similar rebellion was taking place in the world of painting, where the new 'kitchen-sink school' (so called for its alleged preoccupation with domestic squalor) had begun to move into the lead. Even before the events of that May evening it was clear that the post-war generation in Britain had a good deal to say and was in quite a hurry to say it.

Most of the new rebels were leftish-liberal or outright Socialist; a few, like Colin Wilson, had religious aspirations; but on one point nearly all of them agreed. They detested 'the Establishment', a phrase that had lately been coined to describe the hard core of top people – professional monarchists, archbishops, press barons, Etonian Tories, and *Times* leader writers – who still seemed, in spite of a war and a social revolution, to be exerting a disproportionate influence on the country's affairs. Protest against these apparent immovables was very much in the air. So it was, of course, in the 1930s. But the intelligentsia of that period were mostly rebelling against their own class; many of them were Etonians and most came from solid Establishment backgrounds. The new malcontents were chiefly state-educated lower-middles. Their feeling about the country-house class, which had survived into their era like some grotesque coelacanth, was not one of filial resentment. It was closer to outraged boredom.

Into this combustible atmosphere John Osborne, a lean, esurient actor in his twenty-seventh year, flung a play called *Look Back in Anger*, which summed up what many of his contemporaries were feeling about their rulers and elders. It opened, unheralded, at the Royal Court Theatre; and the explosion of that spring night two years ago is still reverberating through the decorous anterooms of English culture. It was as if, in the tiptoe hush of a polite assembly, someone had deafeningly burped. The theatre's press-agent, asked for a description of the iconoclastic young gate-crasher, said he was first and foremost 'an angry young man'. Before long the phrase, in itself not particularly striking, had snowballed into a cult. It did so because it defined a phenomenon that was nationally recognizable. It gave a name to a generation of young intellectuals who disliked being called intellectuals, since they thought the word phoney, affected, and 'wet'.

There is nothing new in young men being angry: in fact, it would be news if they were anything else. Byron and Shelley were classically angry young men. American writing in the 1930s was on fire with anger: Dos Passos, Steinbeck, and Odets come to mind, all brandishing their fists. The very phrase was used in 1951 by an English social philosopher named Leslie Paul as the title of his autobiography: it is the story of a devout left-wing agitator who lost his faith in Russia during the 1930s and turned, like so many others, to a vague sort of Christian humanism. What distinguishes the modern English 'young angries' is that they all came of age around the time that their elders invented the hydrogen bomb. How could they revere 'civilization as we know it' when at any moment it might be transformed into 'civilization as we knew it'? How could they carry the torch of freedom when to do so meant running with it into the ammunition dump? These unanswerable questions set up feelings of uselessness and impotence, which led in some to apathy, in others to a sort of derisive detachment, and in still others to downright rage. And these feelings were intensified by the knowledge that Britain no longer had a voice strong enough to forbid chaos if, by some horrific chance, it should impend.

Somebody, in short, had to say that many young Britons were fed up; that to be young, so far from being very heaven, was in some ways very hell. Osborne was the first in the theatre to say it; and, the theatre being the naked, public place it is, the statement caused a considerable bang. What made it even more shocking was that both the author and his hero, Jimmy Porter, came from low social shelves, yet had the cheek to be highly articulate on a wide variety of subjects, including the sex war, the class war, and war itself. There was no mistaking the portents. A break-through was beginning. The new intelligentsia created by free education and state scholarships was making its first sizeable dents in the façade of public-school culture.

A few months before, in a Christmas message to the readers of the London *Sunday Times*, Somerset Maugham had expressed his opinions of state-aided undergraduates. It was simple and unequivocal: 'They are scum,' said the Old Party. He was in fact referring to Jim Dixon, the hero of Kingsley Amis's immensely successful novel, *Lucky Jim*. Dixon, who lectures at a minor university, is a frankly comic character, much less ferocious than Jimmy Porter; he keeps his anger in check by drinking and pulling dreadful faces; but he shares with Osborne's hero a defiant provincialism, semi-proletarian origins, and the kind of blithe disgruntlement that inspires such phrases as 'the interminable facetiousness of filthy Mozart'. By Mr Maugham's standards *Look Back in Anger* was the apotheosis of scum. The letter columns of the more pompous dailies were soon filled with similar opinions. These young men (said one correspondent) were just envious upstarts: in a decently run society they would have been sent out to work at fourteen with no time to brood about ideas above their station.

Despite his greater violence and dogmatism, it was clear that Jimmy Porter was speaking essentially the same idiom as Lucky Jim and the heroes of John Wain's *Hurry on Down* and Iris Murdoch's *Under the Net*. Both these novels, the work of writers under thirty, had been grouped with Amis's and achieved a comparable celebrity.

Wain's hero was a young provincial iconoclast whose occupations included, at various times, window-cleaning and dope-running: Miss Murdoch's was an aimless pub-crawler with a mordant sense of humour and a talent for sponging. Both were obvious forerunners of Jimmy Porter. All the same, to most of the London critics he was a new and unheard-of disease. They reacted to the play with flustered disapproval; while acknowledging Osborne's command of dialogue, they dismissed his hero as 'a young pup'.

The salient thing about Jimmy Porter was that we – the under-thirty generation in Britain – recognized him on sight. We had met him; we had pub-crawled with him; we had shared bed-sitting-rooms with him. For the first time the theatre was speaking to us in our own language, on our own terms. Most young people had hitherto regarded the English theatre as a dusty anachronism which, as Dylan Thomas said of a certain Welsh museum, ought to be in a museum. Osborne showed them their error; and some of them even began to write plays.

The under-thirties responded to many qualities in Jimmy Porter – his impulsive, unargued leftishness, his anarchic sense of humour, and his suspicion that all the brave causes had been either won or discredited. For too long British culture had languished in a freezing-unit of understatement and 'good taste'. In these chill latitudes Jimmy Porter flamed like a blowtorch. He was not, like Jean Cocteau, '*trop occupé pour être engagé*'; he cared, and cared bitterly. On the one hand, he represented the dismay of many young Britons whose childhood and adolescence were scarred by the depression and the war; who came of age under a Socialist government, yet found, when they went out into the world, that the class system was still mysteriously intact. On the other hand, he reflected the much wider problem of what to do with a liberal education in a technological world. In Britain, as elsewhere, the men who count are the technocrats of whom Sir Charles Snow writes. Jimmy Porter's education fitted him for entry into the intelligentsia at the very moment when the intelligentsia were ceasing to matter. He lurks, a ghostly, snarling dodo, in the scientists' shadow.

In Europe as on Broadway, it is difficult to escape *Look Back in Anger*. Nearly every repertory company in Britain has performed it, and it is being played all over Germany and Scandinavia. Osborne followed it up in 1957 with another hit, *The Entertainer*, which repercussed almost as widely. In just eighteen months an obscure repertory actor had become one of the most prosperous playwrights of the century, with a weekly income in the neighbourhood of £3,500. Osborne married his leading lady, Mary Ure, and moved into a smart little Chelsea backwater, at least a class and a half above Fulham, the suburb of his birth, where he and his mother (a contented barmaid) at one time subsisted on a joint income of less than a pound a week. Once, as a boy, he was out walking with his grandfather, who surprised him by indignantly cutting a passer-by who greeted them. 'That man's a Socialist,' said grandfather in explanation. 'That's a man who doesn't believe in raising his hat.' Osborne has never found a better definition of his own Socialism: its emblem is an untugged forelock rampant. When a master slapped his face at school, he at once riposted by slapping the master; and this, in Britain, takes preternatural guts.

He is passionate in his refusal to venerate what he calls 'the idiot heroes' of patriotic movies; and his fervent republicanism recently led him to describe the British royal family as 'the gold filling in a mouthful of decay'. He will probably always be a bad belonger, to any party or group; his real talent is for dissent. But when his enemies complain that all his opinions are negative, I think they forget that nowadays there is a positive value in merely standing against a current of events which you believe is moving towards suicide. Osborne is a disconcerting, rather impenetrable person to meet: tall and slim, wearing his shoulders in a defensive bunch around his neck; gentle in manner, yet vocally harsh and cawing; sharp-toothed, yet a convinced vegetarian. He looks wan and driven, and is nervously prone to indulge in sudden, wolfish, silly-ass grins. Sartorially he is something of a peacock, and his sideburns add a sinister touch of the Apache. A dandy, if you like: but a dandy with a machine-gun.

Unlike Jimmy Porter, Osborne never went to a university. This is about all he has in common with Colin Wilson, the brash young metaphysical whose first book, *The Outsider*, was hailed as a masterpiece by several middle-aged critics who saw in its philosophy of salvation through despair an antidote to their own disillusion. Although a playwright can get along without the disciplines of higher education, a philosopher cannot, as Wilson's book awfully proved. As one ploughed through its inconsistencies, repetitions, and flights of paranoid illogic (an experience rather like walking knee-deep in hot sand), all one could state with any certainty was that an 'outsider' was anyone whose books happened to have been on the author's recent library list. 'We read Anatole France,' said a French critic, 'to find out what Anatole France has been reading'; and the same is true of Wilson. He was angry, all right, but his anger was more presumptuously cosmic than that of Osborne and the rest. For him we were not just misguided: we were rotten to the core. As far as I could make out, Wilson's philosophic position was somewhere between existentialism and Norman Vincent Peale; but his talk of a spiritual revival, with an élite of outsiders leading the world out of chaos, exerted a hypnotic charm on the lonely and maladjusted, who are always enticed by the promise of words like élite. Shaw was posthumously enrolled in the cult: not Shaw the Fabian Socialist and wit, but that later, lesser Shaw whose belief in the 'life force' led him to condone dictatorship. This, cried Wilson, was the greatest religious thinker of modern times.

In 1957, fresh from unsuccessful flirtations with acting and play-writing, a twenty-four-year-old Yorkshireman named Stuart Holroyd climbed on the Bund-wagon by writing a philosophical work called *Emergence from Chaos*, which more or less followed the Wilson line. According to Holroyd, democracy was 'a myth' and government was best left to 'an expert minority'; but by now it was beginning to dawn on many people that such ideas, if not consciously fascist, were certainly the soil in which fascism grew. Wilson's second book, *Religion and the Rebel*, appeared last autumn. It proved to be a road-company version of the first, and was obliteratingly panned.

Not all the prominent young Britons of today are self-taught. Many of them were at Oxford when I was there, during the four years immediately after the war. As undergraduate generations go, it was disorderly and a bit piratical, but full of gusto and wildfire. There was plenty of gaiety about, but not of the fox-hunting, cork-popping, bounder-debagging kind that followed World War I; most of the new undergraduates were ex-servicemen living on government grants, for whom upper-class prankishness held very little appeal. Kingsley Amis and John Wain both come from the Oxford of that period. Neither of them had an Oxford accent, which is ordinary speech pushed through a constipated flute: that sort of 'poshness' was emphatically out. Both Amis and Wain were (and are) poets and critics as well as novelists, and after graduation both taught at provincial universities; and it is this all-round academicism that makes their writing at once saner and tamer than, for instance, Osborne's. Another post-war Oxonian was Lindsay Anderson, whose anger with the *status quo* has not been off the boil for at least ten years. A formidable film critic, director, and polemicist, he has done more than anyone else to bring the idea of 'committed art' into public controversy. Many Continental critics today speak of Anderson as if he were the dominant force in British cinema. According to one reporter, the party thrown by Mike Todd after the Cannes *première* of *Around the World in Eighty Days* was entirely made up of people anxiously whispering, in eighteen languages: 'Lindsay didn't like it.' He won an Academy Award in 1955 for *Thursday's Children*, a documentary about the education of deaf-mutes, and a Venice Grand Prix two years later for a forty-minute exploration of life in Covent Garden market; and though he has yet to make a feature film, his position as a critical moralist and spokesman for life-embracing cinema is unique in Britain. Quite apart from its A.Y.M.s, the post-war Oxford vintage was a heady one. It also produced Tony Richardson, who directed both of Osborne's plays in London and on Broadway; Sandy Wilson, author of *The Boy Friend*, the most successful of post-war British musicals; and Roger Bannister, the first four-minute miler. In Labour politics it turned out the virulent back-bencher Anthony Wedgwood Benn; and on the Tory side, Sir Edward Boyle, who was the youngest member of the Eden cabinet when he resigned as a protest against the Franco-British invasion of Egypt.

The flag-wagging, wog-flogging assault on Suez was a great promoter of anger. Passions long thought extinct flared everywhere; people who had prided themselves on their detachment suddenly found themselves clobbering their best friends. Reasonably enough, those who were anti-Suez also tended to be supporters of *Look Back in Anger*. In the heat of the crisis, while smoke-bombs were bursting in Downing Street and mounted police charged the crowds in Whitehall, Osborne conceived his second play, *The Entertainer*. When it opened last April, the leading role was played – and played to the hilt – by Sir Laurence Olivier. Significantly, it was he who approached Osborne for a part, presumably on the principle of joining what you can't lick. This was the Establishment's first bow to the 'angries'. It meant that they had officially arrived.

It also established the Royal Court Theatre as the home of forward-looking British drama. Angus Wilson's first play had its London *première* there; so did Nigel Dennis's Swiftian satire, *Cards of Identity*, and the same author's furious parable, *The Making of Moo*, which is the only overtly atheistic play in the English language. Newcomers like Michael Hastings, the ambitious East End teen-ager, saw their work conscientiously staged; and the whole venture throve, and thrives still, in a heady intellectual ferment. Its fiscal keystone, however, was Osborne, who has proved against all augury that you can make a fortune by telling an audience the very things about itself that it wants least to hear.

On the other side of the Thames the National Film Theatre has developed into a comparable oasis of progressive cinema, with the pugnacious film magazine *Sight and Sound* acting as its ally and interpreter. Nor have I yet mentioned such associated phenomena as the rhetorical left-wing poet Christopher Logue or the stoutly committed art critic John Berger, whose influence on the graphic arts is roughly commensurate with Lindsay Anderson's on the cinema.

The newest angry is a fleshy Yorkshireman named John Braine, whose novel *Room at the Top*, an analysis of the means used by an amoral young opportunist to break into the upper stratum of provincial society, was among the larger English best-sellers of 1957. Shrewd and deliberate of speech, Braine has the stamina of a youthful J. B. Priestley, plus a vein of bizarre, unfettered humour that will probably seep into his next novel: its title, *The Vodi*, is the name of a monumentally batty secret society which has figured in his private fantasies for many years. He is at heart a plain old-fashioned Socialist with a common-sense regional brogue, but there is wildness in his background. He was connected, during the war, with a mildly anarchist group in Yorkshire that published a mimeographed broadsheet with an unprintable name. (One of its members, hating regimentation, gathered together a number of cans and fixed them with wire to selected lamp-posts in the town where he lived. On each can he painted the words: 'Please put your Identity Cards in here.'

Before the police removed the cans he had collected, and sub-sequently burned, nearly five thousand cards.)

Braine exudes ambition and may easily outlast many of his fellow angries. His egotism is extremely disarming. After a long conversation some months ago he warned me not to be surprised if much of our talk turned up in his next book. 'And if you complain of being plagiarized,' he said gustily, with his little finger admonitorily raised, 'I shall expose you to the world as one who tried to climb to fame on the back of that colossus of letters – *Braine*.'

In many directions, a lot of unequal talent is exploding. Certain things, however, seem to be agreed on, certain attitudes towards the relationship of the arts to living. The ivory tower has collapsed for good. The lofty, lapidary, 'mandarin' style of writing has been replaced by prose that has its feet on the ground. And the word 'civilized', which had come to mean 'detached, polite, above the tumult', is being restored to its old etymological meaning: to be civilized nowadays is to care about society and to feel oneself a responsible part of it. The books, plays, poems, films, and paintings that the young Britons are trying to turn out may well be ham-fisted and un-Englishly crude, but they will be based on the idea that art is an influence on life, not a refuge from it or an alternative to it. That, really, is what the anger is all about. It is anger that our kind of world is so chary of that kind of art.

If you object that you have heard this sort of thing before, I urge you to remember that the day you stop hearing it will be the day on which art shrugs its shoulders, gives up the ghost, and dies. Britain's angry young men may be jejune and strident, but they are involved in the only belief that matters: that life begins tomorrow.

(*1958*)

A RESOUNDING TINKLE

BY N. F. SIMPSON, AT THE ROYAL COURT

About the highest tribute I can pay N. F. Simpson's *A Resounding Tinkle*, which was tried out at the Royal Court last Sunday, is to say that it does not belong in the English theatrical tradition at all. It derives from the best Benchley lectures, the wildest Thurber cartoons, and the cream of the Goon Shows. It has some affinities with the early revues of Robert Dhéry and many more with the plays of M. Ionesco. In English drama it is, as far as I know, unique. It is also astonishingly funny, and a superb vindication of the judicial acumen that placed it third in the *Observer* play competition.

To sustain anarchic humour for a full evening is among the hardest things a playwright can attempt. Once having espoused the illogical, the irrelevant, the surreal, he is committed: a single lapse into logic, relevance, or reality, and he is undone. A playwright of Mr Simpson's kind comes defenceless to the theatre. He has voluntarily discarded most of the dramatist's conventional weapons. He can have no plot, since plots demand logical development. Lacking a plot, he can make no use of suspense, that miraculous device which, by focusing our attention on what is going to happen next, prevents us from being intelligently critical of what is happening now. Mr Simpson can never free-wheel like that. At every turn he must take us by surprise. His method must be a perpetual ambush. All playwrights must invent, but he must invent incessantly and unpredictably. It is the only weapon left him – he is otherwise naked. As naked, perhaps, as a British Foreign Secretary without an H-bomb; yet unilateral disarmament, even in the theatre, is an extremely disarming thing. At least, the audience seemed to find it so.

What they saw, hilarious though it was, notably differed from the play to which we of the *Observer* awarded the prize. Mr Simpson had revised and reshuffled it, and there were moments when I felt like the American director who, revisiting one of his old productions, found it necessary to call an immediate rehearsal 'to take out the improvements'. The original text began in the suburban home of Bro and

Middie Paradock, a young married couple disturbed by the presence, in their front garden, of an elephant they had not ordered. The question soon arose of how to name it. Middie conservatively favoured 'Mr Trench', their usual name for unexpectedly delivered animals, a suggestion which the radical Bro countered with bravura alternatives such as ''Tis-Pity-She's-A-Whore Hignett'. The debate was interrupted by the arrival of two Comedians, who were lodged in the kitchen, from which they emerged from time to time to discuss, with examples, the nature of comedy. This arrangement set up what I may call, with a deep breath, a sort of counterpoint. Mr Simpson has since decided to lump all the Comedian scenes together into his first act, while reserving the Paradock scenes for the second. I take this to be a back-breaking error, and when the English Stage Company decides (as it surely must) to put on the play for a run, I hope it will amalgamate the two texts and insist on a new ending.

Even as it stands, this is a revolutionarily funny piece of work. In a programme note Mr Simpson declares his indebtedness to the simple fact that the earth, given luck, can support life for another twelve hundred thousand years. How, for so long, are we to keep ourselves amused? This is the problem that faced the tramps in *Waiting for Godot*. An astonished patience is Mr Simpson's answer, as he implies when one of the Comedians doubts the audience's ability to sit through a play full of pauses and the other replies by asking him whether he has ever complained of buying a sponge full of holes.

I prefer Mr Simpson's assumption, which is that we are all on the brink of boredom, to that of most comic writers, which is that we are all on the brink of hilarity. Bro Paradock (Nigel Davenport) is a splendidly sour creation, drab, leather-elbowed, and disgruntled, comic because he reacts with no surprise to circumstances of absolute fantasy. Neither he nor his wife, Middie (Wendy Craig, a pretty study of controlled disgust), is perturbed when their Uncle Ted turns out to be a woman; and he has nothing but quiet scorn for the man who calls and asks him, at six o'clock in the evening, to form a Government. (As he says, that's the Prime Minister's job.)

About a fifth of Mr Simpson's family portrait is *voulu*, polysyllabic, and of a determined quaintness. The rest is pure plutonium, by which I mean something that is rarer than gold.

(1957)

EPITAPH FOR GEORGE DILLON

BY JOHN OSBORNE AND ANTHONY CREIGHTON, AT THE ROYAL COURT

The second act of *Epitaph for George Dillon*, written four years ago by John Osborne and Anthony Creighton, contains a long duologue which in terms of human contact and mutual exploration is better than anything in Mr Osborne's later unaided works. One of the participants is Dillon himself, a *farouche* young actor-dramatist currently sponging on a suburban family straight out of Mr Coward's *Fumed Oak*. (Subject for a thesis: estimate the influence on Mr Osborne's later plays of *The Vortex* and *Red Peppers*, also bearing in mind that the dismissive use of 'little', favoured by Mr Osborne in a plethora of phrases beginning 'nasty little', 'feeble little', 'sordid little', etc., was pioneered by Mr Coward in the twenties.) Dillon has walked out on his wife, a prosperous actress whom he venomously accuses, *à la* Jimmy Porter, of having 'betrayed' him. In his new suburban bolt-hole he meets, as Jimmy never did, his intellectual match.

This is Aunt Ruth, the family outsider, whose life has hit the emotional doldrums. She has just ended two affairs, one of them with Communism and the other with a young writer skilled in the neurotic art of extorting love by means of pathos. The job of playing March-banks to her Candida is temporarily vacant. George volunteers for the part, and the scene in which they come to grips (or, rather, fail to come to grips) is an object lesson in meaty, muscular, dramatic writing.

Ruth, the born giver, slowly recognizes in George a born taker. He savages her cliché-ridden family, whom he regards as part of a universal conspiracy to destroy him. 'I attract hostility,' he declares in a paranoid ecstasy, 'I'm on heat for it.' (Note the female sexual image: one would love to let a good analyst loose on George.) Whenever he goes too far, he resorts to spasms of little-boy charm and bursts of comic improvisation; but though Ruth laughs with him and is sorry for him, she has lived through such scenes before. No more of that sickness for her; no more diving to the rescue of people who scream for help while lying in puddles, achieving by the pretence of drowning a voluptuous fusion of self-pity and power over others. George's only justification for his behaviour is his talent. But where, as Ruth piercingly reminds him, is the evidence that he has any talent at all? And at length George admits to a terrible doubt. He has all the popular symptoms of genius, but perhaps not the disease itself. The admission, however, cuts no ice with Ruth, and George has to console himself by jumping into bed with her teen-age niece.

Up to this point, apart from a few glaring crudities in the handling of flashbacks, the play is entirely successful – powerful, honest, and transfixing. The spirit of suburbia is lovingly captured in Stephen Doncaster's setting and the performances of Alison Leggatt, Wendy Craig, and especially Avril Elgar, whose dowdy spinster daughter, merry as a jerboa, is twin sister to Alec Guinness's unforgotten Abel Drugger. William Gaskill's direction drives shrewdly throughout.

Yvonne Mitchell, though she lacks the years for the part, plays Ruth with a steely, sad directness that is exactly right; and one could not wish for a better George than Robert Stephens, one of the new 'red-brick actors', neither actorish in aspect nor conventionally po-voiced, to whom the English Stage Company has introduced us. Mr Stephens makes George both wolfish and wan, and there is in his voice a cawing note that may even have been modelled on Mr Osborne himself. This is the cleverest portrait I have seen of a certain kind of neurotic artist.

But what kind? Good or bad? And this is where the authors let us down. In the third act George makes one of his plays a provincial hit by spiking it with sex; simultaneously he recovers from an attack of T.B. and agrees to marry Ruth's niece, who is pregnant by him. He ends in tears. But are they the tears of a good writer frustrated by the commercial theatre and suburban morality? Or the tears of a bad writer who has at last met himself face to face? We are given no clue. If George is seriously intended to be a persecuted genius, then the whole play, not just the hero, is paranoid to the point of hysteria. If, on the other hand, he is a mediocre writer forced at length to accept his own mediocrity, it is a play of astounding courage and strength. The authors shrug and allow us to guess which answer is right, which is as if one were to write a play about the crucifixion of a miracle healer without giving the smallest hint as to whether the cures worked. Have we been rooting for a phoney or the real thing? The mere fact of doubt indicates that the play has misfired. Yet the fire is there, boiling and licking, however neurotically; and you must not miss that second act.

(*1958*)

THE POTTING SHED

BY GRAHAM GREENE, AT THE GLOBE

The time is ten years hence, a decade after the London opening of Graham Greene's *The Potting Shed*. A Failed Drama Critic lies abed in his dingy lodgings, up to here in Scotch. Around him are the bleak and grimy symbols of his faith – the cobwebbed bust of Brecht, the mildewed model of the National Theatre, the yellowing autograph of Stanislavsky, the drab little pot of clotted Eulogy, the rusty Panning Pen. He looks somehow void and empty, though of course, as we know, he is up to here. A young Psychiatrist is interrogating him.

P.: But in that case why do you still go to the theatre?

C. (*simply, if indistinctly*): It's my job. Once a critic, always a critic. It's my half of the promise. Sometimes I fall down during the Anthem and disappear for acts on end, and then they have to take my pen away for a while. But I always come back. The people need critics, and a whisky-critic's better than none.

P.: Even if he's lost his vocation?

C.: Even then. But don't misunderstand me. I'm not a bad critic. I go through the motions. I get out of bed every day at seven o'clock in the evening and go to the theatre. Sometimes there isn't a play on, but I go anyway, in case I'm needed. It's a matter of conscience. Have another slug of fire-water.

P.: Not just now. Can you remember exactly where you lost your faith? When did you last have it with you?

C.: I didn't lose it. It was taken away from me one night ten years ago at the old Globe Theatre, before they turned it into a car-park. John Gielgud was in the play. Very wrought-up he was, very curt and brusque – you know how he used to talk to other actors as if he was going to tip them? Irene Worth played his ex-wife. Then there was Gwen Ffrangcon-Davies, very fierce, and a clever little pouter called Sarah Long. And Redmond Phillips – he played a frocked sot on the brink of the shakes. He was the best of a fine lot. No, you couldn't complain about the acting. But somehow that made it worse. (*He sobs controllably.*)

P. (*controllingly*): Tell me about the play. Force yourself back into the theatre. Slump now as you slumped then in D16.

C. (*in a hoarse whisper*): Graham Greene wrote it. It began with the death of a famous atheist, head of a rationalist clan. Greene made them out to be a bunch of decrepit puritans, so old-fashioned that they even enjoyed the company of dowdy dullards like Bertrand Russell. But fair enough: Greene's a Catholic, and the history of Catholicism shows that you can't make an omelette without breaking eggheads. Anti-intellectual jokes are part of the recipe. At first I thought I was in for a whodunit. The old man's son – Sir John – was kept away from the death-bed because of something nameless that had happened to him in the potting shed at the age of fourteen. There were clues all over the place. For one thing, he had recently lost his dog. . . .

P. (*shrewdly*): Dog is God spelled backwards.

C.: The same crude thought occurred to me, but I rejected it (pity my complexity) as being unworthy of the author. How wrong I was! The hero's subsequent investigations into his past revealed that we were indeed dealing not with a whodunit but a God-dunit. He had hanged himself in the dread shed, and demonstrably died. And his uncle, the priest, had begged God to revive him. Make me an offer, haggled the Deity. My faith in exchange for the boy's life, said the priest: and so the repulsive bargain was struck. The boy lived, and uncle lost his faith. My first impulse on hearing these farcical revelations was to protest by the only means at my disposal: a derisive hiccup. But then I looked about me and saw row after row of rapt, attentive faces. *They were taking it seriously!* And suddenly, in a blaze of darkness, I knew that my faith in the theatre and the people who attend it had been withdrawn from me.

P.: But why?

C.: You may not now remember the theatre as it was ten years ago. It seemed on the brink of renaissance. I was one of many who were newly flushed with a great conviction. We recklessly believed that a theatre was a place where human problems could be stated in human terms, a place from which supernatural intervention as a solution to such problems had at long last been ousted. Drama for us was an affirmation of humanism, and its basic maxim was not: 'I die that you may live,' but: 'I *live* that you may live.' *The Potting Shed*, financed by two normally intelligent managements at a highly reputable theatre, shot us back overnight to the dark ages.

P.: But what about Gibbon? 'The Catholic superstition, which is always the enemy of reason, is often the parent of the arts'?

C.: Art that is not allied with reason is today the enemy of life. And now you must excuse me. You have kept me in bed long after my usual time for getting up. And I have a first-night to attend. The play, I understand, is a fearless indictment of a priest who refuses to accompany a murderer to the scaffold because of stupid, heretical, rationalist doubts about the efficacy of prayer to bring the man back to life. The bounder will no doubt be shown his error. Meanwhile (*he takes a deep draught of red-eye*), here's to good old G.G.! Who said the Pope had no divisions? (*He departs, half-clad and half-cut, to perform in a spirit of obedient humility the offices laid down for him by providence and the Society of West End Theatre Managers.*)

(*1958*)

A RESOUNDING TINKLE AND THE HOLE

BY N. F. SIMPSON, AT THE ROYAL COURT

Two years ago last Tuesday there was no English Stage Company. What a dull theatre we must have had! And what on earth did we playgoers find to argue about? After only two years I can scarcely remember the theatrical landscape as it was before George Devine set up shop in Sloane Square and called in John Osborne, the Fulham flamethrower, to scald us with his rhetoric. The climate, on the whole, was listless. We quarrelled among ourselves over Brecht and the future of poetic drama; in debates with foreign visitors we crossed our fingers, swallowed hard, and talked of Terence Rattigan; but if we were critics, we must quite often have felt that we were practising our art in a vacuum.

In two years and twenty-eight productions the Royal Court has changed all that. To an extent unknown since the Ibsen riots, it has made drama a matter of public controversy. It has button-holed us with new voices, some of them bawdy, many of them irreverent, and all of them calculated to bring gooseflesh to the evening of Aunt Edna's life. It has raised hackles, Cain, laughs, and the standards of English dramaturgy. It has given the modern repertoire a permanent London address. At times, perhaps, it has appealed too exclusively to the *côterie*-votaries (Chelsea offshoots of the North American culture-vultures). Yet in spite of this it has reached out and captured popular audiences on television and Broadway and in the West End. Once or twice, quite spectacularly, the Court has fallen on its face, but this is one of the occupational hazards you must expect if you set out to climb mountains. For the most part it has given my mind a whetstone, and my job a meaning, that the English theatre of five years ago showed few signs of providing. If (and the if is crucial) it can hold its present nucleus of talent together, it may very well change the whole course of English drama.

It has celebrated its second birthday by giving us a present: a dazzling new playwright. On the strength of his double bill, *A Resounding Tinkle* and *The Hole*, I am ready to burn my boats and pronounce N. F. Simpson the most gifted comic writer the English stage has discovered since the war. The first of his two plays, which has been drastically cut and revised since it won a third prize in the *Observer* competition, I reviewed when the Court gave it a Sunday showing last year. I indicated its affinities with M. Ionesco, M. Dhéry, and the late Robert Benchley. I tried to explain how and why it had convulsed me, this casual surrealist sketch of a suburban couple with an elephant at their front door; and, had space allowed, I would have applied to Mr Simpson what Sir Max Beerbohm said of humorists in general:

The jester must be able to grapple his theme and hang on to it, twisting it this way and that, and making it yield magically all manner of strange and precious things, one after another, without pause. He must have invention keeping pace with utterance. He must be inexhaustible. Only so can he exhaust us.

But I wondered at the time how Mr Simpson would follow his *tour de force*. Could he bring it off again without repeating himself? *The Hole* proved triumphantly that he could; that he was no mere flash in the pen, but a true lord of language, capable of using words with the sublime, outrageous authority of Humpty Dumpty.

People who believe with John Lehmann that English writers have lost interest in verbal and stylistic experiment should see Mr Simpson's work and recant. Indeed, everyone should see it: for it is not a private highbrow joke, but pure farce, wild and liberated, on a level accessible to anyone who has ever enjoyed the radio Goons (Peter Sellers and Spike Milligan, especially) or treasured the memory of W. C. Fields. I suspect, in fact, that Goon-lovers, who are accustomed to verbal firework displays at which logic is burnt in effigy, may get more sheer pleasure out of Mr Simpson than professional intellectuals, against whose habit of worrying about the meaning of things the play is essentially directed. At heart it is a riotous satire at the expense of people who deal in pigeon-holes, categories, and generalizations, seeking to pin down to a consistent pattern the unrepeatable variety of human existence, working out comprehensive philosophical and religious systems in which somehow one vital thing gets forgotten: the glorious uniqueness of everything that is.

A tramp, who describes himself as 'the nucleus of a queue', is peering into a hole in the road. Others join him, among them a rabid authoritarian, a drifting rubberneck, and a student philosopher: each has a fantastic vision of what is going on down the hole and tries to impose it on the others. They are interrupted, from time to time, by two housewives, one with a husband who desperately wants to be the same as everyone else ('There's nothing Sid wouldn't do to be *identical* with somebody'), the other with a husband who wants, equally desperately, to be different. . . . But here I must stop, for I am falling into the very trap Mr Simpson has laid for us intellectuals.

I am explaining instead of experiencing. And I am in danger of letting you forget that Mr Simpson is ceaselessly, mortally, and unpredictably funny. With Michelet, he cries: '*Mon moi! Ils m'arrachent mon moi!*' – and if that is bourgeois individualism, long may it thrive.

(*1958*)

VARIATIONS ON A THEME
BY TERENCE RATTIGAN, AT THE GLOBE

Let us suppose that Terence Rattigan's Muse, a brisk, tweedy travelling representative of Thalia–Melpomene Co-Productions Ltd, has just returned home after four years' absence. We find her reading the reviews of Mr Rattigan's *Variations on a Theme*. After a while she flings them impatiently down. Her tone, as she addresses us, is querulous:

MUSE: This would never have happened if I'd been here. We get *Separate Tables* launched, I go off on a world cruise, and as soon as my back's turned, what happens? He tries to write a play on his own. Oh, he's threatened to do that before now, but I've always scared him out of it. 'Look what happened to Noël Coward,' I'd say. *That* usually did the trick. 'Just you wait till I'm ready,' I'd say. 'Inspiration doesn't grow on trees, you know.' But Master Terence Slyboots knows better. Thinks you can write plays just like that, haha. The minute I heard what he was up to I came beetling back, but they were already in rehearsal.

'What's the meaning of this?' I said, and I can tell you I was blazing. 'Well, darling,' he said, 'four years is a long time, and –' 'Don't you darling me,' I said. 'I'm a busy Muse. I've got my other clients to consider. You're not the only pebble on the Non-Controversial Western Playwrights' beach, you know. Now let's get down to cases. What's this play about?' 'Well,' he said, 'the central character, who's rich and bored and lives in a villa near Cannes, gets desperately fond of a cocky young boy from the local ballet company, and –' 'Hold your horses,' I said. 'We've never had a play banned yet, and, by

George, we're not starting now. Make it a cocky young *girl*.' 'The central character,' he said, very hoity-toity, 'is a *woman*.'

Black mark to me, I must admit. But once I'd grabbed hold of the script and taken a good dekko at it, my worst fears were confirmed. About the best you could say about it was that it wouldn't be banned. This heroine (he calls her Rose Fish and then, if you please, makes jokes about whether or not she has gills) started out as a typist in Birmingham. She's married four men for money before she meets this ballet-boy. He's been keeping company with a male choreographer, but give the devil his due, Master Terence knows his Lord Chamberlain well enough to keep *that* relationship platonic.

Egged on by the choreographer, Rose gives the lad up for the good of his career. He reforms overnight, but returns to her just as she's in the last throes of succumbing to a wonky lung. And in case you haven't cottoned on to the fact that it's Marguerite Gautier all over again, Rose has a daughter whose pet author is Dumas *fils*. Master Terence makes no bones about his sources. Trouble is, he makes no flesh either. That's where I should have come in. Honestly, I could slap the scamp.

'Interesting subject, don't you think?' he said when I gave the script back to him. 'No,' I said, 'but you've made a real Camille of it, haven't you?' He ignored my barbed word-play. Ruthlessly I pressed on. 'Whatever became,' I asked, 'of that subtle theatrical technique of yours we hear so much about? T.B., indeed, in this day and age! And making the boy symbolically sprain his ankle. And having Rose leave her farewell message to him on a tape-recorder. And giving her a *confidante* I'd have been ashamed to wish on Pinero. And what about that Sherman lover of hers who is talking the so comic English? If you'd written the play well, it would have been bad enough. As it is —' 'I thought the theme would carry it,' he said, 'a young boy living off an older woman.' That made me plain ratty. 'You're not Colette,' I said, 'and don't you think it.'

Anyway, I've told Master Terence that from now on he can whistle for his Muse. I'm not going to come crawling back to him. He thinks the play will succeed in spite of me, in spite of its lack of inspiration. He thinks it's what the public wants. But that reminds me of what Groucho Marx said when three thousand people turned up at the funeral of a rich Hollywood mogul whom everyone loathed.

'You see what I mean?' he said. 'Give the public what they want, and they'll come to see it.' I hope Master Terence heeds the warning. I can get along without him, thank you very much. But he can't get along without me.

(1958)

THE HOSTAGE

BY BRENDAN BEHAN, AT THE THEATRE ROYAL, STRATFORD-ATTE-BOWE

At the end of N. F. Simpson's *A Resounding Tinkle* there is a passage, aberrantly omitted from the Royal Court production, in which four B.B.C. critics discuss the play. It reads, in part:

CHAIRMAN: Denzil Pepper – what do you make of this?
PEPPER: This is a hotchpotch. I think that emerges quite clearly. The thing has been thrown together – a veritable rag-bag of last year's damp fireworks, if a mixed metaphor is in order.
MISS SALT: Yes, I suppose it *is* what we must call a hotchpotch. I do think, though – accepting Denzil Pepper's definition – I do think, and this is the point I feel we ought to make, it is surely, isn't it, an *inspired* hotchpotch?
PEPPER: A hotchpotch de luxe. . . . A theatrical haggis.
CHAIRMAN: Isn't this what our ancestors would have delighted in calling a gallimaufry?
(*Pause*)
MUSTARD: Yes. I'm not sure that I don't prefer the word gallimaufry to Denzil Pepper's hodgepodge.
PEPPER: Hotchpotch. No, I stick, quite unrepentantly, to my own word. . . .

The satanic accuracy of all this is enough to make any critic's elbow fly defensively up. I quote it because it has a chilling relevance to Brendan Behan's *The Hostage*. He would, I fancy, be a pretty perjured critic who could swear that no such thoughts infested his mind while watching Mr Behan's new (careful now) – Mr Behan's new *play*. I use the word advisedly, and have since sacked my advisers –

for conventional terminology is totally inept to describe the uses to which Mr Behan and his director, Joan Littlewood, are trying to put the theatre. The old pigeon-holes will no longer serve.

From a critic's point of view, the history of twentieth-century drama is the history of a collapsing vocabulary. Categories that were formerly thought sacred and separate began to melt and flow together, like images in a dream. Reaching, to steady himself, for words and concepts that had withstood the erosion of centuries, the critic found himself, more often than not, clutching a handful of dust. Already, long before 1900, tragedy and comedy had abandoned the pretence of competition and become a double act, exchanging their masks so rapidly that the effort of distinguishing one from the other was at best a pedantic exercise. Farce and satire, meanwhile, were miscegenating as busily as ever, and both were conducting affairs on the side with revue and musical comedy. Opera, with Brecht and Weill, got into everybody's act; and vaudeville, to cap everything, started to flirt with tragi-comedy in *Waiting for Godot* and *The Entertainer*.

The critic, to whom the correct assignment of compartments is as vital as it is to the employees of Wagons-Lits, reeled in poleaxed confusion. What had happened was that multi-party drama was moving towards coalition government. Polonius did not know the half of it: a modern play can, if it wishes, be tragical-comical-historical-pastoral-farcical-satirical-operatical-musical-music-hall, in any combination or all at the same time. And it is only because we have short memories that we forget that a phrase already exists to cover all these seemingly disparate breeds. It is *commedia dell'arte*. *The Hostage* is a *commedia dell'arte* production.

Its theme is Ireland, seen through the bloodshot prism of Mr Behan's talent. The action, which is noisy and incessant, takes place in a Dublin lodging-house owned by a Blimpish veteran of the Troubles whose Anglophobia is so devout that he calls himself Monsieur instead of Mr. His caretaker is Pat (Howard Goorney), a morose braggart who feels that all the gaiety departed from the cause of Irish liberty when the I.R.A. became temperate, dedicated, and holy. Already, perhaps, this sounds like a normal play; and it may well sound like a tragedy when I add that the plot concerns a kidnapped Cockney soldier who is threatened with death unless his opposite number, an I.R.A. prisoner sentenced to be hanged, is reprieved. Yet there are, in this production, more than twenty songs, many of them blasphemously or lecherously gay, and some of them sung by the hostage himself. Their authorship is attributed to Mr Behan, his uncle, and 'Trad'. Nor can one be sure how much of the dialogue is pure Behan and how much is gifted embroidery; for the whole production sounds spontaneous, a communal achievement based on Miss Littlewood's idea of theatre as a place where people talk to people, not actors to audiences. As with Brecht, actors step in and out of character so readily that phrases like 'dramatic unity' are ruled out of court; we are simply watching a group of human beings who have come together to tell a lively story in speech and song.

Some of the speech is brilliant mock-heroic; some of it is merely crude. Some of the songs are warmly ironic; others are more savagely funny. Some of the acting is sheer vaudeville; some of it (Murray Melvin as the captive, and Celia Salkeld as the country girl whom, briefly and abruptly, he loves) is tenderly realistic. The work ends in a mixed, happy jabber of styles, with a piano playing silent-screen music while the Cockney is rescued and accidentally shot by one of the lodgers, who defiantly cries, in the last line to be audibly uttered: 'I'm a secret policeman, and I don't care who knows it!'

Inchoate as it often is, this is a prophetic and joyously exciting evening. It seems to be Ireland's function, every twenty years or so, to provide a playwright who will kick English drama from the past into the present. Mr Behan may well fill the place vacated by Sean O'Casey. Perhaps more important, Miss Littlewood's production is a boisterous premonition of something we all want – a biting popular drama that does not depend on hit songs, star names, spa sophistication, or the more melodramatic aspects of homosexuality. Sean Kenny's setting, a skeleton stockade of a bedroom surrounded by a towering blind alley of slum windows, is, as often at this theatre, by far the best in London.

(1958)

THE ELDER STATESMAN
BY T. S. ELIOT, AT THE LYCEUM, EDINBURGH

Last week, for the third time in twelve years, the Edinburgh Festival presented the world *première* of a play by T. S. Eliot. It has not always been the same play, though sometimes it has seemed so: in this author's imagination the same themes compulsively (and not always compellingly) recur, among them a guilt-bearing death in a man's past, the human need for contrition and absolution, and the paradox whereby true selfhood can be attained only through self-abnegation.

The Elder Statesman contains all these, together with a rich haul of familiar stylistic devices. Images calculated to evoke well-bred dread cluster together ('The laughter in the doorway, the snicker in the corridor, the sudden silence in the smoking-room'); percipient aphorisms alternate with verbal horseplay, as when an old lag remarks:

> Forgery, I can tell you, is a mug's game.
> I say that with conviction. Ha ha! yes, with conviction.

And Mr Eliot's trick of iteration frequently verges on outright parody:

> I see more and more clearly
> The many many mistakes I have made
> My whole life through, mistake upon mistake,
> The mistaken attempts to correct mistakes
> By methods which proved to be equally mistaken.

At moments like this *The Elder Statesman* comes dangerously near to the competition pages of the *New Statesman*.

But if the old Eliot is well in evidence, the voice of a new Eliot is also heard, unexpectedly endorsing the merits of human love. It is a safe bet that the word 'love' occurs more often in the present play than in all the author's previous work put together: the new Eliot has majored in the Humanities as well as the Eumenides. Often in the past, as the latest Eliot unfolded chill and chaste before us, we have inwardly murmured: 'Poor Tom's a-cold.' Now, by comparison, he is positively aflame.

Encouraging though we may find this step in his spiritual development, it is not by itself enough to make good theatre. In some ways, indeed, it has the opposite effect: Mr Eliot's Indian-summer love-lyrics have little distinction, either literary or dramatic. A new simplicity has certainly entered his style, but so has simplicity's half-wit brother, banality; and at times one longs for the old equivocations, for just one kind of characteristic ambiguity.

This banality extends to the plot. Lord Claverton, politician and tycoon, has retired to a convalescent home, accompanied by his beloved and adoring daughter. Two figures from his past return to plague him, each a reminder of an occasion when he behaved dishonourably. One of them, a prosperous crook from Latin America, was with him when, as an undergraduate motorist, he ran over a man and failed to stop; true, the victim was dead already, but technical innocence, as Claverton knows, is poles apart from moral innocence. His second tormentor is a rich, ageing *chanteuse* whom long ago he seduced and paid off in order to avoid a breach-of-promise action. Other, affiliated sins come home to him. The crook might not have turned to crime, might even have got a First, had not Claverton introduced him to the pleasures of the *luxe* life. Moreover – last item in the catalogue – the old man has sought to dominate his son, who has become in consequence a mutinous wastrel.

By way of expiation Claverton makes a full confession of his misdeeds to his daughter and her fiancé. Duly absolved, having found his true self by sloughing off the sham, he goes off to die mysteriously beneath a great beech tree in the grounds of the sanatorium. He has learned patience and strength; the two lovers, left alone, celebrate their union in language more suggestive of Patience Strong.

It does not help to point out that Mr Eliot has based his play on *Oedipus at Colonus*, in which the guilty, discredited king journeys with his faithful daughters to the sacred grove. Translated into a world of board-rooms and pin-striped trousers, Sophocles becomes Pinero on stilts – the old story of the great man whose past catches up with him, the hero who has Lived a Lie. The more we remember the Sophoclean background, the more we are conscious of the disparity between

Claverton, with his puny sins and facile absolution, and the tremendous obsessing agonies of Oedipus. One's conclusion must be that out of the wisdom of his years and the intensity of his cerebration Mr Eliot has come up with a gigantic platitude. Towards the end, to be sure, he casts over the play a sedative, autumnal glow of considerable beauty, and here and there a scattered phrase reminds us, by its spare precision, that we are listening to a poet. On the whole, however, the evening offers little more than the mild pleasure of hearing ancient verities tepidly restated.

The production, by E. Martin Browne, is careful and suave, with settings by Hutchinson Scott that loyally hint at Attic temples and holy grottoes. Paul Rogers lends Claverton a fine shaggy sonority and the right look of stoic dismay, as of a man staring past the fire into his thoughts. Anna Massey, of the beseeching face and shining eyes, is a first-rate stand-in for Antigone, and Alec McCowen is bonily brilliant as the rebel son.

(*1958*)

KRAPP'S LAST TAPE AND END-GAME

BY SAMUEL BECKETT, AT THE ROYAL COURT

Slamm's Last Knock, a play inspired, if that is the word, by Samuel Beckett's double bill at the Royal Court:

> *The den of Slamm, the critic. Very late yesterday. Large desk with throne behind it. Two waste-paper baskets, one black, one white, filled with crumpled pieces of paper, at either side of the stage. Shambling between them – i.e., from one to the other and back again – an old man: Slamm. Bent gait. Thin, barking voice. Motionless, watching Slamm, is Seck. Bright grey face, holding pad and pencil. One crutch. Slamm goes to black basket, takes out piece of white paper, uncrumples it, reads. Short laugh.*

SLAMM (*reading*): '. . . the validity of an authentic tragic vision, at once personal and by implication cosmic . . .'

Short laugh. He recrumples the paper, replaces it in basket, and crosses to other – i.e., white – basket. He takes out piece of black paper, uncrumples it, reads. Short laugh.

SLAMM (*reading*): '. . . Just another dose of nightmare gibberish from the so-called author of *Waiting for Godot* . . .'

(*Short laugh. He recrumples the paper, replaces it in basket, and sits on throne. Pause. Anguished, he extends fingers of right hand and stares at them. Extends fingers of left hand. Same business. Then brings fingers of right hand towards fingers of left hand, and vice versa, so that fingertips of right hand touch fingertips of left hand. Same business. Breaks wind pensively. Seck writes feverishly on pad.*)

SLAMM: We're getting on. (*He sighs.*) Read that back.

SECK (*produces pince-nez with thick black lenses, places them on bridge of nose, reads*): 'A tragic dose of authentic gibberish from the so-called implication of *Waiting for Godot*.' Shall I go on?

SLAMM (*nodding head*): No. (*Pause.*) A bit of both, then.

SECK (*shaking head*): Or a little of neither.

SLAMM: There's the hell of it. (*Pause. Urgently.*) Is it time for my Roget?

SECK: There are no more Rogets. Use your loaf.

SLAMM: Then wind me up, stink-louse! Stir your stump!

(*Seck hobbles to Slamm, holding rusty key depending from piece of string round his (Seck's) neck, and inserts it into back of Slamm's head. Loud noise of winding.*)

SLAMM: Easy now. Can't you see it's hell in there?

SECK: I haven't looked. (*Pause.*) It's hell out here, too. The ceiling is zero and there's grit in my crotch. Roget and over.

(*He stops winding and watches. Pause.*)

SLAMM (*glazed stare*): Nothing is always starting to happen.

SECK: It's better than something. You're well out of that.

SLAMM: I'm badly into this. (*He tries to yawn but fails.*) It would be better if I could yawn. Or if you could yawn.

SECK: I don't feel excited enough. (*Pause.*) Anything coming?

SLAMM: Nothing, in spades. (*Pause.*) Perhaps I haven't been kissed enough. Or perhaps they put the wrong ash in my gruel. One or the other.

SECK: Nothing will come of nothing. Come again.

SLAMM (*with violence*): Purulent drudge! *You* try, if you've got so much grit in your crotch! Just one pitiless, pathetic, creatively critical phrase!

SECK: I heard you the first time.

SLAMM: You can't have been listening.

SECK: Your word's good enough for me.

SLAMM: I haven't got a word. There's just the light, going. (*Pause.*) Are you trying?

SECK: Less and less.

SLAMM: Try blowing down it.

SECK: It's coming! (*Screws up his face. Tonelessly.*) Sometimes I wonder why I spend the lonely night.

SLAMM: Too many f's. We're bitched. (*Half a pause.*)

SECK: Hold your pauses. It's coming again. (*In a raconteur's voice, dictates to himself.*) Tuesday night, seven-thirty by the paranoid barometer, curtain up at the Court, Sam Beckett unrivalled master of the unravelled revels. Item: *Krapp's Last Tape*, Krapp being a myopic not to say deaf not to say eremitical eater of one and one-half bananas listening and cackling as he listens to a tape-recording of twenty years' antiquity made on a day, the one far gone day, when he laid his hand on a girl in a boat and it worked, as it worked for Molly Bloom in Gibraltar in the long ago. Actor: Patrick Magee, bereaved and aghast-looking grunting into his Grundig, probably perfect performance, fine throughout and highly affecting at third curtain-call though not formerly. Unique, oblique, bleak experience, in other words, and would have had same effect if half the words *were* other words. Or any words. (*Pause.*)

SLAMM: Don't stop. You're boring me.

SECK (*normal voice*): Not enough. You're smiling.

SLAMM: Well, I'm still in the land of the dying.

SECK: Somehow, in spite of everything, death goes on.

SLAMM: Or because of everything. (*Pause.*) Go on.

SECK (*raconteur's voice*): Tuesday night, eight-twenty by the Fahrenheit anonymeter, *End-Game*, translated from the French with loss by excision of the vernacular word for urination and of certain doubts blasphemously cast on the legitimacy of the Deity. Themes, madam? Nay, it *is*, I know not themes. Foreground figure a blind and lordly cripple with superficial mannerisms of Churchill, W., Connolly, C., and Devine, G., director and in this case impersonator. Sawn-off parents in bins, stage right, and shuffling servant, all over the stage, played by Jack MacGowran, binster of this parish. Purpose: to analyse or rather to dissect or rather to define the nature or rather the quality or rather the intensity of the boredom inherent or rather embedded in the twentieth or rather every other century. I am bored, therefore I am. Comment as above, except it would have the same effect if a quarter of the words were other words and another quarter omitted. Critique ended. Thesaurus and out.

SLAMM: Heavy going. I can't see.

SECK: That's because of the light going.

SLAMM: Is that all the review he's getting?

SECK: That's all the play he's written.

(*Pause.*)

SLAMM: But a genius. Could you do as much?

SECK: Not as much. But as little.

(*Tableau. Pause. Curtain.*)

(*1958*)

SUMMING-UP: 1959

As recently as five years ago, popular theatre in the West End of London was virtually dominated by a ruthless three-power coalition consisting of drawing-room comedy and its two junior henchmen, murder melodrama and barrack-room farce. Although competitive among themselves, the members of the combine were united in their determination to prevent the forces of contemporary reality from muscling in on their territory. The average playwright had ceased trying to hold the mirror up to nature, and the fashionable playwright could not possibly hold a mirror up to anything, since genteel idiom demanded the use of the word 'looking-glass'. Nightly, in dozens of theatres, the curtain rose on the same set. French windows were its most prominent feature, backed by a sky-cloth of brilliant and perpetual blue. In the cheaper sort of production, nothing but the sky was visible through the windows, and the impression was conveyed that everyone lived on a hill. There was also a bookcase, which might even – if the producer was in a devil-may-care frame of mind – be three-dimensional and equipped with real books. If we were not at Mark Trevannion's country house in Berkshire, we were probably at Hilary Egleston's flat in Knightsbridge, and, wherever we were, we ran into the same crowd – Rodney Curzon, feeling frightful; a 'really rather nice' American named Kip, Joe, or Calvin McIlhenny III; and, of course, that audacious young Susan Mainwaring, accompanied by her Aunt Gertrude, an obligatory dragoness with strong views about modern youth, the welfare state, and her senile rip of a husband, referred to as 'your poor Uncle Edgar', who never appeared. Offstage characters like Uncle Edgar continually cropped up in remarks such as 'This reminds me of that ghastly evening when Priscilla Mumbles took her owl to the Ritz for cocktails.' Nobody except the gardener was ever called Sidney or Bert, and names like Ethel and Myrtle were reserved for housemaids, paid companions, and pets. To pour the drinks, there was usually somebody's tweedy, middle-aged stick of a husband, who grinned tolerantly at his wife's caprices, offered brandy to her lovers, and never raised his voice above street level; a symbol of sanity in a collapsing world, he was described by the other characters as 'damn decent' or 'rather dim', and by the critics as 'that admirable actor, Cyril Raymond'. (Or any of a dozen other admirable actors.) The language of drawing-room drama was of a rigid deformity. People never just *went* anywhere; they beetled down to Godalming, hurtled up to town, nipped round to Fortnum's, and staggered off home. All bores were cracking, all asses pompous, and the dialogue was sprinkled with epithets of distaste, mostly drawn from the vocabulary of English nannies; for example, 'horrid', 'dreadful', 'nasty', 'sickening', 'disgusting', and 'nauseating'. These were often reinforced by the additional disparagement of 'little', as in 'dreadful little man', 'disgusting little creature', or 'nasty little mind'. (In other contexts, 'mind' was replaced by the classier 'mentality'; e.g., 'You have the mentality of a day-old chick.' For similar reasons, 'visualize' was generally preferred to 'imagine'.) At some point in every play, the hero was required to say, 'That, Celia, is a thoroughly immoral [or 'perfectly revolting'] suggestion.' Minor English place names were relied upon to tinge the baldest statements with wit. A line like 'I am spending the summer in the country' could convulse a whole audience if revised to read 'I am spending the summer at Sidcup/Herne Bay/Budleigh Salterton.'

Five years ago, anyone whose knowledge of England was restricted to its popular theatre would have come to the conclusion that its standard of living was the highest on earth. British plays about people who could not afford villas on the Côte d'Azur were very nearly as rare as British people who could afford them. The poor were seldom with us, except when making antic contributions to broad farce or venturing, tongue-tied with embarrassment and clutching cloth caps, into the gracious salons of middle-class comedy, where they were expected to preface every remark with 'Beggin' yer pardon, Mum.' To become eligible for detailed dramatic treatment, it was usually necessary either to have an annual income of more than three thousand pounds net or to be murdered in the house of someone who did. This state of affairs did not apply during the war years, when everyone pulled together and even Noël Coward wrote tributes to the patriotism of the working classes; otherwise, however, it had persisted since the mid-thirties and *Love on the Dole*. And it had been noticed much earlier than that.

· If our dramatists will condescend to make our acquaintance (or rather cease from trying to persuade themselves that they don't know us), they will find that we, too, the unmentioned by Debrett, the jaded in aspect, have brains and hearts. They will find that we, too, are capable of great joys and griefs, and that such things come our way quite often, really.

Max Beerbohm wrote that in February 1907. It might easily have been written in 1954. I do not think it could be written today.

A change, slight but unmistakable, has taken place; the English theatre has been dragged, as Adlai Stevenson once said of the Republican Party, kicking and screaming into the twentieth century. Only an Englishman, probably, would notice the difference. In the middle of summer there were twenty-one straight plays running in London. Sixteen of them were farces, light comedies, or detective stories, and one at least of the remaining five was a borderline case. I refer to Graham Greene's *The Complaisant Lover*, which bears the same relationship to Mr Greene's earlier plays that his 'entertain-

ments' bear to his more serious novels. It deals with a suburban
dentist whose wife has just started to sleep with a local bookseller.
The adulterous pair arrange to spend a week-end in Amsterdam,
which is interrupted – in a scene of the bitterest farce – by the sand-
blind, unsuspecting cuckold. To force the issue, the lover informs the
husband, by letter, of his wife's infidelity. The trick misfires. It drives
the dentist to tears but not to divorce; instead, he cannily proposes a
ménage à trois – a solution that satisfies him, assuages his wife's guilt,
and utterly disconcerts the bookseller. Perhaps because John Gielgud's
antiseptic direction failed to convince me that the lovers had achieved
any significant carnal contact, perhaps because Ralph Richardson
performed in a vein of fantasy that seemed incompatible with
dentistry, I could not believe a word of it. Or, rather, I believed in
many of the words – Mr Greene's lines have a startling, casual candour – but not in the people who were uttering them. Mastery of
dialogue, I reflected afterwards, is no substitute for mastery of
characterization.

Apart from *The Complaisant Lover*, plays are thriving in central
London with titles like *The French Mistress*, *Caught Napping*, and
Simple Spymen. How, then, can I support my claim that the English
theatre is growing up? I do so by reference to a three-pronged
suburban assault that has lately been launched on the central citadel.
As in a Shakespeare history play, the western region is all afire with
deep-revolving zeal, led by the English Stage Company, which set up
shop in 1955 at the Royal Court Theatre, in Sloane Square, where it
has since presented, in addition to well-known texts by Arthur
Miller, Brecht, Giraudoux, and Ionesco, the first plays of Angus
Wilson, Nigel Dennis, Doris Lessing, N. F. Simpson, and John
Osborne. The Court is run by a stuffy committee and aided by a
meagre subsidy from the Arts Council; even so, it managed to stage,
during the 1958–9 season, two remarkable plays that would never
five years ago have transferred – as these did – to the West End.
One was *The Long and the Short and the Tall*, by a thirty-year-old
television writer named Willis Hall. In construction this was a wartime anecdote of fairly familiar mould. A reconnaissance patrol, cut
off by a Japanese advance in the middle of the Malayan jungle, debates
its chances of getting back to base by breaking through the enemy
lines. The argument is complicated by the fact that the men have

taken a Japanese prisoner; should they let him accompany them, or shoot him out of hand? As in most British war stories, the cast is a cliché microcosm, a 'cross-section of the community' that includes a Scot, a Welshman, a North Countryman, a Cockney, a trigger-happy sadist, and a tough, warmhearted sergeant. They are all, however, deeply individualized; each speaks a language so abundant in racy local metaphor that I could have kicked myself for having acquiesced in the popular myth that the British vernacular is dull wherever it is not Americanized. Mr Hall's play is not only boisterous, exuberant, and accurate; it is also beautifully written. Moreover, it is performed in what, for the London theatre, is a new style of acting. Until a few years ago the English drama schools devoted much of their energy to ironing out of their pupils' accents all trace of regional origin and to replacing it with the neutral, official dialect spoken by B.B.C. announcers. Suddenly, however, a group of plays has sprung up for which B.B.C. English is utterly useless. Out of nowhere – or perhaps out of everywhere – an ambitiously talented bunch of young provincial actors has emerged, ideally fitted to embody the new drama, which treats ordinary people not as helpless victims, stoical jingoists, or clownish vulgarians but as rational human beings. Only two of the eight men in Mr Hall's cast had appeared in the West End, and their director, Lindsay Anderson, had no previous experience of the professional stage, although he has a high reputation as a documentary-film maker. With his actors – Kenji Takaki, Robert Shaw, Edward Judd, Ronald Fraser, David Andrews, Emrys James, Bryan Pringle, and Peter O'Toole – I could find no fault, and in the case of Mr O'Toole, as the cynical Cockney who befriends the Japanese captive, I sensed a technical authority that may, given discipline and purpose, presage greatness. To convey violence beneath banter, and a soured, embarrassed goodness beneath both, is not the simplest task for a young player, yet Mr O'Toole achieved it without sweating a drop. The play lacked stars, and it had a downbeat (that is, anti-war) ending, in which the patrol was decimated. These facts may explain why, despite enthusiastic notices, it ran in the West End for only three months. It will, anyway, be remembered as a portent.

The same can be said of *Roots*, a new piece by Arnold Wesker, who is twenty-seven years old and was born in the East End of London. The subject of his play, which opened at the Court in June and has since moved to the West End, is ignorance. The daughter of a family of agricultural labourers comes home, after a long stay in London, full of progressive ideas she has learned from her lover, who works (as Mr Wesker once worked) in the kitchen of a West End restaurant. Fruitlessly, she tries to explain art and politics to her kinfolk, who regard her with compassionate bewilderment; she plays classical music to her mother on the phonograph, and embarks on a wild dance to illustrate the release it has brought to her. Mother nods, smiling but uncomprehending; how should she care for art, fed as she is by radio pabulum, living as she does with no electricity, an outdoor toilet, and water from a garden tank, on less than five pounds a week? Beatie, the daughter, has returned with a vocabulary that succeeds only in alienating her from her background. In the last scene a family gathering is reluctantly convened to welcome her urban boy friend, who fails to turn up. A smug reaction of I-told-you-so prevents anyone from comforting the shattered Beatie. If this were an English play of the traditional kind, the jilted girl would at this point recognize the futility of her intellectual aspirations and snuggle back to the bosom of the family. Not so Beatie. She rounds on her relatives, blaming their conservatism and their suspicion of independent thought for her own inability to communicate with intelligent people. She has failed because of the *mystique* of humility that has taught her since childhood to keep her place and not waste time on books. At the end of this tirade she realizes that for once she has not been parroting the opinions of her lover but has been thinking for herself. With the wonder that is cognate with one's first sense of identity, she cries, 'I'm beginning. *I'm beginning!*' And the play is over. I stumbled out in a haze of emotion, on a sticky, baking July evening. The theatre, I noticed, was full of young men and women who had been distracted from the movies, from television, and even from love-making by the powerful lure of a show that concerned them and that could help as well as amuse. Joan Plowright played the awakened rustic, and the director was John Dexter, and in neither case can I think of an alternative half as good.

What the future has in store for the Royal Court is anyone's guess. *Roots* was followed by Vivien Leigh in *Look after Lulu!*, Noël Coward's adaptation of Feydeau's *Occupe-toi d'Amélie*, which flopped last season on Broadway. The London critics politely detested it, and

I cannot imagine why it was ever staged at that address. John Osborne told me that he walked into the theatre early in July and found it full of Miss Leigh, Mr Coward, and Hugh Beaumont, the most powerful of West End producers. He wondered for a second if he had come to the wrong place. The original idea had been that the Royal Court should conquer Shaftesbury Avenue; instead, Shaftesbury Avenue seemed to have conquered the Royal Court.

Whatever doubts one may have about the Sloane Square assault on the West End, the two other spearheads look pretty formidable. It is too early yet to pass judgement on the Mermaid Theatre, at Puddle Dock, which was conceived by a dedicated actor-impresario named Bernard Miles, built by public subscription on the brink of the Thames in the financial heart of London, and opened with fanfares last spring. A great concrete hangar, with a raked auditorium, a revolving stage, and an acting area that extends from wall to wall, the Mermaid is physically a director's dream. Its inaugural production – an immediate success – was a free adaptation, augmented by music and song, of *Rape upon Rape*, an eighteenth-century comedy by Henry Fielding, a satirist whose mordancy was such that it impelled Walpole, the Prime Minister, to bring all stage performances under the censorship of the Lord Chamberlain. (Fielding subsequently took up the novel, and England, according to Shaw, was thereby deprived of its finest playwright between Shakespeare and himself.) Intended as a sour indictment of corrupt judges, the play has been adulterated by the addition of insipid tunes and acting of a prevailing coyness; perhaps only Brecht and Weill could have given Fielding the kind of musical staging he needed. The new title, *Lock Up Your Daughters*, indicates the degree of compromise that was involved. But Mr Miles has some valiant plans for his new playhouse. Once this hit has run its course, *on verra*.

By far the most damaging dent in the West End structure has been made by Joan Littlewood, the artistic director of the company known as Theatre Workshop. Two of the smartest playhouses in London – Wyndham's and the Criterion – are occupied, as I write this, by productions that originated at the Theatre Royal, Stratford-atte-Bowe, the East End headquarters of Miss Littlewood's extraordinary troupe. At the Criterion there is *A Taste of Honey*, a first play by Shelagh Delaney, a Lancashire girl who is well over six feet tall and just over twenty years old. It deals joyfully with what might, in other hands, have been a tragic situation. The teen-age heroine, who lives in a ratty tenement bed-sitter, is deserted by her nagging, peroxided mother, who is unaware that her daughter is pregnant by a Negro sailor. Played with tenderly cheeky impulsiveness by a young actress named Frances Cuka, the girl accepts the fact that her child is likely to be fatherless and makes a temporary home with a slender art student whose sexual bent is towards his own sex. Her only qualm is that her own father was mentally deficient: 'He lived in a twilight land, my dad, the land of the daft.' Eventually her mother comes home, the student is summarily evicted, and the curtain falls on preparations for the impending birth. I don't know that I like all of Miss Littlewood's production tricks; I don't see why the mother should address all her lines to the audience, like a vaudeville soloist, and I can't understand why the original ending, in which she accepted the Negro paternity of her daughter's baby, has been altered to permit her to make unattractive jokes about pickaninnies and 'bloody chocolate drops'. All the same, we have here quite a writer, and quite a director.

Brendan Behan's *The Hostage*, currently playing at Wyndham's Theatre, is a perfect embodiment of Miss Littlewood's methods, and well deserved the prize for the best production of the 1959 Paris International Theatre Festival. It is a babble of styles, devoid of form yet full of attack – *Hellz-a-Poppin*, you might say, with a point of view. The scene is a Dublin bawdy-house in which a British service-man is held as hostage for an I.R.A. soldier condemned to death for shooting a policeman. As in *A Taste of Honey*, what sounds tragic turns out to be uproariously comic. The brothel becomes a sort of music hall. The actors chat to the audience, send themselves up in the mock-heroic manner that is Ireland's least imitable contribution to world literature, and sing a number of outstandingly villainous songs, including a devastating tribute to England –

> Old ladies with stern faces,
> And the captains, and the kings

– and a life-embracing chorus called 'There's no place on earth like the world'. No dramatic unity is achieved or aimed at; the players wander in and out of character whenever they, or the events of the play, feel like it. The jokes are unpredictable and often genuinely rude. The brand name of a whisky is clarified as 'Vat 69 – the Pope's telephone number', one of the principal clowns is a male transvestite named Princess Grace, and I particularly liked the Negro prizefighter, who, in a moment of exceptional tumult, strolls across the stage bearing a sign that reads 'Keep Ireland Black'. Finally, the hostage – beautifully played by Alfred Lynch – is accidentally killed in a raid, but no time is allowed for mourning. Mr Lynch jumps up again and joins the rest of the cast in a rousing number entitled 'Oh death, where is thy sting-a-ling-a-ling, oh grave, thy victor-ee!'

Miss Littlewood demands players who can improvise not only in rehearsal but before an audience. She likes the morning's headlines to be incorporated into the evening's performance – a habit that caused her last year to be haled into court and fined for contravening the censorship regulations, which insist that every word spoken on a public stage must first be submitted for approval to the Lord Chamberlain's office. Whether it is desirable for actors to usurp the writer's job and invent their own lines is something I seriously doubt. Whenever I raise the subject, Miss Littlewood starkly replies that as soon as a production is fixed, it is dead, and that she would prefer anything to the inflexible monotony of what she sees in the West End. A stocky, trenchant woman in her forties, she was born in a working-class district of South London and educated at a convent school. She went to the Royal Academy of Dramatic Art on a scholarship, and founded Theatre Workshop in 1945, warning her actors that regular salaries were out of the question; all she could promise them was that the box-office receipts would be equally divided at the end of each week. The company toured England, Germany, Norway, Sweden, and Czechoslovakia for eight years before settling down at the Theatre Royal. To Miss Littlewood's dismay, the local proletariat failed to support her enterprise, and it was not until her productions of *Arden of Faversham* and *Volpone* were thunderously acclaimed at the 1955 Paris International Theatre Festival that the senior London critics began to take her seriously. Her recent conquest of the West End pleases her, but only because it means more money with which to realize her life's obsession – a people's theatre outside the West End. Politically, she stands well to the Left. This is not, I might add, a fact of much significance; it

applies to nearly every theatre company in Europe of any contemporary importance.

Stratford-on-Avon is celebrating this year its hundredth season,
with a troupe of actors led by Dame Edith Evans, Sir Laurence
Olivier, Paul Robeson, Charles Laughton, and Sam Wanamaker. A
stylistic chaos swirled around nearly everything I saw; it was like an
all-star benefit show run mad in doublet and hose and lacking, for
the most part, either unity or purpose. The five guest stars seemed
remote from the rest of the cast – and not surprisingly, when you
consider that Dame Edith and Mr Laughton are playing only two
roles apiece in a total of five plays, while Sir Laurence and the Messrs
Robeson and Wanamaker are confining themselves, respectively, to
Coriolanus, Othello, and Iago. Moreover, it takes a closely knit
company and dynamic direction to offer consistently good work to
an audience that is mainly composed of uncritical tourists and a town
that is frankly apathetic towards theatre. Peter Bull, the English
character actor, has lately recorded – in a highly diverting autobiography called *I Know the Face, But . . .* – his impressions of the
place:

I am here to say, with prejudice, that I personally loathe Stratford-
on-Avon. . . . The atmosphere of old Tudory and brass ornaments
brings my bile to boiling-point, and I did fancy during my short stay
there that no one in the town seemed frightfully keen on the actors,
who are largely responsible for bringing the shop ladies and gentlemen
their revenue.

Mr Bull's testimony may be slightly loaded, since he was fired
during rehearsals; all the same, he has a point.

All's Well That Ends Well, the first Stratford production I saw this
year, is directed by Tyrone Guthrie with his familiar, infuriating
blend of insight and madness. On the one hand we have the great
conductor, the master of visual orchestration, conceivably the most
striking director alive when there are more than six people on stage;
on the other hand we have his zany *Doppelgänger*, darting about with
his pockets full of fireworks and giving the members of the orchestra
hot-feet whenever genuine feeling threatens to impend. He has done
to *All's Well* what he did a few seasons ago to *Troilus and Cressida*
at the Old Vic; that is, set it in a Shavian Ruritania faintly redolent

of *Arms and the Man*. This, of course, would have delighted Shaw, who always held that Helena, the lady doctor who pursues and ensnares the man of her choice, was a harbinger of his own aggressive heroines. Mr Guthrie's modernization enables him to make some telling points that Elizabethan costume often obscures. When Helena, having worked her miracle cure on the king's fistula, claims as her reward the hand of Bertram, the young man's initial reaction is to treat the whole thing as a joke; he cannot believe that the daughter of a medical practitioner could seriously contemplate marrying into the aristocracy. Meanwhile, the braggart Parolles becomes a breezy, overdressed roadhouse cad, foredoomed to failure in his social climbing by the possession of an accent that is ever so slightly 'off'. What Mr Guthrie has done is to make subtle class distinctions where Shakespeare made broad ones; one wonders whether the idea could have occurred to anyone but an Englishman. Until the evening was halfway through, I was beguiled and fascinated. Afterwards Mr Guthrie's love of horseplay obtrudes, and we get – among other things – a long scene, performed mainly in mime, wherein a deaf general reviews the French troops and exhorts them to battle through a faulty public-address system. Two hours of this can be fun; three and a quarter is too much. Lavache, the Countess of Roussillon's clown, who has some of the most haunting prose in Shakespeare, is entirely omitted; to cut a play, yet make what remains last longer than the whole, must argue, I suppose, a kind of dotty genius. The role of the Countess, curiously described by Shaw as the most beautiful old woman's part ever written (it is in fact merely the only old woman's part in Shakespeare that is neither a scold nor a murderess), is played by Dame Edith in her characteristic later manner – tranquillized benevolence cascading from a great height, like royalty opening a bazaar.

Peter Hall, the young man who will next year assume the direction of the Stratford theatre, has staged *A Midsummer Night's Dream* in a manner just as personal as the Guthrie *All's Well.* With sound historical justification, he sees the play as an occasional piece, intended for the celebration of a well-bred marriage; accordingly, he deploys the action in the great hall of an Elizabethan manor house, which gradually, through the cunning of Lila de Nobili's décor, sprouts greenery and develops into a more or less credible forest. Foolishly, the lovers' scenes are played for broad comedy; Mr Hall's sense of stage humour is not of the subtlest, and too many people stumble and fall unfunnily down. His positive contribution is in his handling of the fairies. Fatigued by sinister Oberons with sequins on their eyelids and by Junoesque Titanias attended by sinewy girls flapping romantically about to Mendelssohn, I was delighted by Mr Hall's fresh approach. His fairies are closely related to the lost boys of *Peter Pan*, with Titania as their prim, managing Wendy. Admittedly, they are clad somewhat like insects, and one of them is without doubt a diminutive old lady. But Oberon himself is pure Peter – a petulant, barefoot boy, well-meaning and genuinely magical. Puck, in this interpretation, is not so much his slave as his kid brother. Finally, we have Charles Laughton, a ginger-wigged, ginger-bearded Bottom. I confess I do not know what Mr Laughton is up to, but I am sure I would hate to share a stage with it. He certainly takes the audience into his confidence, but the process seems to exclude from his confidence everyone else in the cast. Fidgeting with a lightness that reminds one (even as one forgets what the other actors are talking about) how expertly bulky men dance, he blinks at the pit his moist, reproachful eyes, softly cajoles and suddenly roars, and behaves throughout in a manner that has nothing to do with acting, although it perfectly hits off the demeanour of a rapscallion uncle dressed up to entertain the children at a Christmas party.

Othello, as directed by Tony Richardson, is full of factitious life – jazz drumming between scenes, rampageous crowds, gestures towards symbolism, like making the Duke of Venice a cripple who has to be carried offstage by a Negro servant, and bizarre climatic effects, as when Othello disembarks on Cyprus in a thick fog and a high wind – and totally devoid of emotional reality. Shakespeare's great indictment of circumstantial evidence comes almost suavely across, without passion or impact. None of the three leading players seems to be operating on the same wave-length as the others, or even to be speaking the same language. Two of them – Mr Robeson and Mr Wanamaker – have had very little Shakespearean experience, and the third – Mary Ure – is vocally ill-equipped for either tragedy or poetry. Miss Ure primly flutes; Mr Wanamaker clips and swallows, playing Iago in a style one would like to call conventional if only he were doing it well. Iago, above all, should be disarming. Mr Wanamaker, to coin an epithet, is profoundly arming. In more appropriate company, I am sure, Mr Robeson would rise to greater heights than he does. As things are, he seems to be murdering a butterfly on the advice of a gossip columnist. His voice, of course, is incomparable – a foundation-shaking boom. It may, however, be too resonant, too musically articulated for the very finest acting. The greatest players – Kean and Irving, for example – have seldom been singers as well. Their voices were human and imperfect, whereas the noise made by Mr Robeson is so nearly perfect as to be nearly inhuman.

We will skim over the inessentials of the Stratford *Coriolanus* as quickly as possible. Boris Aronson's setting is mountainous, which is fine, and full of mountainous steps, which is not – I recalled Alec Guinness's remark, *à propos* of Shakespearean productions in general, that he himself had very few conversations on the stairs of his own house. Harry Andrews is a stolid, muscular Menenius. As Volumnia, the hero's stifling mother, Edith Evans looks overpowering, but her fussy, warbling vibrato swamps all too often the meaning of the lines. Peter Hall's direction is straight and vigorous, with hardly any ideological slanting – a good way with a play that is best served when either everything is slanted or nothing. The lesson to be learned from *Coriolanus* is that although Shakespeare was willing to condemn anyone in the social order, no matter how low or high his position, he would never have condemned the order itself. Any rung in a ladder may be rotten, but there must be a ladder, and rungs.

We can now get down to the heart of the production, which is Olivier's performance of Coriolanus. The first thing to praise is its sheer, intuitive intelligence. Olivier understands that Coriolanus is not an aristocrat; he is a professional soldier, a *Junker*, if you like, reminiscent in many ways of General de Gaulle – a rejected military saviour who returns, after a long and bodeful silence, with an army at his back. Fully aware of the gap between Coriolanus and the patricians he is serving, Olivier uses it to gain for the man an astounding degree of sympathy. With the delicacy that is his hallmark as much as power – few actors are physically as dainty, and none rolls eyes that are half as calf-like – he emphasizes Coriolanus the hater of phoneyness, the plain military man embarrassed by adulation, the awkward adult boy sickened equally by flattery and by the need to flatter. A cocky, jovial commander, he cannot bring himself to feign humility in order to become Consul, and his sulky refusal to apologize to the people takes on, in Olivier's hands, the aspect of high political comedy. We cannot applaud the man, but we like him, and thus the battle of the part is halfway won. What spurs him to betray Rome is not pride but a loathing of false servility.

Olivier also seizes on the fact that Coriolanus was brought up under his mother's thumb. 'There's no man in the world/More bound to 's mother,' says Volumnia. Her opinion always comes first. 'I muse my mother/Does not approve me further' is our initial hint that Coriolanus is doubtful whether he is right to be so intransigent towards the plebeians. Under her persuasion, he consents to make his peace with them, and it is Volumnia who finally dissuades him from sacking Rome, the paternal city. Olivier's ashamed, hesitant collapse is among the truest moments of his performance. Sidling towards Volumnia, he grasps her hand and murmurs, 'Oh – *my mother.* . . .'

This Coriolanus is all-round Olivier. We have the wagging head, the soaring index finger, and the sly, roaming eyes of one of the world's cleverest comic actors, plus the desperate, exhausted moans of one of the world's masters of pathos. But we also confront the nonpareil of heroic tragedians, as athletically lissome as when he played Oedipus a dozen years ago. No actor uses *rubato*, stealing a beat from one line to give to the next, like Olivier. The voice is soft steel that can chill and cut, or melt and scorch. One feels the chill in the icy tirade that begins 'You common cry of curs' and ends 'There is a world elsewhere.' And one is scorched by the gargled snarl of rage with which Olivier rams home, by a wrenching upward inflexion on the last syllable, 'The fires i' th' lowest hell fold in the peo*ple!*' At the close, faithful as ever to the characterization on which he has fixed, Olivier is roused to suicidal frenzy by Aufidius's gibe – 'thou boy of tears'. '*Boy!*' shrieks the overmothered general, in an outburst of strangled fury, and leaps up a flight of precipitous steps to vent his rage. Arrived at the top, he relents and throws his sword away. After letting his voice fly high in the great, swingeing line about how he 'flutter'd your Volscians in *Cor-i-o-li*', he allows a dozen spears to impale him. He is poised, now, on a promontory some twelve feet above the stage, from which he topples forward, to be caught by the ankles so that he dangles, inverted, like the slaughtered Mussolini. A more shocking, less sentimental death I have not seen in the theatre; it is at once proud and ignominious, as befits the titanic fool who dies it.

The image, and the echo, of this astonishing performance have taken root in my mind in the weeks that have passed since I witnessed it. The dark imprint of Olivier's stage presence is something one forgets only with an effort, but the voice is a lifelong possession of those who have heard it at its best. It sounds, distinct and barbaric, across the valley of many centuries, like a horn calling to the hunt, or the neigh of a battle-maddened charger.

(*1959*)

Shakespeare

PREFACE

THE 1950s saw an awful lot of Shakespeare. He was lavishly invoked for Coronation Year; the Old Vic doggedly ploughed through the whole of the First Folio; and the Memorial Theatre at Stratford-upon-Avon staged its annual half-dozen productions, engaging in the course of the decade nearly all of our finest actors. One hesitates to spot trends in an output so vast; but it seems to me indisputable that the romantic approach to Shakespeare has taken a mortal battering in the past dozen years. What one may call, without disrespect, the Gielgud formula has gone into temporary eclipse; Sir John remains a superlative actor from the neck up, but the emphasis he lays on vocal beauty and facial exquisiteness has lost its hold on contemporary taste. The new fashion is to excavate truth, no matter how many diamonds of elocution one may lose in the process.

By this I do not mean merely that the star-system has been supplanted by team-work and the controlling vision of a director, although that is part of the truth; I mean that modern directors have come to regard the plays as fragments of history or as epic fables, rather than as spot-lit studies of individual heroes or lovers. Stars, of course, continue to thrive, as they must as long as all men are not born equally endowed. If I had to single out two high points from my Shakespearean playgoing in the nineteen-fifties, I would choose Olivier's Stratford Macbeth in 1955 and the same actor's Stratford Coriolanus four years later. Power like this confounds theories and fractures patterns, and long may it flourish. But in general we nowadays place Shakespeare in the setting of his own era. We stage the tragedies as if they were histories; instead of trying to make them timeless, we fix them in their own time and social setting. Tragedy, we now suspect, has no meaning apart from historical circumstance. By the same token, the history plays have come into their own. The twin pinnacles of the matchless Old Vic seasons at the close of the war were the productions of *Henry IV*, Parts One and Two, with Richardson and Olivier; the same plays, with Richard Burton,

Michael Redgrave, and Anthony Quayle, set Stratford agog in the early 1950s; and they returned, less starrily cast, to pack the Old Vic in 1955. Shortly afterwards, directed in Paris by Roger Planchon, a whole-hearted disciple of Brecht, they enjoyed a similar success.

If the tale is a fable (as in the comedies it often is), anchor it to earth with solid objects and unsentimental acting. If it is tragic in content, anchor it in place and time. If it is a chronicle, anchor it in historical perspective. Prefer social fact to poetic fiction, the touch of truth to the hypnotic gesture of illusion; and above all, never fall into the error of supposing that high-born characters merit attention and respect more than the rest simply because they sometimes express themselves more beautifully. These, in rough paraphrase, are the Brechtian rules as they have been interpreted by our younger Shakespearean directors – especially, in recent years, under Peter Hall's regime at Stratford-upon-Avon. William Gaskill's Stratford production of *Cymbeline* in 1962, for example, was a resplendent, panoramic achievement that would assuredly never have happened had Mr Gaskill not caught the Brechtian bug while directing *The Caucasian Chalk Circle* for the Royal Shakespeare Company a few months before. The setting, which covered the stage floor and cyclo-rama and overflowed beyond the proscenium, was of pure white netting; into and across it heavy objects of enormous sculptural beauty were respectively lowered or shoved. The designer, Rene Allio, came to Stratford from Roger Planchon's company in Lyons, where Brecht is the bible; and the costumes (also by M. Allio) had a thoroughly Brechtian look, worn and dignified by use. The stage-scape was one of dazzling simplicity, before which events of fabulous complexity were to unfold.

Of all our new Shakespeareans, Mr Gaskill is the best story-teller – lucid and hard-headed, never afraid of a leisurely narrative pace. He presented the ungainly comedy as a tall tale told to a group of Jacobean stage-hands, who helped to shift the scenery between episodes. 'Howsoe'er 'tis strange,' said Cornelius, acting as chorus, '. . . yet is it true;' and we believed him. The relationship between Cloten, the queen's loutish son, and his two attendants was an example of the care Mr Gaskill devotes to accuracy in matters of class distinction. Instead of sniggering at their master's eccentricities (as in conventional productions), the courtiers treated Cloten with a

kind of bored poker-faced deference from which we knew at once
that they had been coping with this Blimpish oaf for years. The
Anglo-Roman war was staged in slow-motion choreography (like
the battles in Roger Planchon's production of Marlowe's *Edward II*);
but Mr Gaskill's visual master-stroke was the dream wherein Posthu-
mus, locked up in a pendent cage, imagines Jupiter descending on an
eagle. The descent actually happened, and the bird had wings of
gold; the effect was classically grand, at once visionary and concrete.
Later in the same season, Clifford Williams directed *The Comedy of
Errors*, using the same general approach; and it was no longer possible
to deny that the Royal Shakespeareans had developed, uniquely in
Britain, a classical style of their own. Its hallmarks (or Hall-marks)
were instantly recognizable: solid, selectively architectural settings
that emphasized wood and metal instead of paint and canvas, and
cogent, deliberate verse-speaking that discarded melodic cadenzas in
favour of meaning and motivation.

But Brecht's way is not the only path to virtue. Simple realism,
shunned by most English Shakespeareans without ever having been
really tried, can pay high emotional dividends; as we learned at the
Old Vic one electrifying October night in 1960, when Franco
Zeffirelli dared to flout the official assumption that all Shakespeare's
characters are 'heightened'. I quote from my review:

Last Tuesday at the Old Vic a foreign director approached Shakespeare with fresh eyes, quick wits, and no stylistic preconceptions; and
what he worked was a miracle. The characters were neither larger nor
smaller than life; they were precisely life-size, and we watched them
living, spontaneously and unpredictably. The director had taken the
simple and startling course of treating them as if they were real people
in a real situation; and of asking himself just how those people, in that
situation, would behave.

It sounds obvious enough; yet the result, in Franco Zeffirelli's production of *Romeo and Juliet*, is a revelation, even perhaps a revolution.
Nobody on stage seems to be aware that he is appearing in an immortal
tragedy, or indeed in a tragedy of any kind; instead, the actors behave
like ordinary human beings, trapped in a quandary whose outcome they
cannot foretell. Handled thus realistically, it is sometimes said, Shakespeare's essential quality gets lost. I passionately demur. What gets lost
is not Shakespeare but the formal, dehumanized stereotype that we
have so often made of him.

It is likewise urged that Signor Zeffirelli robs Shakespeare of his poetry; but this argument is valid only if one agrees with those blinkered zealots who insist that poetry is an arrangement of sounds, instead of an arrangement of words. Last Tuesday I heard every syllable; meaning and character were wedded, and out of their interaction poetry arose. The production evoked a whole town, a whole riotous manner of living; so abundant and compelling was the life on stage that I could not wait to find out what happened next. A young English director of my acquaintance made a true comment in one of the intervals. 'Every director in the audience,' he said, 'is biting his nails and wondering why he never thought of this before.'

It is hard to know where to begin the catalogue of particular praise. The sets (also by Signor Zeffirelli) are spaciously atmospheric, composed of peeling, flaking walls that serve equally well for interiors or exteriors. Children scuffle in the alleys and vendors bawl their wares. We are unmistakably in Verona, or anyway in Italy; the director has even taught his English cast how to shrug. The rival factions are gangs of dawdlers with time on their hands; captives of the streets, like the boys in Fellini's film *I Vitelloni*. Mercutio (electrically played by Alec McCowen) is their unquestioned idol, an intense, fierce, sourly witty young man, always conscious of his intellectual supremacy. His death comes as a chilling shock, since Signor Zeffirelli has caused it to occur by accident. His bout with Tybalt, a basically playful affair, is already over when the mortal thrust is delivered; it is a chance and unintended stroke, yet it kills him, whereafter the feud between the families takes on a new dimension of seriousness. They have squabbled immemorially, but this is their first murder, and it tilts the action towards tragedy.

Romeo, meanwhile, is an idler lured out of sulks into love. His meeting with Juliet at the Capulets' ball is staged with marvellous tact. A crowd has gathered to hear someone sing; around the fringe of it the lovers tentatively edge, ending up together, quietly pressing palm to palm. The balcony scene is heartrendingly good. Here, as everywhere else in the production, grace is subordinated to circumstance, the ideal to the real. The Vic has done nothing better for a decade.

On the one hand, the realists; on the other, the Brechtians. The future of Shakespearean production in England lies, I would guess, somewhere between the two. Presentation à la Brecht: performances à la Stanislavsky. It should make a potent combination.

RICHARD II and HENRY IV, PART ONE
AT STRATFORD-ON-AVON

The Shakespeare Memorial Company at Stratford has now launched *Richard II* and the first part of *Henry IV*. Together, these make up the first half of Shakespeare's tetralogy of kingliness, which is to be presented under the joint direction of Anthony Quayle, Michael Redgrave, and John Kidd. The exterior of the Memorial Theatre retains its touching pink ugliness, lapped on one side by the Avon: but inside, Quayle has made great changes, relining the auditorium to look warmer and more inviting, and erecting on the stage a permanent setting (by Tanya Moiseiwitsch) on which the full quartet of history plays will be acted – an imposing arrangement of beams, incorporating rough approximations of the balcony and inner recess of the Elizabethan stage.

Richard II has been less successful than its next of kin. This is a reclining, effeminate play where the 'Henry' series is upstanding and male, and Miss Moiseiwitsch's timbering is out of key with its lushness. Redgrave, still missing the real heights by an inexplicable inch, makes a fine sketch of Richard, using a shaky tenor voice, a foppish smile, and damp, uncertain eyes to summon up the poor man's instability. In the early scenes, clad in sky-blue doublet and cloak of palest orange, he looked exquisitely over-mothered, a king sculpted in puppy-fat. Alternately malicious and sentimental, Redgrave's Richard is a noble booby, sincerely envious, as well as afraid, of the power to command which is not his. It was not his fault that in the later acts and the slow hysterical slide towards death one tired of him.

There can be no hesitation about *Henry IV*, Part One; oak-beamed and clinker-built, it fits the set perfectly. Memories of Olivier's Hotspur and Richardson's Falstaff inevitably taunt us, but this is undoubtedly a much more thoughtful and balanced production than the Old Vic's. Redgrave now moves into the major key with a raw-boned, shock-headed Hotspur, affecting a rasping Lowlands brogue to account for the references to Harry Percy's thickness of speech; and at least three of the best six English juveniles crop up around him. Alan Badel, the intemperately exciting flyweight whose Fool partnered John Gielgud's Lear last year, plays the tiny part of Poins with fastidious distinction; Duncan Lamont, a sour young actor with a swarthy voice, finds a complete character, glowering and long-sighted, in the involved complottings of Worcester; and, finally, a shrewd Welsh boy shines out with greatness – the first this year.

I am speaking of Richard Burton, whom New York saw last autumn in Gielgud's *The Lady's Not for Burning*. His playing of Prince Hal turned interested speculation to awe almost as soon as he started to speak; in the first intermission the local critics stood agape in the lobbies. Burton is a still, brimming pool, running disturbingly deep; at twenty-five he commands repose and can make silence garrulous. His Prince Hal is never a roaring boy; he sits, hunched or sprawled, with dark unwinking eyes; he hopes to be amused by his bully companions, but the eyes constantly muse beyond them into the time when he must steady himself for the crown. 'He brings his cathedral on with him,' said one dazed member of the company. For all his bold chivalry, this watchful Celt seems surely to have strayed from a wayside pulpit. Fluent and sparing of gesture, compact and spruce of build, Burton smiles where other Hals have guffawed; relaxes where they have strained; and Falstaff (played with affectionate obesity by Anthony Quayle) must work hard to divert him. In battle, Burton's voice cuts urgent and keen – always likeable, always inaccessible. If he can sustain and vary this performance through to the end of *Henry V*, we can safely send him along to swell the thin company of living actors who have shown us the mystery and the power of which heroes are capable.

(*1951*)

OTHELLO

AT THE ST JAMES'S

No doubt about it, Orson Welles has the courage of his restrictions. In last night's boldly staged *Othello* he gave a performance brave and glorious to the eye; but it was the performance of a magnificent amateur. I say this carefully, for I am young enough to have been brought up on rumour of his name, and I sat in my stall conscious that, in a sense, a whole generation was on trial. If Welles was wrong, if a contemporary approach to Shakespeare in his thunder-bolt hands failed, then we were all wrong.

What we saw was a tightly limited acting performance in a bound-bursting production. Welles the producer gave us a new vista (based on five permanent golden pillars) for every scene; he used a russet traverse-curtain to wipe away each setting in the same manner that the films would use a dissolve; he sprinkled the action with some striking background music and realistic recordings – in fact, he sacrificed much to give us a *credible* reading of a play which bristles with illogicalities. The presentation was visually flawless – Cassio's drunk scene became a vivid blaze of mutiny, and the killing of Desdemona, with crimson awnings over a white couch, and a high rostrum towering behind, can never have looked more splendid. The St James's stage seemed as big as a field.

Welles's own performance was a huge shrug. He was grand and gross, and wore some garish costumes superbly. His close-cropped head was starkly military, and he never looked in need of a banjo. But his voice, a musical instrument in one bass octave, lacked range; he toyed moodily with every inflection. His face expressed wryness and strangulation, but little else. And his bodily relaxation frequently verged on sloth. Above all, he never built to a vocal climax: he positively waded through the great speeches, pausing before the key words like a landing-craft breasting a swell. (When dead, his chest went on heaving like the North Sea.) Welles's Othello is the lordly and mannered performance we saw in *Citizen Kane*, slightly adapted to read 'Citizen Coon'.

I think of Othello as a theatrical bullfight, in which the hero is a noble bull, repeatedly charging the handkerchief in the wristy grip of Iago, the dominating matador. Peter Finch gave us none of this. His Iago is a clipped starveling, puny and humourless, pared to the bone. One can accept a charmless Iago, but a bantam-weight is unforgivable. However, Mr Finch seemed a little cowed, both by Mr Welles and the first-nighters, and he will surely improve.

(1951)

TIMON OF ATHENS

AT THE OLD VIC

Watching *Timon* was, I found, rather like going to some scandalously sophisticated party at which, halfway through, the host suddenly falls down drunk and begins to rave from under the piano. It starts superbly, a glittering and rapacious satire on big fleas and the little fleas that bite them, and Tyrone Guthrie's clamorous production gallops breakneck to emphasize the luridity of it all, silhouetting Timon's midget pick-thank toadies against the gilded background of his feasts and pomps. Rightly and unsentimentally, he never lets us overlook the upstart element in Timon's too genial distributions of largesse; rightly, too, he abandons all pretence that Shakespeare's Athens has any connexion with the town whose walls Isocrates saved from ruin bare. Mr Guthrie sets us firmly down in Ben Jonson territory, and the senators come mumbling on like a shady conclave of corrupt borough councillors. All this is modern in the best sense.

What follows, of course, is modern in other, less amiable ways. The berserk jeremiads with which Timon responds to the desertion of his erstwhile cronies; his sick and shapeless railings at man's ingratitude – these have a personal, compulsive note in them, a note struck in many of the plays, from *Titus Andronicus* to *Lear*, but elsewhere relieved by grace-notes from other keys. In *Timon*, as we would churlishly put it, the needle seems to have stuck. Admittedly, as Landor conceded of *Paradise Regained*, muscles sometimes stand out from the vast mass of the collapsed; there are moments of wintry, leafless poetry which eat into the mind; and there is a situation of supreme irony when Timon, having banished himself to the wilderness, stumbles in his cave across a cache of gold – the mineral of his whole undoing. But an unhinged hero can, and here does, unhinge an entire play: the final door will not shut, and the conclusion is botched, hasty, and somehow ashamed.

Mr Guthrie's brilliance in the first half looked like extending itself well into the second, until Andre Morell's Timon laid it low. As the Poet (I do not, of course, mean Shakespeare) says in Act I:

> No levell'd malice
> Infects one comma in the course I hold

– but I must hold it long enough to insist that Mr Morell, a sturdy and disarming actor, has nothing like the power and range demanded by Timon's disjointed miseries. Bay though he might, like some locked-out Alsatian, he could not command my sympathy nor even, at the end, my interest. Mr Morell's eyes seem unable to focus on us; and his voice too lacks grip, being not a little butlerish, and possessed of a hollow, muffled timbre, as if toothache had forced him to thrust cotton-wool into his cheeks. Many lesser things, however, are finely done, among them Leo McKern's squat and spiky Apemantus and John Phillips's robustly effeminate cartoon of a senator. All in all, this is the completest evening the Vic has given us since *Tamburlaine*.

This being a play loaded with references to sums of money, may I add how helpful it would be if the programme were to give some hint of the current exchange-rate in crowns, ducats, and talents? It is much easier, for instance, to form an opinion of a man who owes five talents when you know whether he needs, to restore his credit, a thousand pounds or eight and sixpence. Few bank-managers in the audience, for instance, would be likely to trust a man who owed only eight and sixpence.

(1952)

MACBETH
AT STRATFORD-ON-AVON

Last Tuesday night at the Stratford Memorial Theatre *Macbeth* walked the plank, leaving me, I am afraid, unmoved to the point of paralysis. It was John Gielgud, never let us forget, who did this cryptic thing; Gielgud, as director, who seems to have imagined that Ralph Richardson, with his comic, Robeyesque cheese-face, was equipped to play Macbeth; Gielgud who surrounded the play's fuliginous cruelties with settings of total black, which is about as subtle as setting Saint Joan in total white; Gielgud who commanded dirty tatters for Macbeth's army and brisk, clean tunics for Malcolm's, just to indicate in advance who was going to win. The production assumed, or so I took it, that the audience was either moronic or asleep; it read us a heavily italicized lecture on the play, and left nothing to our own small powers of discovery. When, in the banquet scene, a real table and some real chairs, chalices, and candelabra were brought on, life intervened for a moment; but once the furniture had gone, we were back in the engulfing, the platitudinous void, with its single message: 'Background of evil, get it?' The point about Macbeth is that the murders in it should horrify us; against Mr Gielgud's sable scenery they looked as casual as crochet-work.

In the banquet scene, spurred perhaps by the clever handling of Banquo's ghost, which vanished dazzlingly in one swirl of a cloak, Richardson came to life for several consecutive sentences, and I could not help recalling a line he had uttered earlier in the evening: 'My dull brain was wrought with things forgotten.' Up to this point he had appeared a robot player, a man long past feeling, who had been stumping across the broad stage as if in need of a compass to find the exit. Now, momentarily, he smouldered and made us recall his excelling past, littered with fine things encompassed and performed. And then, and ever after, Sir Ralph's numbness, his apparent mental deafness, returned to chill me: Macbeth became once more a sad facsimile of the Cowardly Lion in *The Wizard of Oz*. At the height of the battle, you remember, Macbeth contemplates suicide, rejecting the thought in the words: 'Why should I play the Roman fool, and die on mine own sword?' Sir Ralph, at this juncture, gripped his blade by the sharp end with both hands and practised putts with it; it was as if the Roman fool had been the local pro.

His feathery, yeasty voice, with its single spring-heeled inflection, starved the part of its richness; he moved dully, as if by numbers, and such charm as he possessed was merely a sort of unfocused bluffness, like a teddy-bear snapped in a bad light by a child holding its first camera. Sir Ralph, who seems to me to have become the glass eye in the forehead of English acting, has now bumped into something quite immovable. His Macbeth is slovenly; and to go further into it would be as frustrating as trying to write with a pencil whose point has long since worn down to the wood.

Sleep-walking, which appeared to be this Macbeth's natural condition, had an unexpectedly tonic effect on his lady. Margaret Leighton seized her big solo opportunity, waking up to give us a gaunt, pasty, compulsive reading of the scene which atoned for many of her earlier inadequacies. But two things are required for an effective Lady Macbeth: first, a husband off whom she can strike sparks – and it would be easier to strike sparks off a rubber dinghy than Sir Ralph. Second, she needs to be sexless; Macbeth is unique among the tragedies in that none of the leading characters ever mentions sexuality. Lady Macbeth is painted granite, and to cast a woman as attractive as Miss Leighton in the part is like casting a gazelle as Medusa. In fact, it is probably a mistake to cast a woman at all, since Lady Macbeth offers none of the openings for nostalgia, yearning, and haggard glamour which attach to every other great female part, from Cleopatra to Blanche DuBois. No, Lady Macbeth is basically a man's role, and none of Miss Leighton's sibilant sulks could convince me otherwise.

Now what to praise? Kenneth Rowell's sculptural costumes, which sat well on everyone save, unaccountably, Sir Ralph; Siobhan McKenna's patient Lady Macduff; and the attack, if nothing else, of Laurence Harvey's Malcolm. And that will have to do. The theatre which gave us, last year, so many pretty lessons in Shakespearean acting and production seems, for the time being, to have unlearned them all.

(1952)

ROMEO AND JULIET

AT THE OLD VIC

I am told that Claire Bloom's performance in the Old Vic's *Romeo and Juliet* is a failure because Miss Bloom ignores the poetry. They say she loses all the music of the verse. To which I can only reply by exposing this alleged defect for the virtue it really is. Let me start by burning my boats and declaring that this is the best Juliet I have ever seen.

'Word-music' is a great maker of reputations. Give an actress a round, resonant voice and a long Shakespearean part, and she will have to enter smoking a pipe to avoid being acclaimed. And everyone will forget (*a*) that the same voice could turn last year's Hansard into poetry, and (*b*) that what Shakespeare demands is not verse-speaking but verse-acting. A golden voice, however angelic, is not enough. Whenever a climax looms up, the actor faces a choice between the poetry and the character, the sound and the fury, because you cannot rage mellifluously or cry out your eyes in tune. Edmund Kean, Irving, and Olivier, on whom our whole tradition of heroic acting rests, have one thing in common: they have all been repeatedly accused of lacking poetry. Miss Bloom sins in good company.

The average Juliet sings the part sweetly, chants it demurely, dismissing passion with a stamp of the foot. Nine tenths of Juliet, as Miss Bloom demonstrates, is not in the least demure: she is impatient and mettlesome, proud and vehement, not a blindfold child of milk. And the result is an illumination. The silly lamb becomes a real, scarred woman, and we see that it is the whole character that is poetic, and not just the lines. When she is quiet, as in the balcony scene, Miss Bloom's candour is as still as a smoke-ring and as lovely. 'I have forgot why I did call thee back' is spoken with a grave amazement: there are no simpers or blushes in this dedicated young creature. From her first meeting with Romeo, as they touch hands at the Capulets' ball, she is no novice, but an initiate in the stately game of love. In silence, as in speech, her communication with Romeo is complete: their minds fit like hand and glove, and his absence wounds her like an amputation. 'Word-music' goes overboard in Miss Bloom's best scene, that in which the Nurse breaks the news of Tybalt's death and Romeo's banishment – first the superb harshness of 'Blistered be thy tongue!' after the old crone has reviled Romeo, and then a desolating panic, crowned at the end by an exit suddenly gentle and bereaved, cradling Romeo's rope-ladder to her breast. I have seen no more moving piece of acting this year. Miss Bloom was not quite adequate to the mighty obstacle of the potion speech, and the death scene seemed to catch her off guard. But enough had been done by then to make the golden statue of remembrance, promised by Romeo's father in the last scene, quite unnecessary. We had already seen pure gold.

Alan Badel, her Romeo, is that freak, a young man with an old man's voice, an old man's snicker, and an old man's leer. Couple with these disadvantages a lack of inches and looks, and you have a problem that no amount of intelligence can solve. Mr Badel is not a romantic actor. He does some daring little things early on, but the later agonies are beyond him. He lingers over them, squirming and yearning, but the total effect is miniature – rather like a restless marmoset.

(1952)

KING LEAR

AT THE KING'S, HAMMERSMITH

It is annoying that the Old Vic did not hold Donald Wolfit in the troupe long enough to show us his *King Lear*, which is now being alternated with *Twelfth Night* at the King's, Hammersmith. His present supporting company explores new horizons of inadequacy. Only Richard Goolden, a macabre Fool with a senile stoop and a child's skipping legs, is of much assistance to the play. Extricate Mr Wolfit's Lear from the preposterous production and you have a great, flawed piece of masonry, making up in weight what it lacks in delicacy: a tribal chieftain rather than a hereditary monarch. Mr Wolfit scorns the trick (known to many lesser actors) of flicking speeches exquisitely to leg; he prefers to bash them towards mid-off and run like a stag. In the mad scenes this impatience with finesse is a weakness: the insanity looks too much like tipsiness. And to play the last unearthly act Lear must land, as it were, by parachute on the top of Parnassus. Mountaineering, however dogged, will not take him there. At these moments Mr Wolfit seems unaccountably grounded.

His mark is still higher up the great slope than anyone else's in our time. He is magnificent in the early scenes, sulking like a beaten dog when Cordelia refuses to play ball with him; and the colloquies with the Fool are horribly moving, with the old man's thoughts staring past his words into the chasm of lunacy. Best·of all is the pause that follows his fit of rage at Cornwall's cruelty. 'Tell the hot duke – ' he begins, and then stops in mid-eruption, veins knotted, fighting hideously to keep his foothold on the tiny ledge which stands between him and madness. Mr Wolfit's Lear is a brilliant compound of earth, fire, and flood. Only the airy element is missing.

(1953)

THE MERCHANT OF VENICE

AT STRATFORD-ON-AVON

Whenever I see *The Merchant of Venice*, I while away the blanker bits of verse by trying to pull the play together in my mind. Does Shylock stand for the Old Testament (an eye for an eye, etc.) and Portia for the New (mercy, etc.)? And if so, what does that make Antonio, the shipping magnate whose bond unites the two plots? Does he represent the spirit of Protestantism? These metaphysical hares chase each other round and round; and when I have done, the play remains the curate's egg it always was. Or, rather, the rabbi's egg, because so much depends on Shylock. Which brings us to the Problem of Michael Redgrave, now, as always, at the turning-point of his career.

The difficulty about judging this actor is that I have to abandon all my standards of great acting (which include relaxation and effortless command) and start all over again. There is, you see, a gulf fixed between good and great performances; but a bridge spans it, over which you may stroll if your visa is in order. Mr Redgrave, ignoring this, always chooses the hard way. He dives into the torrent and tries to swim across, usually sinking within sight of the shore. Olivier pole-vaults over in a single animal leap; Gielgud, seizing a parasol, crosses by tight-rope; Redgrave alone must battle it out with the current. The ensuing spectacle is never dull, but it can be very painful to watch.

His conception of Shylock is highly intelligent – a major prophet with a German accent, a touch of asthma, and lightning playing round his head. But who cares for conceptions? It is the execution that counts. And here Mr Redgrave's smash-and-grab methods tell against him. His performance is a prolonged wrestling match with Shylock, each speech being floored with a tremendous, vein-bursting thump; the process also involves his making a noise like a death-rattle whenever he inhales, and spitting visibly whenever he strikes a 'p' or a 'b'.

Some things he did superbly. At the end of the court scene, even after Portia had warned him that to take the pound of flesh would expose him to the death penalty, you felt that this cheated tyrant would be maniac enough to hang the consequences and start carving. There were also hints that Mr Redgrave did not deny Shylock a sense of humour: he discovered a sensational new pun in his delivery of the speech about 'water-rats' and 'pi-rates'. But he simply could not fuse the villainy of the part with its sardonic comedy. And I begin to think that no English player ever will. It needs a Continental actor to switch from fun to ferocity in a split second: Englishmen take at least half a minute to change gear. And when they are playing in their high-tragedy manner, as Mr Redgrave is, they find it practically impossible to change gear at all.

Shylock is a proud and successful financier with a chip on his shoulder; he is not an abject slave bearing a yoke of lead. Mr Redgrave cringes and crumples every time Antonio opens his mouth – you would think he had never seen a Christian before. He should, of course, outsmile the lot of them. Like the other Shakespearean rogues, Richard III, Iago, and Claudius, Shylock must wear a cloak of charm. Even Antonio describes him as 'kind', and the bond must seem to be what Shylock calls it, 'merry'. Mr Redgrave gives us nothing more merry than a twisted leer. Or perhaps I should say a twisted Lear. Because I shall be much surprised if his performance as the mad king, later in the season, is vocally or physically very different from last Tuesday's Jew. I hope one day to see this actor playing a part insincerely, with his mind on other matters. Then the defences might come down, and the great Shakespearean performance that surges within him might at last be let out.

The jewel of the evening is Peggy Ashcroft's Portia, a creature of exquisite breeding and uncommon sense. She speaks the poetry with the air of a woman who would never commit the social gaffe of reciting in public, with the result that the lines flow out newly minted, as unstrained as the quality of mercy itself. Her handling of the tiresome princelings who come to woo her is an object lesson in wit and good manners; later, in the court-room, we wept at her compassion; and the last act, invariably an anti-climax, bloomed golden at her touch.

Apart from the fiery furnace that is Mr Redgrave and the cool zephyr that is Miss Ashcroft, the production is pretty tepid stuff. The scenery (flimsy pillars, as usual) looks fine in silhouette, and on one occasion, when the sky inadvertently turned green, assumed extraordinary beauty. But I tire of settings that seek to represent nowhere-in-general; how one longs to see everywhere-in-particular! The trial was well staged – but why must Shylock always be alone? Surely all the Jews in Venice would turn up for his triumph?

I cannot imagine what Donald Pleasence was trying to make of Launcelot Gobbo, who is not, I suggest, an organ-grinder's monkey. Yvonne Mitchell is wasted on Jessica. On the credit side, Tony Britton's Bassanio is an attractive scamp; and Robert Shaw, cast as Gratiano, delighted us and himself by giving a fiery and determined performance of Mercutio.

(1953)

KING LEAR

AT STRATFORD-ON-AVON

Michael Redgrave has played *King Lear* and won. For once the complex armoury of this actor's mind has found a foe worthy of its steel. I say 'foe' because Mr Redgrave approaches his big roles as a hunter stalks big game: he does not march up to them with simple friendship in his eyes. The technical apparatus with which he besieges his parts has sometimes looked a little over-elaborate, recalling the old metaphor about the sledge-hammer and the nut. But Lear is a labyrinthine citadel, all but impregnable, and it needed a Redgrave to assault it. On Tuesday night the balloon went up.

He began finely, conveying grief as well as rage at Cordelia's refusal to flatter him. Physically, already, the whole of Lear was there, a skyscraping oak fit to resist all the lightning in the world. The second-act decline into madness was perhaps the least impressive stage of Mr Redgrave's campaign – Mr Wolfit effects this transition more eloquently with less fuss. But once Lear was out on the heath, at odds with the elements, Mr Redgrave found his bearings again, and never lost them to the end. Is it a backhanded compliment to say that this actor is best when maddest? Witness the Dover scene with the eyeless Gloucester: Lear's drifting whims, his sudden, shocking changes of subject, his veering from transcendent silliness to aching desolation were all explored, explained, and definitively expressed. In simple roles Mr Redgrave is often in the predicament of a higher mathematician asked to add two and two together; he may very well hum and haw and come to the conclusion that in certain circumstances they can make five. But give him a scene, like this at Dover, which is the higher mathematics of acting, and he solves it in a flash; here, and throughout the last act, was the cube root of King Lear, 'the thing itself'.

Hamlet without the prince is still a fascinating text; *Lear* without the king is something of a bore. How one wishes that Shakespeare had passed the manuscript to someone like Jonson, with instructions to mend the leaks in the Gloucester sub-plot and provide at least some excuse for the unaccountable behaviour of Edgar! The Stratford company treads water energetically. Joan Sanderson and Rachel Kempson are the creepiest, most credible pair of ugly sisters I can remember; but, apart from his physical appearance, which might be captioned 'Grimaldi as Caliban', Marius Goring makes a surprisingly ordinary Fool, all too obviously intent on pathos-squeezing. There are some dazzling costumes, of primitive Martian cut, but the setting badly lacks variety. To feel the cold of the heath, we must first have felt the warmth of the hearth. The present décor dumps us out of doors at curtain-rise and leaves us there.

(1953)

HENRY IV, PARTS ONE AND TWO

AT THE OLD VIC

I suspected it at Stratford four years ago, and now I am sure: for me the two parts of *Henry IV* are the twin summits of Shakespeare's achievement. Lime-hungry actors have led us always to the tragedies, where a single soul is spotlit and its agony explored; but these private torments dwindle beside the Henries, great public plays in which a whole nation is under scrutiny and on trial. More than anything else in our drama they deserve the name of epic. A way of life is facing dissolution; we are in at the deathbed of the Middle Ages. How shall the crisis be faced? The answer takes us to every social and geographical outpost: to Eastcheap drunks and Gloucestershire gentry, to the Welsh and the Scots, to the minor nobility and the crown itself.

There is much talk of death; to the king it comes as a balm, Falstaff sags at the mention of it, Shallow is resigned to it, and Hotspur meets it with nostrils flared. The odd, irregular rhythm wherein societies die and are reborn is captured as no playwright before or since has ever captured it. In Hal's return to honour and justice the healing of a national sickness is implied. Implied: that is the clue – for there is no overt exhortation in these plays, and no true villain, no Claudius or Iago on whom complacent audiences can fix their righteous indignation. Hotspur is on the wrong side, yet he is a hero; Prince John is on the right one, yet his cynical perfidy at the disarmament conference would have astonished Hitler. Only a handful of plays in the world preserve this divine magnanimity. To conceive the state of mind in which the Henries were written is to feel dizzied by the air of Olympus.

We knew from Douglas Seale's handling of the *Henry VI* trilogy that he was a director of rare historical imagination; and the Old Vic company, which lacks star quality, exactly fits a pair of plays which lack star parts. Note how cleverly Mr Seale lets the two evenings illuminate each other. He gives Falstaff a page in Part I as well as Part II, using the boy as mute audience to the knight's soliloquies; taking his cue from a phrase in Part II – 'wearied and out-breathed' – he makes Hotspur and Hal in Part I so stricken with battle fatigue that they can scarcely lift their swords. The tavern scenes, writhing with squalor and pulsing with visual wit, transport us straight to pre-Crookback England.

Paul Rogers' Falstaff is fussy and perhaps too easily discomfited, but vocally it is a display of rich and immaculate cunning. Rachel Roberts hits off Mrs Quickly to perfection, and few Pistols have been fired more powerfully than John Neville's. The same actor's Hotspur was hampered by a stammer needlessly borrowed from Sir Laurence Olivier; and the best double was that of Paul Daneman, whose malign Worcester was followed by a goatish Justice Shallow, giddy with snobbery and agog with innocence.

Mr Seale's hand seems to stiffen at contact with royalty: his groupings in the court scenes were static, and the episode of the purloined crown was badly staged on a remote rostrum, high and half-visible. Eric Porter gave us all of Henry's guilt but little of his grandeur; and in Robert Hardy's Hal there was too great a show of intelligence. Mr Hardy is rightly proud of his technique, but he is in danger of developing it at the expense of his acting 'innards': the performance was well-timed but soft-centred. Ann Todd and Virginia McKenna intrude briefly and softly into what has been called the smoking-room of Shakespearean drama – though Miss Todd's irruption into the middle of the curtain-call was, to say the least, presumptuous. Audrey Cruddas's permanent setting is both rugged and regal. To sum up, Mr Seale has put the Old Vic in particular and Shakespearean production in general on the right realistic track.

(1955)

MACBETH

AT STRATFORD-ON-AVON

Nobody has ever succeeded as Macbeth, and the reason is not far to seek. Instead of growing as the play proceeds, the hero shrinks; complex and many-levelled to begin with, he ends up a cornered thug, lacking even a death scene with which to regain lost stature. Most Macbeths, mindful of this, let off their big guns as soon as possible, and have usually shot their bolt by the time the dagger speech is out. The marvel of Sir Laurence Olivier's reading is that it reverses this procedure, turns the play inside out, and makes it (for the first time I can remember) a thing of mounting, not waning, excitement. Last Tuesday Sir Laurence shook hands with greatness, and within a week or so the performance will have ripened into a masterpiece: not of the superficial, booming, have-a-bash kind, but the real thing, a structure of perfect forethought and proportion, lit by flashes of intuitive lightning.

He begins in a perilously low key, the reason for which is soon revealed. This Macbeth is paralysed with guilt before the curtain rises, having already killed Duncan time and again in his mind. Far from recoiling and popping his eyes, he greets the air-drawn dagger with sad familiarity; it is a fixture in the crooked furniture of his brain. Uxoriousness leads him to the act, which unexpectedly purges him of remorse. Now the portrait swells; seeking security, he is seized with fits of desperate bewilderment as the prize is snatched out of reach. There was true agony in 'I had else been perfect'; Banquo's ghost was received with horrific torment, as if Macbeth should shriek 'I've been robbed', and the phrase about the dead rising to 'push us from our stools' was accompanied by a convulsive shoving gesture which few other actors would have risked.

The needle of Sir Laurence's compass leads him so directly to the heart of the role that we forget the jagged rocks of laughter over which he is travelling. At the heart we find, beautifully projected, the anguish of the *de facto* ruler who dares not admit that he lacks the essential qualities of kingship. Sir Laurence's Macbeth is like Skule in Ibsen's chronicle play *The Pretenders*, the valiant usurper who can never comprehend what Ibsen calls 'the great kingly thought'. He will always be a monarch *manqué*.

The witches' cookery lesson is directed with amusing literalness; the Turk's nose, the Jew's liver, and the baby's finger are all held up for separate scrutiny; but the apparitions are very unpersuasive, and one felt gooseflesh hardly at all. On the battlements Sir Laurence's throttled fury switches into top gear, and we see a lion, baffled but still colossal. 'I 'gin to be a-weary of the sun' held the very ecstasy of despair, the actor swaying with grief, his voice rising like hair on the crest of a trapped animal. 'Exeunt, fighting' was a poor end for such a giant warrior. We wanted to see how he would die; and it was not he but Shakespeare who let us down.

Vivien Leigh's Lady Macbeth is more niminy-piminy than thundery-blundery, more viper than anaconda, but still quite competent in its small way. Macduff and his wife, actor-proof parts, are played with exceptional power by Keith Michell and Maxine Audley. The midnight hags, with traditional bonhomie, scream with laughter at their own jokes: I long, one day, to see whispering witches, less intent on yelling their sins across the country-side. The production has all the speed and clarity we associate with Glen Byam Shaw, and Roger Furse's settings are bleak and serviceable, except for the England scene, which needs only a cat and a milestone to go straight into *Dick Whittington*.

(*1955*)

TITUS ANDRONICUS

AT STRATFORD-ON-AVON

I have always had a soft spot for *Titus Andronicus*, in spite of the fact that I have often heard it called the worst thing Marlowe ever wrote. Whoever wrote it, whether a member of the Shakespeare syndicate or the chairman himself, he deserves our thanks for having shown us, at the dawn of our drama, just how far drama could go. Like Goya's 'Disasters of War', this is tragedy naked, godless, and unredeemed, a carnival of carnage in which pity is the first man down. We have since learned how to sweeten tragedy, to make it ennobling, but we would do well to remember that *Titus* is the raw material, 'the thing itself', the piling of agony on to a human head until it splits.

It is our English heresy to think of poetry as a gentle way of saying gentle things. *Titus* reminds us that it is also a harsh way of saying harsh things. Seneca's Stoicism, in which the play is drenched, is a cruel doctrine, but it can rise to moments of supernal majesty. Lear himself has nothing more splendid than:

> For now I stand as one upon a rock,
> Environ'd with a wilderness of sea. . . .

The parallel with Lear is sibling-close, and Peter Brook cleverly strengthens it by having the fly-killing scene performed by a wanton boy. But when all its manifold excellences have been listed, the play still falls oddly short. One accepts the ethical code which forces Tamora to avenge herself on Titus, and then Titus to avenge himself on Tamora; it is the casualness of the killing that grows tiresome, as at a bad bullfight. With acknowledgements to Lady Bracknell, to lose one son may be accounted a misfortune; to lose twenty-four, as Titus does, looks like carelessness. Here, indeed, is 'snip, and nip, and cut, and slish, and slash', a series of operations which only a surgeon could describe as a memorable evening in the theatre. When there enters a messenger 'with two heads', one wonders for a lunatic instant whether he is carrying them or was born with them.

Much textual fiddling is required if we are to swallow the crudities, and in this respect Mr Brook is as swift with the styptic pencil as his author was with the knife. He lets the blood, one might say, out of the bath. All visible gore is eliminated from the play, so that Lavinia, tongueless and handless, can no longer be likened to 'a conduit with three issuing spouts'. With similar tact, Mr Brook cuts the last five words of Titus's unspeakable line, 'Why, there they are both, baked in that pie', as he serves to Tamora his cannibalistic speciality – *tête de fils en pâte (pour deux personnes)*.

Adorned by a vast, ribbed setting (the work of Mr Brook, designer) and accompanied by an eerie throbbing of *musique concrète* (the work of Mr Brook, composer), the play is now ready for the attentions of Mr Brook, director. The result is the finest Shakespearean production since the same director tackled *Measure for Measure* five years ago. The vocal attack is such that even the basest lines shine, like Aaron the Moor, 'in pearl and gold'. Anthony Quayle plays the latter role with superbly corrupt flamboyance, and Maxine Audley is a glittering Tamora. As Lavinia, Vivien Leigh receives the news that she is about to be ravished on her husband's corpse with little more than the mild annoyance of one who would have preferred foam rubber. Otherwise, the minor parts are played up to the hilt.

Sir Laurence Olivier's Titus, even with one hand gone, is a five-finger exercise transformed into an unforgettable concerto of grief. This is a performance which ushers us into the presence of one who is, pound for pound, the greatest actor alive. As usual, he raises one's hair with the risks he takes. Titus enters not as a beaming hero but as a battered veteran, stubborn and shambling, long past caring about the people's cheers. A hundred campaigns have tanned his heart to leather, and from the cracking of that heart there issues a terrible music, not untinged by madness. One hears great cries, which, like all of this actor's best effects, seem to have been dredged up from an ocean-bed of fatigue. One recognized, though one had never heard it before, the noise made in its last extremity by the cornered human soul. We knew from his Hotspur and his Richard III that Sir Laurence could explode. Now we know that he can suffer as well. All the grand unplayable parts, after this, are open to him: Skelton's Magnificence, Ibsen's Brand, Goethe's Faust – anything, so long as we can see those lion eyes search for solace, that great jaw sag.

(1955)

HAMLET

AT THE PHOENIX

As he proved seven years ago at Stratford, no living actor is better equipped for Hamlet than Paul Scofield. On him the right sadness sits, and also the right spleen; his gait is a prowl over quicksands; and he can freeze a word with an irony at once mournful and deadly. He plays Hamlet as a man whose skill in smelling falseness extends to himself, thereby breeding self-disgust. He spots the flaw in every stone, which makes him either a born jeweller or a born critic. He sees through Gertrude, Claudius, Rosencrantz, Guildenstern, Polonius, and Ophelia: what remains but to see through himself? And this Mr Scofield does superbly, with a mighty bawl of 'O vengeance!' followed by a rueful stare at his own outflung arms and a decline into moans of derisive laughter. His eulogy of Horatio is not only a hymn to the only honest man in Denmark, it is the tribute enviously paid by complexity to simplicity.

Mr Scofield's outline is impeccable. What is surprising is the crude brushwork with which he fills it in. Vocally and physically he is one long tremendous sulk; a roaring boy is at large, and not (as when he played the part before) a scholar gipsy. The new Mr Scofield protests much too much. The note struck on 'Vengeance!' is thrice repeated, with diminishing returns; too many speeches are mechanically gabbled; and the actor's face is a mask devoid of pathos. To hold our attention he will hit wrong notes or leap up the scale halfway through a line, but the grip seems artificial, as if he had decided that what could not be coaxed into life had better be shouted to death. Potentially, Mr Scofield is still Sir Laurence Olivier's natural heir, but in the technique of realistic acting he is badly out of practice. We have fed him on rhetoric and starved him of life, and if he fails to move us, it is as much our theatre's fault as his.

Peter Brook's production moves like the wind. In a permanent setting (by Wakhevitch) which overhangs the action like a great stone bird-cage, he achieves changes of scene which are both swift and stunning. Yet, though movement is there, destination is lacking. Mr

Brook thrives on plays long unopened, such as *Venice Preserv'd* and *Titus Andronicus*. *Hamlet*, his first attempt at a major tragedy, seems to have overawed him. In the crowd scenes – the play and the duel – he brings off grand slams, but elsewhere his direction is oddly tentative, with niggling cuts and ear-distressing transpositions, and when he seeks to play a trump – by giving the court musicians toy drums and trumpets – one is merely conscious that he has revoked.

Broad fun was never Mr Brook's strong suit. Hence Osric falls flat; Ernest Thesiger's praying-mantis Polonius is annoyingly restrained; and the gravediggers, despite the earthiness of Harry H. Corbett, miss their true *Galgenhumor*. The Gertrude is droopy, the Laertes stiff and hysterical; and though Mary Ure is helped by the substitution of wild flamenco chants for the traditional jingles of Ophelia's madness, her playing has about it a cool calculation which points rather to comedy than to tragedy.

I reserve until last the bloat king, the *bonne bouche* which swallows up the rest. Alec Clunes is not only the best Claudius I have seen, but in most respects the only one. Hamlet speaks of the king as a 'remorseless, treacherous, lecherous, kindless villain', and every Claudius in my memory has played him as such. Mr Clunes, returning to the basic principle of acting, plays Claudius from Claudius's own point of view: as a man who committed a *crime passionnel* after an internal battle which has left scars on his conscience. Into this reading the prayer scene, normally an excrescence, perfectly fits; and the line about Gertrude – 'I could not but by her' – rings a bell-note of pure pathos. We watch the slow crumbling of a man of action who has created through crime a new universe which now falls, stone by stone, about his ears. 'O Gertrude, Gertrude! When sorrows come, they come not single spies, but in battalions!' is a heart-cry rendered doubly moving by the actor's refusal to overstress it and by Gertrude's rejection of his outstretched hand.

To quell Laertes' rebellion, he collects himself, weary yet still majestic. This lonely man engages once again in plotting, of which he is still a master, like the gouty Napoleon at Waterloo. 'That we would do, we should do when we would': this is not only an echo of Macbeth, but a tacit condemnation of Hamlet, who could not when he would. Yet when the plot is laid, a premonition clouds the king's mind, a sigh ominous with defeat. In these scenes of conspiracy (usually regarded merely as a rest for the star) Mr Clunes performs miracles of reclamation which one is lucky to see once in a lifetime of Shakespearean playgoing. For long periods he was the only actor on stage who seemed, supply and subtly, to be listening.

It is objected that he whitewashes Claudius? He shows us a man who has tried and failed to rationalize his faults – and if that is whitewashing, it is how most of us spend our lives. Under his influence *Hamlet* is the tragedy not only of a prince but of a whole doomed family. If my thoughts on Thursday turned to the House of Atreus, it was Mr Clunes' magnificent doing. This is a superb performance.

(*1955*)

OTHELLO

AT THE OLD VIC

Even in prospect, the double *Othello* of John Neville and Richard Burton looked fairly black. The roles of Othello and Iago were to be alternated by two born Cassios: how could they manage overnight the switch from black outside to black inside? And in part one's qualms were justified. The Moor came lame from the struggle, as he must when age is absent. Messrs Burton and Neville are the youngest Othellos the town has seen this century, and if they reply that both Garrick and Kean played the part before reaching thirty, my counter-charge must be that the audience which swallowed the fourteen-year-old Master Betty as Hamlet would swallow anything.

Temperament alone is not enough for Othello, nor is physical beauty. The essence is that unfeignable quality which some call weight and others majesty, and which comes only with age. Frederick Valk had it, a great stunned animal strapped to the rack; but neither Mr Burton, roaring through his whiskers, nor Mr Neville, a tormented sheikh, could give the Moor his proper magnitude. In the grace-notes Mr Neville was exemplary, the moments of sacrificial tenderness; he conveyed, even at the raging climax, a sense of pain at the treachery of Iago, whom once he had loved. The part's quiet dawn and its quiescent sunset were both there. What escaped the actor was the intervening tempest.

Tuesday's performance, with Mr Burton blacked up and Mr Neville a capering spiv, was a drab squabble between the Chocolate Soldier and the Vagabond King. Only the best things in Michael Benthall's production held one's attention: Rosemary Harris's Desdemona, a moth of peace who might profitably have beaten her wings more vigorously, and Richard Wordsworth's Roderigo, a wholly credible ninny. On Wednesday we were in a different world. Mr Burton was playing Iago, and the production rose to him.

Paradoxically, the only way to play Iago is to respect Othello. Let Iago mock the Moor with cheap laughs, and the play collapses: it becomes the farce of an idiot gull instead of the tragedy of a master-spirit. Mr Burton never underestimates Othello; nor, in consequence, do we. His Iago is dour and earthly enough to convince any jury in the world. He does not simulate sincerity, he embodies it; not by the least wink or snicker does his outward action demonstrate the native act and figure of his heart. The imposture is total and terrifying. Like his author, Mr Burton cares little for the question of Iago's motive: mere jealousy of Cassio's rank is not enough, else why should Iago go on hounding Othello after he has supplanted Cassio? Discarding this, Mr Burton gives us a simple, dirty, smouldering drive towards power without responsibility. With a touch more of daemonism in the soliloquies, this will be an incomparable performance.

We may now define this actor's powers. The open expression of emotion is clearly alien to him: he is a pure anti-romantic, ingrowing rather than outgoing. Should a part call for emotional contact with another player, a contemptuous curl of the lip betrays him. Here is no Troilus, no Florizel, no Romeo. Seeking, as Othello, to wear his heart upon his sleeve, he resorts to forced bellowing and perfunctory sobs. Mr Burton 'keeps yet his heart attending on himself', which is why his Iago is so fine and why, five years ago, we all admired his playing of that other classic hypocrite, Prince Hal. Within this actor there is always something reserved, a secret upon which trespassers will be prosecuted, a rooted solitude which his Welsh blood tinges with mystery. Inside these limits he is a master. Beyond them he has much to learn.

(1956)

HAMLET
AT STRATFORD-ON-AVON

The case of Michael Redgrave is perennially absorbing, even to those who deny that he is a great actor. On he plunges, struggling and climbing and stumbling, bursting with will and intelligence, and seeking always to widen the range of his remarkable physical and vocal equipment. Never, to my knowledge, has he run away from an acting problem: he'll wrestle with them all. A serious actor, in short.

Yet something is missing. We admire, but are not involved. 'I wish thar was winders to my Sole,' said Artemus Ward, 'so that you could see some of my feelings.' Mr Redgrave's trouble is that his windows are opaque – one might even say frosted. Sir Laurence Olivier once said he would rather lose his voice or his arms than his eyes. Watch Mr Redgrave's: no matter how he rolls and darts them about, they remain somehow glazed and distant. We know from the evidence of our own that he has two of them, yet something about him persistently suggests the Cyclops. When he looks at other people, either actors or audience, it is as if he saw them only in two dimensions. They are simply 'things in his dream'. Try as he may (and God knows he tries) he cannot establish contact with them as human beings. Just as we think he is about to break through to us, something within him shies and bolts. He withdraws into his solitude, and when next we look, the windows are shuttered again.

Now this business of 'connecting', of getting into emotional touch with others, is at the heart of all acting. It is the very touchstone of the craft. And that is Mr Redgrave's paradox. He has in abundance all the attributes of a great actor, without the basic quality necessary to be a good one.

Even so, he is always fascinating to watch. His present *Hamlet* is a packed, compendious affair, much richer in detail than the one he gave us eight years ago at the Vic. At fifty, Mr Redgrave is the oldest Hamlet to have been seen in England since 1938, when Esmé Beringer struck a glancing blow for feminism by playing the part in her sixty-fourth summer; and it must be conceded that the actor sometimes resembles less a youth approaching murder for the first time than a seasoned Commando colonel suffering from battle fatigue. Nor is the illusion helped by a Gertrude who looks even younger than Googie Withers – a surprising achievement, considering that Miss Withers herself plays the part. Sheer intellectual agility, of which he has plenty, is what Mr Redgrave relies on. He knows the text inside out, and when he offers new readings (such as 'Nilus' for 'eisel' in the grave scene), we trust him as we would trust a walking Variorum Edition of the play. No subtlety of inflexion or punctuation escapes him; at times, indeed, he seems to be giving us three different interpretations of the same line *simultaneously*, which is a bit flustering.

In terms of character, Mr Redgrave presents a man fearful of rousing the sleeping demon within him. Cocteau described the artist as a kind of prison from which works of art escape. This Hamlet is a prison from which fury escapes, in wild frustrated spasms. His lips quake with the effort of containing it. Bottled hysteria is this actor's speciality, as the cellarage scene brilliantly proves. Mr Redgrave's Hamlet, like his Lear, is most convincing when closest to madness. It is, however, entirely unmoving, for the reason mentioned above.

Dorothy Tutin's Ophelia, a mouse on the rack, makes some illuminating minor points, chief among them her horrified reaction, in the play scene, to the mimic death of the Player King. I liked Edward Woodward's Laertes, Paul Hardwick's Rosencrantz (a nervous hearty), and the notion of playing the Second Gravedigger as a supercilious bureaucrat. Almost everything else in Glen Byam Shaw's production is dismal. The courtiers line up like mechanical waxworks, raising their hands in polite embarrassment when the royal family is exterminated before their eyes. The music is Victorian, the costumes are fussy, and the setting, an arrangement of shiny hexagonal pillars, appears to have been inspired by the foyer of the old Paramount Cinema in Birmingham. The best piece of business (Claudius's slapping the face of the Player Murderer) comes from Hugh Hunt's 1950 production. About two of the major performances my feelings are neutral: Cyril Luckham's sane, plodding Polonius and Mark Dignam's Claudius, which very nearly makes up in practical shrewdness what it lacks in dignity and sensuality.

(*1958*)

The American Theatre

PREFACE

I met the American theatre at first hand in 1951, and it bowled me over. It seemed to own the best young actors and actresses (Marlon Brando, Julie Harris, Uta Hagen, Kim Stanley, and their multitudinous like), the most exciting directors (among them Joshua Logan and Elia Kazan), and unquestionably the finest playwrights in the English-speaking theatre – Arthur Miller and Tennessee Williams. It also had the most highly developed tradition of realism in the Western world. While Britain was toying with a return to poetic drama (of a bland, attenuated kind – *vide* Christopher Fry and the later Eliot), and France was preoccupied with the striking but frequently shallow theatricalism of Anouilh, America alone had built on the foundations of realism laid down by Stanislavsky and Chekhov.

The American Group Theatre and its affiliated talents (Clurman, Strasberg, Kazan, Odets, etc.) summed up all that was best in Western drama in the Thirties. Its influence on the wide ranging sister-art of cinema was likewise immense; and when the mid-century arrived, it would have been hard to point to a more fertile orchard of drama anywhere on earth than the one that was ripening around Times Square. *Death of a Salesman* and *A Streetcar Named Desire* were fresh in one's critical mind. A few prophets were already guessing that the second half of the century would bring with it a swing away from realism, as Bertolt Brecht had long predicted, but it was not until the late autumn of 1949 that Brecht formed his Berliner Ensemble, and as far as I was concerned, thirteen years ago the mainstream was realism (i.e. the psychological exploration of contemporary reality). In Russia it had dried up for want of playwrights, and the inheritors – the commanders of the fountainhead – were American.

This much was clear when I landed in New York just before the cold Christmas of 1951. Since then I have returned annually to inspect the Broadway scene, and between 1958 and 1960 I settled not far from the Times Square nexus to write about its output for the *New Yorker*. Slowly, my faith dwindled, my excitement slackened, and I decided, with something approaching horror, that a mighty gang of gifted play-makers were dedicating their talents to the perpetuation of a box-office tyranny that could only get worse as production costs multiplied. I watched the number of theatres diminish, and the proportion of flops increase; I watched costs rise, nut-cases mount, and audiences shrink. As drama critic of the *New Yorker*, I became for the most part an obituarist, writing in the past tense of shows already dead. In the early spring of 1960 it occurred to me that before a decade was out Broadway might very well be a Death Valley of theatre, comprising perhaps a dozen playhouses devoted to musicals, another half-dozen reserved for safe, family comedy, and one respectable auditorium, hallowed each year as the shrine of American drama, in which future equivalents of *J.B.*, *Look Homeward, Angel*, and *The Dark at the Top of the Stairs* would briefly flourish and die unmourned. Recoiling from this vision, I returned to Europe, where theatrical experiment is still relatively cheap, and where it is held self-evident that first-rate theatre is unlikely to emerge except from permanent companies with permanent homes.

No doubt this sounds smug: but I don't think it can be disputed that Europe – with playwrights like Dürrenmatt, Beckett, Genet, Ionesco, Osborne, Pinter, Wesker, and Behan, and acting troupes like the Berliner Ensemble, the Théâtre Nationale Populaire, the Moscow Art Theatre, and Roger Planchon's company in Lyons – was and remains a more provocative source of playgoing pleasure than the United States. *Mutatis mutandis*, the purely commercial theatre in Europe has embarked on the same ruinous road as its Broadway counterpart: what gives Europe the edge is its tradition of subsidized drama, which permits authors and directors to take risks in the name of art, and thereby grants them – to borrow a phrase from a prominent young English director – 'the most important right of all – the right to fail'. Without that privilege, drama stagnates.

Nearly ten years ago I took an American actress to see a West End drawing-room comedy in which gallons of tea were consumed by a cast of sedate middle-aged eccentrics. During the intermission she said to me: 'You know the difference between the British theatre and Broadway? On Broadway you see actors drinking Scotch that's really cold tea. Here they drink tea – but it's really Scotch!' Her implication – that American actors were puritans pretending to be red-blooded, whereas the reverse was true of the British – seemed worth arguing about at the time; but now that drawing-room jollities have all but vanished from the London scene, the question has become academic. The ability to affect gentility is no longer prized in our theatre; and simulated hairy-apeishness has lost much of its *cachet* on Broadway. Today, the basic differences are economic. America plunges its theatre into the midst of the financial jungle and leaves it to fend for itself; whereas we tend more and more to place it in a nationally supported game preserve.

The essays and reviews that follow represent my impressions of American plays and performers I have seen on both sides of the Atlantic in the past dozen years. They record, as I have hinted, a love-affair that gradually cooled and ended in flight. All the same I should like to think of my parting with Broadway as only a trial separation. On page after page I find tributes to the energy, invention, and vivacity of individual American talents; to the partisan activities of the off-Broadway guerrillas; to the enormous potentialities of the projected Repertory Theatre on Lincoln Square; and, above all, to the buoyant, undiscouraged fertility of that marvellous bastard, the Broadway musical.

Leaving music aside, off-Broadway looks like the whitest hope – a sounding-board for new voices like those of Edward Albee (*The Zoo Story*), Jack Gelber (*The Connection*), and Arthur Kopit (*Oh Dad, Poor Dad, Momma's Hung You In The Closet and I'm Feeling So Sad*); and the movement is not a new one. It has old roots, stretching back to the Provincetown Players, who staged O'Neill's early plays before the doughboys went to France; and its revival in the past decade has nourished the skills, formerly darkling, of Geraldine Page, Kim Stanley, Jose Quintero, Ben Gazzara, and many more. What one looks for in vain is a viable bridge between the down-town show-case and the mid-town peep-show; a place in which authors, directors, and actors can pursue their art without diluting their principles or decimating their income. Perhaps the new repertory theatre at Lincoln Square will fill the gap. One hopes so. Otherwise the royal progress will remain, as always: Broadway to Beverly Hills, Brando to *Mutiny on the Bounty*, leaving a residue of uncorrupted souls devoting themselves, in the name of their starving craft, to a martyrdom that would not be necessary if the American theatre received the same measure of municipal support that is granted to libraries, museums, and art galleries. Performers in Broadway hits half-deride and half-envy academies like the Actors' Studio: the reason why classes like this proliferate is that there are so few public opportunities for theatrical talents to spread (or even to test) their wings.

So much vitality; and so few pains taken to preserve it from premature exhaustion! So many lions and tigers; and all condemned to incarceration in a competitive zoo! Such a plenitude of genius, so blithely treated as casual labour! It cannot, surely, be long before someone in America raises the cry that Matthew Arnold raised many years ago in Britain: 'The theatre is irresistible; organize the theatre!'

WINTER JOURNEY

BY CLIFFORD ODETS, AT THE ST JAMES'S

'Quite unimportant,' said one of my colleagues of this play; and I am sick at heart that no one has thus far ambushed and cudgelled him for a critique so recklessly encapsulated. Mr Odets' sin, I suppose, is to have written a play that could be described as 'sheer theatre' – which is to say, it has a compelling reality within its chosen medium, and does not care to invade the debating-chamber, the library, or the church. And so, by an exercise of sophistry similar to that by which indolent essayists, impatiently discussing an unfamiliar poet, resort to dubbing him 'a mere versifier', several popular critics have accepted Mr Odets' skill in hitting his target as *prima-facie* evidence that his talent is second-rate. I cannot conceive why. 'Sheer theatre' (applied disparagingly to Mr Odets, M. Rostand, and Mr Rattigan) will hereafter rank in my mind with 'How well these old craftsmen knew their jobs!' (applied panegyrically to Pinero or Ibsen) as a moribund cliché beloved of intellectual laziness. The primary business of the theatre is to be theatrical; and I refuse to countenance the argument that a play is unimportant simply because it leaves you nothing to discuss in the intervals. *Winter Journey* (or *The Country Girl*, as it was called on Broadway) is intended not to start you talking, but to *stop* you talking.

It remains well worth talking about. Mr Odets offers us what amounts to an Ibsenite thesis. A middle-aged actor, after long and will-ing enslavement to alcohol, is summoned from retirement to play a leading part; we meet his wife, an inscrutable creature who, having devoted herself for a decade to the job of keeping his illusions alive, has become cynically aware of the fact that her principal value to him is as an excuse for his failure. The director of the play for which he is engaged, a spiky and intimidating young idealist, instantly decides that she is the cause of her husband's labefaction; that her apron-strings have strangled him; and his wanton but well-meaning irruption into the actor's domestic life precipitates (as Ibsenites will have guessed) a new, desperate dive into the bottle, after which the play's opening night is all but wrecked. By now both we and the director have realized that the wife is no sorceress, but rather a scapegoat for her husband's infirmity, as well as something of a martyr. Mr Odets' climax – the Broadway first night – I will not reveal, beyond suggesting that his introduction of an additional theme – the director's love for the wife – is ill-prepared and hangs from the play's body with the irrelevance of a donkey's tail pinned to a fighting bull. Even so, the conclusion, that redemption is a compromise which no amount of idealism can achieve unaided, comes across with unimpaired pungency and passion.

The casting is most imaginative. Michael Redgrave must be as delighted as I am with his playing of the mercurial bibber; it is the best serious performance he has given us for years. Mr Redgrave has been passing through what his biographers will probably call 'a dark period', lapsing often into a semaphoring, half-articulate style of playing which one might call algebraic, and which led him, last year at Stratford, almost to *grope* through his parts in a distracted, unavailing attempt to communicate nuance. Eyes bulging, arms windmilling, he gave the impression of being possessed by an adhesive demon that was fiercely resisting exorcism; it was sometimes as if another man's soul were speaking, ventriloquially, through his reluctant jaws. He seemed, like Coleridge, to be beset by a mixture of hyper-sensitivity and insecurity which was numbing his powers of direct statement.

Frank Elgin, the drunk in Mr Odets's play, is just such a performer; and in playing him Mr Redgrave purges himself. 'You are not a technical actor,' says the director (played by Sam Wanamaker), and Mr Redgrave, taking a hint from this true word, battles before our eyes to free himself of the technical preoccupations that have been disfiguring his work. He bounds out of his corner, like a recently defeated heavyweight, fighting, lunging, swinging, and counter-punching; but with a revived authority and victory in his eye, for the uncertainties that are Frank Elgin's enemies are Mr Redgrave's, too. The ensuing duel is convulsive, sudorific, and extremely moving, and the verdict is triumph. Temperamentally, Frank Elgin is a retarded boy, chronically over-mothered, and in this aspect of male psychology Mr Redgrave is deeply versed, as his performance four years ago in Strindberg's *The Father* bore witness. In short, this part is Mr Redgrave's special pasture;

and, the furrow having been ploughed, the transition made, we look to him never to flag again.

Beady-eyed and black-cropped, tautly ironic and especially brilliant in scorn, the young director demands the epithet 'combustible'. Mr Wanamaker is downright dangerous. He enjoys smouldering, and when smouldering is not enough, he throws things – among them a medicine bottle, several articles of clothing, and a hail of half-smoked cigarettes. If there is nothing portable to hand, Mr Wanamaker, profoundly stirred, hits himself on the forehead with a painful and audible smack. This is a most impressive piece of acting. The character itself is fascinating; this director treats his actors in the Buchmanite-cum-revivalist manner popularized by the American Group Theatre, and is satisfied that they have grasped an idea only when one of them is sufficiently moved to hurl a chair halfway across the stage. Mr Wanamaker pads ferally through the debris, wearing that neurotic, almost poetic look which goes, in America, with acute sinus trouble.

Googie Withers, shiny and bespectacled, gives a blisteringly frank and unchivalrous performance as the actor's wife, whose fundamental loyalty has been ravaged by the frustration of too many dead years. She completes one of the most striking trios I have ever watched on a London stage. Add to this some unassuming and cleverly lit settings by Anthony Holland, and you have what seems to me (and, I hope, to Mr Wanamaker, who directed the play) quite an important evening in the English theatre.

(*1952*)

GUYS AND DOLLS

BY FRANK LOESSER, AT THE COLISEUM, LONDON

Guys and Dolls, at which I am privileged to take a peek last evening, is a hundred-per-cent American musical caper, cooked up out of a story called 'The Idyll of Miss Sarah Brown', by the late Damon Runyon, who is such a scribe as delights to give the English language a nice kick in the pants.

This particular fable takes place in and around Times Square in

New York City, where many citizens do nothing but roll dice all night long, which is held by one and all, and especially the gendarmes, to be a great vice. Among the parties hopping around in this neighbourhood is a guy by the name of Nathan Detroit, who operates a floating dice game, and Miss Adelaide, his ever-loving pretty, who is sored up at this Nathan because after fourteen years of engagement they are still nothing but engaged. Anyway, being short of ready scratch, Nathan lays a bet with a large gambler called Sky Masterson, the subject of the wager being whether The Sky can talk a certain Salvation Army doll into joining him on a trip to Havana. Naturally, Nathan figures that a nice doll such as this will die sooner, but by and by she and The Sky get to looking back and forth at each other, and before you know it she is his sweet-pea. What happens next but The Sky gets bopped by religion and shoots craps with Nathan and the boys for their immortal souls. And where do the sinners wind up, with their chalk-striped suits and busted noses, but at a prayer meeting in the doll's mission house, which hands me a very big laugh indeed. The actors who nab the jobs of playing these apes and essences of 42nd Street have me all tuckered out with clapping them.

Nathan Detroit is Sam Levene, who expostulates very good with his arms, which are as long as a monkey's. Stubby Kaye, who plays Nicely-Nicely Johnson, the well-known horse-player, is built on lines which are by no means dinky, for his poundage maybe runs into zillions, but he gives with a voice which is as couth as a choir boy's or maybe couther. He commences the evening by joining in a three-part comedy song about the nags. In fact, it is a fugue, and I will give you plenty of eleven to five that it is the first fugue many patrons of the Coliseum ever hear. Miss Vivian Blaine (Miss Adelaide) is a very choice blonde judy and she gets to sing a song which goes as follows: 'Take back your mink to from whence it came' and which hits me slap-dab in the ear as being supernaturally comical. Myself, I prefer her to Miss Lizbeth Webb, who plays the mission doll, but, naturally, I do not mention such an idea out loud.

The Coliseum is no rabbit hutch, and maybe a show as quick and smart as this *Guys and Dolls* will go better in such a sized theatre as the Cambridge Theatre. Personally, I found myself laughing ha-ha last night more often than a guy in the critical dodge has any right to. And I am ready to up and drop on my knees before Frank Loesser, who writes the music and lyrics. In fact, this Loesser is maybe the best light composer in the world. In fact, the chances are that *Guys and Dolls* is not only a young masterpiece, but the Beggar's Opera of Broadway.

(*1952*)

THE CRUCIBLE

BY ARTHUR MILLER, AT THE BRISTOL OLD VIC

Convictions, as Nietzsche said, are prisons: they exclude from life the fun of doubt and flexibility. In *Death of a Salesman* Arthur Miller observed mankind in detached, compassionate surview; in *The Crucible* he takes sides. And the strength of his convictions breeds the ultimate weakness of his play.

He re-creates the Salem witch-hunt of 1692, which began when a clutch of flighty wantons, discovered dancing naked by moonlight, absolved themselves by accusing others of sending the devil into them. Were they really practising witchcraft, that fertility magic which Christian theology has taught us to call black? Mr Miller evades the issue. For him all oppression is vile, and we must assume that in Salem there was smoke but no fire. A fearful town believes the girls' charges, whereat Mr Miller skins history alive, revealing beneath the surface the familiar ugliness of McCarthyism. Silence is evidence of guilt; he who testifies to a prisoner's innocence is himself suspected. Abigail Williams, the leader of the crypto-coven, seeks to ensnare her ex-lover, John Proctor, by naming his wife as a witch. 'Is the accuser always holy now?' he cries, and, to prove Abigail's malice, confesses his infidelity to the court. But his wife, thinking to shield him, denies it, thereby ensuring her own and her husband's condemnation.

The fierce narrative thrill of the action depends mostly on Mr Miller's mastery of period dialogue. The prose is gnarled, whorled in its gleaming as a stick of polished oak, an incomparable dramatic weapon. Witness Abigail's speech, swearing her friends to secrecy:

Let either of you breathe a word, or the edge of a word . . . and I will come to you in the black of some terrible night, and I will bring a pointy reckoning that will shudder you. . . . I saw Indians smash my dear parents' heads on the pillow next to mine, and I have seen some reddish work done at night, and I can make you wish you had never seen the sun go down.

What pity, then, that Mr Miller's convictions so crucially imprison him! He presents Deputy-Governor Danforth, the judge, as a motive-less monster, which is as if Shaw had omitted the Inquisitor's speech from the trial scene of *Saint Joan*. The enemy is allowed no appeal. Mr Miller writes wrathfully, a state in which the creative muscles tend to seize up; and a hard human tragedy, which one hoped to see irri-gated, is desiccated instead. 'For the Poet,' said Sidney, 'he nothing affirmeth, and therefore never lyeth.' Mr Miller affirmeth plenty, and to support his affirmations he is forced to restrict his sympathies – a fatal abdication from truth. He prejudges those whom he accuses of prejudice, and the last scene, in which Proctor goes to the noose, plays like old melodrama; the words ring heroically hollow, because dramaturgy has declined into martyrology. Men are never wholly right or wholly wrong. The witch-hunters at Salem thought they were, and Mr Miller, the hunters' hunter, flaws a magnificent play by sharing their fallacy.

Rosemary Harris exactly catches the wan aridity of Proctor's wife; and Proctor himself is Edgar Wreford, who, sniffing melodrama in the air, lets the part play him, replacing the firm reins of realism with the loose bit of rhetoric.

(1954)

MOBY DICK

ADAPTED BY ORSON WELLES FROM HERMAN MELVILLE'S NOVEL, AT THE DUKE OF YORK'S, LONDON

At this stage of his career it is absurd to expect Orson Welles to attempt anything less than the impossible. It is all that is left to him. Mere possible things, like Proust or *War and Peace*, would confine him. He must choose *Moby Dick*, a book whose setting is the open sea, whose hero is more mountain than man and more symbol than either, and whose villain is the supremely unstageable whale. He must take as his raw material Melville's prose, itself as stormy as the sea it speaks of, with a thousand wrecked metaphors clinging on its surface to frail spars of sense. (You do not dip into Melville; you jump in, holding your nose and praying not to be drowned. If prose styles were women, Melville's would be painted by Rubens and cartooned by Blake: it is a shot-gun wedding of sensuousness and metaphysics.) Yet out of all these impossibilities Mr Welles has fashioned a piece of pure theatrical megalomania – a sustained assault on the senses which dwarfs anything London has seen since, perhaps, the Great Fire.

It was exactly fifty years ago last Wednesday that Irving made his last appearance in London. I doubt if anyone since then has left his mark more indelibly on every second of a London production than Mr Welles has on this of *Moby Dick*. He serves Melville in three capacities: as adapter, as director, and as star. The adaptation, to begin with, is beautifully adroit. Captain Ahab's self-destructive revenge on the albino whale that tore off his leg is over in less than a hundred and fifty minutes. And two brilliant devices reconcile us to the lushness of Melville's style. Firstly, seeing how readily Melville falls into iambic pentameters, Mr Welles has versified the whole action. Secondly, to prepare us for the bravura acting which is to come, he 'frames' the play as a rehearsal held sixty years ago by a tyrannical brandy-swigging American actor-manager. My only criticism must be that the role of Pip, the mad cabinboy, has been rather too heavily expanded. Mr Welles clearly sees Ahab as Lear and Pip as a cross-breed of the Fool and Cordelia, but the duologue between them was a very ponderous affair, not helped by the agonized inadequacy of the actress (Joan Plowright) to whom Pip's ramblings were given.

The real revelation was Mr Welles's direction. The great, square, rope-hung vault of the bare stage, stabbed with light from every point of the compass, becomes by turns the Nantucket wharf, the whalers' chapel, the deck of the *Pequod*, and the ocean itself. The technique with which Thornton Wilder evoked 'Our Town' is used to evoke 'Our Universe'. The whaling-boat from which Ahab flings himself at Moby Dick is a rostrum projecting into the stalls, and the first-act hurricane is a model of imaginative stagecraft: ropes and beams swing crazily across one's vision, while the crew slides and huddles beneath. Mr Welles's films have already established his mastery of atmospheric sound: here the crash and howl of the sea is alternated with a brisk little mouth-organ theme and strange, foreboding chords played on a harmonium. Dialogue is overlapped, words are timed, syllables are pounced on with a subtlety we have not heard since *The Magnificent Ambersons*. Gordon Jackson, a much-neglected actor, gives Ishmael just the right feeling of perplexity, and Patrick McGoohan as Starbuck, the mate who dares to oppose Ahab's will, is Melville's 'long, earnest man' to the life, whittled out of immemorial teak. His is the best performance of the evening.

When I say that, I am not excepting Mr Welles, who now comes before us as actor. In aspect, he is a leviathan plus. He has a voice of bottled thunder, so deeply encasked that one thinks of those liquor advertisements which boast that not a drop is sold till it's seven years old. The trouble is that everything he does is on such a vast scale that it quickly becomes monotonous. He is too big for the boots of any part. He reminds one of Macaulay's conversation, as Carlyle described it: 'Very well for a while, but one wouldn't *live* under Niagara.' Emotion of any kind he expresses by thrusting out his chin and knitting his his eyebrows. Between these twin promontories there juts out a false and quite unnecessary nose. Sir Laurence Olivier began his film of *Hamlet* with the statement that it was 'the tragedy of a man who could not make up his mind'. At one point Mr Welles's new appendage started to leave its moorings, and *Moby Dick* nearly became the tragedy of a man who could not make up his nose.

Let me now turn about and say that, though Mr Welles plays Ahab less than convincingly, there are few actors alive who could play it at all. Earlier in the evening, as the actor-manager, he makes what seems to be a final statement on the relationship of actor to audience: 'Did you ever,' he says, 'hear of an unemployed audience?' It is a good line; but the truth is that British audiences have been unemployed far too long. If they wish to exert themselves, to have their minds set whirling and their eyes dazzling at sheer theatrical virtuosity, *Moby Dick* is their opportunity. With it, the theatre becomes once more a house of magic.

(1955)

AMERICAN BLUES:

THE PLAYS OF ARTHUR MILLER AND
TENNESSEE WILLIAMS

'Since 1920,' Arthur Miller has said, 'American drama has been a steady, year-by-year documentation of the frustration of man,' and the record supports him. Between the wars most of the serious American playwrights – Odets, for instance, Elmer Rice, Maxwell Anderson, Irwin Shaw, and Lillian Hellman – did their best work in the conviction that modern civilization was committing repeated acts of criminal injustice against the individual. Their heroes were victims, such as Mio in *Winterset*, and they devoted themselves to dramatizing the protests of minorities; it was thus that they ploughed the land cleared for them by O'Neill, the solitary pioneer bulldozer. For his long-sightedness they substituted an absorption in immediate reality; where he was the admonitory lighthouse, they were the prying torches. During the war their batteries ran out: since 1945 none of them has written a first-rate play. The mission of martyrology has been taken up by the younger generation, by Arthur Miller and Tennessee Williams.

Miller and Williams seem, on the face of things, to have even less in common than Ibsen and Bjørnson. Miller, a man of action, belongs to the thirties' tradition of social drama, while Williams, a poet *manqué*, looks ahead to a lyrical, balletic *Gesamtkunstwerk* in which (though I doubt whether he fully recognizes the fact) words as such are likely to have less and less importance. Yet the two men share much. Both echo Jacob in *Awake and Sing*, who says: 'We don't want life printed on dollar bills.' Miller is a rebel against, Williams a refugee from, the familiar ogre of commercialism, the killer of values and the leveller of men. 'You know, *knowledge* – ZZZZpp! *Money* – zzzzpp! POWER! Wham! That's the cycle democracy is built on!' exults the Gentleman Caller in *The Glass Menagerie*. But this is not their only joint exploit. Both reserve their most impassioned utterance for one subject, into which they plunge headlong, sometimes floundering in self-pity, sometimes belly-diving into rhetoric, but often knifing straight and deep: the subject of frustration. Lady Mulligan, in Williams's latest play *Camino Real*, complains to Gutman, the proprietor of her hotel, that he has chosen to shelter some highly undesirable guests. Where-upon:

GUTMAN: They pay the price of admission the same as you.
LADY M.: What price is that?
GUTMAN: Desperation!

Techniques change, but grand themes do not. Whether in a murder trial, a bullfight, a farce like *Charley's Aunt*, or a tragedy like *Lear*, the behaviour of a human being at the end of his tether is the common denominator of all drama. When a man (or woman) arrives at self-knowledge through desperation, he (or she) has become the raw material for a great play. The stature of the work will depend on the dramatist's honesty and skill, but its cornerstone is already laid. Though they take the same theme, Miller and Williams build very differently. In European terms, Miller is the Scandinavian: he has in fact translated Ibsen, whose fierce lucidity, humourlessness, and 'odour of spiritual paraffin' he shares. Williams, on the other hand, is the Mediterranean, the lover of Lorca and D. H. Lawrence, sensuous, funny, verbally luxuriant, prone to immersion in romantic tragedy. Miller's plays are hard, 'patrist', athletic, concerned mostly with men. Williams's are soft, 'matrist', sickly, concerned mostly with women. What links them is their love for the bruised individual soul and its life of 'quiet desperation'. It takes courage, in a sophisticated age, to keep faith with this kind of love, and their refusal to compromise has led both Miller and Williams into some embarrassing pseudo-simplicities. Their reward is in characters like Joe Keller of *All My Sons*, Willy Loman of *Death of a Salesman*, John Proctor of *The Crucible*, Blanche DuBois of *A Streetcar Named Desire*, Laura of *The Glass Menagerie*, Kilroy of *Camino Real*, who live together in the great theatrical line of flawed, victimized innocents.

Arthur Miller, who was born in Brooklyn in 1915, achieved his first Broadway production at the age of twenty-nine. The play, *The Man Who Had All the Luck*, had a framework which Miller (himself a second son) later elaborated in *All My Sons* and *Death of a Salesman*: the relationship of two sons with their father. The protagonist is David, the elder, an unskilled garage hand in a midwestern town. His brother,

Amos, forcibly trained by Pat, a jealous and protective father, to become a baseball pitcher, gets nowhere, while the ignored David thrives, financially as well as maritally. His inability to fail makes David neurotic, and to deaden his sense of unworthiness he falls into the habit of ascribing his success to luck. In the final scene he is made to understand that 'luck' is merely a word used by men less diligent than himself to explain his triumphs. 'You made it all yourself,' cries his wife. 'It was always you.' His hired man, the immigrant Gus, puts the play's case: a man must believe, he says, 'that on this earth he is the boss of his life, not the leafs in the teacups, not the stars. In Europe I see already millions of Davids walking around, millions. They gave up already to know that they are the boss. They gave up to know that they deserve this world.' The point of the *drame à thèse* is weakened because the principal characters are too obviously pawns in Miller's hands; what stays in the mind is the craggy candour of the dialogue. Miller, like Williams, is committed to prose drama, in which both men have uncovered riches which make the English 'poetic revival' seem hollow, retrogressive, and – to use Cyril Connolly's coinage – praeteritist.

Pat, David's father, is guilty only by implication. Joe Keller in *All My Sons*, staged by Elia Kazan in 1947, is a criminal in the legal sense. Shadily, he has been acquitted of manufacturing faulty aircraft parts during the war, and when the play opens his partner is in gaol, taking the rap for him. Of Joe's two sons, one has been killed in action, and the other, Chris, intends to marry his brother's ex-fiancée, the convicted partner's daughter. Chris is a militant idealist ashamed of having survived the war; material possessions sicken him unless they have been purely and honourably acquired – 'Otherwise what you have is loot, and there's blood on it.' Miller concentrates on two shifting relationships: between Chris and his girl, and between Chris and his father. Joe Keller (like Willy Loman) had to compromise in order to live; and Chris (like Biff in the later play) is overwhelmed by the revelation of paternal guilt. How can he marry the daughter of a man who was imprisoned because of his father's perjury? Miller solves this classic impasse with a smart stroke of melodrama: unconvincingly, Keller accepts the burden and shoots himself.

'I'm his father,' says Keller at one point, 'and he's my son, and if there's something bigger than that I'll put a bullet in my head.' This message, more symphonically orchestrated, reappears in Miller's best play, *Death of a Salesman*, which Kazan directed in 1948. *All Our Fathers*, as Daniel Schneider suggested, would be an appropriate alternative title. Willy Loman and his two sons, the sensualist Happy and the mysteriously retarded Biff, are ruined by their belief in 'the wrong dream', the mystique of salesmanship. 'What are you building?' says Ben, Willy's millionaire brother. 'Lay your hand on it. Where is it?' Unlike most hero-victims, Willy is not cynical about the values which are corrupting him; he is pathetic because, brightly and unquestioningly, he reveres them. As the play begins, Biff, the quondam college hero, has returned penniless to his Brooklyn home, where he finds his father going crazy with failure to sell. The ensuing action covers the next twenty-four hours: in a series of beautifully welded interlocking flashbacks we pursue Willy's thoughts into the past, back to the germinal moment of calamity when he was surprised by Biff in a hotel room with a half-dressed tart. This encounter, with its implied destruction of the father-god, stunted Biff's career and left Willy with a load of remorse redoubled by the fact that he, too, was the unsuccessful one of two brothers. Memory explodes the cocoon of illusions within which he preserves his self-respect, and (ostensibly for the insurance money) he commits suicide.

The play is Miller's triumph in the plain style; it rings with phrases which have entered into the contemporary subconscious. 'He's liked, but he's not – well liked'; 'The woods are burning, boys'; Ben's complacent 'The jungle is dark but full of diamonds, Willy.' More memorably, there is Mrs Loman's anguished rebuke to her sons for having scorned their father:

Willy Loman never made a lot of money. His name was never in the papers. He's not the finest character that ever lived. But he's a human being, and a terrible thing is happening to him. So attention must be paid. He's not to be allowed to fall into his grave like a dog. Attention, attention must be finally paid to such a person.

Charley, Willy's neighbour, speaks an epitaph over him which has the same groping, half-articulate power:

And for a salesman, there is no rock bottom to the life. He don't put a bolt to a nut, he don't tell you the law, or give you medicine. . . . Nobody dast blame this man. A salesman is got to dream, boy. It comes with the territory.

There is a fair amount of otiose breast-beating in the script, and Miller's prose sometimes slips into a sentimental rhythm of despair which could be convicted of glibness. But the theatre is an impure craft, and *Death of a Salesman* organizes its impurities with an emotional effect unrivalled in post-war drama.

Willy Loman goes to his fate without knowing exactly why it has overtaken him. The heroes of Miller's last two plays are also defeated, but they know what forces have beaten them: the enemy in each case is identified. In 1950 he adapted *An Enemy of the People*, turning it into a racy contemporary pamphlet. His temperament chimed with what he describes as Ibsen's 'terrible wrath', and the dilemma of Stockmann, the betrayed crusader, duplicated Miller's own, that of the life-long democrat who learns, from the example of his own country, that majority rule is not infallible. Stockmann is vanquished by the pusillanimous stupidity of the mob, on which, in the original, he launches a furious attack. Miller softens it in translation, thereby forfeiting the objectivity which allowed even Ibsen's heroes their weaknesses. Anger is a great simplifier, and Miller is an angry writer. *An Enemy of the People* marks his decision to weight the scales in favour of the oppressed minority man.

'Before many can know something, *one* must know it' – Stockmann's affirmation steers us towards *The Crucible*, Miller's most recent play, produced in New York last January. The bird's-eye compassion of *Salesman* has now been replaced by a worm's-eye sympathy which extends only to the 'right-minded' characters. Though it draws plain contemporary parallels with its subject, the witch-hunt at Salem, it is not an overtly political play: it deals with the refusal of a stubborn intellect to enter into enforced allegiances. 'I like not the smell of this "authority",' says Proctor, the hero. In Salem, as in Stockmann's township, nonconformity was allied with sin, an attitude which Miller detests so savagely that the play often resembles the trial scene from *Saint Joan* with the Inquisitor's speech deleted. The inquisitors in *The Crucible* are unmotivated fiends, and the atmosphere in which they flourished is never explored or accounted for.

The action stays close to historical fact. A group of flighty wantons, charged with engaging in mildly orgiastic rites in a wood near Salem, hit on the notion of exculpating themselves by accusing their neighbours of having sent the devil into them. Their accusations are believed; a tribunal is set up; and the hangings begin. Proctor's wife is arrested, and his attempts to exonerate her lead to his own arrest. In a fine, clinching line he demands: 'Is the accuser always holy now?' If he confesses, giving a list of those who infected him with diabolism, he will be freed; if not, he will be executed. At their last meeting his wife tells him how another of the condemned died:

Great stones they lay upon his chest until he plead aye or nay. They say he give them but two words. 'More weight,' he says. And died.

Head high, as the drums roll, Proctor sacrifices himself for his principles, a commonplace 'Victorian' martyrdom worthy of a mind much less subtle than Miller's. *The Crucible* is disturbing because it suggests a sensibility blunted by the insistence of an outraged conscience: it has the over-simplification of poster art.

In *The Devils of Loudun*, a much more searching analysis of witch-hunting, Aldous Huxley mentions the euphoria of the 'adrenalin addict', a type to which Miller seems at present to belong. 'There are many people,' Huxley says, 'for whom hate and rage pay a higher dividend of immediate satisfaction than love,' this satisfaction being derived from 'their psychically stimulated endocrines'. Bad temper, which produces cramp in the creative muscles, is an enemy of art; and though *The Crucible* is on the right side morally, socially, and politically, it is the artistic equivalent of a closed shop. Full of affirmations, it is also full of emotional half-truths; which will do for a leader writer, but not for a playwright of Miller's stature.

Tennessee Williams's genius has no social commitments, but many aesthetic ones. His faults, like Miller's, are the defects of his virtues. The present cast of Miller's mind traps him in the present, the male preserve wherein history is shaped, and the universal preoccupation is with action and incident; Williams trades in nostalgia and hope, the past and the future, obsessions which we associate most strongly with the great female characters – Marguérite Gautier, Cleopatra, Hedda Gabler, and Chekhov's women, none of whom cares for today half as much as she cares for yesterday or tomorrow. His plays thus have the static quality of dream rather than the dynamic quality of fact; they bring the drama of mood to what may be its final hothouse flowering.

Williams is a Southerner, born forty-two years ago in Columbus, Mississippi, and his work first reached Broadway when his 'memory play', *The Glass Menagerie*, was produced in 1945. It turns a burning-glass on to a storm-proof family unit, insulated against life by its careful preservation of gentility. A stage direction reads:

The apartment faces an alley, and is entered by a fire-escape, a structure whose name is a touch of accidental poetry, for all of these huge buildings are always burning with the slow and implacable fires of human desperation.

Here live Amanda, garrulous and suffocatingly maternal, her cynical son, Tom, and her crippled daughter, Laura. Retrospectively, Tom tells the story of how he invited a Gentleman Caller to dinner as a possible beau for Laura, and how the Caller, affable though he was, revealed that he was already spoken for. Laura's spinsterhood is confirmed; Amanda's hopes are dashed; but neither of these minor disasters is made to sound mawkish. Williams's wry wit acts as a caustic to the wounds. In Amanda, fussy and conventionally archaic, he shows the perfection of his ear for human speech, and also the extent of his tact: she never becomes a grotesque. The play is not a major achievement, but its opacity is as precise and marvellous as a spider's web.

You Touched Me!, on which Williams collaborated with Donald Windham, is of interest only because it dealt (like *The Glass Menagerie*) with the impact of reality on illusions, in this case on two isolated, mutually infectious virgins; and because it was adapted from the short story of the same name by D. H. Lawrence, one of Williams's heroes. It was followed in 1947 by *A Streetcar Named Desire*, which was directed by Kazan, who seems to have an instinct for the best of both Miller and Williams. It is perhaps the most misunderstood of his plays: the English and French productions were both so blatantly sensationalized that Williams's underlying lyric fibre passed unnoticed. If Willy Loman is the desperate average man, Blanche DuBois is the desperate exceptional woman. Willy's collapse began when his son walked into a hotel apartment and found him with a whore; Blanche's when she entered 'a room that I thought was empty' and found her young husband embracing an older man. In each instance the play builds up to a climax involving guilt and concomitant disgust. Blanche, nervously boastful, lives in the leisured past; her defence against actuality is a sort of aristocratic *Bovarysme*, at which her brutish brother-in-law Stanley repeatedly sneers. Characteristically, Williams keeps his detachment and does not take sides: he never denies that Stanley's wife, in spite of her sexual enslavement, is happy and well-adjusted, nor does he exaggerate the cruelty with which Stanley reveals to Blanche's new suitor the secrets of her nymphomaniac past. The play's weakness lies in the fact that the leading role lends itself to grandiose overplaying by unintelligent actresses, who forget that when Blanche complains to her sister about Stanley's animalism, she is expressing, however faintly, an ideal:

Such things as art – as poetry and music – such kinds of new light have come into the world since then! . . . That we have to make *grow*! and *cling* to, and hold as our flag! In this dark march towards whatever it is we're approaching . . . *Don't – don't* hang back with the brutes!

When, finally, she is removed to the mental home, we should feel that a part of civilization is going with her. Where ancient drama teaches us to reach nobility by contemplation of what is noble, modern American drama conjures us to contemplate what might have been noble, but is now humiliated, ignoble in the sight of all but the compassionate.

In 1948 Williams reworked an earlier play, *Summer and Smoke*. Its heroine, Alma, is Blanche ten years younger: a Southern virgin concealing beneath 'literary' affectations a sense of inadequacy in the presence of men. Her next-door neighbour, a notorious rake, tries to seduce her and is boldly repulsed. He shows her an anatomy chart, and explains that the human body is a tree inhabited by three birds, the brain, the belly, and the genitals. Where, he asks, is the soul of which she speaks and for which, in Spanish, her name stands? Ironically, he ends up reformed, whereas Alma, her sexual instincts newly awakened, moves to the other extreme. They exchange attitudes, passing almost without contact. *Summer and Smoke*, a needlessly symbolic morality play, is sentimental in that its characters are too slight to sustain the consuming emotions which are bestowed on them.

Nobody could say that *The Rose Tattoo* (1950) did not contain large characters. It is the most thoroughgoing star vehicle of the last ten years, expressly written for Anna Magnani, whose shaky acquaintance with English unfortunately prevented her from playing the lead in the stage production. Here Williams pleads the cause of sexual love as its own justification. 'So successfully,' he says in his preface, 'have we disguised from ourselves the intensity of our own feelings, the sensibility of our own hearts, that plays in the tragic tradition have begun to seem untrue.' At a time when Miller's plays were growing colder and more intellectualized, Williams's blazed hotter and more sensuous. His heroine is a poor Sicilian immigrant whose husband, a truck-driving smuggler with a fabulous capacity for sexual devotion, has been shot. She learns to her horror that her man had been faithless to her, but the realization does not prevent her from joyously taking as her new lover a man who physically resembles the dead ideal. The play's complex structure – short scenes linked by evocative snatches of music – is too poetic for its theme, but the virtuosity of the writing, alternately ribald and pathetic, is tremendous. Does it alternate between tragedy and farce? That is because it was meant for a great actress whose gift it is to switch emotional gear, change from a Siddonsesque pose to a bout of nose-picking without a moment's hesitation. Williams's fault, as in *Streetcar*, was to have overestimated English-speaking actresses. It would take a Magnani to play the scene in which Serafina, the heroine, entertains her new lover, out of whose pocket, as the poetic tension mounts, there falls a neatly packaged contraceptive. Sardou never asked as much of Bernhardt, nor D'Annunzio of Duse.

Kazan renewed his association with Williams in the spring of 1953, when he directed the violently controversial *Camino Real*. This is a phantasmagoria of decadence, as limpidly rebellious to modern civilization as a Bix Beiderbecke solo is to a Paul Whiteman orchestration. The published text has a unity never achieved by the acting script. It carries to its conclusion Williams's dictum: 'I say that symbols are nothing but the natural speech of drama.' In a preface he adds: 'I have read the works of "thinking playwrights", as distinguished from us who are permitted only to feel. . . .' The result is a tranced play of hypersensitivity, a weird drug-work of wit, terror, and inertia.

It is set in a mythical Central American coastal town. Stage left is the Seven Seas Hotel, where live Byron, Casanova, and Marguérite Gautier, ghosts of the aristocratic way of life; stage right are a pawn-broker's shop, a fortune-teller's tent, and a flophouse, where, among the outcasts, we encounter the Baron de Charlus. Upstage is an arch, giving on to a desert, where a hot wind blows and whither no one dares travel. Williams's hero is Kilroy, the new arrival at this fetid microcosm of modern life: the embodiment of youth and enterprise, he was once a prizefighter but had to abandon his career because 'I've got a heart in my chest as big as the head of a baby'. He is elected the town butt, and the police deck him out in a clown's costume, complete with electrically sparking nose. How does this simpleton fit in with the filth of the Camino Real? Williams answers the question in writing which seems too often to have been composed in a state of *kif*. He indulges in vague, roseate aphorisms; nor can he resist theatrical shortcuts such as a noisy aeroplane crash and *two* chases down the aisles and into the boxes of the theatre, devices which assist the play about as tellingly as a consignment of heroin would help an anti-narcotics campaign. Yet out of the strident blare of the action, Williams's faith in Kilroy's truth, in a child's mistrust of phoneyness, emerges with overwhelming clarity. For those anarchists who escape he has undisguised sympathy. Byron, for example, says of his later works: 'They seem to improve as the wine in the bottle – dwindles. . . . *There is a passion for declivity in this world*'; but when, having roused himself, he departs into the murderous desert, Williams gives him a splendid epitaph: '*Make voyages! – Attempt them!* – there's nothing else!'

Kilroy, too, attempts the voyage, but only after a serio-comic encounter with a character called the Gypsy, who organizes and advertises the local fiesta, at which her daughter, in a loony parody of a fertility ritual, annually recovers her virginity. The Gypsy's garish cynicism ('File this crap under crap') struck the New York critics as the most recognizable thing in the play, along with Kilroy's seduction of the Gypsy's daughter, a grossly comic scene in which the two young people repeat to each other eight times the talismanic words: 'I am sincere.' Surviving a brisk attempt to murder him, Kilroy journeys through the perilous arch, accompanied by Don Quixote, that other liegeman of the lost cause, who ends the play with a movingly symbolic cry: 'The violets in the mountains have broken the rocks!'

Many charges can be brought against *Camino Real*. It has too many italics, too many exclamation marks; it depends too much on boozed writing and aureate diction. Its virtue is in its affectionate championing of the flyblown, inarticulate stratum of humanity. Perhaps when Quixote and Kilroy reach the snowy upper air of the unnamed mountains, they will become subjects for a play by Miller, whose artistic life is dedicated, like Shaw's, to a belief in progress towards an attainable summit. Williams's aspirations are imaginative and hence unattainable; and therein lies the difference between them.

Complementary, yet irreconcilable, Miller and Williams have produced the most powerful body of dramatic prose in modern English. They write with equal virtuosity, Williams about the violets, Miller about the rocks. The vegetable reinforces the mineral; and the animal, a dramatic element feared or ignored in the English theatre, triumphantly reinforces both.

(1954)

SOCIAL DRAMA

The American edition of Arthur Miller's latest work, *A View from the Bridge*, is prefaced by a long essay which Mr Miller entitles: 'On Social Plays'. At which we wince, those of us who remember what the thirties meant by 'social plays' – tracts hoarse with rage and hungry for martyrdom, dramatic tumbrils from which the authors yelled their prophetic curses on us, the complacent *tricoteuses*. Sombre and embittered social plays led us to equate responsibility with solemnity, which we loathed, and irresponsibility with gaiety, which we loved. Mr Miller's purpose is to show us that this dichotomy was false – that there are such things as festal seriousness, responsible gaiety, and triumphant tragedy. He defines theatre in the Greek manner, as 'a dramatic consideration of the way men ought to live', and thence takes off into an artistic credo as stimulating as any of our time.

Just as *Pravda* decries the 'cult of the individual' in politics, Mr Miller decries it in drama. Defying Donne, our modish playwrights see their heroes as islands doomed to be swamped by an impersonal and vanquishing sea. Their prevalent theme is frustration; the hero is either defeated by society or reduced by it to a negative conformity. What has vanished is the positive concept of men living fruitfully together. Modern heroes die sadly in the dark; they 'go gentle into that good night', a pitiful spectacle which has bred in modern audiences an appetite for pathos that amounts to an addiction. Tragedy, by contrast, should happen in sunlight. The hero bends in desperation beneath his burden, but he dies in the service of something larger than himself, and the sun shines the more brightly for his suffering. Ancient tragedy puts the question: 'How are *we* to live?' Modern tragedy asks: 'How am *I* to live?' That is the vital difference.

The first English play to set up personal fulfilment as a tragic ideal happened, unfortunately, to be a masterpiece: *Hamlet*. Here, for the first time, the hero was an outcast, both divorced from and superior to the society around him; for the first time an audience was invited to sympathize with a man's apartness and to ignore his 'togetherness'. Lear stands boldly for England; but Hamlet stands only for Hamlet, the first tragic protagonist to despise and reject every value by which his society lives. One echoes Shaw's stricture:

Hamlet is the tragedy of private life – nay, of individual bachelor-poet life. It belongs to a detached residence, a select library, an exclusive circle, to no occupation, to fathomless boredom, to impenitent mug-wumpism, to the illusion that the futility of these things is the futility of existence. . . .

Hamlet spurns the old idols, dies in the dark, and leaves only a shambles behind him; it is magnificent, but it is not tragedy. As Mr Miller says:

I can no longer take with ultimate seriousness a drama of individual psychology written for its own sake, however full it may be of insight and precise observation. Time is moving: there is a world to make . . . a world in which the human being can live as a naturally political, naturally private, naturally engaged person, a world in which once again a true tragic victory can be scored.

I shall continue to applaud all plays that are honestly frivolous, devoutly disengaged; but I shall reserve my cheers for the play in which man among men, not man against men, is the well-spring of tragedy.

A View from the Bridge is a double bill, in the second half of which one character accuses another of homosexuality; the accusation is false, but it is made clearly enough to have convinced the Lord Chamberlain that the play should be banned in this country. Thus deprived of Mr Miller, where else shall we search for a social playwright? No further, one suggests, than Bertolt Brecht's company in East Berlin, which is acknowledged to be the best theatre company in Europe and has been heavily tipped as the best in the world. Paris has twice capitulated to them; and it is time someone brought them to London, so that we might see in practice what Mr Miller so eloquently preaches – the powerful exhilaration of a true 'social theatre'.

(1956)

VALENTINE TO TENNESSEE WILLIAMS

In Spain, where I saw him last, he looked profoundly Spanish. He might have passed for one of those confidential street dealers who earn their living selling spurious Parker pens in the cafés of Málaga or Valencia. Like them, he wore a faded chalk-striped shirt, a coat slung over his shoulders, a trim, dark moustache, and a sleazy, fat-cat smile. His walk, like theirs, was a raffish saunter, and everything about him seemed slept in, especially his hair, a nest of small, wet serpents. Had we been in Seville and his clothes had been more formal, he could have been mistaken for a pampered elder son idling away a legacy in dribs and on drabs, the sort you see sitting in windows along the Sierpes, apparently stuffed. In Italy he looks Italian; in Greece, Greek; wherever he travels on the Mediterranean coast, Tennessee Williams takes on a protective colouring which melts him into his background, like a lizard on a rock. In New York or London he seems out of place, and is best explained away as a retired bandit. Or a beachcomber: shave the beard off any of the self-portraits Gaugin painted in Tahiti, soften the features a little, and you have a sleepy outcast face that might well be Tennessee's.

It is unmistakably the face of a nomad. Wherever Williams goes he is a stranger, one who lives out of suitcases and has a trick of making any home he acquires resemble, within ten minutes, a hotel apartment. Like most hypochondriacs, he is an uneasy guest on earth. When he sold the film rights of his play *Cat on a Hot Tin Roof* for half a million dollars, he asked that the payment should be spread over ten years, partly out of prudence but mostly out of a mantic suspicion, buzzing in his ears, that in ten years' time he might be dead. He says justly of himself that he is 'a driven person'. The condemned tend always to be lonely, and one of Williams's favourite quotations is a line from a play which runs: 'We're all of us sentenced to solitary confinement inside our own skins.' He says such things quite blandly, with a thick chuckle which is as far from cynicism as it is from self-pity.

To be alone at forty is to be really alone, and Williams has passed forty. In a sense, of course, solitude is a condition of his trade. All writing is an anti-social act, since the writer is a man who can speak freely only when alone; to be himself he must lock himself up, to communicate he must cut himself off from all communication; and in this there is something always a little mad. Many writers loathe above all sounds the closing of the door which seals them up in their privacy. Williams, by contrast, welcomes it: it dispels the haze of uncertainty through which he normally converses, and releases for his pleasure the creatures who people his imaginings – desperate women, men nursing troublesome secrets, untouchables whom he touches with frankness and mercy, society's derelict rag dolls. The theatre, he once said, is a place where one has time for the problems of people to whom one would show the door if they came to one's office for a job. His best-loved characters are people like this, and they are all, in some way, trapped – Blanche DuBois, of *Streetcar*, beating her wings in a slum; Alma of *Summer and Smoke*, stricken with elephantiasis of the soul; Brick in *Cat*, sodden with remorse. As we shall see, much of what has happened to them has also happened to him. He is the most personal of playwrights. Incomplete people obsess him – above all, those who, like himself, have ideals too large for life to accommodate. There is another, opposed kind of incompleteness, that of materialists like the Polack in *Streetcar* and Big Daddy in *Cat*; and in most of Williams's work both kinds are to be found, staring blankly at each other, arguing from different premises and conversing without comprehension. In his mental battlefield the real is perpetually at war with the ideal; what is public wrestles with what is private, what drags men down fights with what draws them up. This struggle is an allegory, by which I mean that it reflects a conflict within Williams himself. He cannot bring himself to believe that the flesh and the spirit can be reconciled, or to admit that the highest emotion can spring from the basest source. As Aldous Huxley has put it: 'Whether it's passion or the desire of the moth for the star, whether it's tenderness or adoration or romantic yearning – love is always accompanied by events in the nerve endings, the skin, the mucous membranes, the glandular and erectile tissue. . . . What we need is another set of words. Words that can express the natural togetherness of things.' For Williams they remain stubbornly apart, and it is this that gives his writing its odd urgency, its note of unfinished exploration. Alone behind the door, sustained by what one critic called the 'comradeship of his introspection', he seeks to bridge the gap between his two selves. His work is a pilgrimage in search of a truce. His typewriter stands on the glass top of a hotel table, and most likely neither he nor it will be there tomorrow.

Though he does not need company, he does not shun it. Leaning back on a bar stool, one of a crowd, he can simulate ease with a barely perceptible effort. Mostly he is silent, sucking on a hygienic cigarette holder full of absorbent crystals, with a vague smile painted on his face, while his mind swats flies in outer space. He says nothing that is not candid and little that is not trite. A mental deafness seems to permeate him, so that he will laugh spasmodically in the wrong places, tell you the time if you ask him the date, or suddenly reopen conversations left for dead three days before. Late at night, part of him may come to life: in shreds of old slang ('We're in like Flynn') or bursts of old songs, remembered from St Louis in the twenties and unexpectedly proceeding, in a voice at once true and blue, from his slumped figure, which you had thought slumbering, in the back seat of somebody else's car. This is Williams on holiday, and you may be sure that his mind is not far from a blank.

He longs for intimacy, but shrinks from its responsibilities. Somewhere in the past, before he became famous, lies the one perfect passion; its object parted from him and afterwards died of cancer. Since then, too cautious to spoil perfection by trying to repeat it, he has kept all emotional relationships deliberately casual. He will incur no more emotional debts, nor extend any more emotional credit. His friendships are many and generous, ranging from Mediterranean remittance men to Carson McCullers; but love is a sickness which he will do anything to avoid. If his deeper instincts crave release, you may find him at a bullfight – or even writing a play.

He was born forty-four years ago in Columbus, Mississippi, the son of an itinerant shoe salesman known throughout the territory as a fiery and accomplished poker player. As a child he lived in Columbus with his mother, his elder sister, and his younger brother at the home of his maternal grandfather, a highly respected Episcopal rector. Here an image took root which has haunted much of his work: the South as a fading mansion of gentility. The first great wrench of his life occurred when he was still very young. His father took a desk job in St Louis and the family left Columbus to join him. 'We suddenly discovered,' Williams says, 'that there were two kinds of people, the rich and the poor, and that we belonged more to the latter.' It was here, in a stuffy back-street apartment, that his world split, amoeba-like, into two irreconcilable halves – the soft, feminine world of the room that he and his sister filled with little glass animals, and the cruel, male world of the alley outside, where cats fought and coupled to a persistent screaming. He entered the University of Missouri and at the age of sixteen got a story into *Weird Tales*, but the depression sent him to work for three memorably detested years in a shoe factory. The result was a heart attack, followed by a complete physical breakdown. He returned to his studies and in 1938 took a B.A. at the University of Iowa. By now his imagination was alive with human voices, and two of his plays had been performed by the St Louis Mummers. The future offered by his father meant going back to the shoe factory. Subjecting his life to its second great wrench, he left home.

'And it don't look like I'm ever gonna cease my wanderin'. . . .' He waited on table in New Orleans and worked on a pigeon ranch in California; then a one-act play won him a prize of a hundred dollars and attracted the attention of a Broadway agent, Audrey Wood. He sent her the script of *Battle of Angels*, an ambitious survey of 'the sometimes conflicting desires of the flesh and the spirit'. To his amazement, the Theatre Guild bought it. It opened in Boston in December 1940 and closed without reaching New York. On top of that, and perhaps because of it, Williams developed a cataract in his left eye. The next two years found him a vulnerable and myopic vagabond in Bohemia, always the victim of a hectic nervous system, which alarmed him by expressing its disquiet as often in illness as in imaginative visions. Back to New Orleans, living from pawnshop to mouth; then to Greenwich Village, where he worked as a waiter, wearing a black eyepatch which someone adorned with a surrealistic white eye-ball.

In 1943 Audrey Wood got him a six-month contract in Hollywood. He spent most of it writing *The Glass Menagerie*, in which his twin worlds of fact and dream came out for the first time distinct and dove-tailed. Its Broadway success a year later gave him security: but 'secu-rity,' he was soon writing, 'is a kind of death. . . .' To escape it he returned to New Orleans, to cheap hotels and rented apartments. On a trip to Taos, New Mexico, he came down with what proved to be a ruptured appendix; but he heard a nun whisper that it might be can-cer, and, spurred by the death sentence, he fled from the hospital. Feverishly he composed what was meant to be his last message to the world.

A new friendship helped him to obey Hemingway's dictum and 'get it out whole'. This was with Carson McCullers. As he wrote to me: 'Carson came to me in the summer of 1946 at the height of my imaginary dying, she came to Nantucket Island, which I had chosen to die on, and the moment she came down the gangplank of the ship from the mainland, in her baseball cap, with that enchant-ingly radiant crooked-toothed grin of hers, something very light hap-pened in me. I dropped my preoccupation with the thought that I was doomed, and from then on there was a process of adjustment to the new situation, and by the late fall of 1947 I was able to release all the emotional content of the long crisis in *Streetcar*.' The play was produced in the same year and fully deserves Williams's description of it: 'saturated with death'.

More studies in desperation followed: *Summer and Smoke* and *The Rose Tattoo*, perhaps the fullest expression of Williams's special kind of romanticism, which is not pale or scented but earthy and robust, the product of a mind vitally infected with the rhythms of human speech. When overheated, however, it can give off lurid fumes, some of which clouded the air in his next play, *Camino Real*. This was Williams's gaudiest rebellion against materialism, conceived in terms of symbols and carried out mainly in italics. Directed by Elia Kazan in the spring of 1953, the play flopped. There ensued one of those low-energy spells from which Williams frequently suffers. Work became a depressant instead of a stimulant; he kept losing sight of the impulse that sent him to the typewriter and felt that his ideas were being smirched and dog-eared by the well-meaning interference of agents, producers, and directors. *Cat on a Hot Tin Roof* was eighteen months in the writing. I now think it his best work, but when I first saw it, it struck me as an edifice somehow tilted, like a giant architectural folly. It was august, all right, and turbulent, but there were moments of unaccountable wrongness, as if a kazoo had intruded into a string quartet. When I saw the published text and read, side by side, the original third act and the version that was presented on Broadway, I guessed at once what had happened. The kazoo was Kazan.

Cat is a birthday party about death. The birthday is that of Big Daddy, a Southern millionaire dying of cancer. His son Brick is a quiet, defeated drinker; and the cat of the title is Maggie, Brick's wife, whose frayed vivacity derives from the fact that she is sexually ignored by her husband. The play deals with the emotional lies that are shockingly exposed as people try to 'reach' each other, to penetrate the inviolable cell in which the soul lives. Williams's trade-marks are all there: the spectre of disease, the imminence of death, the cheating implicit in all emotion, the guilt bound up with sex – plus the technical ability to make tragic characters immeasurably funny. But a play might have all these things and still be bad; what distinguishes *Cat* is the texture of its writing. This is dialogue dead to the eyes alone. It begs for speech so shrilly that you find yourself reading it aloud. 'When you are gone from here,' says Big Daddy, 'you are long gone and no where!' – the words fall from the tongue like 'snow from a bamboo leaf', the image by which Zen Buddhists teach their pupils that 'artless art' which is the goal of contemplation.

But Kazan was not satisfied. He felt that Brick should undergo a change of heart after the showdown with his father; and into Brick's lines a certain hollowness began to creep. In a stage direction Williams had spoken of 'the thundercloud of a common crisis'; with stupefying literalness, Kazan introduced a full-tilt symbolic thunderstorm. Maggie's big lie, uttered to win Big Daddy's inheritance, originally ran: 'Brick and I are going to have a child.' Inflated by Kazan, the line became: 'A child is coming, sired by Brick and out of Maggie the Cat!' The bitterness of the final tableau, when Brick prepares to sleep with Maggie to sustain her lie, was sweetened until the scene seemed to betoken a lasting reconciliation. Williams in no way resents these adjustments, which, he says, 'did not violate the essential truth of the play'. For him, Kazan is 'a very big man, the biggest artist in the theatre of our time'. He is at present working on a film script, which Kazan will direct; but some of his admirers feel that a less creative collaborator might, in the long run, be more helpful.

Discussing the incidence of genius, Somerset Maugham once remarked: 'The lesson of anatomy applies: there is nothing so rare as the normal.' Williams's view of life is always abnormal, heightened and spotlighted, and slashed with bogey shadows. The marvel is that he makes it touch ours, thereby achieving the miracle of communication between human beings which he has always held to be impossible.

Yet he looks anonymous. One ends, as one began, with the enigma. Arthur Miller, after all, looks Lincolnesque, and Anouilh looks hypersensitive, and Sartre looks crazy. Williams, alone of the big playwrights, seems miscast. From that round, rubbery face, those dazed eyes which nothing, no excess or enormity, can surprise – from here the message comes, the latest bulletin from the civil war between purity and squalor. It will always, however long or well I know him, seem wonderfully strange.

(1956)

IN THE FAMILY

FATHER (*heartily concerned*): How come we never get to talk to each other, son?
SON (*sullenly*): We're talking now, aren't we?
FATHER: We're talking, but we're not saying anything, goddammit!

Sometimes it is father and daughter, sometimes mother and son, but that, in a nutshell, is what modern American drama is about. It takes place either in a transparent doll's-house with a porch (the porch is obligatory) or in the past; or both. In this house live a pathetic, ill-matched couple. Mom is driven near-crazy, as she puts it, by dad, who goes on periodical bats. Meanwhile, the porch is full of the children to whom they cannot get through. They are two in number, of whom one is a confused adolescent boy, just awakening to the eternal mysteries of stud poker. There is a strange, stammering poetry in this off-beat child: indeed, it is coming out of his ears. He is about to undergo an emotional upheaval that will scar him for life. Comic relief, for the first half at least, will be provided by friends and neighbours. After that we discover that their lives too are founded on pain and insecurity and lack of togetherness.

Don't mistake me: the failure of generations to communicate with each other is not a bad thing for drama to be about. But there are other things for it to be about, and in the American theatre the theme has become obsessive. Plays lacking it are just not 'serious'; plays with it can usually count on extracting from at least one critic a review beginning: 'With this production the Broadway theatre becomes a palace of truth again.' My present visit to the palace of truth has so far yielded three plays of this breed. All of them have moments of extreme poignancy. All contain performances of the utmost power and subtlety. All of them are as intellectually flabby as they are emotionally redundant.

The most ambitious, already the winner of the New York critics' award for the year's best play, is *Look Homeward, Angel*, adapted from Thomas Wolfe's autobiographical novel. This is a portrait of the artist as a young martyr. The boy here is Wolfe, painfully preparing to be a prose Whitman. The house is a shabby Southern hotel run by his parents. His mother, a covetous drudge, has no time for him. His father, a monumental mason, understands him but, being also a monumental drunk, can all too seldom see him. He has a frustrated love affair and runs away from home. Comic relievers, acting wildly in all directions, round off the play, which is written in starry-eyed, deep-breathing prose that resembles melting butter. Anthony Perkins, pale and filled with tentative fire, is a beautiful sight as Wolfe, and Hugh Griffith comes rowdily freebooting in as his father, albeit from another world.

With the second play, William Inge's *The Dark at the Top of the Stairs*, we move from 1916 to the early twenties. The mood again is personal and reminiscent. The house now is in Oklahoma. Father is a travelling salesman, for ever battling with a suspicious wife. The boy is a tow-haired tot alternately neglected and mother-smothered; his sister has an abortive flirtation with a hypersensitive young Jew who kills himself. This time it is father who runs away. The actor in question behaves throughout as noisily as if he were in *Oklahoma!* rather than Oklahoma; but on the whole, this being a production by Elia Kazan, the performances are electric and intense, especially that of Eileen Heckart, the best thin actress alive. Sharp writing, yet a remote and somehow unnecessary ordeal.

The third, and abysmally the dimmest example of the genre, is called *Blue Denim*, which at times verges on parody. The house, complete with porch, has shifted to Detroit and today. The boy, sensitive as a snail's horn, traditionally gangles. Father is a militant back-slapper, mother a helpless fussbudget. Unable to get through to either of them, he gets a girl pregnant and procures for her an illegal operation. The whole exercise is conducted in dialogue that recalls the Hardy Family films. This one might be called *Abortion Comes to Andy Hardy*.

Why do these plays, even the best of them, seem so ingrowing, so unchallenging, so constricted? I trace the trouble to that house, which is not a house at all but a hothouse. It is an island of shuttered anxieties unrelated (except cursorily) to the society that created it. All criticism, all protest is directed inwards, towards the parents: everything outside is accepted with nothing more rebellious than a shrug. The result is one-eyed drama with a squint induced by staring too long down domestic microscopes and never looking out of the window. If, as these writers allege, the infant bloom is diseased, it is no use merely blaming the stem. It is time to analyse the soil. Arthur Miller did just that in *Death of a Salesman*, striking a balance between soil-analysis and flower-pressing which still awaits a true successor.

(1957)

REQUIEM FOR A NUN

BY WILLIAM FAULKNER, AT THE ROYAL COURT, LONDON

The curtain has just fallen on William Faulkner's *Requiem for a Nun.* It has been performed with imposing devoutness by Ruth Ford, Bertice Reading, Zachary Scott, and John Crawford. The production (by Tony Richardson) and the settings (by Motley) have been austerely hieratic. Let us now imagine that there steps from the wings the Stage Manager of Thornton Wilder's *Our Town*. Pulling on a corn-cob pipe, he speaks.

s.m.: Well, folks, reckon that's about it. End of another day in the city of Jefferson, Yoknapatawpha County, Mississippi. Nothin' much happened. Couple of people got raped, couple more got their teeth kicked in, but way up there those faraway old stars are still doing their old cosmic criss-cross, and there ain't a thing we can do about it. It's pretty quiet now. Folk hereabouts get to bed early, those that can still walk. Down behind the morgue a few of the young people are roastin' a nigger over an open fire, but I guess every town has its night-owls, and afore long they'll be tucked up asleep like anybody else. Nothin' stirring down at the big old plantation house – you can't even hear the hummin' of that electrified barbed-wire fence, 'cause last night some drunk ran slap into it and fused the whole works. That's where Mr Faulkner lives, and he's the fellow that thought this whole place up, kind of like God. Mr Faulkner knows everybody round these parts like the back of his hand, 'n' most everybody round these parts knows the back of Mr Faulkner's hand. But he's not home right now, he's off on a trip round the world as Uncle Sam's culture ambassador, tellin' foreigners about how we've got to love everybody, even niggers, and how integration's bound to happen in a few thousand years anyway, so we might just as well make haste slowly. Ain't a thing we can do about it.

(*He takes out his watch and consults it.*)

Along about now the good folk of Jefferson City usually get around to screamin' in their sleep. Just ordinary people havin' ordinary nightmares, the way most of us do most of the time.

(*An agonized shrieking is briefly heard.*)

Ayeah, there they go. Nothin' wrong there that an overdose of seconal won't fix.

(*He pockets his watch.*)

Like I say, simple folk fussin' and botherin' over simple, eternal problems. Take this Temple Stevens, the one Mr Faulkner's been soundin' off about. 'Course, Mr Faulkner don't pretend to be a real play-writer, 'n' maybe that's why he tells the whole story backwards, 'n' why he takes up so much time gabbin' about people you never met – and what's more, ain't going to meet. By the time he's told you what happened before you got here, it's gettin' to be time to go home. But we were talkin' about Temple. Ain't nothin' special about her. Got herself mixed up in an auto accident – witnessed a killin' – got herself locked up in a sportin' house with one of those seck-sual perverts – witnessed another killin' – got herself married up 'n' bore a couple of fine kids. Then, just's she's fixing to run off with a blackmailer, her maid Nancy – that's the nigger dope-fiend she met in the cathouse – takes a notion to murder her baby boy. That's all about Temple – just a run of bad luck that could happen to anyone. And don't come askin' me why Nancy murders the kid. Accordin' to Mr Faulkner, she does it to keep him from bein' tainted by his mother's sins. Seems to me even an ignorant nigger would know a tainted child was better'n a dead one, but I guess I can't get under their skins the way Mr Faulkner can.

(*He glances up at the sky.*)

Movin' along towards dawn in our town. Pretty soon folks'll start up on that old diurnal round of sufferin' and expiatin' and spoutin' sentences two pages long. One way or another, an awful lot of sufferin' gets done around here. 'Specially by the black folk – 'n' that's how it should be, 'cause they don't feel it like we do, 'n' anyways, they've got that simple primitive faith to lean back on.

(*He consults his watch again.*)

Well, Temple's back with her husband, and in a couple of minutes they'll be hangin' Nancy. Maybe that's why darkies were born – to keep white marriages from bustin' up. Anyways, a lot of things have happened since the curtain went up tonight. Six billion gallons of water have tumbled over Niagara Falls. Three thousand boys and girls took their first puff of marijuana, 'n' a puppy-dog in a flyin' coffin was sighted over Alaska. Most of you out there've been admirin' Miss Ruth Ford's play-actin', 'n' a few of you've been wonderin' whether she left her pay-thos in the dressing-room or whether maybe she didn't have any to begin with. Out in Hollywood a big producer's been readin' Mr Faulkner's book and figurin' whether to buy the movie rights for Miss Joan Crawford. Right enough, all over the world, it's been quite an evening. 'N' now Nancy's due for the drop.

(*A thud offstage. The Stage Manager smiles philosophically.*)

Ayeah, that's it – right on time.

(*He re-pockets his watch.*)

That's the end of the play, friends. You can go out and push dope now, those of you that push dope. Down in our town there's a meetin' of the Deathwish Committee, 'n' a fund-raisin' rally in aid of Holocaust Relief, 'n' all over town the prettiest gals're primping themselves up for the big beauty prize – Miss Cegenation of 1957. There's always somethin' happenin'. Why – over at the school-house an old-fashioned-type humanist just shot himself. *You* get a good rest, too. Good-night.

(*He exits. A sound of Bibles being thumped momentarily fills the air.*)

(*1957*)

THE ICEMAN COMETH
BY EUGENE O'NEILL, AT THE ARTS

CAT ON A HOT TIN ROOF
BY TENNESSEE WILLIAMS, AT THE COMEDY

Paul Valéry once defined the true snob as a man who was afraid to admit that he was bored when he was bored; and he would be a king of snobs indeed who failed to admit to a *mauvais quart d'heure* about halfway through *The Iceman Cometh*. But perhaps, as a colleague suggests, all great art should be slightly boring. A vast structure is to be built, and in the long process there are bound to be moments of tedium: they are the price we pay for size and splendour, and we pay it gladly once the architect has convinced us that we can trust him. O'Neill convinced last Wednesday's audience in thirty minutes flat, after which no doubts remained. This was no crank, planning a folly dependent on sky-hooks: we were safe in the hands of the American theatre's nearest counterpart to Frank Lloyd Wright.

But how did he hold us in our seats through four hours and more of circular alcoholic conversation? By means of verbal magic? I think not. O'Neill writes clumsily and top-heavily. He never achieves the lumi-nous, crystallizing phrase, nor has he the opposite virtue of earthy authenticity: his gin-mill dialogue has the stagey swagger of melo-drama. If it isn't the language, then, is it the universality of the theme? Again, no. Most of the characters are special cases, confirmed alco-holics out of touch with any kind of reality that cannot be bottled. When Hickey, the reformed drunk, urges these red-eyed wet-brains to abandon their pipe-dreams and face the truth about themselves, we know that the cure will kill them; but we cannot relate this knowledge to our own lives as we can, for instance, when Gregers Werle strips Ekdal of his illusions in *The Wild Duck*. Many of us, like Ekdal, have a dark-room of the soul where we develop dreams that the light of day would obliterate. But very few of us actually live in the dark-room, so enslaved to our fantasies that we would rather have D.T.s than give them up.

No, what holds us about the play is the insight it gives us into O'Neill himself. It is a dramatized neurosis, with no holds barred, written in a vein of unsparing, implacable honesty. 'Speak, that I may see thee,' said Ben Jonson; and when O'Neill speaks, he hides nothing. Instead of listening to a story, we are shaking hands with a man, and a man whose vision of life is as profoundly dark as any since Aeschylus. It is this autobiographical intensity that grips us throughout the *longueurs* of the narrative and the gawkiness (I had almost said Gorki-ness) of the style. For O'Neill, a pipe-dream is not just one alternative to despair: it is the only alternative. His bar-room derelicts comfort and sustain one another as long as each tolerates the others' illusions. Once Hickey has removed the illusions, nothing remains but guilt and mutual accusation. One may not agree with O'Neill's conclusions, but one cannot escape the look in his eye, which is as magnetic as the Ancient Mariner's. He speaks like a man who has touched bottom himself; for whom words like 'inferior' no longer have meaning. He is one of the few writers who can enter, without condescension or contempt, the world of those whom the world has rejected.

The play demands and gets superb direction. Peter Wood's produc-tion is better in many respects than the New York version I saw and admired last spring. Like all good directors, Mr Wood is loyal to the text; he is also constructively disloyal to the hysterical punctuation and overheated stage-directions of which American playwrights are so fond. His cast deserves individual attention. Nicholas Meredith plays a cashiered Blimp, making a character out of a caricature by discreet understatement; Lee Montague is funny, dour, and truthful as an Italian barkeep who cannot bring himself to admit that he is also a pimp; and Jack MacGowran, pinch-faced and baggy-trousered, plays the tetchy proprietor with a weasel brilliance I have not seen since the hey-day of F. J. McCormick. In the sketchily written role of a drunken Harvard alumnus, Michael Bryant gets closer to the raw nerve of reality than any West End débutant I can remember. The pale, shaky smile, the carefully preserved sophistication, the glib, hectic delivery all converge to make a rounded, original whole, half clown, half martyr.

Of the three central characters, Patrick Magee does not quite get the rock-sombre melancholy of Larry, the disgusted nihilist who has deserted anarchism for drink; but the other two are perfect – Vivian Matalon as a guilty young stool-pigeon, pathetically ripe for suicide, and Ian Bannen as Hickey, the manic salesman, driving his friends to destruction with the enthusiasm of a revivalist. I winced a bit at the Kensington cosiness of Mr Wood's three waterfront tarts. Otherwise, the production is flawless. It makes a wonderfully worrying evening.

By a useful coincidence, *Cat on a Hot Tin Roof* also explores the impact of truth on illusion, the difference being that where O'Neill thinks pipe-dreams necessary, Tennessee Williams condemns them under the generic heading of 'mendacity'. A world war separates the two plays. In jazz terms, *The Iceman Cometh* (1939) is a collective improvisation on a traditional blues theme. *Cat on a Hot Tin Roof* (1954) belongs to the modernist school, its three acts being in essence three long introspective solos (by, respectively, Maggie, Big Daddy, and Big Mama), accompanied throughout by the groundbass of Brick's pervasive melancholy.

The first act lays bare a breaking marriage: Brick, the liquor-loving son of a Southern millionaire, can no longer sleep with Maggie, his wife. The second act tells us why, in the course of a scorching duologue between father and son which reveals that Brick is a latent homosexual, consumed with guilt because he spurned a college friend who loved him and died, shortly after the spurning, of drink. Brutally reacting to this harsh dose of truth, Brick ripostes in kind, and Big Daddy learns what the rest of the family already knows: that he is suffering from inoperable cancer. In the last act the relations gather round Big Mama to batten on the inheritance. Maggie wins it by pretending to be pregnant. To support her lie, Brick must sleep with her; and thus mendacity breeds mendacity.

A magnificent play: but modern jazz, to pursue the metaphor, calls for much greater technical virtuosity than Dixieland. Williams's quasi-tragedy needs superlative soloists, superlatively directed. After seeing Peter Hall's production I feel I owe an apology to Elia Kazan. I still prefer the author's third act (here played for the first time) to the modified version approved by Mr Kazan; but I missed, more than I would ever have thought possible, the galvanic inspiration of Mr Kazan's direction. Mr Hall's pace is lethargic: he stresses everything except what needs stressing. General sloth may account for the cutting of (among others) Big Daddy's best speech; but I cannot think what could account for the omission of the play's last vital line, in which Brick ironically queries Maggie's protestations of love, unless it was the inadequacy of the actor playing the part. Paul Massie, to whom I refer, is callow and absurdly unprepared for a searching test like Brick. All the same, he ought to have been allowed to utter, however lamely, the final clinching statement of the play.

Leo McKern, with crudely padded shoulders, uses enormous vocal exertions to become Big Daddy; but the more he tries, the more he fails, for the whole point about the character is that his cynical, animal zest should flow without effort. Which leaves us with Kim Stanley, the gifted Broadway actress who plays Maggie the Cat. Miss Stanley has all the qualities for the part, an anxious lyricism, a limpid voice, tear-puffed eyes, and indomitable gallantry; but, as pregnant women are said to be eating for two, she found herself quite early on acting for four. It was like watching a first-rate squash player hammering away at a court without walls.

(*1958*)

LONG DAY'S JOURNEY INTO NIGHT

BY EUGENE O'NEILL, AT THE GLOBE

Eugene O'Neill died five years ago. The eclipse of reputation that commonly befalls great men as soon as they die has not yet happened to him; and now that *Long Day's Journey into Night* has followed *The Iceman Cometh* into London, I doubt if it ever will. O'Neill has conquered. We have the measure of him at last, and it is vast indeed. His work stretches like a mountain range across more than three decades, rising at the end to these two tenebrous peaks, in which the nature of his immense, hard-pressed talent most clearly reveals itself. As Johnson said of Milton, he could not carve heads upon cherry-stones; but he could cut a colossus from a rock. Sometimes the huge groups of his imagination stayed stubbornly buried within the rock; worse, they would sometimes emerge lopsided and unwieldy, so that people smiled at them – not without reason, for it is widely felt that there is nothing funnier than a deformed giant.

Many charges, during his lifetime, were levelled at O'Neill by the cherry-stone connoisseurs of criticism. That he could not think; that he was no poet; that his attempts at comedy were even more pathetic than his aspirations to tragedy. The odd thing is that all of these charges are entirely true. The defence admits them: it does not wish even to cross-examine the witnesses. Their testimony, which would be enough to annihilate most other playwrights, is in O'Neill's case irrelevant. His strength lies elsewhere. It has nothing to do with intellect, verbal beauty, or the accepted definitions of tragedy and comedy. It exists independently of them: indeed, they might even have cramped and depleted it.

What is this strength, this durable virtue? I got the clue to it from the American critic Stark Young, into whose reviews I have lately been dipping. Mr Young is sometimes a windy writer, but the wind is usually blowing in the right direction. As early as 1926 he saw that O'Neill's theatrical power did not arise from any 'strong dramatic expertness', but that 'what moved us was *the cost to the dramatist of what he handled'*. (My italics.) Two years later, reviewing *Dynamo*, he developed this idea. He found in the play an 'individual poignancy' to which he responded no matter how tritely or unevenly it was expressed. From this it was a short step to the truth. 'Even when we are not at all touched by the feeling itself or the idea presented,' he wrote, 'we are stabbed to our depths by the importance of this feeling to him, and we are all his, not because of what he says but because saying it meant so much to him.'

Thirty years later we are stabbed in the same way, and for the same reason. The writing of *Long Day's Journey* must have cost O'Neill more than Mr Young could ever have conceived, for its subject is that rarest and most painful of all *dramatis personae*, the dramatist himself. No more honest or unsparing autobiographical play exists in dramatic literature. Yet what grips us about it is not the craft of a playwright. It is the need, the vital, driving plaint, of a human being.

We are watching a crucial day in O'Neill's late youth, covered with a thin gauze of fiction; events are telescoped, and the family's name is Tyrone. They live in a gaunt, loveless New England house. Father is a rich retired actor, now beetle-browed with drink, whose upbringing as an immigrant Irish pauper has made him a miser: he recognizes the fault, but cannot cure it. His wife suffered badly at the birth of their second son (Edmund, otherwise Eugene), and he hired a cheap quack to ease her pain, with the result that she has become a morphine addict. The elder boy is a failed actor, something of a whoremaster, and a great deal of a drunk. His brother, Edmund, who has been to sea and is ambitious to be a poet, also drinks and detests more than he wholesomely should.

We catch the quartet on the desperate day when mother, after a long abstinence, returns to drugs, and Edmund learns that he has T.B. With these urgent, terrible realities the family cannot cope. Old rows, old resentments keep boiling up; the pressures and recriminations of the past will not let the present live. Every conversation leads inexorably to the utterance of some sudden, unforgivable, scab-tearing cruelty. At every turn O'Neill points the contrast between official Irish-Catholic morality and the sordid facts of drink and dope. The family goes round and round in that worst of domestic rituals, the Blame Game. I blame my agony on you; you blame yours on her; she blames hers on me. Father blames his past; mother blames father; elder son blames both; and younger son blames all of them. If the play has a flaw, it is that O'Neill, the younger son, lets nobody blame him – though I recall, as I write this, the moment when his mother cries out that she would not be what she is had he never been born. The wheel, coming full circle, runs over all of them. Shortly after the events covered in the play, O'Neill entered a sanatorium, where, he wrote later, 'the urge to write first came to me'. It was more than an urge, it was a compulsion.

The London production is much shorter than those I saw in Berlin and New York; about a quarter of the text has been cut away. This is shrewd pruning, since a non-American English-speaking cast might not have been able to carry the full four-hour burden. Alan Bates, shock-haired and forlorn, approaches Edmund with just the right abandon. Once inside the part, however, he stumbles over a distracting North Country accent. Ian Bannen, on the other hand, gets easily to the heart of the elder brother, especially in the last-act debauch when he confesses to Edmund how much he hates and envies him: what he lacks is the exterior of the seedy Broadway masher. He falls short of his New York counterpart, Jason Robards, Jr, just as far as Anthony Quayle falls short of Fredric March. Mr March, with his corrugated face and burning eyes, looked as weighty as if he were made of iron. Mr Quayle, though he conveys every syllable of the part's meaning, never seems to be heavier than tin.

By West End standards, let me add, all these performances are exceptionally good. That of Gwen Ffrangcon-Davies is by any standards magnificent. In this production mother is the central figure: a guileful, silver-topped doll, her hands clenched by rheumatism into claws, her voice drooping except when drugs tighten it into a tingling, bird-like, tight-rope brightness. Her sons stare at her, and she knows why they are staring, but: 'Is my hair coming down?' she pipes, warding off the truth with a defensive flirtatiousness. At the end, when the men are slumped in a stupor, she tells us in a delicate quaver how the whole mess began. 'Then I married James Tyrone, and I was happy for a time. . . .' The curtain falls on a stupendous evening. One goes expecting to hear a playwright, and one meets a man.

(1958)

WEST SIDE STORY

BY LEONARD BERNSTEIN, STEPHEN SONDHEIM, AND ARTHUR LAURENTS, AT THE WINTER GARDEN

American musicals traditionally divide into two opposed categories: folksy optimism (Rodgers and Hammerstein) versus city cynicism (Rodgers and Hart) – rural versus urban, grass roots versus asphalt jungle. The king of the jungle is *West Side Story*, which comes screaming out of the tall island's Western tenements, where Puerto Ricans carve and are carved by bands of less recent immigrants. A 'P.R.' girl falls in love with a boy from the enemy gang, and the tragedy of Verona, with appropriate adjustments, is retold. He kills a member of her family; a rumour is spitefully spread of her death; and as he sees her across a square and runs to grasp her, he is cut down by a volley of Puerto Rican bullets.

The score, by Leonard Bernstein, is as smooth and savage as a cobra; it sounds as if Puccini and Stravinsky had gone on a roller-coaster ride into the precincts of modern jazz. Jerome Robbins, the director-choreographer, projects the show as a rampaging ballet, with bodies flying through the air as if shot from guns, leaping, shrieking, and somersaulting; yet he finds room for a peaceful dream-sequence, full of that hankering for a golden age that runs right through American musicals, in which both gangs imagine a paradise where they can touch hands in love, without fear or loss of face. The jokes are necessarily few and sardonic, as when the delinquents express their scorn of social therapists who regard them as symptoms rather than as individuals:

> My sister wears a moustache,
> My brother wears a dress –
> Goodness gracious, that's why I'm a mess!

Mr Robbins has probably over-stylized a situation too fresh and bloody to respond to such treatment. The boys are too kempt; their clothes are too pretty; they dope not, neither do they drink. This makes them unreal, and gives the show an air of sociological slumming. Yet it compromises only on the brink of greatness; and that, surely, is triumph enough.

(1958)

MY FAIR LADY

BY FREDERICK LOEWE AND ALAN JAY LERNER, AT DRURY LANE, LONDON

'Was all the hysteria justified?' one read on Thursday morning, à propos of the uproar at Drury Lane last Wednesday night. The nerve of the question took one's breath away, coming as it did from the very journalists who had created the hysteria. Those who beat drums are in no position to complain of being deafened. Let us forget about the hysteria associated with *My Fair Lady* and point instead to the rare, serene pleasure it communicates, a pleasure arising from the fact that it treats both the audience and *Pygmalion* with civilized respect.

This winning show honours our intelligence as well as Shaw's. It does not bully us with noise: the tone throughout is intimate, light, and lyrical, and even Doolittle's *lion-comique* numbers are sung, not shouted. It does not go in for irrelevant displays of physical agility: the dustman's pre-nuptial rout at Covent Garden is the only choreographic set-piece. Following the film, it restores Eliza to Higgins at the end, but no other sentimental concessions are made: the score contains only two love songs. Never do we feel that numbers have been shoe-horned, with a beady eye on the hit parade, into situations that do not concern them. Where most musical adaptations tend to exploit their originals, this one is content to explore.

Everything in the score grows naturally out of the text and the characters; the authors have trusted Shaw, and we, accordingly, trust them. Consider the four solo numbers they have provided for Higgins. In the first he rails against the English for neglecting their native tongue; in the second he congratulates himself on the sweetness of his disposition. In the third he damns women for their refusal to behave like men; and in the fourth, a wonderful blend of rage and regret, he furiously acknowledges his attachment to a woman who is unlike him in every respect. All four songs are right in character, and all four are written more to be acted than sung. Rex Harrison, performing them in a sort of reedy *Sprechgesang*, is not merely doing the best he can; he is doing just what the authors wanted. For all its grace and buoyancy, what holds the show together at the last is its determination to put character first.

On this resolve all its talents converge. A feeling of concord positively flows across the footlights. In a sense, the outstanding thing about the evening is that there is nothing outstanding about it, no self-assertion, no sore thumbs. The keyword is consonance. Oliver Smith's décor, lovely in itself, both enhances and is enhanced by Cecil Beaton's dashing dresses. Frederick Loewe, the composer, and Alan Jay Lerner, the lyricist, have produced a score as sensitive to Shavian nuance as litmus to acid. They have drawn song out of Shaw's people, not imposed it on them. Mr Lerner's words are wily enough for Gilbert, and Mr Loewe's contribution, enriched by the creative arrangements of Robert Russell Bennett, is far more than a series of pleasant songs: it is a tapestry of interwoven themes, crisscrossing and unexpectedly recurring, so that a late number will, by a sudden switch of tempo, echo an apt phrase from an earlier one. Apart from all this, the cast itself, directed by the hawk-eyed Moss Hart, is among the best ever assembled for *Pygmalion*.

Stanley Holloway is the fruitiest of Doolittles, Robert Coote the most subtly pompous of Pickerings. Nothing in Julie Andrews's Cockney becomes her like the leaving it; but she blossoms, once she has shed her fraudulent accent, into a first-rate Eliza, with a voice as limpid as outer space. And I don't doubt that Mr Harrison, who seemed a bit edgy on Wednesday, is by now giving the effortless, finger-tip performance I saw last year on Broadway. The moment when he, Miss Andrews, and Mr Coote erupt into that ecstatic, improvised tango, 'The Rain in Spain', is still the happiest of the night. Ten years ago, I learn, Shaw was approached for permission to turn his play into a musical. Outraged, he replied: 'If *Pygmalion* is not good enough for your friends with its own verbal music, their talent must be altogether extraordinary.' In this instance, it is.

(*1958*)

SWEET BIRD OF YOUTH
BY TENNESSEE WILLIAMS, AT THE MARTIN BECK

RAISIN IN THE SUN
BY LORRAINE HANSBERRY, AT THE ETHEL BARRYMORE

Apart from the performance of Geraldine Page, a display of knock-down flamboyance and drag-out authority that triumphantly quells all doubts about this actress's ability to transcend her mannerisms, almost everything connected with *Sweet Bird of Youth*, Tennessee Williams's new play at the Martin Beck, dismayed and alarmed me. The staging, by Elia Kazan, is operatic and hysterical; so is the writing; and both seem somehow unreplenished, as if they had long been out of touch with observable reality. A dust bowl, one feels, is being savagely, obsessively ploughed, in defiance of the known facts about soil depletion and the need for irrigation. The heroine (Miss Page) is a decaying movie queen, querulous, doped, alcoholic, hypochondriac, and exorbitantly sexed. She fears heart attacks, and admits, like her author, that she has been 'accused of having a death wish'. Her current gigolo is a blond lad whose past history includes a spell in the chorus of *Oklahoma!* and a brief, reluctant participation in the Korean War; since then he has devoted himself to selling his virility to the highest bidder. He escorts Miss Page on a trip to his home town on the Gulf Coast. His purpose is to see once more a girl named Heavenly, whom he loved, seduced, and photographed in the nude when she was barely fifteen. He is not, however, aware that his youthful attentions left the girl physically tainted, so virulently that the curative operation has robbed her of the power to bear children. Heavenly's father, a political boss, has determined to avenge his daughter by gelding her seducer. In the second act we meet the boss – Big Daddy rewritten in the deep dyes of Victorian villainy – and see him delivering, for reasons that may have to do with directorial panache, a racist speech on a TV screen that covers the whole cyclorama. The obvious and unmistakable *scène à faire*, between his daughter and her ex-lover, never takes place and appears to have been forgotten. And after the first act the film star contributes nothing to the plot beyond offering her boy friend a lift to the next town; he turns it down, out of an obscure awareness that he must stay and surrender himself to be castrated. He begs us, in parting, to understand him, and to recognize ourselves in him.

For my part, I recognized nothing but a special, rarefied situation that had been carried to extremes of cruelty with a total disregard for probability, human relevance, and the laws of dramatic structure. My brain was buzzing with questions. How does it happen that the boy has not heard about the operation to which his beloved has submitted herself? Come to that, why is he ignorant of his mother's death? Can the postal service be that bad? And why is it emphasized that the action begins on Easter Sunday? Is castration to be equated with resurrection? By what convention, moreover, are weighty rhetorical asides, pages long, addressed directly to the audience while the other characters on stage freeze and pretend not to listen? Are Jo Mielziner's settings bleak and wall-less for symbolic reasons or because the lines would have been unspeakable against décor more realistic? Are we, in short, listening to anything more significant than antique melodrama pepped up with fashionable details about tape-recorders, coronaries, happy pills, and the price of diamond clips? Frankly, I doubt it. And I suspect that *Sweet Bird of Youth* will be of more interest to Mr Williams's biographers than to lovers of the theatre. The hero of *Orpheus Descending*, his play before last, was torn to shreds by dogs. In *Suddenly Last Summer*, which succeeded it, the poet was slain and partly devoured by Spanish urchins, and the heroine was threatened with mental castration in the form of brain surgery. Now, it seems, the urge is out in the open; in *Sweet Bird of Youth* the *ingénue* has lost the use of her sexual organs before the curtain rises, and an analogous deprivation awaits the hero immediately after it falls. Let us hope that the theme is at last exhausted, that by exhausting it Mr Williams has achieved some kind of personal fulfilment, and that in the future he will be able to write with fewer nerve ends trailing and in a style less dependent on the dictates of inner anguish. 'The age of some people,' says Paul Newman, as the gigolo, doing everything possible to clothe a symbol in credible flesh, 'can only be calculated by the level of rot in them.' In *Sweet Bird of Youth* the level is dangerously high; none of Mr Williams's plays has contained so much rot. It is as if the author were hypnotized by his subject, like a rabbit by a snake, or a Puritan by sin. Under hypnosis a man may reveal much about himself that would otherwise remain hidden, but the process of revelation involves the loss of his ability either to control what he is doing or to relate it to objective reality. And without this ability art is impossible.

On the evidence of *Sweet Bird of Youth*, Mr Williams seems at present to be wholly alienated from the tangible, diurnal world that formerly nourished his talent. The supreme virtue of *A Raisin in the Sun*, by Lorraine Hansberry, is its proud, joyous proximity to its source, which is life as the dramatist has lived it. I will not pretend to be impervious to the facts; this is the first Broadway production of a work by a coloured authoress, and it is also the first Broadway production to have been staged by a coloured director. (His name is Lloyd Richards, and he has done a sensible, sensitive, and impeccable job.) I do not see why these facts should be ignored, for a play is not an entity in itself, it is a part of history, and I have no doubt that my knowledge of the historical context predisposed me to like *A Raisin in the Sun* long before the house lights dimmed. Within ten minutes, however, liking had matured into absorption. The relaxed, free-wheeling interplay of a magnificent team of Negro actors drew me unresisting into a world of their making, their suffering, their thinking, and their rejoicing. Walter Lee Younger's family lives in a roach-ridden Chicago tenement. The father, at thirty-five, is still a chauffeur, deluded by dreams of financial success that nag at the nerves and tighten the lips of his anxious wife, who ekes out their income by working in white kitchens. If she wants a day off, her mother-in-law advises her to plead flu, because it's respectable. ('Otherwise they'll think you've been cut up or something.') Five people – the others being Walter Lee's progressive young sister and his only child, an amiable small boy – share three rooms. They want to escape, and their chance comes when Walter Lee's mother receives the insurance money to which her recent widowhood has entitled her. She rejects her son's plan, which is to invest the cash in a liquor store; instead, she buys a house for the family in a district where no Negro has ever lived. Almost at once white opinion asserts itself, in the shape of a deferential little man from the local Improvement Association, who puts the segregationist case so gently that it almost sounds like a plea for modified togetherness. At the end of a beautifully written scene he offers to buy back the house, in order – as he explains – to spare the Youngers any possible embarrassment. His proposal is turned down. But before long Walter Lee has lost what remains of the money to a deceitful chum. He announces forthwith that he will go down on his knees to any white man who will buy the house for more than its face value. From this degradation he is finally saved; shame brings him to his feet. The Youngers move out, and move on; a rung has been scaled, a point has been made, a step into the future has been soberly taken.

Miss Hansberry's piece is not without sentimentality, particularly in its reverent treatment of Walter Lee's mother; brilliantly though Claudia McNeil plays the part, monumentally trudging, upbraiding, disapproving, and consoling, I wish the dramatist had refrained from idealizing such a stolid old conservative. (She forces her daughter, an agnostic, to repeat after her, 'In my mother's house there is still God.') But elsewhere I have no quibbles. Sidney Poitier blends skittishness, apathy, and riotous despair into his portrait of the mercurial Walter Lee, and Ruby Dee, as his wife, is not afraid to let friction and frankness get the better of conventional affection. Diana Sands is a buoyantly assured kid sister, and Ivan Dixon plays a Nigerian intellectual who replies, when she asks him whether Negroes in power would not be just as vicious and corrupt as whites, 'I *live* the answer.' The cast is flawless, and the teamwork on the first night was as effortless and exuberant as if the play had been running for a hundred performances. I was not present at the opening, twenty-four years ago, of Mr Odets's *Awake and Sing*, but it must have been a similar occasion, generating the same kind of sympathy and communicating the same kind of warmth. After several curtain calls the audience began to shout for the author, whereupon Mr Poitier leaped down into the auditorium and dragged Miss Hansberry on to the stage. It was a glorious gesture, but it did no more than the play had already done for all of us. In spirit, we were up there ahead of her.

(*1959*)

THE BACKSTAGE JUNGLE

William Gibson's *The Seesaw Log*, published in a volume that also contains the text of Mr Gibson's Broadway hit *Two for the Seesaw*, is a blow-by-blow, cut-by-cut account of an ordeal that occupied two years of the author's life and left him, at the end, financially enriched and spiritually depleted. In short, it is a success story. At the same time it is a study of defeat. In the course of a hundred and forty pages, the rugged-individualist theory of art, which regards the author's intentions as sacrosanct, is eroded and finally overwhelmed by the rugged collectivism of an industry in which nothing is more sacred than the will of the audience. *Per se*, the struggle is old stuff. The cry of the betrayed dramatist ('That's not my play!') is among the more easily identifiable night sounds of Broadway, and if the theme of ideals versus commercialism were to be banished from literature today, a tidy heap of American writers would be out of work tomorrow. Mr Gibson's book, however, has three qualities that, conjoined, give it a special fascination. One is the sturdy excellence of its prose. The second is its attention to detail; this is the fullest factual record I can remember of the daily hazards involved in getting a Broadway show on the road and bringing it back alive. Thirdly, and personally, I was fascinated by the ambiguity of Mr Gibson's conclusions. By a strange exercise of doublethink, he seems to have felt simultaneously fulfilled and frustrated when his play became a hit. While resenting the changes he had been called on to make, he was grateful to those who had asked him to make them. After a characteristic agony of rewriting in Philadelphia, he describes himself as suffering 'the paradoxical experience of seeing his work improve by becoming poorer'. No student of semantics could resist a phrase like that.

For non-playgoers, let me explain that *Two for the Seesaw* is a dialogue for two lovers – a Nebraska lawyer on the brink of divorcing a rich wife, and an ebullient girl from the Bronx with whom he has a temporary, solacing affair. When Mr Gibson finished the first draft, in April 1956, he was in his early forties; he had already written five unstaged plays, a novel, a television script, and a lot of poetry, but Broadway was new to him – just how new he learned seven months later when a New York producer bought an option on his dramatized duet. In the fall of 1957 Henry Fonda agreed to play the lead opposite an unknown *gamine* named Anne Bancroft. Rehearsals started in November, whereupon all hell, quietly at first but rapidly mounting to tantrum intensity, began to break loose. Mr Fonda, on whose presence in the cast the show's backing depended, belatedly realized that the hero was not only dull by comparison with the heroine but pretty nasty in his own right. Accordingly, changes were suggested, and Mr Gibson's attempts to reconcile his own convictions with those of the star, the director, the producer, and the audience kept him sweating until the Broadway opening on 16 January 1958. By this time he had been – by turns – sick, furious, conciliatory, disgusted, delighted, and sick again. He had slept through performances of rewrites that had cost him sleepless nights, and he had entered in his diary such confidences as this, written during the Washington tryout:

The play grew more and more effective, and I felt less fulfilled as a writer.

After Washington he went back to his home in Massachusetts, where he lacerated himself for his subservience and decided that we – every man jack of us – had lost 'some religious component in ourselves, and this component was the difference between art and entertainment'. Yet a few days later, when the Philadelphia critics had expressed approval of the production, we read:

The fact was unblinkable, after such reviews, that the hammering my script and head had undergone . . . had issued in a much better play.

His conclusion, after the New York dailies had conceded him a hit, is that the American theatre is 'primarily a place not in which to be serious, but in which to be likable'.

As acted, *Two for the Seesaw* is funny, accurate, and often poignant. Since Mr Gibson offers no specific examples of the alterations he was required to make, and since he informs us that the printed text contains elements of several versions, it is almost impossible to tell whether we have lost a masterpiece or gained a smash. For a fledgling playwright, Mr Gibson seems to have gone in for an awful lot of backstage hectoring, lecturing, and quasi-directing, so that one is tempted to wonder how much his own behaviour contributed to the general uproar. Be that as it may, his main point is that he was forced to modify his original conception under pressure from his co-workers and his audience. How humiliating that sounds! Yet Chekhov rewrote at the behest of Stanislavsky, and Bertolt Brecht, perhaps the most original dramatist of our century, was not only ready but positively eager to learn from his spectators and to incorporate into his work the suggestions of fellow intellectuals. It was Brecht who spoke of what he called 'the romantic concept of individual creation', by which he meant that nobody can write a play singlehanded; it emerges from, and is aimed at, a particular social, political, and historical climate, and in its final form, if it is a good play, all the influences implied in those adjectives will coalesce. No dramatist, in other words, is an island. To think otherwise is a form of solipsism.

Mr Gibson writes as if only two choices lay open to the playwright; he can either make compromises for the sake of the box office or refuse them in the name of artistic integrity. There is in fact a third choice – that of adapting one's play so that it will have the maximum impact on the audience, small or large, dumb or smart, for which it was intended. That, unfortunately, is feasible only in a non-commercial subsidized theatre. Mr Gibson, meanwhile, is trapped in a false antithesis. The true source of his torment is not that he was asked to make his play appeal to its own audience but that he was asked to make it appeal to *every* audience. His tale is hypnotically readable, and I urge him, in the light of what I have said, to dramatize it. It would make a provocative and alarming evening.

It is disturbing to reflect that to a Russian about three quarters of *The Seesaw Log* would seem either mad or meaningless. In the Soviet theatre there are no tryouts and no investors to consider. No star's reputation is at stake, nor is there a first-night panic, since the Moscow critics seldom review a play until they have seen it at least twice. Russian theatres are institutions, and institutions sometimes turn into museums. Our theatres are shopwindows, and shopwindows sometimes turn into peepshows. The danger with the Russian system is that economic security has been known to breed complacency; the trouble with ours is that economic insecurity frequently breeds hysteria. Of both worlds, one cannot help feeling, there must be a borrowable best.

(1959)

THE GREAT GOD BROWN

BY EUGENE O'NEILL, AT THE CORONET

For a short season at the Coronet, the Phoenix Theatre Company is presenting a revival of O'Neill's *The Great God Brown*. It makes a fascinating evening. When the play was first performed, in 1926, most of those who took the trouble to analyse it came to the conclusion that the author was writing about the conflict between Art, symbolized by Dion Anthony, and Crass Materialism, represented by Billy Brown. And so, on the surface, he was. Anthony, painter and compulsive lush, has all the attributes we popularly associate with genius. He is hypersensitive and converses, for the most part, either in sentences ending with exclamation marks or in elaborate rhetorical questions, such as 'Why was I born without a skin, O God, that I must wear armour in order to touch or to be touched?' His power over women is infallible, as witness the ease with which he defeats Brown, poor baffled clod, in their rivalry over the girl Margaret. Once married, he goes in heavily for night-long tippling and after-noon rising, thus providing further evidence that he has an artist's soul; it was, I think, Desmond MacCarthy who said that whenever he turned up at someone's house for tea and found his host shaving in front of the drawing-room mirror, he was tempted to believe that he might be among bohemians. Still conforming to aesthetic type, Anthony spends much of his spare time – and his time is mostly spare – in the company of a bovine tart named Cybel, who mothers him, and to whom he skittishly refers as Mother Earth, Old Filth, or 'you sentimental old pig'. Utter the phrase 'a characteristic O'Neill hero', and at once I see a tearful, ageless adolescent with his face buried in the lap of a prostitute. (There's nothing like a bordello for a man who needs a captive audience.) To complete the picture, Anthony habitually addresses his intimates in the self-pitying, ponderously ironic manner of a drunken Irish tragedian – a sure sign that O'Neill means us to accept him as a frustrated genius. Brown, on the other hand, is just as obviously the incarnation of material success. He lacks imagination, toils all day at his desk, and smoothly passes off Anthony's ideas as his own. Envious of his friend's sexual magnetism, he uses his wealth to buy Cybel's affection, and when Anthony dies in his presence, of a heart attack, he carries his envy to the maniacal extreme of deciding to impersonate the dead man and thus to sleep with his wife. In the last (and by far the worst) act he is shot down by the cops as an escaping murderer.

That, in outline, is the play O'Neill's early admirers thought he had written – a straight fight between a frail introvert full of hidden love and a hardy extrovert full of hidden hate. But did he mean no more than that? Today, looking back on the body of O'Neill's work, we know better. Consider Anthony's speech – his best, and least exclamatory – at the close of the first act. He is speaking of his father:

What aliens we were to each other! When he lay dead, his face looked so familiar that I wondered where I had met that man before. Only at the second of my conception. After that, we grew hostile with concealed shame. And my mother? I remember a sweet, strange girl, with affectionate, bewildered eyes, as if God had locked her in a dark closet without any explanation. I was the sole doll our ogre, her husband, allowed her and she played mother and child with me for many years in that house until at last through two years I watched her die with the shy pride of one who has lengthened her dress and put up her hair. And I felt like a forsaken toy and cried to be buried with her, because her hands alone had caressed without clawing. She lived long and aged greatly in the two days before they closed her coffin. The last time I looked, her purity had forgotten me, she was stainless and imperishable, and I knew my sobs were ugly and meaningless to her virginity; so I shrank away, back into life, with naked nerves jumping like fleas. . . .

This is the voice of O'Neill himself, bursting through the artifice of the play like a bareback rider plunging through a paper hoop. These parents, as we know from his later work, are his parents, and *The Great God Brown* reveals itself as one of the many tentative sketches he made for the final, brutal family portrait, *Long Day's Journey into*

Night. Billy Brown, the pseudo-chum who loathes Anthony under the guise of love, is O'Neill's first attempt to express what he felt about his elder brother, the secret enemy with whom he constantly competed – not, however, for the love of Margaret but for the affection of his mother. One of the sternest objections to *The Great God Brown* is that it fails to establish its postulate; we meet Anthony's parents only briefly, in a prologue, and this short acquaintance does not explain why he feels so furious, bereft, and forlorn. The truth is that the prologue itself needs a prologue, in the shape of *Long Day's Journey into Night*.

In the light shed by the latter play, the first two acts of *The Great God Brown* make sharp dramatic sense. Freud and Ibsen, O'Neill's joint literary progenitors, are supplemented by loans from Pirandello and the Greeks; property masks are donned to indicate the social self, as opposed to the private self. To protect himself against society, Anthony wears a mask of cynical sensuality; when he removes it, exposing the naked face beneath, his wife is terrified. Similarly, she herself, who needs no disguise with her husband, puts on a mask of idealized girlhood when talking to Billy Brown. Only to Cybel, the whore, can Anthony speak freely without a false face; on one occasion he visits her masked, which prompts her to inquire, 'Haven't I told you to take off your mask in the house?' The reproach might have been better phrased, but I don't think it destroys the validity of the convention. The destruction occurs later, when Brown steals the mask of the dead Anthony; and it wrecks the last two acts. A device hitherto employed to explore character is suddenly enlisted to advance the plot. I am ready to concede that a man might assume an alien façade in order to deceive the world, but that a wife might allow an old friend to pass himself off as her husband is totally incredible. We are transported into a soggy realm of bad fantasy; either Billy is a brilliant mimic or Margaret is a blockhead. If the former is the case, I simply don't believe it; if the latter, I lose interest.

(*1959*)

CULTURE IN TROUBLE

Since this year ends in a nought and is thus divisible by ten, nearly all the leading American magazines have lately been firing at their readers such stark, factitious questions as 'What Trends Will Guide Our Culture in the Coming Decade?' and 'Have We a Viable Stance for the Sixties?' A man from a national weekly telephoned me a few weeks ago to ask the former question. He caught me at a bad time. I had just seen a TV programme in which Jacques Barzun, Lionel Trilling, and W. H. Auden had discussed 'The Crisis in Our Culture' with such fussy incoherence that they seemed to be not so much debating the crisis as embodying it. Mr Barzun sat bolt upright and smirked, while Mr Trilling leaned so far forward in cerebration that he appeared, in close shots, about to butt the camera. Mr Auden, looking like a rumpled, bulkier version of Somerset Maugham, slumped in his chair and squinted gaily at everyone, flicking ash at random, grinning mysteriously in the manner of Mr Amis's Professor Welch, and displaying throughout the show the sartorial hallmark of the middle-aged English intellectual – a collar tip curling up over the lapel of his jacket. From time to time he made eccentric interventions, as when he said he was ashamed to admit that he read newspapers, and when he suddenly asked Messrs Trilling and Barzun how old they were. 'Videowise', he emerged as a distinct individual with little to say; they, on the other hand, had plenty to say, but seemed devoid of individuality. They spoke with the corporate drone of a house organ (Mr Barzun's 'House of Intellect', no doubt), beside which Mr Auden sounded like a mouth organ – i.e., a very human instrument, capable of expressing great skittishness and great melancholy, but difficult to integrate into an orchestra. Together they formed a triptych of official American culture, and their appeal, especially to intelligent viewers under forty, must have been almost nil.

What will happen to American culture at that level of punditry I would not care to predict. Yet elsewhere, in the theatre and among the younger writers, I do discern a trend – or, to be more exact, a strong and growing preoccupation with two themes. The first of these, mainly noticeable on Broadway, has to do with biography. Popular shows are tending more and more to be based on the careers of people still living or fairly recently dead. Two years ago we had Dore Schary's *Sunrise at Campobello*, which was concerned with Franklin Roosevelt's battle against polio; *Gypsy*, last season's biggest musical hit, explained how the youthful Gypsy Rose Lee became a successful stripper; and the most prosperous shows of the new season – *Fiorello!*, *The Miracle Worker*, and *The Sound of Music* – deal respectively with the early triumphs of Fiorello LaGuardia, Helen Keller's childhood struggle against physical handicaps, and the adventures of an Austrian family called Trapp, who escaped from the Nazis and became famous in America for their singing. We have also had a play founded on the efforts of Harry Golden, a Jewish editor living in the South, to fight segregation through ridicule; and before long Judy Holliday is to appear in a dramatized biography of Laurette Taylor, whose problem was the bottle.

I won't go into the quality of these shows, which, apart from *Gypsy* and *Fiorello!*, has so far been pretty poor; what concerns us here is their prevalence and popularity. In no other country has the theatre ever devoted itself so zealously to biographical studies of the recent national past. The trend began in Hollywood with films like *The Jolson Story*, *The Glenn Miller Story*, and their numerous successors, all of which offered quasi-factual proof that it was possible for anyone, given enough talent and energy, to rise from the utmost obscurity to the topmost celebrity. Broadway has now followed suit, and American drama, which has hitherto given most of its serious attention to fictional characters defeated by circumstance, appears to be changing its course; the new emphasis is on real-life characters who triumph over circumstances. The individual, spurred on by courage, faith, and good will, not only survives adversity but emerges from it an object of national admiration. And if we complain (as we might in the case of an ordinary play) that this picture of life is facile and wishfully optimistic, we are easily refuted, because: 'It actually happened.' American audiences have an unbounded faith in victorious individualism; all the same, it does their suspension of disbelief no harm to know that the victory in question can be historically verified.

(*1957*)

Along with this interest in upbeat biography goes a second trend, which I hesitate to call religious or even spiritual, since in some of its manifestations it is neither. Less precisely, and therefore more accurately, it concerns the belief that what happens inside a human being is more important than what happens outside. This notion, of course, is usually expressed in Freudian terms: man is said to be ruled by the internal trinity of Ego, Superego, and Id. Sometimes, stated in another form, it declares that the summit of human aspiration and responsibility is achieved when one person learns to love another. The hero of *J.B.*, the modern Job play with which Archibald Mac-Leish won a Pulitzer Prize last year, sees no hope in politics, psychiatry, or organized religion; discarding all three, he 'finds fulfilment', as they say, by loving his wife. A similar conclusion is reached in *The Tenth Man*, a heartily acclaimed new play by Paddy Chayefsky. The central character, a suicidal Jewish ex-Communist in the throes of analysis, is cured of his disenchantment with mankind by taking part in a ceremony held to exorcise a supposed demon from the body of a young girl. 'It is better to believe in dybbuks,' an old rabbi tells him, 'than in nothing.' This eminently disputable statement weans the hero away from nihilism, and he achieves personal salvation by falling in love with the girl.

In plays like this it is never suggested that society's relationship with man might be among the causes of his distress, and the idea that man might have a constructive relationship with society has clearly been abandoned as impossibly Utopian. Happiness lies within, and nowhere else; the world outside, brutal and immutable, is best ignored, since it can only bruise you and damage the inviolability of your soul. This doctrine of inner illumination crops up *passim* in contemporary American writing. J. D. Salinger's Glass family, for instance, is mainly composed of latter-day mystics and self-slaughtered saints whose offers of disinterested love are constantly being slapped down by a society which their humility forbids them to criticize. The Beat extremists go much further, dedicating themselves to reaching enlightenment through lysergic acid or opium; and the most memorable theatrical experience at present accessible in New York is an Off-Broadway play called *The Connection*, which deals, somewhat in the manner of *Waiting for Godot*, with the mystique and the technique of dope addiction, including the lassitude that precedes the 'fix' and the illusion of spiritual insight, soaring and super-human, that follows it. (The author's name is Jack Gelber.) Nor must I omit Norman Mailer and the philosophy of Hipsterism that he expounds in his controversial new book, *Advertisements for Myself*, which is partly a Mailer anthology and partly an exercise in self-revelation. Soon after he wrote *The Naked and the Dead* Mr Mailer became an active Socialist; now, symptomatically, he has swung to the opposite extreme and embraced a religion of outright, psycho-pathic (his own word) egocentricity. The Hipster, in brief, is a man who has divorced himself from history as well as from society; who lives exclusively in the present; who thinks of himself as a white Negro; and whose aim is self-discovery through sexual pleasure, enhanced if need be by the aid of marijuana.

Christopher Caudwell, in his brilliant *Studies in a Dying Culture*, attributed the decline of bourgeois art to two forces:

On the one hand there is production for the market – vulgarization, commercialization. On the other there is hypostatization of the art work as the goal of the art process, and the relation between art work and individual as paramount. This necessarily leads to a dissolution of those social values which make the art in question a social relation, and therefore ultimately results in the art work's ceasing to be an art work and becoming a mere private phantasy.

A ham-fisted paragraph, but not without relevance. Mr Caudwell, who died more than twenty years ago, could not have predicted that Broadway, the theatre market, would take to selling the life stories of famous contemporaries; and if he had, it would merely have con-firmed his opinion of commercialism. Meanwhile, what he says about art developing into 'private phantasy' is disturbingly borne out by the cult of inner fulfilment that I have just described.

This movement, according to some observers, represents nothing more serious than – to quote one of them – 'a transient reaction to Soviet atheism and materialism'. I hope they are right. In fact, they had better be; American culture is tilting far too heavily in one direction, and it is becoming quite urgent that the balance should be restored.

(*1960*)

The European Theatre

PREFACE

The theatre of experiment in Europe is now drawn up in battle formation, and the shape of the conflict is that of a cold war in little. On one side, there are the playwrights who believe that the key to a man's soul is his social and political environment, and on the other, those who believe that the key to his social and political environment is to be found in his soul. The former group is predominantly Leftist, concerned with social change and the necessity of communicating with the many as well as the few; its leaders since the last war have been Sartre and Brecht – especially the latter, my growing allegiance to whom is elaborately documented in the pages that follow. (His own company, the Berliner Ensemble, has suffered lately from the artistic quarantine imposed on it by the Berlin wall; but the influence of his work and production methods has continued to spread on both sides of the iron curtain.) The opposition group is anarchic and in the main pessimistic; uninterested in social change, and rejecting all political solutions, it concentrates on exploring individual *malaise* in a world where communication between human beings has become (it contends) a virtual impossibility. The best-known exponents of this position are of course Samuel Beckett and Eugène Ionesco, of whom the latter dismisses Sartre and Brecht as a pair of ephemeral journalists. Meanwhile, oscillating between the two extremes, there are the Swiss playwrights Max Frisch and Friedrich Dürrenmatt, who like to demonstrate, in parables such as *Andorra* (Frisch) and *The Visit* (Dürrenmatt), the personal nightmares to which corrupt societies can give rise.

Plays of the Beckett–Ionesco genre are essentially Western, addressed to and written by members of a sophisticated intelligentsia in countries with a high standard of living. The questions they pose could be summarized thus: once a man's physical needs are satisfied, what is the purpose of living? The Brechtian approach is at once more earthy and more international, which is why it is sometimes accused of being naïve. It is addressed to the under-privileged as well as the

highly developed countries, and its aim is to show the human consequences of social and economic injustice – the causal connexion, for
instance, between the economic structure of a society and the private
morality its citizens profess. Brechtian drama puts first things first,
and insists that mankind must be raised to the same level of opportunity before one starts worrying about whether equality of opportunity means anything more than an equal chance to be spiritually
unhappy. In any society, says the Ionesco supporter, misery is
constant. Certain kinds of misery, argues the Brechtian, are curable;
as to the rest, let us postpone judgement until we have built a new
society.

Though I favour the latter, I recognize the legitimacy of both
views. My quarrel with Ionesco, conducted in 1958 in the columns of
the *Observer*, arose from the claim, repeatedly made by his adherents,
that his was the only road to the future of European drama. At this I
raised my eyebrows; and I responded with much the same scepticism
when I read, four years later, Martin Esslin's *The Theatre of the
Absurd*, an authoritative survey of the achievement, antecedents, and
influence of Beckett, Ionesco, Arthur Adamov, and Jean Genet.

Mr Esslin defines his subject as 'the lyrical, poetical theatre of the
world within, the theatre of dream, mood, and being'; and he cites
a crucial passage from Camus:

A world that can be explained by reasoning, however faulty, is a
familiar world. But in a universe that is suddenly deprived of illusions
and of light, man feels a stranger. . . . This divorce between man and his
life, the actor and the setting, truly constitutes the feeling of Absurdity.

By their repudiation of verbal logic, psychological consistency, and
any kind of ideological commitment, the dramatists of the Absurd
try to shock us into awareness of our new and grievous plight – await-
ing death in a universe without a God, ungoverned by reason, and
devoid of purpose. Towards the end of the book, Mr Esslin sums up
his case:

Concerned as it is with the ultimate realities of the human condition,
the Theatre of the Absurd, however grotesque, frivolous, and irreverent
it may appear, represents a return to the original, religious function of
the theatre – the confrontation of man with the spheres of myth and
religious reality.

These are large claims indeed, and Mr Esslin works hard to sub-stantiate them. With Beckett he succeeds completely: that bleak, de-nuded vision of man as a forlorn biped condemned to die alone has a tragic honesty that Aeschylus would have recognized, if not compre-hended. He defends Ionesco as an antic poet of despair, and whets one's appetite for Adamov, the scope and size of whose output I had never before suspected: how has London dared to ignore *Le Ping-Pong*, *Paolo Paoli*, *Le Professeur Taranne*, and the Adamov adaptation of Gogol's *Dead Souls*?

Tracing the forebears of the Absurd, Mr Esslin leads us back to the mime plays of antiquity; to the *Commedia dell' Arte*; to Edward Lear and Lewis Carroll; to Jarry, Strindberg, and the young, Rim-baud-impregnated Brecht; to the Dadaists and Tristan Tzara (who called one of his plays 'the biggest swindle of the century in three acts'); to the Surrealists and Antonin Artaud's *Theatre of Cruelty*; to Kafka, and to Joyce.

All this is helpful and credible. But when Mr Esslin ropes in Shakespeare, Goethe, and Ibsen as harbingers of the Absurd, one begins to feel that the whole history of dramatic literature has been nothing but a prelude to the glorious emergence of Beckett and Ionesco. Overstatement and Mr Esslin are not strangers, as may be guessed from the fact that he calls N. F. Simpson 'a more powerful social critic than any of the social realists'; and I wish I had an extra month of life for every playwright in connexion with whose work Mr Esslin refers to 'the human condition'.

My present reaction to the Absurdists is to enjoy them as poets while mistrusting them as philosophers. How are we to judge what they write? According to Mr Esslin, by whether it 'springs from deep layers of profoundly experienced emotion' and 'mirrors real obses-sions, dreams, and valid images in the subconscious mind of its author'. If it fulfils these conditions (he continues), it will have a 'general, as distinct from merely private, validity'.

But what does 'valid' mean? A schizophrenic is as totally alienated from everyday reality as any Absurdist: do his perceptions therefore qualify as art? The man who reacts to the universe with a cry of im-potent anguish is acceptable as an artist only if he can persuade us that he has sanely considered the other possible reactions and found them inadequate. Despair must speak from experience. When they wrote their first plays, Beckett, Ionesco, Adamov, and Genet were all in their late thirties, which is the earliest reasonable age for wanhope. They are conceivably among the last and certainly among the most *outré* representatives of disillusioned Western individualism in the arts – an attitude summed up by the neurotic hero of Aldous Huxley's novel, *Island,* who confesses, when faced with a workable modern Utopia, that he 'can't take yes for an answer'.

Adamov has recently changed his mind. He now maintains that 'the theatre must show . . . both the curable and the incurable aspect of things. The incurable aspect, we all know, is that of the inevitability of death. The curable aspect is the social one.' He has thus espoused Marxism, not in order to make men equally happy, but to allow them to contemplate their condition on equal terms:

> When the material obstacles are overcome, when man will no longer be able to deceive himself as to the nature of his unhappiness, then there will arise an anxiety all the more powerful, all the more fruitful, for being stripped of anything that might have hindered its realization.

This seems to me to get the priorities exactly right. What irks one most about the Absurdists is their pervasive tone of privileged despair.

TIGER AT THE GATES

BY JEAN GIRAUDOUX, TRANSLATED BY
CHRISTOPHER FRY, AT THE APOLLO

In spite of a few bad performances and a setting uniquely hideous, I do not believe that anyone could emerge from *Tiger at the Gates* unaware that what had just hit him was a masterpiece. For this is Giraudoux' *La Guerre de Troie n'aura pas lieu*, brought to us at last, after twenty years of impatience, in a methodical translation by Christopher Fry. It remains the final comment on the superfluity of war, and the highest peak in the mountain-range of modern French theatre. At the lowest estimate, it is a great occasional play, in the sense that its impact might be doubled if war seemed imminent; but to call it dated because nowadays we are at peace is to ignore its truest warning, which is that nothing more surely rouses the sleeping tiger of war than the prospect of universal tranquillity.

What is to engage us is the process whereby the Trojan war nearly failed to happen. Returning disillusioned from one campaign, Hector finds another impending; to send Helen back to the Greeks he will undergo any humiliation, even the dishonour of his wife. Paris, his brother, gives in to him easily, but Helen is harder to persuade. The fates, in choosing her for their instrument, have endowed her with an icy indifference to Hector's enormous compassion. 'I'm sure,' she says, 'that people pity each other to the same extent that they pity themselves.' Yet she, too, puts herself in his hands.

Breaking all precedents, Hector refuses to make the traditional speech of homage to his fallen soldiers; instead, we have the majestic tirade in which he rejoices with those who survived, the cowards who live to make love to the wives of the dead. His last stumbling-block is Ulysses, wily and circumspect, who reminds him, as they amicably chat, that a convivial 'meeting at the summit' is always the preamble to war; but even he agrees to gamble against destiny and take Helen home in peace. In the play's closing moments, war is declared. To reveal how would be an insult to those who know the text and a terrible deprivation to those who do not. Enough to say that history passes into the keeping of (Max Beerbohm's phrase) 'those incomparable poets, Homer'.

I cannot but marvel at the virtuosity of Giraudoux' prose. It embraces grandeur and littleness in one gigantic clasp; having carved a heroic group in granite, it can turn to the working of tiny heads on cherry-stones. No playwright of our time can change gear so subtly, from majestic gloom to crystalline wit. Sometimes, in the mass debates, the verbal glitter is overpowering, but in duologues Giraudoux has no rival. Hector's scenes with Helen in the first act and with Ulysses in the second ring in the mind like doubloons flung down on marble. Is it objected that English actors jib at long stretches of ornate prose? Or that they are unused to playing tragic scenes for laughs and comic scenes for tears? If so, they had better relearn their craft. The player who thinks Giraudoux unactable is in the wrong profession. Harold Clurman, the director, has tried hard to teach old dogs new tricks, but the right note of vocal aristocracy is only intermittently struck. Listening to Giraudoux should be like watching a series of lightning water-colours, dashed off by a master; some of the present company make do with ponderous cartoons, licking the lead and plunging it deep into the paper. This is the case with Walter Fitzgerald's Ulysses, a dour and laboured performance; and Diane Cilento, though fetchingly got up in what I can best describe as a Freudian slip, gives us paste jewellery instead of the baleful diamond Giraudoux had in mind for Helen. It is Michael Redgrave, as Hector, who bears the evening's brunt. He is clearly much happier in the emotional bits than in the flicks of wit which spark and speckle them; but, even so, this is a monumental piece of acting, immensely moving, intelligent in action, and in repose never less than a demi-god. In the presence of such an actor and such a play, I will forgive much. Especially do I feel for anyone unlucky enough to have to stumble and clamber over the obstacle-course of Loudon Sainthill's set. It is enough to make a chamois nervy.

(*1955*)

ONDINE

BY JEAN GIRAUDOUX, AT THE BRISTOL OLD VIC

Why, during his lifetime, did we so sorely neglect the author of
Ondine? If we picture European drama between the wars as a house,
Jean Giraudoux was the decorator, and he did it up so imposingly
that only Shaw, Brecht, Pirandello, and O'Casey could live in it
without feeling dwarfed. We travel through his plays as through a
luminous grotto, glimpsing murals of time-suspending wit and loveliness; and it would be churlish, after such a journey, to complain that
the labyrinth seemed shapeless, that there were too many blind alleys,
or that every picture did not tell a story. As well might one condemn
the Uffizi Gallery for lacking narrative impact.

Life as Giraudoux perceived it was life as it appeared to Mr Huxley while mescalin was tickling his cerebral cortex: cleansed, pure,
alive with colour, and so transformed in the matter of dimensions that
a turn of phrase was as tangible as a column of alabaster. Though he
preferred what Thomas Mann called the 'finer and much less obvious
rhythmical laws' of prose, Giraudoux was arguably the greatest theatrical poet of his time. As a prose architect he easily eclipsed Shaw in
the art, now forgotten but once obligatory, of providing long speeches
for crucial moments. Not for him the clipped, chopped scurry of
most modern dialogue. At regular intervals Giraudoux feels a set-
piece coming on, and the plot must pause while it blazes; when this
occurs, we get marvels like the Madwoman's account of her daily
ritual in *La Folle de Chaillot*, or the Judge's speech in the present play,
which describes the unearthly calm that hung over the world one
summer afternoon when all the attendant spirits, celestial and infernal
alike, ran off for a few hours and left mankind to its solitude.

A playwright is a man who can forget himself long enough to be
other people; and a poet is a man who can forget other people long
enough to be himself. In Giraudoux, as in few others, the two vocations are fused like Siamese twins. The playwright sets the scene, and
in the *tirades* the poet takes over; and by a miracle of collaboration the
poet's eloquence nearly always crowns an arch which the playwright

has built. So it is with the Judge's speech in *Ondine*. The play has been making one of Giraudoux's pet points, that once humanity acquires knowledge of the supernatural it is lost. A brave but doltish knight-errant has married a water-sprite, unaware that if he is unfaithful to her he must die. We have squandered much time in the second act on glittering trivialities, Giraudoux in his rhinestone vein; but now, in the third, we return to the main theme. The loyal Ondine is on trial; but it is the disloyal knight who will die. One thinks of the warning delivered to the heroine of *Intermezzo*: 'Ne touchez pas aux bornes de la vie, à ses limites.' We have to live in the same universe as the agents of the supernatural; but we must beware of trying to live on the same plane.

The tone of this beautiful play is half festal seriousness and half momentous levity. It gets from John Moody and his Bristol troupe a far better production than the pantomime extravaganza, directed by Alfred Lunt, which bore its name on Broadway two seasons ago. And this, amazingly, in spite of having no Ondine to speak of. In New York Audrey Hepburn flouted the text by having hair which was short and dark instead of long and blonde, and menaced the mood by wearing fish-net tights; yet she gave the character its one vital quality: a destructive innocence. Beyond the charm of her supulchral little voice, one saw the ruthlessness of the troll. Moira Shearer has the harmless innocence of Miranda in her brave new world, and her voice issues not from the anteroom of eternity but from the pump-room at Bath. It is the cool, collected voice of a Jane Austen heroine. Miss Shearer's dancing had a lyricism which her acting has not, and henceforth she had better steer clear of naiads. Her real line, I suspect, is comedy, and contemporary comedy at that.

(*1955*)

THE BALD PRIMA DONNA AND THE NEW TENANT

BY EUGÈNE IONESCO, AT THE ARTS

The new double bill of plays by Eugène Ionesco is explosively, liberatingly funny. Its first half is a maniacal assault on the banality of English suburbia. A family is discussed, every member of which, past or present, is named Bobby Watson; a young couple are alarmed to find, after lengthy mutual cross-examination, that they have been married for years; and the arrival of the Captain of the Fire Brigade completes a *reductio* that is not only *ad absurdum* but way beyond it.

Yet this is not the untethered nonsense of Lear; rather, it is a loony parody of the aunts and uncles in *The Family Reunion*, uncertain of who they are and of why they exist. M. Ionesco's *petits bourgeois* are so wildly confused that quite often they get their sexes mixed: the only person secure in her identity is the maid, who sternly declares: 'My name is Sherlock Holmes.' For such people words have no verifiable meaning, since they relate to nothing real, and the climax is an orgy of *non-sequiturs*, at the height of which someone screams: 'Stop grinding my teeth!' Acted with a swifter abandon, and stripped of the cuckoo-clock with which its director, Peter Wood, has facetiously seen fit to adorn it, this little masterpiece would be irresistible.

The New Tenant is a macabre anecdote about a man who moves into an attic room and fills it with so much furniture that all access to the outside world is blotted out; happy and submerged, his last wish is that the light should be turned off. The nature of sanity is to move out into the world; the nature of disease is to be drawn back into the womb, to which dark constriction M. Ionesco's hero is inescapably attracted. Nowhere is there a fuller and funnier portrait of introversion. Robert Eddison plays the part to perfection, and splits with Michael Bates the lion's share of a memorable evening.

(*1956*)

AMÉDÉE

BY EUGÈNE IONESCO, AT THE ARTS, CAMBRIDGE

Many good plays, as James Agate used to say, are built in two storeys – a ground floor of realism and a first floor of symbolism. M. Ionesco goes further than that: farcical at street level, he is tragic one flight up. *Amédée* is a perfect example of this unique architectural audacity.

On the ground floor the play is a macabre farcical anecdote about a married couple with an unusual problem. There is a corpse in their flat. Neither of them can recall how it got there or who killed it, but its presence has kept them indoors for the best part of fifteen years. In one corner of the living-room Amédée sits working on a play (average annual output: one word). In the opposite corner, at the top of her voice, his wife operates a busy telephone switchboard. Meanwhile, the corpse, recumbent in the bedroom, begins to grow; and, as if this were not inconvenient enough, its growth is accompanied by a sickening proliferation of poisonous mushrooms all over the walls of the apartment. For Amédée's wife, a short-tempered woman at the best of times, it is the last straw when the bedroom doors burst open to admit a pair of outsize, cadaverous, and extremely unwelcome feet.

Before long the room is full of mushrooms, feet, and furniture, a scenic demand brilliantly met by Peter Zadek's production and Feliks Topolski's designs; and the harassed couple are discussing 'How to Get Rid of It' (the play's alternative title) in tones that are certainly exasperated, but no more so than if the problem in hand were a dead mouse or a smell in the sink. Their very imperviousness to calamity is what makes Amédée and his wife so persistently funny. The horror of their plight simply does not occur to them; if they are irritated, it is more with each other than with the corpse. The whole mood of the play is like Alexander Woollcott's famous tale of the housemaster who, coming upon a mutilated torso in the school bootcupboard, briskly remarked: 'Some dangerous clown has been here.'

The *dénouement*, never Ionesco's strongest point, is a messy phantasmagoria that is probably as unstageable as Mr Zadek makes it seem. The upshot of it is that Amédée pulls the house down and plunges to his death, in which condition he takes on the appearance of the corpse he was trying to extricate.

And now, if you will just step upstairs to the symbolic level, watching out for the dustbins that Mr Beckett has carelessly left on the landing, we will examine the meaning of what we have just been laughing at; for up here sits Ionesco the puppet-master, inscrutably pulling the strings. Something, in the bourgeois marriage whose last hours we have witnessed, died long ago. Neither partner will take the blame for it; but the wife protests her innocence a thought too shrilly; and this, coupled with the fact that the victimized male is a pet Ionesco figure, is enough to convince me that she is the principal culprit. But what has she killed? What is the dead thing that won't lie down, that so hilariously tumesces? A tableau from the play springs to mind: Amédée, the writer unable to communicate, vainly repeating the two lines which represent fifteen years' work, while his wife sits at the switchboard, communicating like mad in glad contrapuntal cries of: 'I'm putting you through! I'm putting you through!' What has died is the creative spark that was the real Amédée, and the tragedy is that he doesn't know it. In the loveless hot-house of his marriage the dead tissue has flowered into a cancerous life of its own, which eventually destroys him. Only as he dies does he realize that the corpse in the bedroom was himself.

If I have made the play sound obscure, I have blundered. Its meaning is always there, staring at us through the veil of glittering farce that disguises it; and such is Ionesco's mastery that we are most aware of it when our laughter is loudest. This, the best of his plays that I have seen, is also the neatest proof that his philosophy of despair is pure humbug. A man who triumphantly succeeds in communicating his belief that it is impossible to communicate anything is in the grip, I cannot help thinking, of a considerable logical error. The scratch cast is led ably by Kathleen Michael and unforgettably by Jack MacGowran, who resembles (if you can imagine such a thing) a panicky Manolete.

(*1957*)

THE BALCONY

BY JEAN GENET, AT THE ARTS

The great virtue of Jean Genet's *The Balcony* is that it seeks to relate sexual habits to social institutions. According to M. Genet, the bishop's mitre, the monarch's sceptre, the judge's robes, and the general's jackboots are symbols that inspire common men to sexual fantasies of domination and submission. In Madame Irma's House of Illusions their dreams become facts. The man from the gas company, episcopally garbed, forgives a penitent her sins; a repressed bank clerk defiles the Virgin Mary, while other clients prefer to disguise themselves as flagellant judges or victorious warriors. M. Genet regards these scabrous rituals with a sort of furious pity. What else, he implies, can we expect of a society whose only absolute values are those of conquest and authority?

That is the indictment. M. Genet dramatizes it by setting his quaint bordello in the midst of a revolution that has already wiped out all the real holders of power save one, the Chief of Police, who now enlists the regular customers to play out their fantasy roles in earnest. Overnight, the revolt is quelled; and soon afterwards a new figure takes its place in the mythology of the brothel. A stranger asks permission to dress up as the Chief of Police, in which guise he promptly gelds himself. This horrific act completes M. Genet's argument. The image of power is erotic, but power itself is sexless. The reality survives by enslaving mankind to the symbol.

To object that the play's view of life is extremely personal is merely to say that only one man could have written it. Some power symbols are clearly more erotic than others. I myself would not place Sir Winston's cigar in quite the same category as Mussolini's fasces, but Baldwin's pipe is a disquieting thought; and the histories of Roman Catholicism and English Protestantism alike attest to the fact that the idea of female virginity is a potent and highly seductive thing. Nor can one rationally object to the violence of M. Genet's language: only dolts would contend that playgoers, who are numbered in thousands, should be protected against words and situations with which library subscribers, who run into millions, have long been familiar. The true objection to the play is that, although nobody but M. Genet could have written the first half at all, almost anyone else could have written the second half better.

The first, or expository, half is flawless; out of an anarchic, unfettered imagination there emerges a perfect nightmare world. But the second half is argumentative, and logic is necessarily a fettered thing, bound by rules to which M. Genet, who has flouted rules all his life, is temperamentally opposed. Just when the play cries out for an incisive, satiric mind like M. Sartre's, it branches off into a confusion so wild that I still cannot understand what the scenes in the rebel camp were meant to convey. As an evoker, M. Genet is magnificent; as an explainer, he is a maddening novice. He cannot think in cold blood – as witness his statement that the Arts Theatre had coarsened his play, when in fact (if Bernard Frechtmann's translation is to be trusted) it had softened it. Apart from Selma Vaz Dias and Hazel Penwarden, Peter Zadek's cast is shamelessly feeble; but many good actors, one guesses, took one look at the text and turned it down in a huff. For all its faults, this is a theatrical experience as startling as anything since Ibsen's revelation, seventy-six years ago, that there was such a thing as syphilis.

(*1957*)

THE CHAIRS
BY EUGÈNE IONESCO

L'APOLLON DE BELLAC
BY JEAN GIRAUDOUX, AT THE ROYAL COURT

The two prime assumptions of French literature are that there is no humour without satire and no truth without logic. Eugène Ionesco denies both propositions, and hence the French adore him. He flouts both of their household gods. The words he utters are those of an anarch, of a logical negativist who believes that nothing in the dictionary has a verifiable meaning. In his plays the light of verbal communication is extinguished. People collide in the dark; and when, fleetingly, a phrase kindles the heart, it is as if a match had been struck and we glimpsed, for a second, a human face, lonely and deeply appalled.

In England, where satire and logic lost their literary hegemony two centuries ago, we are less likely than the French to be overwhelmed by the originality of a style based on nonsense-humour and nonsense-logic. That it is virtuoso nonsense nobody denies: Ionesco is a poet of double-talk. But this is at best a minor gift. It does not explain why *The Chairs* is such an enthralling experience.

It is night on an island. In a round house of many doors sit a nona-genarian couple who will soon fling themselves suicidally into the river. At first, however, all is tranquil. Mad scraps of reminiscence are swapped, the old man bemoans his failure in life, the old woman babies and consoles him. From their moonstruck chatter we gather that he has a message to the world which he has bidden everyone to hear. The guests start to arrive, at first singly, then in pairs, soon in unmanageable droves, until the old-age *pension* resembles Groucho's cabin in *A Night at the Opera*. With this difference: that all the guests are invisible. They are creatures of the old man's dream, and before long he and his wife are plunging in and out of doors with yet more chairs for the unseen multitude, whom they engage, from time to time, in phantom conversation.

The audacity of the idea is breathtaking; here is pure theatre, the stage doing what only the stage can do. As the doorbell rings and the numbers crazily swell, one sees that Ionesco is more than a word-juggler. He is a supreme theatrical conjurer. And what does the trick mean? A hired orator, at the end, speaks the old man's message to the listening throng. Or rather, he would speak it, were he not dumb; and they would listen if they existed. Moral: truth is a tale told without words to people who cannot hear it. Communication between human beings is impossible.

I mention this facile and despondent philosophy because it leads us to Ionesco's second great virtue. He knows the secret of creating comic people. It derives from the Jacobean comedy of humours; and there are hints of it in Bergson, who says somewhere that the comic character 'slackens in the attention that is due to life . . . in some way or other he is *absent*'; but what it boils down to is that a person who pursues an obsession, who sees life through the blinkers of a fixed idea, who is blind to the world and the people around him, is by definition comic. If I stroll into a peace conference and quietly apply hot feet to the assembled statesmen, I am comic; but the moment I apologize and begin to explain myself, the joke is over. I must not hesitate: my special bent must be at once irrational and unreasonable-with.

The Old Man in *The Chairs* is such a character; so is the hero of Ionesco's *The New Tenant*; so are Jacques Tati and the amiable zanies of *La Plume de ma Tante*, not to mention most of the great drolls of world literature. Each is gripped by an obsession he cannot be bothered to account for. If they paused to give a rational explanation of their actions, the comedic contrast between their private world and the observable world would be irretrievably lost. It is precisely because they don't 'communicate', either with us or with each other, that Ionesco's people are funny. As a thinker he is banal; as a word-trickster he is no more than ingenious; but as a comic inventor he is superb and classical.

Tony Richardson's direction has the right, spooky enthusiasm. The Old Man really needs an actor less *voulu* in his eccentricity than the dogged George Devine; but Joan Plowright, all boggling fervour and timorous glee, makes a wonderful North-Country mouse of the Old Woman. The same director does considerable damage to the curtain-raiser, Giraudoux's *Apollon de Bellac*, which you would be wise to miss, in spite of a summery performance by Heather Sears. At one point Miss Sears informs a chandelier that it is beautiful. According to Giraudoux, '*Le lustre s'allume de lui-même*'; according to Mr Richardson, Apollo switches it on at the door. Thus can poetry, in a single gesture, become irrevocable prose.

(*1957*)

THRICE BLESSED

Theatrically, Paris makes us all sybarites. The English critic, accustomed to begging and yapping for the veriest crumb of quality, rapidly finds that his taste for caviare is regarded not as a bizarre craving but as a natural appetite which not to satisfy would be a gross discourtesy.

Consider those Temples of Dramatic Gastronomy, the three great repertory theatres of France. Most ancient and blessed is the Comédie-Française, whose twin shrines owe their dignity to the fact that, unlike any theatre in England, they are of the blood royal, created by Louis XIV's express decree. The English court patronized the theatre: the French court adopted it; and therein lies the difference. To support its company of thirty *sociétaires* (elected for twenty years) and fifty *pensionnaires* (engaged for a season), the Comédie receives an annual subsidy of some £380,000 – more than twenty times the sum granted to the Old Vic – with which it is able not only to keep new plays and established classics permanently alternating in its repertoire, but also to stage *reprises* of lesser works applauded in their day and now revived to test their endurance, thereby ensuring that no masterpiece dies of neglect.

The point about the Comédie is that it is the touchstone, the standard of measurement, the guarantee of continuity, the rule which must be learned before it can be broken; the central blazing sun which, no matter how many satellites whirl off from its periphery, provides the dramatic universe with a constant *punctum referens*. Its acting style, clear as a chessboard and taut as a drum, blends the rhetorical past with the realistic present, welding the players together into an orchestra of concerted expertise. French is a language that easily petrifies into cliché and formula. The end of the world, when it arrives, will surely be announced in French; but this very hardness and finality of outline has forced the French to bend the language to their will by means of gesture and inflection. What their tongue prohibited, their temperament has achieved. By making an unnatural effort, they became 'natural actors'; and the Comédie enshrines the result. To see its production of de Montherlant's *Port-Royal* is to feel a bridge of solid architecture beneath one's feet; to see anything at the Old Vic is to leap from one greasy stepping-stone of individual talent to another. True style is a weapon which, though it may split mountains, can also crack nuts. Witness Molière's *Les Amants Magnifiques*, the gracious frailty of which is exactly matched by Suzanne Lalique's settings, soaring and dissolving, shining in pearl and gold.

Beyond question it was the Comédie that created the audience for classical repertory on which Jean-Louis Barrault drew when he seceded in 1946 to set up the non-subsidized Compagnie Renaud-

Barrault at the Marigny. This is another Temple, but one in which the high priest preaches too many of the sermons. Barrault, a born director of high intellectual vigour, lacks both the stature and the presence of a great actor. About Alceste in *Le Misanthrope* there must hang a ruinous Byronic grandeur: Barrault, unable to supply more than a petulant asperity, is acted out of sight by Pierre Bertin as Oronte, a bland pink trout of a poet *manqué*. Barrault's supreme virtue is that he will fly at anything; Shakespeare, Kafka, Fry – and even Chekhov, whose genius shrivels under the searchlight of the French language, which brusquely dispels his mists, sharpening his vague evocative outlines into razor-edged silhouettes. One yearned, in Barrault's production of *The Cherry Orchard*, for the looseness of English. Chekhov's vital third dimension is achieved only by Jean Desailly as Lopakhin, the only character in the play whose approach to life is calculated, realistic, and thoroughly French.

Any other nation would have been satisfied with two such repertories. France insisted on a third and got it: Jean Vilar's Théâtre National Populaire, installed at the Palais de Chaillot at a cost to the public of £55,000 a year. Low prices and a programme ranging from Corneille to Brecht keep the gigantic fan-shaped auditorium regularly filled. I am myself antipathetic to the French classics; their starved vocabulary is a penance to my ear, and I agree with Stendhal that '*l'alexandrin est un cache-sottise*'. For me Corneille's *Cid* does not flower, and I gloated when the audience failed to spot such transpositions as '*honneur*' for '*devoir*' and '*violence*' for '*impatience*'. Yet from this prolonged display of baleful pomp one fact clearly emerged: that in Gérard Philipe the T.N.P. has the best *jeune premier* in the world, a limpid, lyrical young animal about whom the only reservation must be that animals seldom age well: an ideal Cid rarely grows up into an ideal Lear. About the T.N.P's production of Brecht's *Mère Courage* I have no reservations at all: a glorious performance of a contemporary classic which has been acclaimed everywhere in Europe save in London. Into this ribald epic of the Thirty Years' War the squalor of all wars is somehow compressed. Does Germaine Montero, as the sleazy, irresistible heroine, nag where she should dominate? Yes – but the play carries her. Never before have I seen a thousand people rise cheering and weeping in their seats.

The three Temples, as international in scope as only truly national theatres can be, cruelly expose our shortcomings. Next year M. Julien, the ebullient impresario of the Théâtre Sarah-Bernhardt, intends to repeat the international drama festival he held so successfully last summer. On that occasion the English contribution was a somewhat depleted company of *The Confidential Clerk*. M. Julien is already worried. How shall he find an English group fit to compete with the French, German, and Russian contingents? Where, in the absence of a national playhouse, is our best to be sought? Must we forever shrink from committing ourselves to a theatre which should enshrine our drama, cradle and nourish it, presenting eight times a week a performance of which we can say to our guests: 'This is English acting. This is our style'? If it be argued that there is no audience for such an experiment, I answer in the traditional maxim of French actors: 'The public always follows the crowd.' And in any theatre, from Shakespeare's to our own, the intelligent public is ultimately the crowd.

(*1955*)

LA PLUME DE MA TANTE

AT THE GARRICK, LONDON

My allegiance to M. Robert Dhéry, the star and author of *La Plume de Ma Tante*, dates from a rainy evening in Paris last winter when I attended a revue of his devising called *Ah! Les Belles Bacchantes!* Within ten minutes I had entered a new dimension of comedy, the dimension of calamity.

Everything in the show went wrong: not loudly wrong but mildly, shiftily, provoking those tiny tremors that plague the nervous system when, in a large quiet room, a small object falls thunderously to the floor. While announcing the first item (a modest scena depicting the creation of the universe), the *compère* paused and stared, without comment but with immense disquiet, at something that was happening on the stage a few feet in front of him. Whatever it was (and he did not explain), it disturbed other members of the troupe as well; they would break off, in the middle of songs and sketches, to contemplate it. Glances of horror would be exchanged, and mute appeals flashed towards the wings. At length the truth transpired: what everyone on stage knew, and had determined to hide from us, was that gas was escaping from the footlights. No action was taken, because by now the cast had other things on its mind: a lion was at large in the backstage corridors, and one of the dressing-rooms was on fire.

M. Dhéry has been presenting shows like this for more than seven years, and I was a late-comer to the cult. In *La Plume de Ma Tante* he and his squadron of harassed stoics make their London début. Over some of their work, it must be admitted, there hangs a pall of slip-shod improvisation; and they are without their greatest clown, the irreplaceable Louis de Funès. Yet enough remains to throw serious doubt on the English definition of revue as an entertainment in which acid, modish people say acid, modish things. Nothing in the present show is satirical, and nothing is topical – how could it be, since M. Dhéry's sense of humour has no malice and is quite untethered to time and place? If we seek a parallel, we may find it in the films of M. Jacques Tati and nowhere else on earth.

The deviser himself takes part, with a touch of Chaplin in his method and of *commedia dell'arte* in his lineage. He treats his company, a bright-eyed troupe to whom ghastly things are constantly hap-pening, with enormous compassion. I am not sure why he introduces M. Christian Duvaleix as 'my brother-in-law, Amsterdam', but when M. Duvaleix slinks ogling into view, the penalty is swift: his electric guitar blows up in his face. At this he betrays absolutely no surprise. Imagine the convulsions with which an English comedian would greet a similar mischance and you have the measure of M. Dhéry's directorial tact, which amounts to a minor revolution in comic tech-nique. Or consider Mlle Colette Brosset's appearance as an under-study involved in a *pas de deux* with an Eton-cropped ballerina whose interest in her is not exclusively professional; vaguely aghast, Mlle Brosset confides to the audience no more than a single, horrified whisper: 'She must be *mad*!' And I have not yet mentioned the superb M. Jacques Legras, whose face is a fish-mask of utter despair and who eats dog-biscuits for solace; nor would it be fair to omit my delight in the brief item entitled 'Domingo Blazes and His Courage-ous Latin-American Band'. (Courageous in what sense I do not know, though I suppose it takes courage of a sort to work for a band-leader three feet high.) M. Gérard Calvi's music is wanly haunting, and the dances are led with long-limbed abandon by Mlle Nicole Parent, who shows in a bullfight ballet that she really knows something about how bulls are fought.

M. Dhéry's speciality is the comedy of disaster, the gaiety of quiet desperation, and because of this he provides the perfect response to the alarming events of our time. He teaches us, when confronted with calamity, to react with only the faintest of shrugs. We may look foolish, but we have kept our dignity. His basic theme is embarrassment, the agony of a man discovered in a moment of private aberration, of anti-social lunacy; and he implies that such lunacy is not only funny, but healthy. I shall often return to the Garrick in the weeks to come, knowing that, however much I may chafe at the passing crudities, there will always be golden moments at which, suddenly and without warning, tears of laughter will stand in my eyes. Either M. Dhéry is a genius or the word has no meaning.

(*1955*)

PAUVRE BITOS

BY JEAN ANOUILH, AT THE THÉÂTRE MONTPARNASSE-GASTON BATY

A sensation being bruited, I went last week to see M. Anouilh's new play, *Pauvre Bitos, ou Le Dîner de Têtes*, which has split Paris into two camps – those who dislike it, and those who detest it. Mere dislike is the Right-Wing reaction, while active loathing issues from the Left: both camps, needless to say, are packing the theatre. Far more than *Antigone*, *Bitos* is M. Anouilh's political manifesto. It is a cruel, discordant work, as bitterly imagined as written, in mood as violent as that of a neurotic schoolboy locked up in a dormitory while his classmates frolic in the sun; and its conclusion lies somewhere between 'A plague on both your houses' and 'I'll be revenged on the whole pack of you.' It is the blackest by far of M. Anouilh's plays. It is also the most cunningly constructed, a dirty act done with the utmost art, a torture-chamber designed by a master builder.

In shape it resembles a fox-hunt, except that the fox in this instance has envenomed teeth. A truer similitude, perhaps, would be the slow tearing of wings from a wasp. Maxime, an arrogant young land-owner, has inherited a derelict priory where in 1793 the revolutionary tribunal condemned several of his ancestors to death. Thither he summons his rich friends to a dinner at which each must impersonate a figure of the Revolution. Their aim is to vilify and humiliate the guest-of-honour, a Communist deputy named Bitos, who was once a lowly scholarship boy at Maxime's school. His entrance, as Robespierre, is a stupefying *coup de théâtre*. The other guests are correctly clad in periwigs and ordinary dinner jackets; the ignorant Bitos arrives in full eighteenth-century fig, complete with knee-breeches and buckle-shoes. Atop his *perruque* there rests, absurdly, a bowler hat. Stifling his shame, he tries to pass off as high-born banter the increasingly savage gibes of his tormentors, who scorned him even as a child because, as Maxime icily observes, '*vous manquiez de grâce*'. The charade now begins to bare its fangs, declaring its contempt for the common man and his pitiful efforts to set up 'an aristocracy of mediocrity'.

From taunts they proceed to direct intimidation. Robespierre was shot in the face on the eve of his execution; so a pistol, loaded with blanks, is fired at little Bitos, who promptly swoons. In a dream he re-lives Robespierre's life in counterpoint to his own, and finds that the melody is the same: both were sullen, unloved tots who grew up to condemn in others the qualities they lacked themselves. Unable to please, Bitos has devoted his life to denouncing pleasure. This explanation of revolutionary zeal is painfully familiar, but it has seldom been advanced so liverishly, and never with so complete an absence of pity. Michel Bouquet, rightly divining his author's wish, allows no hint of pathos to soften his portrait of Bitos as a smug and blood-less puppet. But M. Anouilh's spleen is far from spent. Out, in the last act, come the thumb-screws. The revived Bitos is plied with drink until he consents to accompany the jokers to a night-club, where they plan to involve him in an unsavoury brawl. They are unexpectedly foiled. As a wise insurance against the charge of total misanthropy, M. Anouilh has admitted to the cast two people in whom human feeling is not quite extinct. One of them, a young schoolteacher, leaves the dining-room with a short and half-hearted paean to what he vaguely calls '*le vrai peuple*'. The other is a girl who now urges Bitos to quit the party before further ignominy befalls him. He takes her advice, but turns in the doorway to inform her, in a frenzy of spite, that nothing is as crushing as pity; and that it is she, in consequence, whom he will remember with the purest hatred.

As an essay in political thought, the play is imitative and negligible. As a study of human character, it is hysterical and often foul-mouthed. As a piece of dramatic architecture, it is, as I have said, exquisitely gripping. But it fascinates me most in another aspect: as an exercise in self-revelation. Whose side is the author on? The question has agitated Paris ever since the play opened a fortnight ago. To be sure, M. Anouilh's aristos are heartless sadists; but I have little doubt that his real enemy is Bitos, in whose wounds no knife is left unturned. This despised provincial upstart is drawn with an ugly, obsessive passion, almost as if he were a ghost that the haunted author were struggling to exorcise. The name Bitos called up an odd echo. I found myself thinking of the derisive nickname, 'Anouilh le Miteux', that Jouvet bestowed on the young upstart from Bordeaux; scruffy Anouilh, at whose work the maestro laughed, saying that it reeked of old socks. In every Anouilh play there is mockery, and in many there is hatred; but in this one I smell self-hatred. Perhaps, as Max Beerbohm said of Ibsen's attack on the artistic temperament in *When We Dead Awaken*, 'it is but another instance of his egoism that he has reserved his most vicious kick for himself'. *Pauvre Jean*, in fact: but how brilliant, how distastefully brilliant!

(1956)

PHÈDRE

BY RACINE, AT THE PALACE, LONDON

'*Poussez le rôle vers la douleur et non vers la fureur, tout le monde y gagnera, même Racine.*' That was Régnier's advice to Bernhardt when she first approached *Phèdre* in 1874, and Sarah heeded it. As well she might, for to adopt the 'furious' reading would have been to court comparison with the apocalyptic performance of Rachel twenty years earlier. That this was an earthquake of acting nobody need doubt.

Hear Lewes on her entrance: 'You felt that she was wasting away under the fire within, that she was standing on the verge of the grave with pallid face, hot eyes, emaciated frame – an awful, ghastly apparition. . . .' Her fourth act was a tempest, the actress being driven by a gale of emotion as horrifying as it was uncontrollable.

Since Sarah, however, the '*douleur*' interpretation has been in vogue: Phèdre is seen as the catspaw of the gods, more sinned against than sinning in her passion for her stepson. Arguing this case, the defence traditionally calls Racine himself, who insists in his preface to the play that his heroine, essentially virtuous, is the pitiable victim of destiny, not of her own desires. But here, surely, the author was simply insuring himself against possible charges of immorality, being fully aware that the woman he had created was not only the prey of Venus but an active collaborator as well. In short, though she knows she is doing wrong, she cannot help doing it; there is a tigress within her that must be fed. Without the tigress, the play has no motive force, and the calmer passages, with their anguished envy of innocence, go for nothing.

On Monday night Edwige Feuillère essayed the part for the first time, and it was soon clear that she favoured the passive, quietist reading. An imposing stillness, a tranquil desolation – these were the phrases that crept to mind. The last act was so delicately cadenced as to be almost inaudible, and the actress throughout made her most touching effects with those lines, expressive of romantic resignation, to which her talents naturally incline her. In the fourth-act tirades she came, very nearly, to the boil; her voice, until then strangely fuzzed and bottled, achieved vibrations of considerable intensity; but her only downright concession to the Grand Manner was her death-fall. No one drops dead like Mme Feuillère. Shatteringly, she slumped, and there, almost before the eye could register it, was mortality.

Yet chance after chance was inexplicably missed.

Soleil! je te viens voir pour la dernière fois

was thrown away. Nothing was made of

On ne voit point deux fois le rivage des morts.

And the seizing of Hippolyte's sword, which should be tremendous, was most strangely fumbled, as if not a sword but a compromising letter were in question.

The plain truth is that this actress is wanting in the majestic attack that should compel awe. Never does she command the stage; rather than lead the action, she is led by it. Never is she eaten up with desire: one does not feel that the plague within her is ambitious and contagious. The part should be, in the literal meaning of the word, terrific. With Mme Feuillère one gets no sense of danger. Her performance is an immensely graceful apology for Phèdre, a sort of obituary notice composed by a well-wishing friend; but it is never a life nakedly lived before our eyes.

On top of this, and through no remediable fault of her own, she fails to satisfy the *optique du théâtre*. The hunted, ravaged look of the great sufferers is beyond her means. She lacks the tragic mask. Her face is immovably serene, and it cannot, how grimly soever she purse her lips, how fiercely knit her eyebrows, assume the lineaments of total agony. For this reason, if for no other, the performance must be accounted a gallant failure. The Hippolyte, Jean-François Calvé, is game but immature, and the best feature of a somewhat stodgy supporting cast is the eloquent Thésée of Bernard Noel.

(*1957*)

FIN DE PARTIE AND
ACTE SANS PAROLES

BY SAMUEL BECKETT, AT THE ROYAL COURT, LONDON

You began Catholic, that is to say, you began with a system of values in stark opposition to reality. . . . You really believe in chastity, purity, and the personal God, and that is why you are always breaking out into cries of c—, s—, and hell. As I don't believe in these things except as quite provisional values, my mind has never been shocked to outcries by the existence of water closets – and undeserved misfortunes. . . . Your work is an extraordinary experiment and I would go out of my way to save it from destruction or restrictive interruption. It has its believers and its following. Let them rejoice in it. To me it is a dead end.

That is Wells, writing in 1928 to James Joyce. After seeing *Fin de Partie*, which closed last night, I offer it as an admonitory text to Samuel Beckett, formerly Joyce's friend. I do not wish to press too far the comparison between the two men. Their styles are utterly different: one gorges on Joyce and slims on Beckett. But they share an Irish gallows-humour, an absorption in psychiatry, and a grudge against God that the godless never feel. But above all, in Beckett's private world, one hears the cry that George Orwell attributed to Joyce: 'Here is life without God. Just look at it!'

As produced in London, *Waiting for Godot* made Beckett's world valid and persuasive. Though deserted by God, the tramps survived, and did so with gaiety, dignity, and a moving interdependence; a human affirmation was made. I had heard, and discounted, rumours that Beckett disliked the London production. These rumours I now believe. The new play, directed by Roger Blin under the author's supervision, makes it clear that his purpose is neither to move nor to help us. For him, man is a pygmy who connives at his own inevitable degradation. There, says Beckett, stamping on the face of mankind: there, that is how life is. And when protest is absent, the step from 'how life is' to 'how life should be' is horrifyingly short.

Before going any further, I ought to explain what I think the play is about. I take it to be an analysis of the power-complex. The hero, a sightless old despot robed in scarlet, has more than a passing affinity with Francis Bacon's paintings of shrieking cardinals. He lives in a womb-shaped cell, attended by Clov, his shambling slave, on whose eyes he is totally dependent. His throne is flanked by two dust-bins, wombs within the womb, inhabited by his parents, Nagg and Nell. Eventually Nell dies, whereupon the tyrant asks Clov to see what Nagg is up to. '*Il pleure*,' says Clov. '*Donc*,' says the boss, '*il vit.*' The curtain falls on a symbolic stalemate: King (Nagg) versus King and Knight (Boss and Clov). The boss is imprisoned for ever in the womb. He can never escape from his father.

Schopenhauer once said: 'The will is the strong blind man who carries on his shoulders the lame man who can see.' Beckett reverses the positions. It is the lame man, Clov – representing perception and imagination – who is bowed down by the blind bully of naked will. The play is an allegory about authority, an attempt to dramatize the neurosis that makes men love power. So far, so good. I part company with Beckett only when he insists that the problem is insoluble, that this is a deterministic world. '*Quelque chose suit son cours*': and there is nothing we can do about it. My interpretation may be incomplete, but it illuminates at least one of the play's facets. The blind irascible hero, Hamm, is working on an interminable novel: does this not bring to mind the blind 'cantankerous Irishman' by whom Beckett was once employed? Hamm stands for many things: for the Church, the State, and even Godot himself; for all the forms of capricious authority. One of them may perhaps be Joyce.

When I read the play, I enjoyed long stretches of it – laconic exchanges that seemed to satirize despair, vaudeville *non sequiturs* that savagely parodied logic. Within the dark framework I even discerned glimmers of hope. I now see that I was wrong. Last week's production, portentously stylized, piled on the agony until I thought my skull would split. Little variation, either of pace or emphasis, was permitted: a cosmic comedy was delivered as humourlessly as if its author had been Racine. Georges Adet, peeping gnome-like from his bin, performed with charming finesse; otherwise, moaning was the rule, to which Jean Martin (Clov) conformed with especial intensity. I suddenly realized that Beckett wanted his private fantasy to be accepted as objective truth. And that nothing less would satisfy him. For a short time I am prepared to listen in any theatre to any message, however antipathetic. But when it is not only disagreeable but forced down my throat, I demur.

I was influenced, I admit, by *Acte sans Paroles*, the solo mime which followed the play. Here Man (Deryk Mendel) is a shuffling puppet, obedient to the imperious blasts of a whistle which send him vainly clambering after a flask of water, lowered from above only to be whisked out of reach. He is foiled even when he tries to hang himself, and ends up inert, unresponsive to whistle and carafe alike. This kind of facile pessimism is dismaying in an author of Beckett's stature. It is not only the projection of a personal sickness, but a conclusion reached on inadequate evidence. I am ready to believe that the world is a stifling, constricting place – but not if my informant is an Egyptian mummy.

(*1957*)

POSTSCRIPT ON IONESCO

The position towards which M. Ionesco is moving is that which regards art as if it were something different from and independent of everything else in the world; as if it not only did not but *should* not correspond to anything outside the mind of the artist. The end of that line, of course, is Action Painting. M. Ionesco has not yet gone so far. He is stuck in an earlier groove, the groove of cubism, which has fascinated him so much that he has begun to confuse ends and means. The cubists employed distortion to make discoveries about the nature of objective reality. M. Ionesco, I fear, is on the brink of believing that his distortions are more valid and important than the external world it is their proper function to interpret. To adapt Johnson, I am not yet so lost in drama criticism as to forget that plays are the daughters of earth, and that things are the sons of heaven. But M. Ionesco is in danger of forgetting; of locking himself up in that hall of mirrors which in philosophy is known as solipsism.

Art is parasitic on life, just as criticism is parasitic on art. M. Ionesco and his followers are breaking the chain, applying the tourniquet, aspiring as writers to a condition of stasis. At their best, of course, they don't succeed; the alarming thing is that they try. As in physiology, note how quickly the brain starved of blood produces hallucinations and delusions of grandeur. 'A work of art,' says M. Ionesco, 'is the source and the raw material of ideologies to come.' O *hubris*! Art and ideology often interact on each other, but the plain fact is that both spring from a common source. Both draw on human experience to explain mankind to itself; both attempt, in very different ways, to assemble coherence from seemingly unrelated phenomena; both stand guard for us against chaos. They are brothers, not child and parent. To say, as M. Ionesco has said, that Freud was inspired by Sophocles is the direst nonsense. Freud merely found in Sophocles confirmation of a theory he had formed on the basis of empirical evidence. This does not make Sophocles a Freudian, or vice versa: it is simply a pleasing instance of fraternal corroboration.

You may wonder why M. Ionesco is so keen on this phantom notion of art as a world of its own, answerable to none but its own laws. Wonder no more: he is merely seeking to exempt himself from any kind of value-judgement. His aim is to blind us to the fact that we are all in some sense critics, who bring to the theatre not only those 'nostalgias and anxieties' by which, as he rightly says, world history has largely been governed, but also a whole series of new ideas – moral, social, psychological, political – through which we hope some day to free ourselves from the rusty hegemony of *Angst*. These fond ideas, M. Ionesco quickly assures us, do not belong in the theatre. Our job, as critics, is just to hear the play and 'simply say whether it is true to its own nature'. Not, you notice, whether it is true to ours, or even relevant; for we, as an audience, have forfeited our right to a hearing as conscious, sentient beings. 'Clear evidence of cancer here, sir.' 'Very well, leave it alone: it's being true to its own nature.'

Whether M. Ionesco admits it or not, every play worth serious consideration is a statement. It is a statement addressed in the first person singular to the first person plural; and the latter must retain the right of dissent. I am rebuked in the current issue of *Encounter* for having disagreed with the nihilistic philosophy expressed in Strindberg's *Dream Play*. 'The important thing,' says my interviewer, 'seems to me to be not the rightness of Strindberg's belief, but rather how he has expressed it. . . .' Strindberg expressed it very vividly, but there are things more important than that. If a man tells me something I believe to be an untruth, am I forbidden to do more than congratulate him on the brilliance of his lying?

Cyril Connolly once said, once and wanly, that it was closing time in the gardens of the West; but I deny the rest of that suavely cadenced sentence, which asserts that 'from now on an artist will be judged only by the resonance of his solitude or the quality of his despair'. Not by me he won't. I shall, I hope, respond to the honesty of such testimonies, but I shall be looking for something more, something harder: for evidence of the artist who is not content with the passive role of a symptom, but concerns himself, from time to time, with such things as healing. M. Ionesco correctly says that no ideology has yet abolished fear, pain, or sadness. Nor has any work of art. But both are in the business of trying. What other business is there?

(1958)

SUMMING-UP: 1959

The office of André Malraux, Minister of State in Charge of Cultural Affairs in General de Gaulle's government, overlooks the courtyard of the Palais Royal and commands a splendid rear view of the Comédie-Française, which backs on to the other side of the great enclosed plaza. When escorting visitors on to his balcony, the Minister is apt to fling up one elbow in a mock-defensive gesture, as if he expected at any moment to be picked off by a sniper from the House of Molière. This jocular piece of mime, as few Parisians would need to be told, has its origin in the celebrated press conference of 9 April 1959, at which M. Malraux analysed, briskly and tartly, the faults of the Comédie and announced his scheme for setting them right. A weak administration, he said, had allowed effective control of the company to pass into the hands of a clique of expert light comedians who had concentrated on farce while neglecting the French heritage of classical tragedy; during the six months that ended in February, the troupe had given a hundred and thirteen performances of Labiche and only six of Racine. As a sort of punishment for imbalance, for offending against the sacred principle of equilibrium, one of its two theatres was to be taken away from the company; the Salle Luxembourg, renamed the Théâtre de France, would he handed over to Jean-Louis Barrault in the autumn, whereafter the Comédie would confine its Parisian activities to the Salle Richelieu. The present administrator was to be summarily replaced by Claude Bréart de Boisanger, a career diplomat with no theatrical experience. As if these bombshells were not enough for one spring morning, M. Malraux went on to explode several more. The current standard of productions at the Opéra and the Opéra-Comique reminded him, he said, of the Comédie-Française in the twenties, or even in the nineties; henceforth, the *théâtres lyriques* were to be united under the leadership of A.-M. Julien, the bustling founder of the Paris International Drama Festival. Two more prizes remained to be distributed. The Théâtre Récamier, a smart little Left Bank playhouse, was to be given to Jean Vilar, the director of the Théâtre National Populaire, as a showcase for apprentice playwrights, and Albert Camus was to have a theatre of his own, in which to produce spurned, forgotten, or undiscovered masterpieces. Finally, M. Malraux explained the purpose of his plan: he hoped to attract to the national theatres those members of the younger generation who had come to believe that live drama was dull, archaic, and no longer their concern.

The repercussions began at once, and are still noisily audible. The Comédie was up in arms; one of its former administrators, writing as temperately as he could, bade M. Malraux remember that, except in the epochs of great actresses such as Rachel and Bernhardt, tragedy had never been very popular with the company's audiences, while a talent for comedy, he added, did not strike him as undesirable in a theatre dedicated to the name of Molière. *L'Express* came out with a cartoon depicting a lachrymose M. Malraux addressing the spectators at the Salle Richelieu with the words *'Aux larmes, citoyens'*. The accompanying article supported the plan as a whole, but was dubious about some of its implications. The author feared that state aid for *avant-garde* theatres (i.e., those of Camus and Vilar) might inhibit the true spirit of experiment and induce conformism and self-censorship. Moreover, since there was no evidence that the Ministry of Finance intended to increase its annual theatrical allotment, the Malraux proposals, with their exclusively Parisian emphasis, might constitute a setback for the provincial theatre. The five National Centres of Drama outside Paris were already in a shaky financial condition; needing more money, they might, under the new dispensation, get even less, and the best they could hope for was the continuation of an unsatisfactory *status quo*. These doubts were echoed and amplified by members of the theatrical Left, who declared that a cultural dictatorship was imminent; what M. Malraux wanted, they said, was a safe, centralized theatre that could be bribed into connivance with Gaullism. 'André Malraux,' one young writer said to me, adapting Cocteau's famous remark about Victor Hugo, 'is a madman who thinks he's André Malraux.' The most exciting productions in France, he went on, were being staged in Lyon at the Théâtre de la Cité de Villeurbanne, directed by Roger Planchon, an avowed disciple of Bertolt Brecht. 'Malraux says he admires Planchon, but will he dare to subsidize him?' Meanwhile, the traditionalists are complaining that the new set-up bestows too many favours on people of Leftist sympathies, such as MM. Vilar, Camus, and Julien. Accused by the conservatives of being a revolutionary and by the Leftists of tendencies towards Fascism, M. Malraux thus finds himself between two fires. The situation is fascinating and in one respect unique: for the first time in history, official responsibility for a country's cultural health has been placed in the hands of an internationally respected man of letters. Can an artist work for a government without letting that government's policies colour his view of art? Are intellectuals capable of translating theory into action? The results of the Malraux plan will provide answers, partial but empirical, to questions like these.

Most people I met in Paris this summer agreed with the Minister on two points: that the Comédie-Française was ripe for reform, and that youth had lost interest in drama. Françoise Sagan was undoubtedly speaking for many of her contemporaries when she said to me, 'I never go to the theatre. I don't know anyone who does.' I almost apologized for having brought the subject up; the tone of her voice, decorously bored, made me feel as if I had confessed to some tedious minor eccentricity, like collecting bus tickets. For Mlle Sagan and her coevals, the cinema is the only performing art that counts. Even so, the fact that Paris has around sixty stages on which live actors appear nightly suggests that the theatre is not exactly moribund. After two weeks of intense playgoing I had a long, informal conversation with M. Malraux, in order to match my impressions against his. Darkly dressed, compulsively blinking, and snorting with sinus, he talked readily and electrically. Here, grouped under various headings, is a contrapuntal account of what I saw and what he said:

(1) The Comédie-Française. I spent an evening at *Le Dindon*, one of Georges Feydeau's hotel-bedroom farces, which was directed by Jean Meyer and played with slippery glibness by a cast that included Robert Hirsch and the wonderfully effusive Jacques Charon. MM. Meyer, Hirsch, and Charon are founder-members of the cabal that M. Malraux holds responsible for the company's decadence. Accomplished though they are, one understands his objections. It is idiotic, as he said, to devote 600,000,000 francs (£400,000) a year to bolstering the reputations of Feydeau and Labiche. I also saw a revival of François Mauriac's *Les Mal-Aimés*, a sombre closet drama about a rich alcoholic who, deserted by his wife, employs emotional black-

mail to force his elder daughter into staying with him and giving up the man she loves to her younger sister; the point of the play is to show the terrible skill with which people who cannot command love revenge themselves on people who can. I thought the production admirable, in a slightly musty way, but I can't say I relished the round of applause that greeted the father's description of French politics as a squalid zoo badly in need of an animal trainer – '*Tant qu'en France il n'y aura pas de dompteur, je me désintéresserai de la ménagerie.*'

Mauriac's plays are among the few in the French repertoire that occupy the middle ground between stylized tragedy and stylized comedy (or satire); in other words, they belong in the realistic tradition, which, despite its success in Russia, Scandinavia, Germany, Britain, and the United States, never really took root in the French theatre. I asked M. Malraux why this was so. He replied that Corneille and Racine had created, in the seventeenth century, a form of drama that resembled, in the dignity of its proportions and the magnitude of its moral architecture, a palace, and that this image had dominated the French theatre ever since. What appalled Voltaire about Shakespeare was, *au fond*, that he made no attempt to be 'palatial' in the manner of Racine. Whenever the French wrote plays, said M. Malraux, they were trying – often without knowing it – to 'rediscover the palace'. Even comedy was regarded as a palace annex. He added that this theory would have to be modified a little to fit Claudel, whom he considers a modern giant. (As he put it, Claudel may be a cathedral, but he certainly isn't a palace.) I suggested that this aversion to realism applied to actors as well as to playwrights; one seldom saw a good French performance of Chekhov or Ibsen. M. Malraux agreed, but he thought that this was a Latin, rather than a peculiarly French, characteristic. Latin civilizations were made up of people who behaved as if they were permanently on stage. Their idea of a great man was '*une conception de parade*', involving large gestures and romantic display, and they felt the same way about great acting. It would have been impossible, he said, for Bernhardt to play a Chekhov heroine, because her conception, not so much of the role as of the whole purpose of acting, would have been alien and inappropriate.

Since realistic drama presented such problems, and since he had already committed himself on the subject of farce, I wondered what plays, apart from the French classics, M. Malraux would like to see in the programme of the Comédie. Neatly side-stepping, he said that the choice of plays was not his business but that of the new administration. He himself was not especially enamoured of Racine; he merely hoped that more use might be made of tragediennes like Annie Ducaux and Marie Bell. It did not matter enormously that neither of these actresses was a Rachel, because nowadays the appeal of tragedy depended not on star performers but on star productions, as Jean Vilar had shown at the T.N.P. The grand objective, M. Malraux repeated, was to bring young people into the national theatre, and he would go to any lengths to achieve it. Public funds would be used to make good seats cheaply available to youth; efforts were being made to sign up Maurice Chevalier for a season of Molière; and whenever the home company was away on tour, its place would be taken by visiting troupes from the provincial centres. At worst, I decided, the Malraux plan could do no harm to the Comédie-Française, and at best it could do a vast amount of good.

(2) The Compagnie Renaud-Barrault, which will open at the Salle Luxembourg in October, operating on an annual subsidy of 130,000,000 francs, to be deducted from the former Comédie-Française allowance of 600,000,000. M. Barrault, who left the Comédie after the war to form the company he now co-directs with his wife, Madeleine Renaud, has in recent years shown a weakness for whimsy that cannot wholly be blamed on the necessity of pleasing the fashionable bourgeois audience. An actor whose charm is as boundless as his emotional range is limited, he has too often played parts – such as Alceste in *Le Misanthrope* – for which he patently lacks the guns, while the talents of his wife, a twinkling adept in all the caprices and condescensions of high comedy, have been seen in too many nearly identical roles. All the same, M. Barrault's directorial energy is immense, and he has a rare cementing power that has enabled him, over more than a decade, to command the allegiance of such gifted players as Simone Valère, Jean Desailly, and Pierre Bertin. Last season, at the Palais Royal, he revived Offenbach's *La Vie Parisienne* with such verve and aplomb that it has filled the theatre ever since; the whole company sang and danced as buoyantly as it spoke, and free rein was given to the antic genius of Jean Parédès, a fleshy, fish-eyed droll, debonair as a sea-lion, who played three parts under as many wigs and convinced me, not for the first time, that he was the

funniest actor in France. I am certain, however, that what endeared M. Barrault to M. Malraux was not *La Vie Parisienne* but his production, at the same theatre, of Claudel's *Le Soulier de Satin*. When M. Barrault moves into the Salle Luxembourg, his inaugural task will be the staging of *Tête d'Or*, an early Claudel play that has never been publicly performed. This will be followed by Jean Anouilh's *La Petite Molière*, which was tried out by the Barrault company at the Bordeaux Music Festival at the beginning of June.

The latter piece has a bizarre history. Some years ago M. Anouilh wrote a film script about the life of Molière; the front office rejected it, whereupon he sent it to M. Barrault, wondering whether it might somehow be revamped into a play. He got a startling reply: M. Barrault declared himself perfectly willing to stage it unchanged – long shots, close-ups, and all. And that, more or less, is what he did in Bordeaux. The text is trite and fact-bound: Molière the artist is weaned away from tragedy to comedy while Molière the man moves from happiness to misery, deserting his mistress to marry her convent-trained sister, who promptly and casually cuckolds him. I liked the moment when Molière, played by Barrault, sonorously remarks that '*L'homme est un animal inconsolable et gai*', and, when asked who said that, retorts that, of course, he did – the joke being that the phrase was coined by the hero of *L'Hurluberlu*, M. Anouilh's latest Paris success. But most of the evening's pleasure comes from the stagecraft. No sooner has a group of live actors left an inn than a gilded frame drops into sight, behind which we see a miniature facsimile of the inn's exterior and the surrounding landscape; tiny puppets trot out of the door and drive off in a tiny coach. This is the long shot. Immediately afterwards another picture frame slides down and we get the close-up – three actors sitting and jogging in the back seat while a painted avenue of trees recedes behind them. It is all very clever, and all very superficial. At dinner a few nights later I badgered M. Barrault about his obsession with stylized trickery. He smiled, like an artful urchin caught sticky-fingered in the act of filching candy, and then got down to definitions. There were, he said, three possible ways of staging a play, of which two were valid. 'To explain how the three differ,' he went on, 'let us take a chair.' Realism, which was good, meant a real chair in a real setting. Stylization, which was bad, meant a deformed chair in a deformed setting. Transposed realism, which was better than either, meant a real chair in an unreal setting. He implied that Stanislavsky and Brecht, whom one associates, respectively, with the first and last categories, had it over the Surrealists and Expressionists, who are sandwiched together in the second. As a theory, this is unexceptionable; all that remains is for M. Barrault to put it into practice. I felt a passing twinge of alarm, however, when he told me that his third production at the Salle Luxembourg would be *Le Rhinocéros*, by Eugène Ionesco, the king of the Surrealist conjurers.

(3) The Théâtre National Populaire. Jean Vilar has done some tremendous things at the Palais de Chaillot – I think of Germaine Montero in *Mother Courage* and Maria Casarès as Phèdre – but that colossal auditorium, with its wasteland of a stage, is a great destroyer of subtlety, and the company has long needed a second, smaller home in which to try its hand at intimacy and close quarters. The Théâtre Récamier, M. Malraux's gift, looks like an ideal choice.

I have just mentioned M. Ionesco, and this may be the place to say something about his *Tueur sans Gages*, which was the last independent production to be presented at the Récamier. Apart from *Le Rhinocéros*, as yet unseen, this is the only full-length play M. Ionesco has written, and it confirmed my opinion of him as a brilliant, anarchic sprinter unfitted by temperament for the steady, provident mountaineering of the three-act form. The first two hours are a tiresome blur. An architect, symbolizing bureaucracy, escorts the hero, a Chaplinesque innocent, around a Utopian city whose peace has been shattered by a series of unexplained murders. Determined to solve them, the innocent is frustrated, Kafka-fashion, by the police, who care about nothing but traffic control, and by politics, in the person of a raging harridan who, quoting Orwell without acknowledgement, bawls that under her regime war will be called peace, tyranny liberty, and misery happiness. The play comes to life only in the last half-hour, during which, ironically, it also comes to death. The killer appears, squat-nosed, slack-lipped, cretinous, clad in jeans, and swaying gently back and forth on the soles of his shoes. The hero begs him to give up killing, to which he makes no reply beyond a quiet, detached, commiserating snicker. And as the scene progresses, we realize that this is no murderer but death himself, the unslaked and unbribable principle of mortality. Jean Saudray played the part, and I saw no better performance in Paris.

(4) Albert Camus. Many European theatres are named after famous playwrights, and many fine companies have had resident dramatists, as the Moscow Art Theatre had Chekhov and the Compagnie
Louis Jouvet had Giraudoux, but for a government to engage a celebrated author to direct his own playhouse is something unknown
since Molière. The nearest modern analogy, I suppose, would be
Bertolt Brecht's Berliner Ensemble, and even there the parallel is not
precise, because the titular head of the troupe was not Brecht himself
but his wife, Helene Weigel, who has continued to run it since his
death. For all pertinent purposes, M. Camus will be working without
precedents. Whatever happens, I feel pretty sure that the emphasis
will be on words and ideas rather than on *mise en scène*. I base this
prediction on the adaptation of Dostoevsky's *The Possessed* that M.
Camus wrote and directed in Paris last season. Considering the length
and complexity of the novel, I thought it a surprisingly successful
job; I don't know when I last saw on the stage such an elaborate
study of the motives that impel non-proletarians to become revolu-
tionaries, or of the ways in which such motives, if imperfectly com-
prehended, may lead to actions that are inhuman, self-destructive, or
both. On the one hand we have Pierre, the plotter and fanatic, who
is quite unaware that his reasons for executing the student Shatov are
founded on personal resentment and not, as he imagines, on revolutionary zeal. This very lack of self-knowledge is what makes Pierre
indestructible; he survives through ignorance. Stavrogin, on the other
hand, whom Pierre worships, achieves a sort of self-knowledge and
commits suicide, realizing that the savage, nihilistic behaviour for
which he is notorious arises out of an expiatory need to be regarded
as an unpardonable monster – a need that, in turn, springs from a
moment in his past when he felt himself responsible for the death of a
twelve-year-old girl. Stavrogin, in fact, is the literary progenitor of
Arthur Koestler's hero in *Arrival and Departure*, who discovered that
he was doing the right revolutionary things for the wrong psychological reasons. There is a lot to carp at in M. Camus' dramatization.
Although it goes on for nearly four hours, many of the domestic and
romantic relationships are left scamped or nebulous, and the end is a
concertina of catastrophe, with the deaths of Shatov, Pierre's father,
and Stavrogin following on each other's heels like melodramatic
clockwork. The best performance was that of Michel Bouquet as

Pierre – pallid and gimlet-eyed, his hair like a combed mop that had been dyed jet black, and shuffling around the stage on tiptoe, as if fearful of making full pedal contact with the earth. My high opinion of M. Bouquet may be partly due to the fact that he had the most self-absorbed role; impregnable egotism is the quality that French actors play most easily. (If you doubt this, go to a comedy in Paris. You will find the leading performers so enchanted by their own voices that they will cut short their own laughs rather than allow the audience to usurp the floor; they regard laughter as a form of heckling.) After seeing *The Possessed* I decided that M. Camus had attempted the impossible with a great deal of literary skill; that he was an uneven director of actors; and that he had a lot to learn about lighting and stage illusion. My mind looks forward to his new venture rather more eagerly than my eyes and ears.

As far as it goes, therefore – and I needn't add that it goes infinitely further than any British or American scheme for helping the theatre has ever gone – the Malraux plan seems to me provocative and invigorating. I wish, however, that it had found room for the Théâtre de la Cité de Villeurbanne, directed by Roger Planchon, whose remarkable productions of both parts of Shakespeare's *Henry IV* I attended at the Théâtre Montparnasse-Gaston Baty. Like Brecht, his mentor, M. Planchon sees drama as a public statement of something useful, and believes in the beauty of useful things. Also like Brecht he is quite prepared to take a text and slash, paraphrase, and reshuffle it to make a contemporary impact. He did this with the two Henries. No translator was named in the programme, but the plays were boiled down to the bare social bones; each point was made, coolly and pungently, on a rostrum backed by a map of medieval England, and each scene was prefaced by a caption, projected on to a screen, that summed up the import of what we were about to see. Individual characterization was subjected to the larger image of declining feudalism. The result was not Shakespeare; it was abundance reduced to relevance, riches cut down to a living wage, a jungle turned into a cartographical survey. The audience was held not so much by what was happening to the characters as by what was happening to the whole society. I admired what I saw, and understood why Arthur Adamov, the leading Socialist in the theatrical *avant-garde*, thinks M. Planchon the best director in France. He is not alone in this opinion.

Soon after I left Paris, M. Planchon presented Marivaux's *La Seconde Surprise de l'Amour* in a production that was described by the critic of *Arts*, an ostentatiously neutral weekly, as a revelation. Henceforth, it would be impossible, said the review, to stage Marivaux without reference to M. Planchon's *mise en scène*, which was, apparently, bold enough to suggest that the servants in the play led lives as vivid and vital as those of their masters and mistresses.

Meanwhile, the commercial theatre is tenuously prosperous, most of the right-bank houses being occupied by comedies with titles like *Déshabillez-vous, Madame*. Sterner stuff runs up against the problem of apathy. Tennessee Williams's *Orpheus Descending* was playing, when I saw it, to dwindling audiences, despite the faunlike magnetism of Jean Babilée as the martyred hero, the cluttered eloquence of Lila de Nobili's set, and the detailed control of Raymond Rouleau's direction. (Apart from MM. Rouleau, Barrault, Planchon, Vilar, and André Barsacq, few French directors pay much attention to detail.) The Swedish Lars Schmidt, who produced *Orpheus Descending*, has lately become the most active Parisian backer of American plays; in the past two seasons *Cat on a Hot Tin Roof*, *The Diary of Anne Frank*, *Twelve Angry Men*, and *Two for the Seesaw* have opened under his patronage. He is a soft, anxious, harassed man. Production costs, he says, are as high in Paris as in London; *Orpheus* ran up a bill of ten million francs before the curtain rose. On top of that, the Société des Auteurs insists that managements stage at least as many native plays as foreign ones, and the opportunities created by the Malraux plan will make it even more difficult to get hold of new manuscripts. Even so, I am not madly worried about Mr Schmidt's solvency. Against rising costs, for instance, one must set the fact that theatre rents in Paris amount to no more than fifteen per cent of the box-office take, whereas in London the figure is forty per cent.

The two great popular hits of the last Paris season were Félicien Marceau's *La Bonne Soupe* and M. Anouilh's *L'Hurluberlu; ou Le Réactionnaire Amoureux*. I can't say I was bowled over by either of them. The latter, a windy and posturing work, sets out to be a sort of moralizing farce, which involves the author in a certain amount of unfairness, as when the *jeune premier*, having behaved towards a young woman as cynically as farce tradition demands, is treated to a serious lecture on the vileness of cynicism. The whole play is ambiguous;

we are never sure whether we are listening to Anouilh the boulevard Thersites or Anouilh the right-bank conformist. His hero is a retired general who has resigned from the Army in disgust and settled in the country, where he plots ineffectively against the established order. His grandiose plans for governing the nation are contrasted with his incompetence at running his own family – his daughter is seduced and abandoned by a young idler who reads radical papers, and he suspects his wife of having taken a lover. Throughout the play M. Anouilh uses the general as his mouthpiece to attack those aspects of modern life that affluent French theatregoers find most distasteful. On one occasion the hero inquires, at thunderous length, why the opinion of a million imbeciles should be regarded as sacred; this anti-democratic tirade brought the house down, and I felt I must have been one of the few people present who questioned the infallibility of retired generals when it comes to deciding who is an imbecile and who is not. Again (and again and again), M. Anouilh's spokesman asserts that France must regain her sense of honour. Life must be made harder; there must be obedient effort and respect for authority, with no more nonsense about social security. It is true that in the second half many of the general's ideals are shown to be unworkable, but there is no doubt that M. Anouilh wants us to sympathize with them, just as he wants us to detest the oafish milkman who dashes in from time to time, bawling about the rights of the workers. I thought, as I watched the play, of Cyril Connolly's remark about right-wing satire – that it was doomed to ultimate peevishness because it was directed at a moving staircase from a stationary one. There are odd flashes of the earlier, better Anouilh, especially when the subject is marriage. The production was notable for the kind of décor, not uncommon in Paris, that confuses slapdash fragility with visual poetry, and for a lot of effective, loud-mouthed acting.

In *La Bonne Soupe*, as in *L'Oeuf*, his great success of the season before last, M. Marceau tells the story of an obscure member of society who beats the system at its own game and comes out on top. Also, as in *L'Oeuf*, the action is composed of a multitude of short scenes narrated in the first person by the central character. In this case the protagonist is a shopgirl from Carcassonne who runs away to Paris with a married man and ends up, after a number of ticklish reverses, as a highly prosperous *grande cocotte*. The heroine, rampageously played by Marie Bell, tells her tale to a croupier at a casino; she is on stage throughout, commenting on the action. Nicole Courcel appears as her younger self, a provincial *ingénue* slowly donning the armour of urban cynicism. The play is not without virtues; I remember a speech that superbly conveyed the atmosphere of a prostitutes' hotel, which reminds Mlle Courcel, in its silence, its secrecy, its perpetual twilight, and the lethargic motion of its inhabitants, of a film she once saw about the bottom of the sea. And I think of a moment in the last act when the narrator announces that it is time for her to replace Mlle Courcel. Rising from the roulette table, Mme Bell interrupts the scene and tells the girl to withdraw, which she does, slowly and calmly, moving backward as she waves farewell. '*Adieu, ma jeunesse,*' murmurs Mme Bell, and briskly, drying her tears, takes over. There are several scenes as affecting as this; unfortunately, there are many more that are crude and naïve, so that the play's pseudo-sophistication appears as *voulu* and false as magenta lipstick on a ten-year-old schoolgirl. I must add that André Barsacq's staging is impeccably speedy and does everything possible to give the piece the raffish poetry it aims at and misses.

If I had to choose the best French play of the year, I would probably go for *Tchin–Tchin*, by a young writer named François Billetdoux, which I saw at a pocket theatre in Montparnasse. From the title and the locale, you might forgivably imagine it to be an experimental work of the kind that one associates with M. Ionesco and Samuel Beckett. In fact, it is a simple tragi-comedy, composed in a style that can only, if drably, be described as poetic realism. The two main characters are a guarded young-middle-aged Englishwoman called Mrs Puffy-Picq, whose husband has just left her, and Cesareo, a rueful Italian whose wife has just run off with Mr Puffy-Picq. The Italian pays a nervous visit to the Englishwoman. Tentatively, they drink. They drink a lot; hence the title. Gradually, hopelessly, they try to complete the classic pattern by falling in love themselves. It doesn't work; they mistrust each other too much, and, anyway, the equation doesn't balance. Yet by the end of the play they have achieved, after a series of violent ups and downs, something that approaches consolation. Neither of them will now collapse or commit suicide, though it is likely that both will go on drinking quite heavily. They remain, to the end, essentially comic characters, and that is what makes them moving; they will survive without sentimentality, suspecting that they may be fairly silly and not caring very much if they are. The curtain falls on a note of true, hard-earned optimism, which I prefer to the facile pessimism of so much left-bank writing. The leading roles are beautifully played by Katharina Renn, as the bereft wife, and by the author, as the bereft husband. M. Billetdoux is in his early thirties and has plenty of time to lure the younger French playwrights out of the blind alley into which Messrs Beckett and Ionesco have beguiled them. To assert that all communication between human beings is impossible is rather like putting on a strait jacket and then complaining about the impossibility of shaking hands. If I understand him rightly, M. Billetdoux is saying that communication is desperate and rare, always difficult and seldom total; but possible, with whatever qualifications; possible, all the same.

(1959)

MOTHER COURAGE

BY BERTOLT BRECHT, AT THE DEVON ARTS
FESTIVAL

Bertolt Brecht's *Mother Courage*, which had its English premièr last week, is a chronicle play about warfare in which warfare scarcely appears. It is *Henry V* without the dear friends and the breach and th nonsense about not wishing one man more. Brecht's subject is th decimating tumult of the Thirty Years' War, yet no plumes nod from his heroes' helmets and no rhetoric glitters on their lips. Instead w have rags and curses, for we are dealing with the underside of battle the rowdy hordes of parasites whose only care is the strategy of sur vival. They batten on war, profiting when they can, and suffering i they must, but knowing always that the price of their wares, drin and food and clothing, varies in direct ratio to the fury of the fightin We see war reflected in the eyes of a nomadic camp-follower calle Mother Courage, her three children, and the guests who share he covered wagon – a fugitive priest and a lecherous cook.

It is well known that Brecht leans eastward in his politics: must w

therefore expect Mother Courage's family to be downtrodden peas-
ants oppressed by Fascist beasts? Nothing of the sort. Mother Courage
is a bawdy cynic who can barely recall the names of the men who
sired her children. Her code of honour is Falstaff's, and her moral
code Doll Tearsheet's. She is in the war for what she can make out
of it; and in return the war robs her of her children, the very reasons
for her avarice. Her younger son is shot for theft. Her elder son
commits a murder during a moment of truce, and is executed for his
error in timing. And her daughter, a mute, dies at the end of the most
tremendous scene to have enriched the drama for many years.

Sheltering in a lonely farmhouse, she overhears soldiers plotting to
massacre the townsfolk sleeping below. She seizes a drum, climbs
onto the roof of the barn, pulls the ladder up behind her, and beats
out a frenzied tattoo of warning. The troop commander begs her to
stop, promising immunity for her friends on his honour as a gentleman. There is a pause: and she beats harder, until a musket is fetched
to silence her. The aftermath is written in the same vein of dis-
passionate, ironic tragedy. Mother Courage is keening a lullaby over
her dead child when the sound of a marching army is heard. The
war is moving on; and she goes with it, hauling her wagon and
singing her song of defiance. There is no room for self-pity in drama
like this.

By any definition, the play is an epic: a tale of endurance set in
the open air (there are no interior scenes) of any war-bruised country.
It is also a folk opera. Its earthy language, dotted with imagery as
mountains are dotted with edelweiss, takes frequent flight into song,
accompanied by Paul Dessau's trenchant music. Theatre Workshop,
the company chosen to play it, was dismally unequal to the strain.
Ants can lift objects many times their size and weight, but actors
cannot. Mother Courage is a role calling for the combined talents
of Anna Magnani and Siobhan McKenna: Joan Littlewood plays it in
a lifeless mumble, looking both over-parted and under-rehearsed.
Lacking a voice, she has had to cut Mother Courage's song, which is
like omitting the Hallelujah Chorus from the *Messiah*.

As director, she has sought to present, with fourteen players in a
concert hall, a play which the author intended for a company of
fifty in a fully equipped theatre with a revolving stage. She has made
a vice of economy by allowing her actors to change the scenery in

full view of the audience, a device at which Brecht would boggle. Some of her blunders are attributable not so much to financial straits as to sheer perverseness. She adds music where Brecht indicates none, uses Dessau's score in the wrong places, and has it sung badly where she uses it rightly. The result is a production in which discourtesy to a masterpiece borders on insult, as if Wagner were to be staged in a school gymnasium. Barbara Brown does well as the mute Kattrin, and Harry Corbett's decaying chaplain abounds in hints of the performance this actor might have given in more favourable surroundings.

(1955)

THE GOOD WOMAN OF SETZUAN
BY BERTOLT BRECHT, AT THE ROYAL COURT

'What is style?' asked Cocteau, and answered: 'For many people a very complicated way of saying very simple things. According to us, a very simple way of saying very complicated things.'

Many local critics have roundly consigned *The Good Woman of Setzuan* to the first category. Why, they demand, does Brecht need three hours, fourteen scenes, and thirty actors to prove that poor people are often a grasping lot? And, indeed, if that were all he was saying, we could write the play off and turn to something more important – a musical, perhaps, needing three hours, fourteen scenes, and thirty actors to say precisely nothing. But in fact the rapacity of the poor is a point made only in the play's first act. Shen Te, a genial harlot whose goodness the gods reward with a large cash prize, is instantly fleeced by the neighbours she has been enjoined to love, and is saved from bankruptcy only by the ruse of inventing and impersonating a ruthless male cousin named Shui Ta.

So far, so simple. Now watch the plot proliferate, burgeoning into paradoxes that only a simpleton could find simple. Shen Te falls in love with a shiftless airman who needs money to buy himself a job, and how better can she supply it than in the guise of the go-getting Shui Ta? Only this time it is not she alone who suffers: she raises the money, but learns that 'you cannot help one poor man without trampling down twelve others'. Pregnant and deserted, betrayed by two kinds of love, she devotes herself to a third – love for her unborn child, to safeguard whose future she once more summons Shui Ta. With fearful results: she rapidly becomes the richest inhabitant of Setzuan, and the most diligently hated.

The final trial scene is one of those high moments of art when character and symbol coalesce. Shui Ta is accused of murdering Shen Te. 'You were her greatest enemy!' shouts an angry peasant. 'I was her only friend,' is the sad reply. Irony as august, as bitterly conclusive, as this is seldom heard anywhere, least of all in the theatre. A fallacy has been exposed: that of seeking to be perfect in an imperfect society. Hastily mumbling a few vague exhortations, the gods who rewarded Shen Te nip back to heaven. Their commandments clearly don't work – but whose will? Must good ends always be achieved by base means? An epilogue, rashly omitted in the present production, poses the question to the audience, inviting it to choose between changing human nature and changing the world. Brecht implies, of course, a Marxist solution: let us change human nature *by* changing the world; and China embarked on just such an experiment several years after he wrote the play.

First fill a man's stomach and then talk to him about morality – that is Brecht's springboard, as it was in *The Threepenny Opera*; but the new dive is far more sophisticated. Macheath, after all, was a criminal; Shui Ta causes far more pain without ever breaking the law. Rather the opposite: 'he' is regarded by the authorities as a pillar of society. Similarly, the worthless pilot earns promotion in Shui Ta's sweat-shop by an impeccably moral act; he refuses to accept from a kindly timekeeper more money than is his due, and thereby wins the boss's eternal respect. This is a scene of the most biting subtlety.

At every turn emotion floods through that celebrated dam, the 'alienation-effect'. More and more one sees Brecht as a man whose feelings were so violent that he needed a theory to curb them. Human sympathy, time and again, smashes his self-imposed dyke: when Shen Te meets her airman on a park-bench in the rain; when she learns (disguised as Shui Ta) that he means to abandon her; when, alone on the stage, she shows her unborn son the glory of the world; and, most poignantly, at the close, when she begs the gods for aid and enlightenment.

In George Devine's production the great challenge is partly muffed. Honourably bent on directing his cast along cool, detached Brechtian lines, Mr Devine forgets that the Brechtian method works only with team-actors of great technical maturity. With greener players it looks like casual dawdling. Conscious of my heresy, I wish he had chosen an easier style and presented the play as a sort of *Teahouse of the October Revolution*. Teo Otto's tubular setting would still have fitted, and Eric Bentley's clumsy translation would, I hope, have come in for drastic revision. Anything would be preferable to hearing Mr Bentley's Americanisms spoken with North Country inflections.

Peggy Ashcroft, in the taxing central role, is only halfway fine. As Shui Ta, flattened by a tight half-mask which helps her to produce a grinding nasal voice, she is superb; nothing tougher has been heard since Montgomery last harangued the troops. Yet her Shen Te won't do. Sexily though she blinks, all hints of whorish earthiness are expunged by those tell-tale Kensingtonian vowels. What remains is a portrait of Aladdin as it might be sketched by Princess Badroulbadour.

All the same, the production must not be missed by anyone interested in hearing the fundamental problems of human (as opposed to Western European) existence discussed in the theatre. In the context of our present prosperity, these problems may appear irrelevant. They are still cruelly relevant to more than half of the inhabited world.

(*1956*)

BERLIN AT PLAY

West Berlin, now busy with its annual arts festival, is superficially gayer than the denuded Eastern sector of the city, and one has to guard against the pathetic fallacy of judging the spirit of a place by the energy of its advertising industry. Over the Kurfürstendamm the slim street-lights lean like sea-serpents, illuminating a long, low avenue that is all dressed up for a party to which no one appears to be going. Here there are no visiting trippers to pack the pavements, and by midnight the Berliners are mostly in bed. Half a mile to the east begins the great dust bowl that separates the two camps. The Reichstag, as befits a senior ruin, presides over the chaos, staring across unkempt parkland at a smashed railway station, where flowers grow between the tracks. The man-made horizons are hereabouts limitless. Those two shallow steps, leading nowhere, are the Reich Chancellery; that drunkenly tilted cone of bricks in the back yard is the Bunker – only now the whole district is back yard. Presumably in a mood of what-the-hell, the East Germans themselves demolished the Imperial Palace, thereby knocking two squares into one to make Marx-Engels-Platz. It is the largest in Europe, and the loneliest.

How has this flattened, sundered city managed to re-establish itself as the European capital of serious drama? It has no playwrights of stature now that Brecht is dead, and many of its best actors are working in Hamburg, Düsseldorf, and elsewhere. What holds its theatre together is something very German: a tenacious belief that great plays belong in great playhouses as surely as great paintings belong in great museums, and that it is a public responsibility to keep them there. Germany long ago outgrew the folly of trying to make plays pay; besides Berlin's broad canvas, the London theatre resembles a pigmy boudoir *vignette*. We call our system democratic because it submits every new production to the test of popular opinion; in fact it is a dictatorship, ruled by economic pressure. In the West End all plays are equal, but farces and melodramas are more equal than others.

The lesson of Berlin is that there is no theatrical freedom without theatrical subsidies. The Western Sector has six legitimate playhouses, two of which are directly state-aided, while the rest are subsidized indirectly by the Volksbühne, a municipal organization that distributes seats at cut prices to a myriad subscribers. (The situation is roughly the same in the East.) The result is a repertory which makes some Western critics feel that theatre in Berlin is, if anything, too free: it stages too many great plays. One sees their point. Swollen with *haute cuisine* (Ibsen, Strindberg, Büchner, O'Neill, Lorca, Miller, Shaw, Giraudoux, Molière, Schnitzler, Faulkner, and Shakespeare were on the menu last week), a man might well yearn for a doughnut.

Very loosely, you might say that West Berlin likes its plays to be introspective and retrospective; the East prefers a more extrovert drama. In the West one's first stop is the Schiller-Theater, which is London Airport with good acoustics – a functional paradise, hushed by pile carpets, where at once one feels a respected guest, not just a source of income. Its new production of *Measure for Measure*, a rather formal, choreographic affair, has both the vices and the virtues of West German taste. The major vice, probably incurable, is a submerged hysteria in the acting. Whenever a famous speech comes up, there bursts through the façade that shrieking teutonic demon that Brecht tried so hard to exorcise. The compensating virtue is an intense imaginative thoroughness. The director (Sellner) must have read the text to tatters before it yielded up a simple question which, as far as I know, has never been asked before: how old is Angelo? Traditionally he is middle-aged. Sellner, with startling logic, sees him as a vain, attractive youngster, an interpretation which makes sense of the part, sense of the relationship with Mariana, and sense of the play.

The veteran director Erwin Piscator, who invented 'Epic Theatre' in the twenties, is curtly dismissed by many Berlin intellectuals as a back number. By local standards, they may be right; by ours, his production of *Danton's Death* is wildly exciting. The setting (by Caspar Neher, still the *doyen* of German designers) is a wide curved ramp spiralling up to a height of about fifteen feet and then spiralling centrally down again; at the highest point stands the guillotine. Symbolic? Yes: but capable of presenting crowd scenes worthy of Eisenstein, and of showing us, as it spins on the revolve, a revolution that has got out of hand and forgotten that violence is self-perpetuating.

In Büchner's masterpiece the disillusioned Danton ('We haven't made the Revolution: the Revolution has made us') and the doctrinaire Robespierre are both drawn with equal sympathy. Piscator slants his production against both of them. Danton is played as a bombastic sensualist and Robespierre as a frigid fanatic: the play becomes an attack on the principle of revolution, rather than a sad dissection of revolutionary practice. Still, this production is a gauntlet flung down by Piscator to Brecht; and Brecht has done some slanting in his time.

Brecht's heir apparent as the kingpin of Berlin theatre seems to be Oscar Fritz Schuh, who runs the Theater am Kurfürstendamm. His festival offering is the German *première* of Eugene O'Neill's posthumous play *Long Day's Journey into Night* – four hours of introspection, 'written', as the preface unpromisingly bodes, 'in tears and blood'. At greater length and in greater depth than usual, this is the familiar American tragedy of two sons alienated from their father. The younger son is Edmund (O'Neill himself), who has T.B. His brother secretly hates him, and his father is a miser; all three drink heavily. Mother, meanwhile, takes dope in the attic. The play is a throbbing, repetitive essay in self-justification: it goes round and round the family circle to prove that Edmund's weaknesses are entirely due to the wickedness of his relations. The translation, even in a city where translating is a large minor industry, misses the Irishness of the text, and the sinister, gauzy setting (Neher again) suggests a household wrongly akin to the Mannons of *Mourning Becomes Electra*. Schuh's handling of the actors, however, is miraculous. I shall never forget the haggard, twitching, elderly child that Grete Mosheim makes of Mama; and the hectic fragility of Hans Christian Blech's Edmund is astounding in an actor whose temperament and appearance are those of a young James Cagney.

(1956)

BERLIN POSTSCRIPT

'Our theatre,' an East Berlin actor said to me, 'looks at the state of the world and asks: why? The Western theatre shrugs and says: why not?'

But nothing in Berlin is as simple and clear-cut as that. The East accuses the West of clinging to the star system, forgetting that there are star personalities even in that holy of Eastern holies, the Berliner Ensemble itself. The West retorts that the East irons out all individuality, forgetting that teamwork is so deeply rooted in German theatre that no actor, whatever his politics, can escape it. The only safe truths are these: that Berlin has no knockdown stars like Olivier or Edith Evans; that its actors have never developed that elaborate technique of charm with which French and English actors make bad plays commercial; and that its general theatrical level is higher than anywhere west of Moscow's best.

The Brechtless Berliner Ensemble maintains a standard of production unbeaten in either sector. The plays it produces are sometimes another matter. One, written by the Minister of Culture, yawningly chronicles the Nazi defeat outside Moscow – sad stuff, redeemed only by Brechtian stagecraft and settings that seem to have been broken off from naked reality by a giant hand. Visually, their *Playboy of the Western World* (renamed *The Hero of the Western World*) is equally ravishing, down to the last pecking hen and hunk of peat, but all the poetry has gone from Synge's text, which is interpreted as a satire on the Western cult of violence. (Hitler and Mickey Spillane are mentioned tersely in the programme.) The acting style, of course, is as deft and clear as ever. The question is whether it, and the company, will hold together now that their great energumen is dead. Their average age is already perilously low, and some of the older actors are on the brink of defecting.

The West has two answers to the Berliner Ensemble. One is the director Oscar Fritz Schuh, whom I discussed last week. The other is the entire repertory of the Schlosspark-Theater, the smaller of the two state playhouses. Here one sees plays for which we London critics are frankly out of training. Strindberg's *Road to Damascus*, for instance, the whole massive trilogy trimmed to fit into a single evening. Its hero is an unnamed Stranger (the author, lightly disguised) pursued by fantasies of guilt: at first he rejects the consolation of religion, since it would compel him to hate his neighbour as himself, but later undergoes a half-hearted, quasi-Pauline conversion. Dank and arid, I thought it; yet I was glad to have seen it, and gladder still to acclaim Martin Held, in the dual role of the Beggar and the Confessor, as a supreme mimetic talent, with the repose of a lizard and the attack of a lion.

Next day I saw William Faulkner's *Requiem for a Nun*, staged by Piscator in black and white for the rather dreary reason that the leading characters are a spade and a spook – a Negress, that is to say, and a white woman. The Negress is to die for the murder of her mistress's baby, and the play's purpose is to show that the real responsibility for the crime lies with the nymphomaniac mother. I never expected to relish the droning stammer of Faulkner's style, but Joana Maria

Gorvin almost converted me, a haunting actress with a pinched face, eyes full of dread, and a downhearted-frail voice that carried me with her at least halfway to expiation.

And at the Schlosspark last Monday I survived the most drastic emotional experience the theatre has ever given me. It had little to do with art, for the play was not a great one; yet its effect, in Berlin, at that moment of history, transcended anything that art has yet learned to achieve. It invaded the privacy of the whole audience: I tried hard to stay detached, but the general catharsis engulfed me. Like all great theatrical occasions, this was not only a theatrical occasion: it involved the world outside. The first page of the programme prepared one: a short, stark essay on collective guilt. Turn over for the title: *The Diary of Anne Frank*, directed by Boleslaw Barlog, *première* performance. It is not a vengeful dramatization. Quietly, often gaily, it re-creates the daily life of eight Jews who hid for two years in an Amsterdam attic before the Gestapo broke in. Otto Frank was the sole survivor: Anne was killed in Belsen.

When I saw the play in New York, it vaguely perturbed me. There seemed no *need* to do it: it smacked of exploitation. The Berlin actors (especially Johanna von Koczian and Walter Franck) were better, on the whole, and devouter than the Americans, but I do not think that was why the play seemed so much more urgent and necessary on Monday night. After the interval the man in front of me put his head in his hands and did not afterwards look at the stage. He was not, I believe, Jewish. It was not until the end that one fully appreciated Barlog's wisdom and valour in using an entirely non-Jewish cast. Having read the last lines of the diary, which affirm, movingly and irrationally, Anne Frank's unshattered trust in human goodness, Otto Frank closes the book and says, very slowly: 'She puts us to shame.'

Thus the play ended. The house-lights went up on an audience that sat drained and ashen, some staring straight ahead, others staring at the ground, for a full half-minute. Then, as if awakening from a nightmare, they rose and filed out in total silence, not looking at each other, avoiding even the customary nods of recognition with which friend greets friend. There was no applause, and there were no curtain-calls.

All of this, I am well aware, is not drama criticism. In the shadow

of an event so desperate and traumatic, criticism would be an irrelevance. I can only record an emotion that I felt, would not have
missed, and pray never to feel again.

(1956)

STARS FROM THE EAST

The second Paris Drama Festival, now entering the seventh of its
ten weeks, is already a resounding success. Every theatrical capital
has sent a team except Moscow, and this will be remedied next year,
when we are promised the Maly Theatre in Chekhov. One of the
few flops has been Judith Anderson, playing *Medea* in a Widow
Twankey wig and a style describable only as armpit rhetoric. One of
my special joys was the great Neapolitan comedian Eduardo da
Filippo, appearing in his own play *Questi Fantasmi!* and giving a performance that combined the urbane authority of Louis Jouvet with
the deadpan melancholy of Buster Keaton. But Paris, so far, has kept
its loudest cheers for the Berliner Ensemble of Bertolt Brecht and –
hors de catégorie – the Peking Opera.

Brecht's troupe, a post-war phenomenon, is some twelve hundred
years younger than the Chinese opera, yet both have much in common. They presage an era in which drama, ballet, and opera are no
longer separate arts requiring separate critics. They mix dance, mime,
speech, and song in the service of the ultimate god: narrative. And
both are popular forms, untouched by anything esoteric. The
Chinese programme, made up of excerpts from longer works, contains little we would call opera; most of it is brilliant tumbling, acro-
batics put to the task of telling a good story. An old man takes a girl
across a river in a punt, but there is no river and no punt: the performers mime the action, with the delicacy of cats. Two warriors
fight in a darkened room, miming even the darkness (for the stage is
brightly lit), missing each other by inches, prowling and swooping
through fifteen minutes of ceaseless comic invention. You may object
that nothing very profound takes place; but I cannot call superficial
an art that explores, with entranced and exquisite love, the very

wellsprings of physical movement, speaking the language of the body so ardently that a flexed arm becomes a simile and a simple somersault a metaphor.

Bertolt Brecht's Epic Theatre borrows heavily from the Chinese: the emphasis is classically on how events happen, not romantically on the emotions of the people they happen to. Once in a generation the world discovers a new way of telling a story. This generation's pathfinder is Brecht, both as playwright and as director of the Berliner Ensemble. Last year he electrified Paris with *Mother Courage*; this year he brought *The Caucasian Chalk Circle*. My first impression was of petrified amazement at the amount of money involved. From East Berlin Brecht has transported dozens of impressionistic settings, hundreds of costumes, a new revolving stage for the Sarah-Bernhardt, a new curtain, and seventy-six people – scarcely a quarter of his permanent staff. Brecht has adapted the Oriental tale of the Chalk Circle to medieval Georgia. An army rebellion unseats the governor of a city, whose wife flees in panic, leaving her baby son behind; Grusha, her maid, protects the child, finds it a father, and then, when the revolt is quelled, disputes possession of it with the real mother, now returned to power. The judge gives the child to Grusha because, in Brecht's words: 'Each thing belongs to him who can do it the most good.' If I was unmoved by what Brecht had to say, I was overwhelmed by the way in which he said it. It is as shocking and revolutionary as a cold shower. In the British theatre everything is sacrificed to obtain sympathy for the leading characters. *Chez* Brecht, sympathy is nowhere; everything is sacrificed for clarity of narrative. No time is wasted on emotional climaxes. Situations which our playwrights would regard as cues for sentimental tirades are drowned by the clatter of horses' hooves or cut off by the whirr of the closing curtain. Three commentators, seated at the side of the stage, then outline in song what is going to happen next.

I have read a great deal about Brecht's theory of acting, the famous *Verfremdungseffekt*, or 'alienation effect'. What it boils down to in practice is something extremely simple. The small parts are all generalized. They wear masks down to their lips, fashioned like faces in Bosch or Brueghel and so exaggerated that we know at a glance what kind of people they are meant to be – drunken, prying, lecherous,

miserly, what have you. We can thus concentrate on the principals,
who wear no masks or make-up and play with absolute realism. These
include Ernst Busch as the Judge and Angelica Hurwicz as Grusha (a
fat girl, because Brecht does not want us to judge his characters on
the easy grounds of physical attractiveness); but the supporting players are not neglected. Helene Weigel, the governor's wife, leaves no
doubt that she is a great actress: she has eyes like the glint of hatchets,
a clarion voice, and a physical technique as supple as that of Martha
Graham.

The whole production is superb: a legend for today told in Flemish
and Oriental terms. One sees why Brecht feels that our method is as
different from his as driving a carriage-and-four is from driving a car.
Unless we learn it soon, a familiar process will take place. Thirty years
from now Brecht will be introduced to the English critics, who will
at once decry him for being thirty years out of date. The ideal way of
staging *Henry IV*, *Tamburlaine*, *Peer Gynt*, and a hundred plays yet
unwritten will have been ignored; and the future of the theatre may
have been strangled in its cot.

(1956)

THE CAUCASIAN CHALK CIRCLE
AND MOTHER COURAGE

BY BERTOLT BRECHT

TRUMPETS AND DRUMS

ADAPTED BY BERTOLT BRECHT FROM GEORGE
FARQUHAR'S *THE RECRUITING OFFICER*, AT THE
PALACE, LONDON

When the house-lights went up at the end of *The Caucasian Chalk
Circle*, the audience looked to me like a serried congress of tailor's
dummies. I probably looked the same to them. By contrast with the
blinding sincerity of the Berliner Ensemble, we all seemed unreal and
stagey. Many of us must have felt cheated. Brecht's actors do not
behave like Western actors; they neither bludgeon us with per-

sonality nor woo us with charm; they look shockingly like people – real potato-faced people such as one might meet in a bus-queue.

Let me instance the peasant wedding in *The Caucasian Chalk Circle*, a scene more brilliantly directed than any other in London. A tiny cell of a room, ten by ten, is cumulatively jammed with about two dozen neighbours and a sottish monk. The chances for broad farce are obvious, but they are all rejected. Reality is preferred, reality of a memorable and sculptural ruggedness. I defy anyone to forget Brecht's stage pictures. No steps or rostra encumber the platform; the dominant colours are browns and greys; and against a high, encircling, off-white backcloth we see nothing but solid, selected objects – the twin gates in *The Caucasian Chalk Circle* or Mother Courage's covered wagon. The beauty of Brechtian settings is not of the dazzling kind that begs for applause. It is the more durable beauty of *use*.

The same applies to the actors. They look capable and practical, accustomed to living in the open air. Angelica Hurwicz is a lumpy girl with a face as round as an apple. Our theatre would cast her, if at all, as a fat comic maid. Brecht makes her his heroine, the servant who saves the governor's child when its mother flees from a palace rebellion. London would have cast a gallant little waif, pinched and pathetic: Miss Hurwicz, an energetic young woman too busy for pathos, expresses petulance where we expect her to 'register' terror, and shrugs where other actresses would more likely weep. She strengthens the situation by ignoring its implications: it is by what it omits that we recognize hers as a great performance.

As Eric Bentley said, 'Brecht does not believe in an inner reality, a higher reality, or a deeper reality, but simply in reality.' It is something for which we have lost the taste: raised on a diet of gin and goulash, we call Brecht ingenuous when he gives us bread and wine. He wrote morality plays and directed them as such, and if we of the West End and Broadway find them as tiresome as religion, we are in a shrinking minority. There is a world elsewhere. 'I was bored to death,' said a bright Chelsea girl after *Mother Courage*. 'Bored to life' would have been apter.

The famous 'alienation effect' was originally intended to counterbalance the extravagant rhetoric of German classical acting: to a debauched emotionalism, Brecht opposed a rigorous chastity. *Mother Courage* cries out for rich and rowdy performances. Brecht has staged it in a style light, swift, and ironic. In the central part Helene Weigel is never allowed to become a bawdy and flamboyant old darling: her performance is casual and ascetic: we are to observe but not to embrace her. Twice, and agonizingly, she moves us: elsewhere, even in Paul Dessau's magnificent songs, we must never sympathize with Mother Courage. She has battened on the Thirty Years' War, and must suffer for her complicity by losing her daughter and both her sons. But the clearest illustration of the 'A-effect' comes in the national anthem, which the Berliner Ensemble have so arranged that it provokes, instead of patriotic ardour, laughter. The melody is backed by a trumpet *obbligato* so feeble and pompous that it suggests a boy bugler on a rapidly sinking ship. The orchestration is a criticism of the lyrics, and a double flavour results, the ironic flavour which is 'A-effect'.

Irony crops up throughout *Trumpets and Drums*, Brecht's expansion of Farquhar's *The Recruiting Officer*, advanced by a hundred years so as to coincide with the American Revolution. This involves propaganda, but it is propaganda as blithe and irrefutable as the remark made by an American wit on first seeing the playing-fields of Eton: 'Here,' he cried, 'is where the battle of Yorktown was lost!' Farquhar's text has been surveyed by cool new eyes, against the larger vista of England at war, and there is evidence that the director (Benno Besson) does not find enforced recruitment particularly hilarious.

Captain Plume is the kind of role in which, formerly, John Clements was wont to cut a charming dash. Dieter Knaup plays him realistically, as a sallow and calculating seducer. The costumes look as if people and not puppets had worn them, and the settings, shiny Hogarthian etchings suspended on wires, are amusing without being 'amusing'. And to show that Brecht can throw his bonnet over the windmill, we have Wolf Kaiser as Captain Brazen, who does just that, entering every time with a new hat which he whips off and flings irretrievably over the nearest rooftop.

Is it mere decadence that makes us want more of this, more attack, more abandon? I think not. Brecht's rejection of false emotions sometimes means that the baby is poured out with the bath-water: the tight-wire of tension slackens so much that the actors fall off, and instead of single-mindedness, we have half-heartedness. Yet as a corrective he is indispensable. It is possible to enter the Palace Theatre wearing the familiar British smile of so-unsophisticated-my-dear-and-after-all-we've-rather-*had*-Expressionism (what *do* such people think Expressionism was?) and it is possible to leave with the same faint smile intact. It is possible: but not pleasant to contemplate.

(*1956*)

SUMMING-UP: 1959

Drama in Germany is a wounded art, still recovering from the casualties it suffered between 1933 and 1945. Exile accounts for some of them, death for the rest. In the case of the refugees, the damage was measurable and vast; with the coming of Hitler, Germany lost many of its best writers, directors, and actors, and for a decade and more its theatre resembled a decapitated giant with a megaphone instead of a mind. But there is no way of calculating how much potential talent was killed off in the war. Travelling around German theatres today, you rapidly notice that something is missing, and before long you realize what it is. A whole age group has almost disappeared; there are hardly any actors in their forties.

The wartime losses were, of course, architectural as well as human; most of the great playhouses were shattered by bombs. After twelve years of sickness a cultural tradition had to be revived amid ruins, with rubble still smoking underfoot. It is customary, when discussing the post-war German theatre, to applaud its technical efficiency and the speed of its recuperation, and then to complain that it has turned out no new playwrights of any importance. The complaint is accurate, but niggling. It is remarkable enough that post-war Germany has an organized theatre at all; what is astonishing, not to say eerie, is that in range of repertoire and general excellence of production there is no theatre in Europe to match it. I am not speaking in terms of individual talent. The finest actor in Europe is not a German; several other countries have directors as good as Germany's best; and in the matter of living dramatists the French and the British hold an authoritative lead. Where the German theatre scores, and ultimately wins, is in versatility, consistency, and national extensiveness. From one end of the sundered country to the other, every town big enough to have an art gallery and a public library also has a municipal playhouse, which automatically gets a civic subsidy, since the Germans believe that if a citizen has a right to good paintings, good sculpture, and good books, he has a right to good drama as well. Every such theatre has an *Intendant*, or administrator, who engages the company and selects the plays, many of which he is likely to direct himself; an average season's repertoire consists of around half a dozen new productions, augmented by a few left over from previous years. In any given week you can usually see at least four different shows, and sometimes as many as six. The lucky Düsseldorfers, I noticed as I flashed through their city this summer, could take in Schiller, Molière, and *Waiting for Godot* on consecutive nights at the local *Stadttheater*, and there are fewer Düsseldorfers than there are inhabitants of Buffalo.

To the outsider, the most flabbergasting thing about the German theatre is its eclecticism; the country we associate most closely with nationalism is the one that offers the widest international choice of plays. This was true thirty years ago, and it is even truer now that Germany is split. On both sides of the East-West border the European classics are the backbone of the repertory; but while the West performs contemporary French, English, and American plays that are seldom seen in the East, the East puts on modern Russian, Chinese, Hungarian, Rumanian, Polish, and Czech plays that are seldom, if ever, staged in the West. The result, *in toto*, is theatre of a diversity unparalleled anywhere in the world. The Federal Republic has a number of 'private' (i.e., commercially run) playhouses, which have no counterparts in the Eastern Zone. Otherwise, both Germanys adhere to a principle much older than their latter-day antagonisms; namely, that it is a permanent public responsibility to make serious professional drama readily available, by means of subsidy, to everyone who wants to see it.

A few statistics, and we can get down to particulars. At the last count, West Germany, with a population of 53,000,000, had 121 theatres, or one to every 430,000 people. The equivalent figures for the East are 18,000,000 inhabitants and 86 theatres, or one to every 209,000. Just why the East should be so much more saturated theatrically is something that has never been fully explained to me. Its supporters say that Marxism and culture, its opponents that Marxism and propaganda, are synonymous.

Berlin is a city with two centres—the cluster of expensive hotels, bars, cinemas, shops round the Memorial Church, a sparkling nucleus of light, like a sham diamond, in the shabby twilight of the town; and the self-conscious civic centre of buildings round the Unter den Linden. . . .

This admirable description of the city today was written in 1932 by Christopher Isherwood – a fact that rather makes one doubt the validity of pointing modern political morals by contrasting the glittering opulence of the Western sector with the bureaucratic austerity of the East. Berlin seems always to have been split – once atmospherically and now geographically. Despite its bisected nature, it remains the artistic capital of the nation as a whole. In some ways, competition between the two sectors has had a stimulating effect on the theatre; in others, it has created enervating tensions. If, for instance, a West Berlin actor takes a job in an East Berlin production of an anti-capitalist play, he is liable to be reviled by the West-sector press. Similarly, an East Berlin director would have very ambiguous feelings if one of his shows got a rave review from a reactionary West Berlin critic. On one point, however, civic pride overrules political rivalry. Few West Berliners, no matter how rabid their allegiance to the Bonn government, would deny that the finest productions in the city are those of the Berliner Ensemble, which operates at the Theater am Schiffbauerdamm, in the East. Founded and inspired by Bertolt Brecht, this celebrated troupe was described in the London *Spectator* as 'the only theatre that can be named in the same breath with the Moscow Art or the Abbey at the height of their powers' – a judgement with which I concur, and on which I shall enlarge later.

Being Germany in little, Berlin offers a theatrical diet that is an open incitement to gluttony. The Western sector has six legitimate playhouses, the Eastern sector five – not counting the Theater der Freundschaft, which puts on plays for children. During a sample week in June the West was doing Sophocles, Calderón, Goldoni, Chekhov, Giraudoux, and John Osborne, while the East was busy with Shakespeare, Jonson, Goethe, Lessing, Shaw, Synge, and Brecht. And in both sectors, inevitably, there were productions of Molière and Schiller. Most of the serious work in West Berlin takes place at the Schiller-Theater, a great grey pleasure dome that has been rebuilt since the war, and at its affiliated suburban house, the Schlosspark; their joint Intendant, Boleslaw Barlog, receives an annual grant of four million marks (£350,000), on which to struggle through the season. Understandably, he manages to keep up a fairly high standard, with plenty of room for experiment. This summer I saw an extremely far-out production, at the Schiller, of Sophocles's *Trachiniae*, in a German version of Ezra Pound's brisk colloquial translation. On the stage, which projected jaggedly out into the auditorium, there was a lopsided abstract construction in polished steel, a long ramp that went zigzagging up into distant darkness, and practically nothing else except the cast. The choral bits were intoned by a group of young women in green gym tunics, who carried out, from time to time, little choreographic stunts reminiscent of a eurhythmics class celebrating the opening of the new playing field. Yet, despite these vagaries, the tragedy came across like thunder. The Heracles (Fritz Eberth) never went off into the daemonic, shrieking, self-hypnotized trance that is the plague of so many Germany actors, not to mention politicians, when they are faced with a solid patch of rhetoric, and Hilde Krahl was memorably guilt-ravaged as the slave bride who gives her husband the corrosive, undoffable shirt of Nessus, under the impression that it is a garment magically endowed with the power of preserving love. I felt at the end, as I seldom do after watching, say, *Medea*, that I knew several marriages exactly like that. Next day the company presented *The Madwoman of Chaillot*, Giraudoux's ravishing fantasy about a flamboyant old beldam who saves Paris from destruction at the hands of an oil combine by walling up the entire board of directors in a sewer. This, I'm afraid, is the kind of play the Germans do least well. As performers, they are incomparable in logic, clarity, and head-on emotional impact; call upon them, however, for elegance, grace, and the subtler nuances of charm, and you will often be disappointed. It is not by chance that there are no good German ballet companies. The Schiller production missed none of Giraudoux's points, but blunted many; lyricism, like a bird frightened by traps set to snare it, flew out of the window. The leading role was played – graciously, though slothfully – by a venerable actress in her eighties, making what was probably her farewell appearance. I decided that I pitied her. The German theatre is predominantly a male province; Moissi, Krauss, Bassermann, Deutsch, and Gründgens are the players whose names come first to mind. (In France, of course, acting is female; one thinks of Rachel, Bernhardt, Feuillère.) At the Schiller the central character in *The Madwoman* was not the Madwoman but the Ragpicker, performed with overwhelming zest and dynamism by Martin Held, the best all-round actor in Germany today. A sturdy, pink-faced man in his forties (a decimated age group, as I've said), he has enormous pathos and an attacking style full of the simplicity that we sometimes, and stupidly, call naïveté. In the Giraudoux he played not only the Ragpicker, who is a proletarian droll, but the president of the oil company – a brilliant trick worthy of Pirandello, since it is the Ragpicker who volunteers, during the second act, to impersonate the president at a mock trial, wherein he improvises a riotous defence of money-making as a healthy way of life. We thus hear the same actor twice extolling the mystique of wealth – first sincerely, then tongue in cheek.

At the Schlosspark I saw a production, by Hans Lietzau, of John Osborne's *The Entertainer* that made me radically reconsider my strictures on the play as it was presented in London and New York. I had formerly maintained that the role of Jean, Archie Rice's disillusioned daughter, was ineffectual and underwritten. The last act tapered off, I had snarled; the girl's part came to nothing. I have now changed my mind. To be sure, the German version lacked an Olivier, but not without reason; there is no music-hall tradition in Germany, and hence no model for the seedy, bawdy raconteur that Sir Laurence played. Martin Held compromised by making Archie a German-cabaret M.C., cruder and sweatier than Olivier, and drunker, too, in a stiff-backed, stolid way, emphasizing his jokes with a ghastly, crowing laugh. A lot of subtleties were lost, but the play as a whole took on, almost by default, much more cogency and shape. In Lietzau's production the centre of the stage was occupied by daughter Jean, a tight-lipped blonde, forever watching her father, and reacting with tremors of pity and disgust to each new evidence of disintegration, each new proof that the man was spiritually dead. We saw the action through her eyes, and the play achieved a unity I had never thought it possessed.

The Schiller-Schlosspark pattern of variety, thoroughness, and efficiency recurs all over the country. In a short week-end at Hamburg – a city for whose green, water-girt beauty I was, by the way, completely unprepared, having expected Pittsburgh with mud-wrestling – I was able to see three first-rate works at the Schauspielhaus, which is run by the veteran Gustav Gründgens, and to spend an evening at the local experimental theatre, which advertised something called *Mississippi-Melodie*, by Tennessee Williams (not, as I'd hoped, a minstrel show culled from Mr Williams's juvenilia but a quadruple bill, dowdily cast, of his better-known one-act plays). The Schauspielhaus presented Schiller's *Mary Stuart*, which was played with thumping soundness, despite someone's decision to garb Queen Elizabeth in a negligée trimmed with pink marabou; the first part of Goethe's *Faust*, in a lively new staging by Gründgens; and Brecht's *Saint Joan of the Stockyards*, which had had its world *première* at the same theatre earlier in the season. Written just after the 1929 unpleasantness, Brecht's piece is a bitter attempt to illustrate the interdependence of capitalism and religion, or – to put it more precisely – of profiteering and charity. It revolves around the friendship between Pierpont Mauler, a sentimental Chicago meat king, and a Salvation Army girl named Joan Dark. Warmed at first by Mauler's private good-heartedness, Joan slowly discovers that in an economic pinch he will go to any lengths to safeguard his profits, whereafter she realizes that by distributing soup and moral sustenance to the poor she is not alleviating hardship but accepting it as an immutable fact of life, and therefore encouraging its perpetuation. With this message on her lips, she returns to the mission hall, which Mauler and his friends have equipped with a gaudy new golden-piped organ. But her voice is drowned by the choir; exhausted by tramping the winter streets, she collapses and dies, and is thereupon hailed by the meat king's spokesman as 'a fighter, and a sacrifice in the service of God'. As a portrait of Chicago, the play is less than convincing, but as a satire on the relationship between those who take and those who give, its pungency is tremendous; it was by far the most successful show of the Hamburg season.

Wherever you go in Germany, Brecht is inescapable. Frankfurt, which has staged five Brecht plays since 1952, added a sixth last spring, to critical applause so tumultuous that it made half a column in the *New York Times*. The occasion was the West German *première* of *Schweik in the Second World War*, Brecht's version of the adventures that might have befallen Jaroslav Hašek's Good Soldier had he been conscripted by the Nazis to fight against Russia. Schweik, the beaming innocent who makes authority look most foolish when most he seems to embrace it, had an abiding appeal for Brecht, who once said that Hašek's book was one of the three literary works of this century most likely to become classics. In Brecht's play, as Schweik blunders into the Army and towards Stalingrad, the action is constantly interrupted by Hitler and his lieutenants, on a platform high above the stage; the Führer persistently, and pathetically, inquires whether Schweik, the little man, still loves him, because without the love of the little man he cannot go on. Finally, Schweik rejects his advances with unctuous obscenity. Although it is embellished with some of the loveliest lyrics Brecht ever wrote, the text is rough, acid, and brutally contemptuous of Nazi sympathizers. The night I was there, the Frankfurt audience cheered it.

The ubiquity and the influence of Brecht have been growing ever since his death, three years ago, at the age of fifty-eight. In the 1957–8 season he set a record; for the first time in the history of the German theatre a contemporary native playwright was among the four dramatists whose works were most often performed in the German-speaking countries. Shakespeare, as always, came first, with 2,674 performances, and he was followed by Schiller, with 2,000; Goethe, with 1,200; and Brecht, with 1,120. (Molière, Shaw, and Hauptmann, in that order, were the runners-up.) It is doubtful whether any dramatist in history has made a greater impact on his own country in his own era than this stubby, ribald Marxist, who spent his mature creative years – from 1933 to 1948 – away from home, exiled and almost penniless, first in Scandinavia and then in the United States.

I have paid many visits to Brecht's Berliner Ensemble in the five years since it took up residence at the Theater am Schiffbauerdamm, but whenever I approach the place, I still feel a *frisson* of expectation, an anticipatory lift, that no other theatre evokes. Western taxis charge double to go East, since they are unlikely to pick up a returning fare, but the trip is worth it: the arrow-straight drive up to the grandiose, bullet-chipped pillars of the Brandenburg Gate, the perfunctory salutes of the guards on both sides of the frontier; the short sally past the skinny trees and bland neo-classical façades of Unter den Linden (surely the emptiest of the world's great streets), and the left turn that leads you across the meagre, oily stream of the Spree and into the square-*cum*-parking-lot where the theatre stands, with a circular neon sign – 'BERLINER ENSEMBLE' – revolving on its roof like a sluggish weather vane. You enter an unimposing foyer, present your ticket, buy a superbly designed programme, and take your seat in an auditorium that is encrusted with gilt cupids and cushioned in plush. When the curtain, adorned with its Picasso dove, goes up, one is usually shocked, so abrupt is the contrast between the baroque prettiness of the house and the chaste, stripped beauty of what one sees on the expanses, relatively enormous, of the stage. No attempt is made at realistic illusion. Instead of being absorbed by a slice of life, we are sitting in a theatre while a group of actors tell us a story that happened some time ago. By means of songs, and captions projected on to a screen, Brecht explains what conclusions he draws from the tale, but he wants us to quarrel with him – to argue that this scene need not have ended as it did, or that this character might have behaved otherwise. He detested the reverence of most theatre audiences, much preferring the detached, critical expertise that he noted in spectators at sporting events. Theatrical trickery, such as lighting and scene changes, should not, he felt, be concealed from the customer. In his own words,

> . . . don't show him too much
> But show something. And let him observe
> That this is not magic but
> Work, my friends.

Always, as a director, he told his actors that the mere fact of passing through a stage door did not make them separate, sanctified creatures cut off from the mass of humanity – hence his practice, which is still followed to some extent by the Ensemble, of allowing outsiders to wander into rehearsals, as long as they keep quiet. He abhorred the idea that the production of plays is a secret, holy business, like the nurture of some rare hothouse plant. If actors can spend their spare time watching ditchdiggers, he said, why shouldn't ditchdiggers watch actors? Initially, the Ensemble actors were embarrassed by this open-door policy; later, however, they realized how much it had helped them to shed inhibitions. A cast that has rehearsed for weeks before strangers is unlikely to dread an opening night.

I arrived at the theatre this year during a rehearsal, and one that was loaded with nostalgia. *The Threepenny Opera*, Brecht's first decisive success, was being prepared for revival on the same stage that had seen its *première* thirty-one years earlier, with the same director in charge – Erich Engel, now looking gaunt and unwell, despite the jaunty cock-sureness of his beret. As I entered, somebody was singing 'Mack the Knife' with the tinny, nasal vibrato that one remembers from the old Telefunken records. Engel and two young assistants interrupted from time to time, talking with the easy, probing frankness that comes of no haste, no pressure, no need to worry about publicity, deadlines, or out-of-town reviews. I noticed that Mr Peachum, a part usually given to a rubicund butterball, was being played by Norbert Christian, a slim soft-eyed actor in his thirties. Brecht, I reflected, would have liked that; he always detested physical type-casting. In Brecht's theatre it is what people do, not what they feel or how they look, that counts. Action takes precedence over emotion, fact over fantasy. '*Die Wahrheit ist konkret*' ('Truth is concrete') was Brecht's favourite maxim; for him there could be no such thing as abstract truth. Some-body once asked him what the purpose of a good play ought to be. He answered by describing a photograph he had seen in a magazine, a double-page spread of Tokyo after the earthquake. Amid the deva-station, one building remained upright. The caption consisted of two words: 'Steel Stood'. That, said Brecht, was the purpose of drama – to teach us how to survive.

The rehearsal continued, the patient denuding process that would ultimately achieve the naked simplicity and directness on which the Ensemble prides itself. To encourage the players to look at themselves objectively, a large mirror had been placed in the footlights, and throughout the session photographers were taking pictures of every-thing that happened, providing a visual record that would afterwards be used to point out to the actors just where, and how, they had gone wrong. One of the most impressive women alive had meanwhile come to sit beside me – Helene Weigel, Brecht's widow, who has directed the Ensemble since its inception ten years ago and plays several of the leading roles. At sixty, she has a lean, nut-brown face that suggests, with its high cheekbones, shrewdly hooded eyes, and total absence of make-up, a certain kind of Spanish peasant matriarch; her whole manner implies a long life of commanding and comforting, of which she clearly regrets not an instant. Her warmth is adventurous, her honesty contagious, and her sophistication extreme, and that is the best I can do to sum up a woman who would, I think, be proud to be called worldly, since a scolding, tenacious affection for the world is the main article of her faith. The Weigel – to adopt the German manner of referring to an actress – has no real counterpart in the American theatre; in appearance, and in dedication, she resembles Martha Graham, but a Martha Graham altogether earthier and more mischievous than the one Americans know. At the end of the rehearsal we exchanged gifts and greetings. I got a scarf, designed by Picasso in the company's honour; a book about the Ensemble's seminal production, *Mother Courage*; a photographic dossier comparing the performances of Charles Laughton and Ernst Busch in the title role of Brecht's *The Life of Galileo*; and – unexpectedly – a complicated game of the do-it-yourself variety, invented by Mozart to teach children how to compose country dances by throwing dice. The Weigel, alas, got only a cigarette lighter. Talking about the state of the company, she said, 'When Brecht died, I was afraid this place might become a museum.' Her fears have turned out to be unjustified. It is true that the Ensemble mostly performs Brecht plays, but the plays are acted and directed by people steeped in the Brecht spirit. Throughout the theatre his ghost is alive and muscular.

Or, rather, his ghosts, because there were many different Brechts, as I discovered while reading John Willett's invaluable book *The Theatre of Bertolt Brecht* and Martin Esslin's biographical study, *Brecht: A Choice of Evils*. The early Brecht was a touchy child, with a Bavarian accent, whose father ran a paper mill in Augsburg. After serving as a medical orderly in the First World War – an experience that inspired his lifelong hatred of militarism – Brecht plunged into the German *avant-garde* of the twenties, making a name for himself as an outspoken, nihilistic poet-playwright with a gift for turning gutter idiom into poetry. In Germany, where literature had always spoken a high-flying language unknown to human tongues, this was something new; as Ernest Borneman lately remarked in the *Kenyon Review*, 'There was no precedent (a) for colloquial poetry; (b) for plain storytelling. There was no German equivalent to writers like Kipling,

Mark Twain, or Hemingway.' Brecht was impressed by, and freely borrowed from, the work of writers as disparate as Villon, Rimbaud, Büchner, Wedekind, Shakespeare, Kipling, and Luther, and he positively welcomed the charge of plagiarism, retorting that in literature, as in life, he rejected the idea of private property. Through the mouth of Herr Keuner, an imaginary character on whom he fathered many anecdotes and aphorisms, he scoffed at authors whose egotism compelled them to exclude from their work all notions and phrases that were not of their own invention: 'They know no larger buildings than those a man can build by himself.' (In this respect, as in several others, Brecht resembles Picasso, who once remarked, 'To copy others is necessary, but to copy oneself is pathetic.' In the early Montmartre days, according to Roland Penrose's recent biography, Picasso's reading matter included Verlaine, Rimbaud, Diderot, and the adventures of Sherlock Holmes, Nick Carter, and Buffalo Bill; the same list, or one very similar, would serve for the young Brecht. In addition, both men embraced Communism, yet expressed themselves in styles that were utterly antipathetic to Socialist realism; both revolutionized the arts of their choice; and both, despite shortness of stature and slovenliness of dress, were immoderately attractive to women.)

Brecht's early manner was summed up in 1922 by the German critic Herbert Ihering:

This language can be felt on the tongue, on the palate, in one's ears, in one's spine. . . . It is brutally sensuous and melancholically tender. It contains malice and bottomless sadness, grim wit, and plaintive lyricism.

A little later there was the Brecht who, in collaboration with Kurt Weill, revolutionized the popular musical stage with *The Threepenny Opera* and *The Rise and Fall of the City of Mahagonny*, using the rhythms and slang of a depressed urban society to lacerate Western decadence, and bringing into the 'serious' theatre the sardonic street-corner poetry of post-war Berlin. Already he was moving towards the vantage point that he was to make his own – 'that interesting and largely neglected area', as Mr Willett describes it, 'where ethics, politics, and economics meet.' In 1926 Brecht read *Das Kapital* for the first time. Marxism supplied a corrective to his anarchic tendencies, a remedy for his disgust with the world around him, and a mental discipline that delighted his love of logic and paradox. Hence, after 1928 we get Brecht the Communist didact, writing instructional plays in a new, sparse, bony style:

> When I address you
> Cold and broadly
> In the driest terms
> Without looking at you
> (I apparently fail to recognize you,
> Your particular manner and difficulties),
>
> I address you merely
> Like reality itself
> (Sober, incorruptible, thanks to your manner,
> Tired of your difficulties),
> Which you seem to me to be disregarding.

From this period come *Die Massnahme*, an austere analysis of revolutionary self-abnegation that is, intellectually, the masterpiece of Communist drama, and *Die Mutter*, Brecht's stage adaptation of the famous Gorki novel. Both plays were savagely attacked in the Marxist press – the latter for being out of touch with working-class reality, the former because it denied the thesis that a good Communist is never torn between the claims of reason and emotion. (Brecht's failure to reconcile these rival claims accounts, in Mr Esslin's view, for the fascinating ambiguity that runs through his work. The bald statement he wants to make and the poetry with which he makes it often pull in different directions; matter and manner are exquisitely at odds.) Like many of his Leftist contemporaries, Brecht was seeking a method whereby economic processes could be effectively dramatized; he hoped to see money and food some day displace power and sex as the drama's major themes. With most bourgeois writers, he said, 'the fact that moneymaking is never the subject of their work makes one suspect that . . . it may be the object instead.'

The next Brecht was the director who practised, and the theorist who preached, 'Epic Theatre' – a phrase he borrowed from Erwin Piscator in the twenties and went on defining until the end of his life. This, perhaps, is the Brecht who is best known in America, thanks to the energetic proselytizing of Eric Bentley. For every American who has seen a Brecht production, there are probably a thousand who are armchair experts on the 'alienation effect', the abolition of suspense, the prefacing of scenes with projected captions, the use of music not to intensify emotion but to neutralize it, the rejection of 'atmospheric' lighting in favour of general illumination, and the outright ban on costumes and props that do not look worn or handled.

> Of all works, my favourites
> Are those which show usage.
> The copper vessels with bumps and dented edges,
> The knives and forks whose wooden handles are
> Worn down by many hands: such forms
> To me are the noblest.

Brecht's opposition to naturalistic acting was really, as he often insisted, a return to the older forms of popular theatre, including (the list is Mr Esslin's) 'the Elizabethan, the Chinese, Japanese, and Indian theatre, the use of the chorus in Greek tragedy, the techniques of clowns and fairground entertainers, the Austrian and Bavarian folk play, and many others'. His refusal to permit actors to 'identify' with their roles, and thus to create strongly individualized characters, sprang from his conviction that human identity is not fixed but infinitely mutable, dependent on particular social and economic circumstances; this is the leftwing equivalent of Pirandello's theories, at once frivolous and despondent, about the many-faceted impermanence of the human ego. What Pirandello fatalistically accepted, Brecht sought to explain. His loathing of stage emotionalism is more easily accounted for. It was a violent reaction against the bombast of the conventional German theatre. Life in a Brecht production is laid out before you as comprehensively as in a Brueghel painting, and with many of the same colours – browns, greys, and off-whites. It does not seize you by the lapel and yell secrets into your ear; humanity itself, not the romantic individualist, is what it is seeking to explore. In 1936 Brecht stated his attitude:

The spectator of the *dramatic* theatre says: 'Yes, I have felt the same. I am just like this. This is only natural. It will always be like this. This human being's suffering moves me because there is no way out for him. This is great art; it bears the mark of the inevitable. I am weeping with those who weep on the stage, laughing with those who laugh.'

The spectator of the *epic* theatre says: 'I should never have thought so. That is not the way to do it. This is most surprising, hardly credible. This will have to stop. This human being's suffering moves me because there would have been a way out for him. This is great art; nothing here seems inevitable. I am laughing about those who weep on the stage, weeping about those who laugh.'

Nobody of any critical intelligence who is familiar with what passes for 'great art' in London or New York could fail to applaud this succinct, startling, and unforgettable distinction between the audience that is all heart and nerves and the audience that tempers feeling with knowledge and observation.

Two more Brechts, and the outline is complete. One was the mellow playwright who reached the peak of his creativity in exile. Between 1937 and 1945 Brecht wrote eleven plays, among them *The Life of Galileo*, *Mother Courage*, *The Good Woman of Setzuan*, *Puntila*, and *The Caucasian Chalk Circle*. By that time the ideological element was assumed or implied more often than it was stated. The five works I have named all deal with the tension between instinct, love, and emotion, on the one hand, and, on the other, a society that perverts or exploits all three. The church defeats Galileo by playing on his weakness for the good, sensual life. Mother Courage tries to protect her family by making money out of the Thirty Years' War, but the war, in the end, destroys her children. Shen Te, of Setzuan, finds that you cannot help those you love without injuring your neighbours. The landowner Puntila, all charity and generosity when drunk, is an efficient businessman during bouts of cold-blooded sobriety, from which, unavailingly, he begs to be delivered. In the last of the great plays, *The Caucasian Chalk Circle*, good-heartedness defeats the system. Grusha, the maid, is brought to trial for having kidnapped a high-born baby, but the judge decrees that the child belongs to her, since everything should belong to those who serve it best.

The last Brecht was the sage of East Berlin, at once the pride and the embarrassment of the Communist régime, which saw him laurelled in the West (especially at the Paris International Theatre Festivals of 1954 and 1955) and accused in Russia of being a 'formalist' opponent of Socialist realism. Mr Esslin's book goes deeply into Brecht's ambivalent relationship with the Party when he returned to Germany in

1948 after an inconclusive velitation with the Un-American Activities Committee. Before moving to East Berlin, he not only contrived, with characteristic guile, to obtain an Austrian passport, which would allow him easy access to the West, but gave the copyrights of his works to a West German publisher, who still owns them. When someone asked him, towards the end of his life, why he had elected to stay in the East, he is said to have likened himself to a doctor with a limited supply of drugs who is forced to choose between two patients – a syphilitic old roué and a diseased prostitute who is, however, pregnant. It seems clear, too, that Brecht's acquaintance with Hitlerism had left him with very little faith in the possibility of turning Germany into a true democracy overnight; hence he felt able to support an authoritarian government that, whatever its faults, was at least anti-Nazi and anti-capitalist. (I suddenly remember the occasion when I took Helene Weigel to the West Berlin *première*, three years ago, of *The Diary of Anne Frank*. At the final curtain the audience sat shocked and motionless; Frau Weigel's face was rigid and masklike. Shortly afterwards, in the restaurant next door to the theatre, she wept; and I should think she weeps seldom. Wiping her eyes, she shook her head and said firmly, 'I know my dear Germans. They would do this again. Tomorrow.')

Early in 1949, in collaboration with his old friend Erich Engel, Brecht staged *Mother Courage* at the Deutsches-Theater in East Berlin. The style – light, relaxed, and ascetically spare – set the pattern for all his subsequent productions. As the tireless old protagonist, dragging her canteen wagon across the battlefields of the Thirty Years' War, Helene Weigel played in a manner that shrank utterly from flamboyance; her performance was graphic yet casual, like a shrug. At two carefully selected moments she was piercingly and unforgettably moving – first in the soundless cry that doubles her up when her son is executed, and again when, to avoid incriminating herself, she must pretend not to recognize his body. She walks over to the stretcher, wearing a feigned, frozen smile that does not budge from her lips until she has surveyed the corpse, shaken her head, and returned to her seat on the other side of the stage. Then she turns to the audience, and we see for an instant the drained, stone face of absolute grief. These moments apart, the production achieved a new kind of theatrical beauty, cool and meaningful, by deliberately avoiding climaxes of individual emotion; with *Mother Courage* the broad canvas and the eagle's-eye view of humanity were restored to European drama after too long an absence.

That autumn the company formally adopted the name Berliner Ensemble, and for the next five years it spent most of its time on tour. In 1952 a detailed, illustrated account of its first six presentations, complete with an analysis of the acting techniques and methods of stagecraft, was published in a huge volume of well over four hundred pages, laconically entitled *Theaterarbeit* (*Theatre Work*). In the spring of 1954 the Ensemble moved into the Theater am Schiffbauerdamm, and Brecht celebrated his homecoming with an extraordinary production of the *Caucasian Chalk Circle*, which opened in June and later astonished Paris and London. A concave white curtain covered the back of the stage, a convex white curtain swept to and fro across the front; between them, the vast revolve whirled around, bearing fragmentary settings for the journeying heroine to encounter, and long silken sheets adorned with Oriental landscapes came billowing down to indicate place and climate. Lee Strasberg, the artistic director of the Actors' Studio and a passionate upholder of Stanislavsky's quest for emotional truth in acting, as opposed to the social truth sought by Brecht, saw the play while the Ensemble was in London. He concluded that what Brecht practised was by no means incompatible with what Stanislavsky preached, and declared that the production was one of the best half-dozen he had ever witnessed.

I met Brecht, for the first and only time, in Paris during the summer of 1955, the year before his death. Ovally built, and blinking behind iron-rimmed glasses, he sported a grey tunic of vaguely Russian cut and conversed in wry, smiling obliquities, puffing on a damp little cigar. To judge by Ernest Borneman's description of him in the twenties, exile had changed his appearance hardly at all: 'He was an eccentric in behaviour, speech, and dress, as well as in politics. He wore clothes that kept a neat balance between those of a soldier, a workman, and a hobo. . . . The hair was sliced off abruptly after two or three inches growth, all around the head, and hung down . . . like the coiffure you see on busts of Roman emperors.' Max Frisch, the Swiss playwright and novelist, has set down perhaps the best portrait of Brecht in his later years, and I am indebted to Mr Esslin for introducing me to it. Brecht met Frisch in Zurich in 1947 and would often, when the latter was embarking on a train journey, go to the station to see him off:

Avoiding the crowd, he leaves the platform with rapid, short, rather light steps, his arms hardly swinging, his head held slightly sideways, his cap drawn on to the forehead as if to conceal his face, half conspiratorially, half bashfully. . . . He gives the impression of a workman, a metalworker; yet he is too slight, too graceful for a workman, too much awake for a peasant . . . reserved, yet observant, a refugee who has left innumerable stations, too shy for a man of the world, too experienced for a scholar, too knowing not to be anxious, a stateless person . . . a passer-by of our time, a man called Brecht, a scientist, a poet without incense.

After the Master's death many people in the company, as well as outside it, wondered whether it could survive without his fiery presence. An interim answer was supplied by the Ensemble's triumphant East Berlin presentation, in January 1957, of *The Life of Galileo* – a production begun by Brecht and finished by Engel. I saw it again this summer, and the play still seems to me, as it did at the first night, an incomparable theatrical statement of the social responsibilities of the intellectual. At the outset it looks as if we were in for a straight fight between religious obscurantism and scientific discovery. The only progressive art, says Galileo, is 'the art of doubt', a remark that echoes Brecht's own dictum: 'Scepticism moves mountains.' But before long we arrive at the author's real purpose, which is to condemn Galileo for cowardice. Intimidated by the threat of torture, cajoled by the promise of a cossetted life, he abjectly recants, and emerges from the Inquisition chamber to be shunned by his pupils, one of whom shouts at him, 'Unhappy is the land that lacks a hero!' Wanly, Galileo responds, 'Unhappy is the land that needs a hero.' Brecht goes on to show how one such concession brings a hundred in its train; within months Galileo is backing the Church in social and political, as well as scientific and theological, affairs. The final tableau epitomizes the argument: in the foreground a choir polyphonously hymns the power of science, while in the background Galileo wolfs a fat roast goose. The play contains two scenes that exemplify, as sharply as anything Brecht ever wrote, his ability to make an intellectual position visible and tangible. In the first of them a provincial ballad singer hails Galileo's challenge to Rome. As he does so, a riotous procession, reminiscent of a painting by Hieronymus Bosch, streams across the stage. Some of the marchers are clad in obscene masks, and coax a jangling music out of saucepans and brass bedsteads; others toss a straw effigy of a cardinal in a blanket; one, a child, is attired as the earth, with water squirting from its eyes at the loss of its position at the centre of the universe; another clumps in horrendously on twenty-foot stilts, surmounted by a gigantic facsimile, acclaimed on all sides, of Galileo's head. The second scene that sticks in my mind is the one in which the liberal Cardinal Barberini, newly installed as Pope, turns against Galileo. At first, skinny in his underwear, waiting to be robed, Barberini refuses to countenance the Inquisitor's demand that the scientist be brought to trial, but as the robing proceeds and he is draped, encased, and almost buried in the ceremonial vestments of his office, the Pope grows more and more receptive to the Inquisitor's plea, to which, at last, he consents. It is instructive, by the way, to contrast Brecht's attitude towards Galileo with Arthur Koestler's in *The Sleepwalkers* – bearing in mind, of course, that Mr Koestler's Marxism was once as deeply ingrained as Brecht's. According to the Koestler version, Galileo's pride brought about a disastrous and un-necessary breach between science and religion. Brecht, on the other hand, accuses Galileo of not having had enough pride (or self-respect) to make a breach that was healthy and necessary. Koestler wants to reconcile the physical with the metaphysical; Brecht strives to keep them apart. But, whatever one thinks of the argument, it is impossible to deny the unassertive loveliness of Caspar Neher's décor for *The Life of Galileo* – three towering panelled walls of darkly glowing copper, enclosing an area into which informatively beautiful objects, such as Roman bas-reliefs and silver models of the Aristotelian uni-verse, are occasionally lowered. The production proved that the spheres of the Ensemble would continue to revolve without the animating zeal of their great mover. Brecht thus demonstrated, post-humously, the truth of his own apophthegm that no man is indispens-able, or, if he is, he is up to no good.

The Ensemble today consists of sixty-two actors, plus a staff of administrators, office workers, stagehands, musicians, designers, dress-makers, scene builders, electricians, ushers, waitresses, and cooks that brings the grand total of employees up to nearly three hundred. Its yearly subsidy, paid by the Ministry of Culture, amounts to more than three million marks. Rehearsals, in this happy set-up, may go on for anything between two and six months; when I was there in June, the cast of *The Threepenny Opera* was already wearing full costume and make-up, although the opening was not scheduled until October. It sometimes worries Helene Weigel that in all its ten years of operation the Ensemble has presented no more than twenty-five plays. She need not disturb herself unduly, because the main reason for the company's low output is, quite simply, its fame. Its productions are being reverently filmed for the East Berlin archives, it is constantly being invited to foreign countries (Hungary and Rumania this summer, Scandinavia in the fall, England and China next year), and it spends a lot of time polishing and recasting its existing repertoire.

This summer I attended two productions I had not seen before. One was *Die Mütter*, Brecht's expansion of the Gorky novel about an illiterate Russian mother who begins by urging her son to abandon his revolutionary activities and ends up, after he has been shot, a convinced supporter of the cause. The play is outright *agitprop*, a mosaic of Marxist exhortations, and the last scene shows the whole cast singing in praise of Communism while a film projector fills the backcloth with newsreel shots of Lenin, Khrushchev, Mao Tse-tung, and even – fleetingly – Stalin. It all sounds crudely hysterical until one sees the stealth and subtlety of the performance. There are no exaggerated Czarist villains, no exuberantly heroic proletarians; everyone acts with a detached calm that, if anything, reinforces the message. Weigel plays the mother as a quiet but relentless nagger. ('I picked out the nagging and decided to use it all through,' she told me later. 'I wanted to show that nagging could be constructive as well as nasty.') Looking like Nefertiti lined by years of labour over a hot stove, she permits herself one moment of pure lyricism. Her son, who has escaped from Siberia, appears without warning at a house where his mother is employed as housekeeper. Entering from the kitchen, she sees him and instinctively registers chiding disapproval; then, uncontrollably, she flies to his arms, as weightlessly as Ulanova's Juliet flies to Romeo, letting both legs swing round the boy's waist as he catches her. Throughout the evening one feels Brecht's passion for objects that have been durably used – a sofa, a soup tureen, a hand-operated printing press. Once, in a poem, he said that his wife chose her props with the same loving precision as that with which a poet chooses his words. Weigel's props, he declared, were selected

> . . . for age, purpose, and beauty
> By the eyes of the knowing,
> The hands of the bread-baking, net-weaving,
> Soup-cooking comprehender
> Of reality.

After this, one of the company's oldest productions, I went to see the newest – *The Resistible Rise of Arturo Ui*, described in the programme as '*ein Gangster-Spektakel von Bertolt Brecht*'. Written in 1941, it is a jagged, raucous parody of Hitler's rise to power, told in terms of Chicago in the twenties, composed mostly in blank verse, and including several malicious revampings of scenes from Shakespeare and Goethe. Hitler-Ui is a small-time thug who, taking advantage of a falling market, blackmails the mayor of the city (Hindenburg) into allowing him to organize a really prosperous protection racket. When the mayor dies, Ui succeeds him. His plans to take over the suburb of Cicero (Austria) are disputed by some of the mob; he slaughters the dissidents with as merry a lack of compunction as Hitler showed in disposing of Ernst Roehm and his friends on the Night of the Long Knives. In the final scene Ui is the boss, high on a rostrum spiky with microphones, through which he shrieks an oration that is cacophonously reproduced, at intervals of roughly half a second, by loudspeakers all over the theatre. The whole play is performed in a style that is somewhere between Erich von Stroheim and the Keystone Cops. The Roehm murders are staged like the St Valentine's Day massacre; a truck drives into a garage, its headlights blazing straight at the audience, and silhouetted gunmen mow down the victims. The entire cast wears the sort of distorted make-up that one associates with puppets; the revolve whizzes around; and squalling Dixieland jazz interlards the scenes. Macabre farce on this level of inventiveness was something I had never struck before in any theatre. Its quality was condensed in the performance of Ekkehard Schall as Ui – one of the most transfixing human experiments I have ever seen on a stage, and a perfect image of Brechtian acting. Schall, who is under thirty, plays Ui with a ginger moustache, a ginger forelock, a trench coat, and a hat with the brim completely turned down. He invests the part with all the deadpan gymnastic agility of the young Chaplin: clambering on to the back of a hotel armchair and toppling abruptly out of sight; biting his knuckles, and almost his whole fist, when momentarily frustrated; indulging, when left alone with wo-men, in displays of ghastly skittishness; and learning, from a hired ham actor, that the golden rule of public speaking is to preserve one's chastity by shielding – as Hitler always did – the lower part of one's belly. Yet Schall can change gears without warning, swerving from pure knockabout to sudden glooms of fearful intensity; from Chaplin, one might say, to Brando; for the virtue of Brechtian training, as of Brechtian thinking, is that it teaches the infinite flexibility of man-kind. The play itself is rowdy and Chaplinesque. What the production – and Schall, above all – has added to it is a fever, a venom, and a fury that make laughter freeze, like cold sweat, on one's lips.

> In me are contending
> Delight at the apple trees in blossom
> And horror at the house-painter's speeches.
> But only the second
> Drives me to my desk.

Thus Brecht; and this production makes one glad that he was so driven. Its directors – Peter Palitzsch and Manfred Wekwerth – are both, like Schall, young men who were shaped by his tuition. The tradition, I would hazard, is safe.

(1959)

THEATRE IN MOSCOW

Last November, having signed a customs form vouching that my baggage contained no antelope horns, Manchurian deer, hashish, 'negative or clichés', I entered Russia via Leningrad. A company of British actors, directed by Peter Brook, had been invited by the Ministry of Culture to perform *Hamlet* in Moscow. For the first time since the October Revolution, English was to be spoken on a Russian stage; and I took advantage of the cultural thaw to ride in on the actors' wake and take a first-hand look at the Moscow theatre.

The city itself had first to be digested. Its very layout is dramatic, monumentally gaunt and gaping, like a convention of huge warehouses held on an open plain. The new university soars upward like Rockefeller Centre in New York, though the Russians do not thank you for making the comparison; and by night the city suggests America, fantastically stripped of bars and grills and ads. How comforting, in memory, is neon lighting, symbol of salesmanship and hence of ingratiation! By day the great impersonal squares unfold: there must be half a dozen open places in the centre of Moscow where the battle of Waterloo could be fought without breaking a single window. For colour one looks at the domes and minarets of St Basil's Cathedral, which is Brighton Pavilion in war-paint and, as far as I could see, the only thing in Moscow that wears make-up. The squares surge with wind-bruised, shiny-cheeked people conversing in condensed steam. There are thousands of Chinese faces, many of them belonging to Chinese. Wandering unescorted, you rapidly get lost, for maps and phone books are as closely guarded as the two embalmed dynasts in the bakelite mausoleum on Red Square. In Moscow, as in most other great cities, the best landmarks are the theatres.

Seven of these are occupied by music hall, puppetry, opera, operetta, and ballet; the rest – twenty-one in number – are legitimate theatres, including three entirely devoted to plays for children. The same principles of organization apply to all of them. Every theatre has a permanent company of between eighty and a hundred and fifty actors, recruited in most cases from an affiliated drama school; and a repertoire of some twenty plays, so alternated that the same piece is never performed for more than two consecutive nights. This means that in any given week the visitor has a choice of about a hundred and fifty different shows. The thought of playing the same part night after night fills Russian actors with horror and incredulity; the idea of a 'long run' exists only in the theatres of London, Paris, and New York, and can scarcely be expressed in the Russian language.

And here let me pause to shatter a popular fallacy. With two exceptions, the Moscow theatre is not supported by government money. State subsidies were withdrawn in 1948 from every playhouse except the Bolshoi (meaning 'big') and the Maly (meaning 'little'). These are the two repositories of theatrical tradition. The Bolshoi is the home of opera and ballet, a gaudy pleasure dome where no fantasy goes unindulged; before your eyes the river Neva bursts its banks and a whole palace, staircase and all, subsides in flames. Nowhere on earth is the art of theatrical magic more extravagantly practised. The Maly, founded in 1824, is the oldest straight theatre in Moscow, and is known as the 'House of Ostrovsky' in much the same way as the Comédie-Française is known as the House of Molière. All the other theatres are autonomous and self-supporting. This seems unbelievable, in view of the splendour of the productions and the size of the companies, until you remember that they pay no theatre rent or entertainment tax, and that it is a rare season when average attendances drop below ninety-five per cent of capacity.

The British *Hamlet*, a middling specimen of West End Shakespeare, had its *première* at the second house of the Moscow Art Theatre; or, to give it its full title, the Affiliated House of the Moscow Academic Art Theatre in the Name of Gorky. The audience reactions were immensely revealing. Accustomed to constant changes of scenery, they were baffled when the curtain rose again and again on the same gray permanent setting. Nor, in a theatre where doubling is unknown, could they comprehend why so many members of the cast were playing more than one part apiece. During the interval one critic expressed his delight at the subtle stroke of interpretation whereby the same actor played the Player Queen and the Second Gravedigger, and I had not the heart to tell him that the reason for this was not theatrical invention but economic necessity. Some of the older Russian actors were shocked at the speed with which the verse was spoken. 'Cinema technique!' moaned one. 'Is Shakespeare not allowed to draw breath in Britain?' The admiring comments made by many people on the relative cheapness of the production must, I imagine, have fallen rather brutally on the ears of the producer, Hugh Beaumont, for it was one of the most costly shows he had ever backed. Physically, the acting looked wooden and inexpressive beside the rich mobility of Russian players; but if the audience thought so, it kept its counsel, and the applause at the end was long and stormy.

Russian directors have of course made *Hamlet* very much their own property. To Akimov in 1932 he was a revolutionary who staged a fake ghost in order to overthrow the tyrant Claudius; and in the spring of 1955 Nikolai Okhlopkov, with a cast of a hundred and eighty and a full orchestra booming Tchaikovsky, directed a Hamlet who represented Renaissance Man casting off the fetters of the Middle Ages. Paul Scofield's British Hamlet, by contrast, represented only Paul Scofield, which struck some Russian theorists as a trifle meagre. The director of the Maly Theatre, however, called it 'a three-octave performance', and *Pravda* congratulated the actor on seeing Hamlet as a positive, dynamic hero rather than as a pessimistic weakling. At the British Embassy reception after the first night much else emerged, and I was able to piece together a picture of the Russian attitude towards drama as a whole.

To begin with, our notion of an opening night as a nerve-racked occasion on which everything depends is quite inexplicable to a Russian. In Moscow plays are rehearsed for many months with at least two separate casts; and the critics are expected to see the new production several times before reviewing it, which gives them time to ponder the relative contributions of author, actors, and director. Bad notices never mean unemployment; if the new show fails to draw, it is dropped, and that is that; the repertoire rolls on unhindered. I made the childish error of asking an actor to name the star of his company, and my interpreter gently signified to me that the concept of a 'star' was something his language was barely capable of rendering. Outside Russian theatres the names of the plays are billed, but never the names of the actors. Against each important character the programme usually lists two or three names, with a pencilled tick beside the one who will be playing it at that particular performance.

Maturity and consistent excellence are rewarded with the title of Honoured Artist of the Soviet Union, which is as close as Russia gets to the idea of a 'star'. Even so, you will see Honoured Artists playing Lear on Tuesday and a three-line bit part on Wednesday. The great drawing card in Moscow is not the actor but the theatre he works for. Above all, the Embassy reception showed me that the great gulf of sensibility which in London makes it almost impossible for an actor to converse intelligibly with a politician simply did not exist in Moscow. In Russia man is assumed to be a political animal, and the theatre to be a limb of the body politic; and the politician who cannot talk theatre is regarded as culpably myopic.

Yet much less of the theatre than I had expected is politically slanted. The classics are no longer twisted to make debating points; Shaw, Wilde, and Dickens are played with absolute fidelity to the letter and spirit of the text. And nothing could be falser than the Western idea that the Russians treat Chekhov as a satirical farce: he is handled with the solemn respect due to a classic. Propaganda in the Moscow theatre (which is about one tenth of it) seeks primarily to stimulate enthusiasm for hard work. One of our most popular philosophers once remarked regretfully: 'Man is the only animal that works'; in Moscow it would be said triumphantly. Life in the town is Spartan, as befits the training camp of a heavyweight contender; and the basic tenet of all propaganda is that life imitates art. You work because art shows you the pleasures of work, and this is even true of the Children's Theatre, where dashing new plays urge the young to leave home and build community centres in Siberia.

But for some Russian tastes the theatre has grown too hortatory of late. People have been complaining that art ought to imitate life a little more. In the past year, and for the first time since the Revolution, some theatres have been reporting empty seats; and too many bad playwrights, it has been hinted, are getting preferential treatment purely because they toe the party line. In November Mr Mikhailov, the Minister of Culture, called a public meeting to find out what had gone wrong. One speaker recalled the great days when squads of police had to be summoned to control the queues outside the Art Theatre. Now, he added bitterly, you could sometimes get seats by walking in on the day of performance. The case for more imitation of life was strongly pressed, especially by a woman called Engineer Ginsburg, who said: 'We want to see ordinary people on the stage. The villains now are too black, and the heroes are like the dishes in a dietetic restaurant – no salt, no pepper, nothing with a tang to it.' Another speaker reminded the audience that plays critical of the régime were now approved, such as the one in which a commissar's daughter forms a decadent yearning for jeans, jazz, and pony-tail hairdos; but the consensus was that the revolutionary theatre needed more realistic fuel. In a speech a few days later Mr Mikhailov roundly condemned those theatre directors and playwrights who had failed to come through with their quota of new plays, and exhorted them to go out and look at life in the raw.

At present the revolutionary theatre of experiment has almost ceased to exist, except at the little Satirical Theatre. Vakhtangov, Meyerhold, and Tairov are dead; Okhlopkov directs very seldom;

and the only active survivor of the pre-war group is the sixty-four-year-old Alexei Popov, who has been in charge of the Red Army Theatre since 1936. The great Russian theatres today are homes of the solid bourgeois virtues, performing nineteenth-century plays in surroundings of weighty scenic opulence; the Maly, for instance, and the Moscow Art. The joy of seeing master craftsmen working in unison, with the humane poetry and not just the neurotic trimmings of naturalism, is something I had never known until I saw these perdurable players. This is Stanislavsky without Freud, physiological acting without the psychiatric glosses beloved of so many American 'Method' actors; it has subtlety and absolute inevitability, plus what Stark Young once described as 'a magnificent dignity and grave, warm beauty like nature's'. To say that youth is not at the helm of the Russian theatre is an understatement: it is lucky if it is allowed to scrub the decks. The power and the glory of Soviet theatre resides in its older actors, who are by far the finest I have ever seen.

With age they do not wither or grow frail, as our actors often do. They expand in mind and muscle, a formidable parade of which every member resembles Blake's Ancient of Days. There is a simple reason for this continuity of development: economic security. Once an actor has been accepted by a company and proved himself in it, he has no financial worries. Variation of repertoire keeps him from going stale or gaga; he is seldom asked to act more than four times a week, and when he retires the state steps in with a liberal pension. Compare the plight of the old actor in England, ashamed of his age and doubtful whether he can learn his lines in three weeks' rehearsal.

In Moscow age is a badge of merit, and there is time for certainty and for perfection. To see an Ostrovsky play at the Maly is like spending a week-end with old friends. Onto the stage the giants trundle, hawk-eyed spectacular dowagers like Turchaninova, ancient intriguers like Vladislavsky, all playing with a selfless economy and precision that recalls a group of champions at a chess tournament. It is the same at the Moscow Art Theatre; ripe in years, robust as oaks, beaming in their beards and their supreme authority, the masters play together as Stanislavsky taught them and as they can still teach the world. Tonight Konsky, sardonic and lantern-jawed, will delight you in *An Ideal Husband*. The next night in Tolstoy, it is Gribov, as a jaundiced, fish-eyed *moujik*, who sets you cheering; a day later Zhiltsov, with his effortless barrel-chested thunder, will transfix you, or Tarassova, who weeps as readily as most British actresses simper.

Finally, in Gorky's *The Lower Depths*, a dozen new faces will be thrust before you, faces from a Bosch crucifixion, crapulous faces, swollen and condemned. Every step that is taken has beneath it, you feel, a tradition of immortal rock; the characters' roots are sunk deep into the stage. These players tend to sit heavily (I saw a chair break under one of them at the Maly: he instantly turned the mishap to theatrical advantage). They fan themselves, gesture with their eyebrows and fingertips, and never lose the thread of the tapestry they are weaving. Theirs is the greatness that can come only to actors who do not need to worry about how great they are. The surfaces of life, audible and visible, are flawlessly captured: every moment a sudden, eccentric, but obviously *right* gesture catches your eye, yet each fragment fits smoothly into the general mosaic.

If their actors are older than ours, their audiences are younger. Nevertheless, the system has its drawbacks. The old actors tend to cling to the roles of their youth, and surrender them to younger players only under considerable pressure. Mr Mikhailov made this point when he said in a recent speech that the dearth of new Russian plays was partly due to the necessity of writing parts for middle-aged actors. Yet there are other reasons for the thinness of contemporary Soviet drama. One is the cultural iron curtain.

The only American playwrights known in Russia are Howard Fast, Lillian Hellman, and Arthur Miller. The only French author performed is Jean-Paul Sartre. His *Edmund Kean* is already in rehearsal, and *The Respectful Prostitute* was a sensation last winter because it portrayed a tart with something approaching realism. In Paris the play was a virulent one-act squib lasting just over an hour; in Moscow it lasts over three hours, has six settings, and ends with a heroic tableau in which the tart and the Negro, hand in hand, look forward into a new dawn of enlightenment. This was greeted with cheers. My interpreter said, and I agreed with him, that all culture needed a strain of naïveté to survive; but the whole point of the original play was its sophisticated irony. This had been banished at the author's suggestion. It was ruin by consent.

The real reason for the lack of new plays lies in the basis of Communism as a whole. By definition, the U.S.S.R. has abolished nostalgia.

Nobody looks back on the past with regret, which means that there can be no more playwrights like Turgenev and Chekhov, who half-loathed the old way of life yet were half-committed to it. That delicate tension has gone. At the same time the Western sense of humour strikes Russians as gloomy or macabre. I showed a few old *New Yorkers* to a Russian actor, and his comment was that things in the west couldn't be as bad as that. To him the cartoons were either un-intelligible (jokes about advertising, sugar daddies, and commercial TV) or unimaginably cynical. Thurber's humour of quiet desperation only made him sigh with compassion; he could not see why we laughed at anything so close to despair. The comedy of surrealism has no meaning in Moscow. Revolutionary comedy is always moral, which is to say it is never pure comedy but always satire.

The most imaginative production I saw was of a satire, Mayakov-sky's *Klop* (*The Bedbug*), written in 1929. Yutkevich has restaged it at the Satirical Theatre with an ebullient technique compounded of vaudeville, revue, and cartoon film. Its hero is a backsliding worker who reverts to bourgeois habits once the first stage of the revolution is completed and he has money to spend – not, of course, to multiply, for in Russia you cannot make money breed. Deserting his prole-tarian sweetheart, he marries into a family of social climbers, from whom he learns vulgarity, the inevitable by-product of class distinc-tions. The willing oaf is taught to overdress ('But don't wear two ties at once, especially of different colours!') and to dance the tango with his little finger crooked. To symbolize its loyalty to the revolution, the family holds a winter wedding party dressed and lit entirely in shades of red. This develops into a nightmare orgy, rather like a parody of *The Boy Friend* held in a brothel. With the rout at its height, fire breaks out, and the guests perish in a scabrous cartoon sequence, brilliantly filmed; we see their wigs and eyelashes going up in flames and their cosmetic-laden faces melting down like wax dummies. Only the hero survives, frozen in a block of ice as the firemen's hoses play on him. Fifty years later he is discovered and defrosted by a world which, now having reached the final stage of Communism, regards him as an alien monster or zoological specimen. His vodka-tainted breath prostrates all who approach him, and six electric fans whirr to keep the air pure. If he touches a dog, it is at once infected with the plague of servility and will do nothing thereafter but sit up and beg.

In consequence he is placed in a zoo, where his atavistic habits of smoking, gambling, drinking, and singing sentimental songs are watched rather as we in London watch the chimpanzees' tea party.

The comedian playing the 'bedbug' was a fine low comic rather like Bert Lahr, and I relished the production until the hero's jilted fiancée, now an old woman, said: 'And to think I nearly killed myself for filth like that!' Compassion, I suddenly realized, was banished, even for this misguided moon-calf. *Saeva indignatio* was the correct reaction. We were not to pity him, since that would imply some degree of identification and might even lead to our tolerating him. At once my tainted heart was with him in his cage, beside his vodka, his cigarettes, and his ukulele; and it remained there to the end, though my mind acknowledged the impact of a staggeringly clever production. On the way out of the theatre I lit a cigarette, feeling as defiant as if I were peroxiding my hair.

But if pure comedy is rare, pure tragedy is nonexistent. To our mind, the spectacle of a man hounded and suffering, defeated by society or strangled by fate, constitutes tragedy, from which we derive a refinement of our knowledge of the human condition. But in Utopia that kind of tragedy is impossible. Since there is always a way out, no one can ever be trapped. Mr Zubov, the director of the Maly Theatre, put the case to me quite frankly. Domestic tragedy, he said, was still conceivable, though it was fast disappearing; but social tragedy was unthinkable. In Soviet society a man could never be crushed. He quoted Vishnevsky's *An Optimistic Tragedy* as an example of Soviet tragedy in that it had a happy ending. I mentioned *Hamlet*. He smiled.

'Ah,' he said, 'that is a golden page of the past.' He added that in Russia the circumstances necessary to create the anguish of a Hamlet or Lear simply did not exist. 'In our society,' he concluded, 'there may be occasional collisions, but there are no defeats.' That is the attitude, and the theatre reflects it. A generation of actors has thus grown up whose only acquaintance with tragic emotion is restricted to the classics. Another theatre director, going still further, explained to me why Communists regarded individualism, in our eyes the wellspring of tragedy, as a doubtful social virtue. 'You think of artists as crazy individuals,' he said, 'and you do not mind sacrificing a whole generation as long as a few individual rebels turn out a few poems of suffering and despair. We would rather save the generation and do without the poets.'

Our conception of the artist as an individual rebel was, I realized, badly in need of revaluation. If Russia is right, the pressures which produce lyric artists, passionately affirming their own selfhood, are inexorably being removed. Collective art is taking their place, for how can one *épater les bourgeois* when there are no *bourgeois* to *épater*? J. D. Salinger's latest story, 'Raise High the Roofbeam, Carpenters', is a gloriously moving piece of writing about the martyrdom of a saint in a vulgarized society. The saint eventually, and with tremendous pathos, commits suicide. But in Utopia, one asks, what would Mr Salinger write about?

There are many bad plays in Moscow today. Many breasts are beaten, many flags wagged, and many lectures read. But there are no plays that are merely, in Mr Zubov's phrase, 'aids to digestion'. The theatre of mindless farce and meaningless melodrama is unknown. One would like to see a Western theatre organized on Russian lines without Russian ideology; but without some ideology or other the theatres would never be built and the organization never imposed.

I was revolving these things in my mind as my plane rose, bearing me away from the *shashlik* territory, across the *bœuf Stroganoff* belt into the *Schnitzel* country. I landed for a while at Prague – sour word, which rhymes with nothing. At Brussels vulgarity and fecklessness started to flow back into my system. By the time we reached London my moral disintegration was complete; yet I felt an individual once more, a little lost and purposeless perhaps, but still an individual, going to hell in my own way instead of to heaven in somebody else's. I felt specific, and no longer generic.

For this freedom I paid the ultimate price. My first duty on leaving the airport was to attend the first night of a farce about pre-marital sex. It satirized the future (universal television and progressive education) where Russian plays satirize the past. By Russian standards it had scarcely been rehearsed at all, yet it looked over-rehearsed to the point of seeming mechanical. The actors imitated not life but other actors; the sets drew their inspiration not from the world but from other sets. If it was a success the management might, in six months' time, be tempted to gamble some of its profits on a play of moderate intelligence. I thought of Moscow, swallowed my doubts, and decided that ours was just a difference of approach. Just a simple difference of approach.

(1956)

THE CHERRY ORCHARD AND THREE SISTERS

BY ANTON CHEKHOV, AT SADLER'S WELLS, LONDON

The great thing about the Moscow Art Theatre's production of *The Cherry Orchard* is that it blows the cobwebs off the play. And who put them there? Why, we ourselves. We have remade Chekhov's last play in our image just as drastically as the Germans have remade *Hamlet* in theirs. Our *Cherry Orchard* is a pathetic symphony, to be played in a mood of elegy. We invest it with a nostalgia for the past which, though it runs right through our culture, is alien to Chekhov's. His people are country gentry: we make them into decadent aristocrats.

Next, we romanticize them. Their silliness becomes pitiable grotesquerie; and at this point our hearts warm to them. They are not Russians at all: they belong in the great line of English eccentrics. The upstart Lopakhin, who buys up their heritage, cannot be other than a barbarous bounder. Having foisted on Chekhov a collection of patrician mental cases, we then congratulate him on having achieved honorary English citizenship. Meanwhile the calm, genial sanity of the play has flown out of the window. In M. Stanitsyn's production it is magnificently restored. Common-sense is not a quality we like to attribute to our artists; we prefer them slightly deranged; but Chekhov had it in full measure, and so have his present, peerless interpreters. Did I say this was Chekhov without the cobwebs? It is more: it is a total spring-cleaning.

Part of its freshness comes from the fact that it is a brand-new production, with new décor and several newly graduated players: on this tour the Art Theatre is clearly experimenting with youth. But there is more to it than that. The real novelty lies in its attitude towards Mme Ranevsky's feckless household. This is not the old régime, crazily expiring with a pathetic jest on its lips. It is a real family, capricious perhaps and irresponsible, but essentially normal and un-doomed. The play becomes what Chekhov called it: a comedy. 'In places, even a farce,' he added, but M. Stanitsyn does not go as far as that. He simply treats the characters as recognizable human beings in a mess, rather than as freaks trapped in a tragic *impasse*.

M. Massalsky's Gayev, for example, is no crumbling dodderer but the man of 'suavity and elegance' whom Chekhov imagined: the decay is internal and moral. Nor is there anything of the neurotic spinster in Mlle Lennikova's Varya: she is a practical, good-hearted girl who blushes too much to be easily marriageable; and her collapse, when Lopakhin lets her down, is the more moving for its lack of neurotic preparation. Lopakhin himself behaves, as Chekhov de-manded, 'with the utmost courtesy and decorum': no thrusting vul-garity here, but a mature impatience which rises, in the third-act announcement that he is the master now, to an astonishing climax of dismayed exasperation. The actor, M. Lukyanov, plays like a master throughout.

One crucial test remains: what does the production invite us to make of Trofimov, the eternal student with his vision of a transformed Russia? The English habit is to present him as a hare-brained booby whom no one could possibly take seriously. Yet the Czarist censor took him seriously enough to expunge several of his more critical speeches. M. Gubanov's performance is delicately right: a bundle of nerves, forever fingering his spectacles, and a fumbler in matters of emotion, but intelligent and sincere withal – a true misfit, but also a true prophet. This is straight Chekhov, not propagandist distortion. It is we who, by turning the other members of Ranevsky's household into caricatures of high-born futility, have infected the text with un-necessary social significance.

There are many more actors to salute – it is in the nature of this glowing troupe that it bats all the way down the list. I think of M. Leonidov's Yasha, more cad's cad than gent's gent, embracing the maid Dunyasha and blowing cigar-smoke into her eyes as she smiles at him. Of M. Yanshin's earth-larding Pischchik, frantically feeling for his purse after the conjuring tricks have been played. Of M. Kornukov's plump Epikhodov, pocketing an apple to make up for his rejection by Dunyasha. And I have not yet mentioned Alexis Gribov, one of the great actors of the world, who plays the tiny part of Firs, the ancient butler – fixed like a statue, in jaundiced petrifaction, and held upright only by handy walking-sticks or tables. Are there no weaknesses? For me, yes: I thought Mme Tarassova inexpressive and unmoving. This is not a failure of conception; Chekhov expressly forbade the romantic agonies which most actresses bring to Mme Ranevsky. It is a failure of execution. The actress is simply monotonous.

Peter Ustinov contends that team-work and Chekhov are, in acting terms, incompatible. The characters, he maintains, are all soloists who occasionally interrupt each other's monologues but never listen to what anyone else is saying. They are deaf and blind to the world outside them – which is why they are funny and also why they are appalling. Fair comment, and in *Three Sisters*, a much more complex work than *The Cherry Orchard*, this technique is carried as far as it can go without blowing the play centrifugally apart. The very theme is estrangement: a brief brushing of lips is as close as anyone ever gets to another's soul. Of the three girls yearning for Moscow, Olga will never marry, Masha has married badly, and Irina is cheated of marriage by a tragic duel. Their brother, Andrey, is yoked to a prolific and faithless shrew. Two nihilists look on: one active – the savage Solyony, who scents his hands because, like Lear's, they smell of mortality – and the other passive: Chebutikin, the doctor, jilted by the girls' mother and now drunk past caring. And so all sit, mourning and mumbling, making out of their inconsequence a choral lament on human isolation.

The Moscow production, based on the original staging by Nemirovich-Danchenko, gets all of this and infuses it with that strange dynamic apathy that is Chekhov's greatest demand on his actors. The sisters themselves are new to the roles and as yet unsettled in them: Mlle Yurieva's Masha comes nearest to the wry fatalism we are looking for. Her Vershinin, M. Massalsky, is unduly restrained, tarred with the pomade of the *matinée* idol; but the elder parts are filled to overflowing with beard and rasp and detail. M. Gribov's Chebutikin, in particular, is all I had heard of it; encrusted with corruption, a ponderous fish-eyed shrug of a man, he is yet capable, while remembering his dead love, of a sudden and transfixing pathos. The last act is, I suppose, the high-water mark of twentieth-century drama, yet this superb company meets its challenge as if opening the door to an old friend. The sound-effects and lighting are brilliant throughout: we weep, apart from anything else, for a lost world so lovingly revived. How these actors eat; and listen; and fail to listen; and grunt and exist, roundly and egocentrically exist! They have become, with long rehearsal, the people they are playing: they do not need, as our actors do, to depend on the lines alone for their characterization. We act with our voices, they with their lives. Where we leave off, they begin. Don't be deterred by the language barrier. This is not verbal acting, like ours, but total acting: Stanislavsky often made his players rehearse without words, to be sure that their faces and bodies were performing as well. Read the play before going, and you will be safe. Safe, and enriched.

By a shaming coincidence, our theatre last week offered what should have been its best: Edith Evans, John Gielgud, and Harry Andrews in *Henry VIII* at the Old Vic. This sprawling chronicle has four good scenes: Buckingham's downfall and Wolsey's, and Katharine's trial and death. The rest slumps without galvanic direction, which here it doesn't get. The style is ceremonial and listless, bogged down by leaden costumes and drab settings. The end of an era, I thought during the first act, when Dame Edith and Mr Andrews, ludicrously under-rehearsed, were groping for lines like children playing at blind-man's-buff. And though Sir John made good use of his poker back and door-knob face, he never for a moment suggested Wolsey the self-made 'butcher's cur': all was rigid declamation, issuing from a tense and meagre tenor.

Certes, he wept: which is to say, he moved himself. Dame Edith, by contrast, moved me. Her death scene lifted her to those serene, unassertive heights where at her best she has no rivals. The quiet, large face, with its prehensile upper lip, shifted and quaked according to the dictates of the character, an unabashed queen in great extremity. Dame Edith ignored the 'verbal music', and thereby made a truer music, having to do with the experience of dying. Alone in the company at what foreigners are wrongly encouraged to regard as our national theatre, she could have wandered on to the stage at Sadler's Wells and seemed at home.

(*1958*)

UNCLE VANYA

BY ANTON CHEKHOV

THE TROUBLED PAST

BY RAKHMANOV, AT SADLER'S WELLS, LONDON

In *Uncle Vanya* Chekhov created one of the most improbable and least playable heroes in dramatic literature. Everything about him is either negative or ridiculous. Vanya has wasted his life running the estate for his brother-in-law, a transparent old fraud whom he once mistook for a literary genius. His fumbling advances to the dotard's second wife have been wearily repelled. His status in the household is that of a tolerated clown. About all of this he grumbles incessantly, yet does nothing; nothing, that is, until the ancient locust proposes to sell the estate from under him: whereat we plunge into the farce of his botched suicide attempt and the pot-shot that fails even to wing his intended victim. Self-pitying in repose, ineffectual in action, how can we take him seriously? Yet if we don't, the play collapses. I expected the Moscow Art Theatre to have solved the problem, but I could never have guessed how. M. Orlov and his director, M. Kedrov, have found in Vanya a wholly unsuspected quality: dignity.

On the surface this Vanya is a man of weight and substance. His aspect is grave, and his beard, though a lightish brown, is none the less a serious beard. The tie gives us our first hint of weakness – it is somehow too fussy – and his voice, when he addresses his mother, gets a little too petulant for comfort. Yet the external man is robustly mature. Only in flashes do we glimpse the man within, an adolescent who can neither be his age nor live up to his looks. It is a lightweight who peers out through the pale eyes of the heavyweight face. He knows he has squandered his life on an old humbug; knows he has lost the power to live for himself; yet always he keeps up appearances. Dignity never deserts him. He clings to it even in the shooting spree, which becomes in its mad way a matter of honour, an assertion of principle rather than a display of temperament; and in tenacity like this there is a kind of heroism. M. Orlov's clumsy nobility puts us in mind, as it should, of Don Quixote. This Vanya always looks capable of tragedy: his tragedy is that he is capable only of comedy.

Around this superb performance a constellated production revolves. M. Khtorov misses nothing of Serebryakov, a literary lion in the last stages of mange; and instead of the glittering *mondaine* our actresses like to make of Elena (or any other part, given half a chance), Mlle Anastasieva gives us both a credible wife for the old beast and a woman to whom Vanya and Astrov can be drawn without looking too much like doomed moths. The Astrov himself (M. Gubanov, so good as Trofimov in *The Cherry Orchard*) is a failure, partly because the actor is too young and partly because he falls too readily into that vein of stolid, sententious rhetoric which tempts even the best Russian players from time to time. Of course Astrov sees through the phoneys around him, and of course he has visions of a revived Russia: but he is also a self-disgusted cynic and a hard drinker, and of these M. Gubanov shows us nothing. Against this signal disappointment I can set Mlle Lennikova's shining Sonya and the Telyegin, plump and wheezing, of M. Yanshin, whose performance as Mr Pickwick must be as perfect as Moscow says it is.

But the true stars of the show, M. Orlov apart, are the second-act storm and the dawn that succeeds it. This is a storm with a personality of its own; a special, authentic, Stanislavsky-trained storm, not just a shaking of thundersheets and a dribble of peas in a drum. It begins far off, with a premonitory rumble and a hiss of light rain. The curtains faintly billow. Then, with a catarrhal explosion that makes the theatre throb, it is upon us: the curtains flare like flags, and the rain pelts down, so savagely that we can hear it splashing off the porch into its own puddles. Capriciously, it subsides, and as capriciously resumes, without for an instant distracting our attention from the actors. It is followed by the gaunt electric blue of dawn, which seeps across the room from the drenched garden and finally, when the first spikes of sunlight reinforce it, persuades even Chekhov's night-long talkers to go to bed. Technicians, as much as actors, make up the magic of the M.A.T. ensemble: and my main complaint about the production is that, by setting the first act indoors instead of out, it cheated us of seeing and hearing what these unseen *virtuosi* could make of a garden at sunset.

It is by their last acts that most of us will remember this Chekhov cycle: all three plays end with protracted and desolate leave-takings.

The fourth production, Rakhmanov's *The Troubled Past*, also ends on a farewell, but this time the mood is triumphant: the revolutionary army of 1918 is marching off to repulse the invading capitalist hordes. This pedestrian play, written in 1935, celebrates the decision of the eminent Russian naturalist Timiryazev to throw in his lot with the rebels. The old man's instinctive faith is contrasted with the qualms of his assistant, who thinks the intelligentsia should stay aloof; but 'intelligentsia', says the professor, is a 'bragging, boastful word', since it implies a separation of the intellectual from the worker to whom he must be allied if social progress is to be made.

The conclusion is unexceptionable: what is dismaying is the absence of argument that precedes it. Nobody challenges the professor's points, everything is taken as read, and the dialectic passion that lights up the best propaganda plays is totally lacking. The piece is frankly designed to remind students and *savants* of their duty to support the régime: and the congratulatory phone-call from Lenin which the hero receives at the end is a clear promise of official laurels for all who heed the message. I see no reason why a Soviet company should not bring over a play with a Soviet emphasis, but I wish they could have picked a better one. Needless to say, the M.A.T. humanizes the text magnificently: M. Koltsov's professor is a sharp, querulous creature of eccentric impulse, and Mme Androvskaya positively embraces the role of his aghast, admiring wife – this is the couple out of Angus Wilson's *The Mulberry Bush*, long before they became darling dodos.

People who wonder exactly what this company stands for should note that two of the tiniest crowd-parts in *The Troubled Past* are played by Mlle Maximova and M. Gubanov, both of whom play leads in the Chekhovs. It is also worth remembering that, while the touring troupe is appearing in London, the M.A.T. is keeping two Moscow theatres open with a full repertory of plays. Theatre on this scale is something we in England have not even begun to contemplate. I wish the M.A.T. had brought us their version of Dickens or their resplendent production of Wilde's *Ideal Husband*, both of which were suggested by Moscow but rejected by the host-impresario, Peter Daubeny: an error, I feel sure, for the comparisons would have been instructive. But I am niggling. We have entered an Aladdin's cave of acting to which, without Mr Daubeny, we would never have had access at all. I feel pelted with pearls.

(*1958*)

Portraits

VISIT TO THE PAST

I went to see Gordon Craig partly because he is among the last of
the great Edwardians and partly because a blue-haired and brilliant
American authoress had spent several hours exhorting me with considerable violence to meet the ageing giants of art while yet they lived.
'Don't just read their books,' she had said. 'That's like just eating the
meat of the lobster. Be a gourmet; go to the head and suck the brains.
There's tasty chewing there!' Spurred by this daunting advice, I drove
up from Nice one Sunday this midsummer to talk to a man who was
born in the same year as Aubrey Beardsley.

Although he is eighty-four years old and has published little for a
quarter of a century, Gordon Craig is still several lengths ahead of the
theatrical *avant-garde*. Ideas that he expounded fifty years ago, in his
breathless prophetic prose, are nowadays bearing fruit all over Europe.
He anticipated Bert Brecht when he said of actors: 'Today they
impersonate and interpret; tomorrow they must *represent* and interpret. . . .' His notion that true drama was a one-man responsibility,
in which words, direction, décor, lighting, and music should all proceed from the same organizing brain, once seemed a fatuous vanity;
yet last year Peter Brook, directing *Titus Andronicus*, undertook all
these tasks save that of writing the play. Nor would Craig hold this
omission against him, since he regards the hegemony of the writer as
the supreme tragedy of theatrical history: literary men, he says, are
intruders, despoilers of the purity of theatre as a separate art. Dismissed as a crank, he none the less brought modern staging to birth
with his productions, a memorable few which include *Hamlet* at the
Moscow Art Theatre and Eleanora Duse in *Rosmersholm*. If today we
call 'stage-managers' directors and 'scene-painters' designers, it is
largely Craig's doing.

He last saw England in 1929, when C. B. Cochran invited him to
take on a new production of his own choice. There was a dispute over
expenditure, after which Craig left the country in a permanent huff.
He lived in France until the Nazis arrived and shut him up in an intern-

ment camp. A few months later a German intelligence officer, asking for one of his books at a Paris store, learned from the assistant that its author was imprisoned; shocked, he contrived to have Craig released. For the rest of the war the old theorist worked unmolested in his Paris studio. He now occupies a single cluttered room in a modest *pension de famille* at Vence, high in the hills that overlook Nice. Here, last spring, he learned that a tardily grateful nation had created him a Companion of Honour. He was flattered, but at the same time embarrassed, because he could not afford to come to London and be royally congratulated. His only regular income derives from investments made by his mother, Ellen Terry. It amounts to just over £6 a week.

I arrived in fear of finding a testy sage steeped in pathos and embittered by neglect. As soon as the car drew up in front of the *pension* I knew my error. The figure that greeted me was surely bowed and slightly crumpled, but what it exuded was neither pathos nor rancour, but mischief. You might have taken him for the oldest truant schoolboy alive – or, more extravagantly, for an indomitable old lady who had just, by some constitutional fantasy, been elected President of the French Republic. He wore a snuff tweed suit with six pens clipped to the breast pocket, a neat cream stock around his neck, a shawl-like garment draped across his shoulders, and a broad-brimmed hat on top of wild white curls.

He clambered into the car, crowing with conspiratorial glee, and told the driver to take us down to a nearby inn for lunch. '*Prenez garde!*' he cried as we moved off. 'Bad corner! Hoot, hoot!' Grinning wickedly and waving his mottled, curry-coloured hands, he began to talk in a voice of such vagrant music that I found myself listening as much to its cadences as to its meaning. He peeped at me from time to time across a nose as sharp as a quill. I was already reassured. There was no bitterness here: only resilience, magnanimity, and a great appetite for joy.

'You have the right face for a critic,' he said as we disembarked. 'You have the look of a blooming martyr.' Having ordered the meal in genial and execrable French, he opened the briefcase he was carrying: it contained two razor-edged knives, in case the management had been slack in sharpening its cutlery. We were talking vaguely about Edward Lear when Craig whisked me back eighty years in a single sentence. 'One day,' he said, 'when I was very small, that man Charles Dodgson came to tea. Tried to divert me with a puzzle about ferrying six cows across a river on a raft. Very tiresome . . .'

Trowelling sauce-drenched food ('I hate a dry plate') into his mouth, the almost toothless lion avidly reminisced. Irving was the greatest director he had ever known, and as an actor: 'We've had no one so *dangerously* good.' The Terrys, he said, were always a slapdash sort of family: the Irvings were precision instruments. Granville Barker was 'a small man among giants' – this in a whisper, as if Barker himself might spectrally be eavesdropping on the conversation. 'Rather an affected man,' said Craig, securely merry and patriarchal.

Far from being pent up in the past, Craig keeps in touch with every new development in theatre, cinema, and even television. He was soon urging me to see the new French underwater documentary, *Le Monde du Silence*: 'It's like nothing you've ever dreamed of. Or, rather, it's like *everything* you've ever dreamed of.' He showed a keen interest in 'this fellow Orson Well-ess', of whose films he had heard much. 'I'll tell you a thing about Well-ess,' he said. 'A Paris paper published an interview with him, in which he said that one day he was standing in the American Express in Paris when the door *flew* open to reveal a cloaked figure in a funny hat. *Me!* He threw himself to the ground in veneration. I gathered him up and took him to my studio and spent six months teaching him the art of the theatre.' Craig was now shaking with glee. 'Magnificent, isn't it? *Because I've never met the fellow in my life!*' He nudged me and we rocked.

After lunch he conducted me on foot round the baked medieval village of Tourrette, leading the way in his rangy shuffle and talking of his memoirs, extracts from which are to be published in the autumn under the title *Index to the Story of My Days*. He spoke glowingly of Picasso ('Those eyes!' he said, stabbing two fingers at me like prongs), and gaily of his own poverty: 'I'm as poor as a fish!'

He has a collection of theatrical souvenirs – books, prints, letters, and designs – which is worth around £20,000. So far he has rejected all offers for it, mostly because he suspects the buyers of planning to break up the collection and resell it piecemeal. 'A few years ago,' he confided, 'an American made a handsome bid. But I knew as soon as we started to talk business that he wasn't quite the man. He said to me: "Please sit down, Mr Craig." And I said: "It's *my* room – *you* sit down!" Not quite the fellow, you see. . . .' I reflected that it would be a generous thing if the Arts Council were to purchase his treasures; and the sooner the better. 'I count my life in days now, not in years or months or even weeks.'

Back in the *pension*, he led me up to the dark little room where he sleeps and works. Masks of his own carving hung on the walls (there is more than a touch in him of William Morris); day-books and journals were piled on the floors; implements for painting and writing littered the tables. On a shelf beside the brass bedstead stood a cork into which was stuck a photograph of a composed and smiling beauty: 'My mother,' said Craig. He talked, as he pottered, of his plans for the future. He is making a collection of English farces of the last century; 'and', he said, 'I'm beginning to solve the problem of staging the cauldron scene in *Macbeth*. I'm not certain yet, mind you, but it's getting clearer. It's getting clearer every day. . . .' Suddenly: 'Did you ever think that Shakespeare had a cat? Look at the sonnets. Most of them aren't written to a woman or a boy. They're addressed to a *cat*.'

But there was one thing he specially wanted to show me, and he flipped through his scrapbooks to find it. He raced past priceless letters from Irving and Stanislavsky until: 'There!' he said. Following his finger, I stared at an advertisement, cut out of an American magazine, for stainless steel. 'Stainless steel!' he cried. 'There's something serious there!' I pictured towering settings of steel taking shape in that restless, hungry mind. From one of his journals, volume after volume of fastidious, spidery script, there floated to the floor a newspaper cutting. I picked it up. Its headline ran: '£105 m. for New Schools.' In the margin was an annotation in Craig's hand: 'Why not educate by the stage?' Seeing that I had read it, he laughed joyously. 'We only need five millions for our theatre,' he said, 'but they'll never let us have it. Never.'

I took my leave, exhausted, though he was not. He explained that he had much to do: there were some new ideas about *The Tempest* that needed his attention. As I drove away, he waved, winked, and loped back to his den. The theatre is not yet ripe for Gordon Craig. Perhaps, indeed, it will never be. But meanwhile, at Vence, work is still in progress. When the theatrical millennium arrives, he will be its first harbinger and surest witness.

(1956)

A TRIBUTE TO MR COWARD

To be famous young and to make fame last – the secret of combining the two is glandular: it depends on energy. Someone once asked Demosthenes what was the most important quality in an orator. 'Action,' he said. And the second? 'Action.' And the third? 'Action.' So with a talent.

Noël Coward, who was performing in public at ten, has never stopped being in action; at fifty-three he retains all the heady zest of adolescence. Forty years ago he was Slightly in *Peter Pan*, and you might say that he has been wholly in *Peter Pan* ever since. No private considerations have been allowed to deflect the drive of his career; like Gielgud and Rattigan, like the late Ivor Novello, he is a congenital bachelor. He began, like many other satirists (Evelyn Waugh, for instance), by rebelling against conformity, and ended up making his peace with it, even becoming its outspoken advocate.

Any child with a spark of fantasy in its soul is prone to react against the English middle classes, into which Coward was born. The circumstances of his early upbringing, in Teddington, were 'liable', he wrote afterwards, 'to degenerate into refined gentility unless carefully watched'. He promptly reacted against them, and also against his first school-teacher, whom he bit in the arm – 'an action which I have never for an instant regretted'. From this orgy of rebellion he excepted his mother, a tiny octogenarian who is now comfortably installed in a flat in Eaton Square. With the production of *The Vortex*, in 1924, notoriety hit him. He had already written two other plays and most of a revue, meanwhile announcing that his own wit and Ivor Novello's profile were the first and second wonders of the modern world.

The Vortex, a jeremiad against narcotics with dialogue that sounds today not so much stilted as high-heeled, was described by Beverley Nichols as 'immortal'. Others, whom it shocked, were encouraged in their heresy by an unfortunate photograph for which Coward posed supine on a knobbly brass bedstead, wearing a dressing-gown and 'looking', as he said, 'like a heavily-doped Chinese illusionist'. From this sprang the myth that he wrote all his plays in an absinthe-drenched coma; in fact, as he has been patiently explaining for nearly thirty years, he drinks little and usually starts punishing his typewriter at seven a.m. His triumph has been to unite two things ever dissociated in the English mind: hard work and wit. Toil is commonly the chum of serious-mindedness; and though, within Coward, a social historian and philosopher are constantly campaigning to be let out, they seldom escape into his work. His wit in print is variable – he has not written a really funny play since *Present Laughter* in 1942 – but in private it is unflagging. It took Coward to describe an American adaptation of *The Cherry Orchard*, set in the deep South, as 'A Month in the Wrong Country'; and many other theatrical *mots* have been fathered on him. We may never know, for example, whether it was he who, after seeing a certain actress as Queen Victoria, left the theatre murmuring: 'I never realized before that Albert married beneath him.'

To see him whole, public and private personalities conjoined, you must see him in cabaret. Just before his first season at the Café de Paris, I noticed him watching his predecessor, whose act was not going too well. I asked him how he was enjoying the performance, and, with a stark, stunned, take-it-or-leave-it stare, he hissed: 'Sauce! Sheer sauce!' A few weeks later he padded down the celebrated stairs himself, halted before the microphone on black-suede-clad feet, and, upraising both hands in a gesture of benediction, set about demonstrating how these things should be done. Baring his teeth as if unveiling some grotesque monument, and cooing like a baritone dove, he gave us 'I'll See You Again' and the other bat's-wing melodies of his youth. Nothing he does on these occasions sounds strained or arid; his tanned, leathery face is still an enthusiast's.

All the time the hands are at their task, affectionately calming your too-kind applause. Amused by his own frolicsomeness, he sways from side to side, waggling a finger if your attention looks like wandering. If it is possible to romp fastidiously, that is what Coward does. He owes little to earlier wits, such as Wilde or Labouchère. Their best things need to be delivered slowly, even lazily. Coward's emerge with the staccato, blind impulsiveness of a machine-gun.

I have heard him accused of having enervated English comedy by making it languid and blasé. The truth, of course, is the opposite: Coward took sophistication out of the refrigerator and set it bubbling on the hob. He doses his sentences with pauses, as you dose epileptics with drugs. To be with him for any length of time is exhausting and invigorating in roughly equal proportions. He is perfectly well aware that he possesses 'star quality', which is the lodestar of his life. In his case, it might be defined as the ability to project, without effort, the outline of a unique personality, which had never existed before him in print or paint.

Even the youngest of us will know, in fifty years' time, exactly what we mean by 'a very Noël Coward sort of person'.

(1953)

PRECIOUS LILLIE

Debrett's Peerage, a thick, comely, and infallible volume, correctly refers to Beatrice Gladys Lillie by her married name, Lady Peel. *Who's Who in the Theatre* is also thick and comely, but it is not quite infallible, and one of the most fallible things about it is its habit, in edition after edition, of describing Miss Lillie as an 'actress'. Technically, I suppose the blunder might be defended, since she has been known to impinge on the legitimate stage; in 1921 she appeared in *Up in Mabel's Room* and eleven years later played the Nurse in Shaw's *Too True to Be Good*. But these were transient whims. To call her an actress first and foremost is rather like calling Winston Churchill a bricklayer who has dabbled in politics. If acting means sinking your own personality into somebody else's, Beatrice Lillie has never acted in her life. There may be some mechanical means of disguising that true and tinny voice, or of suppressing that cockeyed nonchalance; but the means might very well involve the use of masks and gags, and the end would not be worth it. She would never be much good at impersonation. One of her recurrent delusions is that she is a mistress of dialects, but in fact the only one she has really mastered is her own brand of Berkeley Square Canadian; and she can hardly open a door on stage without squaring up to the operation as if she were about to burgle a safe.

To some extent, an actress can be judged by measuring her performance against the character she is meant to be playing; but there is nothing against which to measure Miss Lillie. She is *sui generis*. She resembles nothing that ever was, and to see her is to experience, every time, the simple joy of discovery that might come to an astronomer who observed, one maddened night, a new and disorderly comet shooting backwards across the firmament. But if she is not an actress, no more is she a parodist, as some of her fans insist; she parodies nothing and no one except herself. Nor does she belong in the main stream of North American female comics. Almost without exception, American comediennes get their laughs by pretending to be pop-eyed, man-hunting spinsters. Miss Lillie is as far removed from these as a butterfly is from a guided missile. The miracle is that this non-acting non-satirist has managed to become the most achingly funny woman on earth.

Twentieth-century show business has a small and incomparable élite: the streamlined international entertainers of the twenties and thirties. Noël Coward, Gertrude Lawrence, Maurice Chevalier, Alfred Lunt, and Lynn Fontanne were among the founder-members of this shining and exclusive gang. Miss Lillie is the Commonwealth representative. She was born fifty-eight years ago in Toronto, the second daughter of John Lillie, a volatile Irish schoolmaster who had served in the British Army under Kitchener. The first recorded event in her life was her summary ejection, at the age of eight, from the choir of the local Presbyterian church. It seems she upset the congregation by pulling faces during the hymns. Both her father, who died in 1933, and her mother, who lives in a Thames-side house near London, achieved an early and lasting tolerance of their child's eccentricities. Sensing that she had something to express, but not knowing exactly what it was, they sent her to a man named Harry Rich – of whom nothing else is known – for lessons in gesture. She loathed the lessons, but they stuck, and many of the odder poses in which she nowadays finds herself are directly attributable to Mr Rich.

At fifteen she left school and embarked with her mother and sister for England, with the idea of becoming a child soprano. Her official repertoire included such ballads as 'I Hear You Calling Me' and 'Until', but secretly she and her sister Muriel were rehearsing something a little wilder, entitled 'The Next Horse I Ride On I'm Going to Be Tied On'. This clandestine seed was later to bear lunatic fruit; for the moment, however, it got nowhere.

Her career as a straight singer languished until the summer of 1914, when she was engaged for a week at the Chatham Music Hall on the outskirts of London. Here she sang Irving Berlin's 'When I Lost You', and the audience reaction indicated that she had lost them for good. Without much hope, she attended an audition held by the Anglo-French impresario André Charlot. Idly, she guyed a serious romantic number, smiled wanly, and was about to leave the theatre when Charlot, in a state verging on apoplexy, seized her arm and offered her forty-two dollars a week to appear in his next revue, *Not Likely!* She accepted, and soon the panic was on. Charlot adored and fostered the madness of her method, constantly giving her bigger spots, and it was under his banner that she made her triumphant Broadway debut in *Charlot's Revue of 1924*.

Around this time she had her hair cut off, for reasons that may give some hint of the devious way her mind works. With Michael Arlen, H. G. Wells, Frederick Lonsdale, and Lonsdale's two daughters, she was cruising on Lord Beaverbrook's yacht. The Lonsdale girls were close-cropped, and Miss Lillie, who favoured plaits, was powerfully impressed by the advantages of short hair for swimming. Back in London she ordered her coiffeur to give her what would now be known as a brush cut. Only when he had finished did it occur to her that there was more to life than swimming. For a while she wore false plaits attached to her ears by rubber bands. One day the elastic snapped, and she has remained, ever since, cropped for immersion. Nowadays she hides her hair beneath a bright pink fez. There is no good reason for this, either. It is just one *idée fixe* on top of another.

Meanwhile, she had fallen in love. In 1920 Robert Peel, a young and toweringly handsome great-grandson of Sir Robert Peel, resigned his commission in the Guards and married Charlot's zany soubrette. They spent a raffish honeymoon at Monte Carlo, winning $25,000 at the tables a few hours after arriving and losing $30,000 a few hours before departing. In 1925 Robert's father, the fourth baronet, died, and Miss Lillie became Lady Peel. Her husband, a man of devouring energies, was at various times a sheep farmer in Australia and a race-horse owner in England. During the slump he generously formed an orchestra of unemployed miners and toured the country with it, often losing as much as £500 a week. He died in 1934, leaving one son. Eight years later the young Sir Robert, who had just passed his twenty-first birthday, was killed when the British destroyer *Hermes* was sunk by Japanese dive-bombers in the Indian Ocean. His mother received the news in a Manchester dressing-room, where she was putting on make-up to appear in a new Cochran revue. It is one of the paradoxes of the theatre that though every actor's ambition is to stop the show, his instructions are that it must go on. The revue went on that night with Miss Lillie clowning on schedule and wishing herself ten thousand miles away. Thereafter an inner withdrawal took place; since her son's death she has entered into no binding personal relationships with anyone.

In forty years on the stage she has been seen in nearly forty shows, many of them bearing prankish, exclamatory titles like *Cheep!* and *Oh! Joy!* and most of them remembered chiefly for her part in them. Apart from the war years, when she sang for the troops in the Mediterranean area, she has seldom been far away from the big money. The movies have intermittently attracted her, but, like Coward and the Lunts, she has never thought of depending on them for a living. Pre-war residents of Hollywood remember her vividly, swinging an enormous handbag within which there rattled a motley haul of jewellery known as 'The Peel Poils'. For a talent so deeply spontaneous, the stage was always the best place. In New York, just before the war, she was paid $8,000 for a week at the Palace, and today one imagines even Las Vegas baulking at her cabaret fee.

Her title sits drolly on her, like a tiara on an emu, and for a certain kind of audience there is an irresistible savour in the spectacle of a baronet's wife shuffling off to Buffalo. There have, however, been moments of embarrassment. In 1936, billed as Lady Peel, Miss Lillie appeared in an Ohio city and rashly chose as her opening number a travesty of a suburban snob. 'Ladies and gentlemen,' she began, 'I'm sure you will appreciate what a comedown this is for me – me that's always 'ad me own 'orses. . . .' Few acts can have fallen flatter. Many women in the house began to sniff audibly, and at the end of the monologue, according to Miss Lillie, some attempt was made to take a collection to sustain her in her fight against poverty.

Offstage she leads a fairly intense social life, and has arguably slept through more hours of daylight than of dark. Her conversation is an unpunctuated flow of irrelevancies which only acute ears can render into sense. As a maker of epigrams her rating is low. It is rumoured that she once said of a tactless friend that 'he doesn't know the difference between tongue-in-cheek and foot-in-mouth', but remarks like that need a degree of premeditation to which she is a stranger. She excels at the casual impromptu, as when a pigeon flew in at the window of her apartment and she, looking up, briskly inquired: 'Any messages?' To surprise her friends, she will go to considerable lengths. Her last Christmas present to Noël Coward was a baby alligator, to whose neck she attached a label reading: 'So what else is new?' Last year she stood for several hours on a draughty street corner in Liverpool in order to wave maniacally at the Duke of Edinburgh as he drove by with the Queen. She received from the carriage a royal double-take, which she regarded as ample compensation. At parties, with a little pressing, she will try out her newest hallucinations, nursery rhymes villainously revamped or bizarre attempts at mimicry; I once saw her spread-eagled on top of an upright piano, pretending to be Marilyn Monroe.

Some of her leisure time is spent painting, a difficult art for which she has evolved impossible working habits. 'I do children's heads out of my nut,' she told an interviewer. 'I paint on the floor and show my work on the piano in the dark. I call myself Beatrice Van Gone.' She habitually uses as canvases the cardboard lids of laundry boxes. One of her sitters was the child actor Brandon de Wilde. He is also one of her closest confidants. Whenever Miss Lillie is in New York, she calls up Brandon and the two journey to Coney Island, where they frequently end up in the Tunnel of Love. A radio commentator once asked Brandon what Miss Lillie did in the tunnel. 'It's very dark in there,' the child explained, as to a child, 'so naturally she doesn't do anything.' De Wilde's ingenuous imagination appeals strongly to Miss Lillie, who has a great deal of urchin in her and very little *grande dame*. She also has the kind of knockdown spontaneity that one associates with Zen masters, together with something much more mysterious – that ambiguous, asexual look that so often recurs among the greatest performers.

Her last show, *An Evening with Beatrice Lillie*, took three quarters of a million dollars at the Broadway box office three seasons ago, and then ran for eight successful months in Britain. It enshrined her art in what seems likely to be its final form. The rebuke to Maud for her rottenness, the lament about wind round my heart – they were all there, presented with a relaxed finesse that astonished even her oldest eulogists. She looked like Peter Pan as Saul Steinberg might sketch him, and the only phrase for her face was one that a French critic used many years ago to describe Réjane – '*une petite frimousse éveillée*', which means, in James Agate's rough translation, 'a wide-awake little mug'. A supreme economy distinguished all she did. By twirling four Oriental fingers, she could imply a whole handspring, and instead of underlining her gags in red pencil she could bring down the house with a marginal tick. For any line that struck her as touching on the sentimental she would provide a withering facial comment, as if to say (the expression is one of her pets): 'Get *me*!' She would survey the audience with wintry amazement, until it began to wonder why it had come; she would then overwhelm it with some monstrous act of madness, such as wearing an osprey feather fan as a hat, banging her head against the proscenium arch, or impersonating Pavlova and a roller-skating bear, one after the other, in a sketch bearing no relation either to ballet or zoology.

Once, in an effort at self-analysis, she said: 'I guess it's my nose that makes them laugh,' but the explanation is as perfunctory as the nose. One thing is certain: she wrecks the old theory that all great clowns have a breaking heart. Miss Lillie has no more pathos than Ohrbach's basement. Nothing on stage seems to her tragic, though many things arouse in her a sort of cool curiosity. If a ton of scenery were to fall at her feet, she would regard the débris with interest, but not with dismay; after a light shrug and a piercing little smile, she would go on with whatever she was doing. (In wartime this insouciance was a rare asset. Quentin Reynolds, who was often her companion during the blitz, testifies that in the midst of the bombing her demeanour was positively sunny.) She reminds one of a bony, tomboyish little girl attending what, if her behaviour does not improve, will surely be her last party. Her attitude towards events, if she has one, might be summed up in the comment: 'Hmmmm . . .'

I have two theories about her: one about what she does, and another about the way she does it. What she has been doing for the last forty years is conducting guerrilla warfare against words as a means of communication. Having no message to convey, she has no need of language as most of us understand it, so she either abandons words altogether or presents them in combinations aberrant enough to crack a ouija board. Faced with the drab possibility of consecutive thought, she draws herself up to her full lunacy. She will do anything to avoid making sense – lapse into a clog dance, trap her foot under an arm-chair, or wordlessly subside beneath the weight of a mink coat.

Mime attracts her as an alternative to words. This imperial urchin can let winsome candour, beady-eyed tartness, and appalled confu-sion chase each other across her face in a matter of seconds. Consider the frosty, appraising regard she bestows on the waistcoat of the huge baritone who suddenly interrupts her act to sing 'Come into the Garden, Maud' straight down her throat. Though she takes an early opportunity to seize a chair in self-defence, she betrays none of her apprehension in words.

The traditional comic formula is: Tell them what you're going to do; do it; then tell them you've done it. Miss Lillie's is: Tell them what you might do; do something else; then deny having done it. Even the famous purchase of the double-damask dinner napkins embodies her basic theme: the utter futility of the English language. Nobody is a more devout anthologist of the whimpers, sighs, and twitters that the human race emits in its historic struggle against intelligibility. It is not surprising that she turns to French when delivering her demented salute to the home life of cats: '*Bonjour*, all the little kittens all over the world!' When someone in another number fails to understand a question, she tries German, brusquely demanding: '*Sprechen Sie Deutsch?*' And once, into a Cockney sketch already obscured by her inability to speak Cockney, she inserted a sudden moan of Italian. If ever a monument is erected to her, it should be modelled on the Tower of Babel. She is like Eliza Doolittle at Mrs Higgins's tea party in *Pygmalion*, using what seems to her perfectly acceptable verbal coinage but to everyone else counterfeit gibberish. In certain moods she becomes quite convinced that she is an authority on bird talk. Coward once wrote for her a comic folk song that contained the line: 'And the robin sings ho! on the bough.' Every time she reached it she would pause. 'The robin,' she would firmly declare, 'does *not* say ho.'

In 1954, on a trip to Japan, she visited the Kabuki Theatre and was fascinated by what she saw: the colour, the weirdness, and the elabo-rate stylization. The idea of using Kabuki technique in a sketch at once took hold of her mind, and she was not in the least perturbed when someone pointed out that British audiences (for whom the sketch was intended) might be slightly befuddled by a parody of something they had never seen. Following instinct, she devised a number called 'Kabuki Lil'. When it was still in the formative stage, by which I mean a condition of nightmarish inconsequence, she described it to me:

'These Kabuki plays, you see, they go on for six months with only one intermission. All the women are men, *of course*, and they're simply furious most of the time, waving swords round their heads and *hissing* at each other. They take off their boots when they come on, and kneel down on cushions. There's a lot of work done with cushions, so I shall have cushions too. And they play some kind of musical instrument that goes right round the back of my neck, only one string, but I expect I shall manage. I don't think I shall say a word of English – after all, *they* don't – but I wish I could get hold of one of those terrific rostrums they have in Tokyo that sail right down the aisle and out of the theatre. I think they have rollers underneath them, or perhaps it's men? Anyway, I think I've got the spirit of the thing. . . .'

Something was dimly taking shape in the chaos of her mind, but what emerged on stage was beyond all imagining. It varied notably from night to night, but the general layout remained the same. Miss Lillie shuffled on attired as a geisha, with a knitting needle through her wig and a papoose strapped to her back. After performing some cryptic act of obeisance, she sat cross-legged on a pile of cushions. Thereafter, for about ten minutes, she mewed like an asthmatic seagull: the sketch contained not one recognizable word. Tea was served at one point, and the star produced from her sleeve a tiny bottle of Gordon's gin with which to spike it. From time to time she would grasp a hammer and savagely bang a gong, whereupon music would sound, jittery and Oriental. This seemed to placate her; until the sixth bang, which evoked from the wings a sudden, deafeningly amplified blast of 'Three Coins in the Fountain', sung by Frank Sinatra.

It was while watching this sketch, so pointless, yet so hysterical, that I hit on the clue to her method. I reveal it without hesitation, because I do not believe that anyone could copy it. The key to Beatrice Lillie's success is that she ignores her audience. This is an act of daring that amounts to a revolution. Maurice Chevalier was speaking for most of his profession when he said in his autobiography: 'An artist carries on throughout his life a mysterious, uninterrupted conversation with his public.' To get into contact with the dark blur of faces out front is the Holy Grail of every personality performer except Miss Lillie, who converses not with her public but with herself. Belly laughter, for which most comedians sweat out their life's blood, only disconcerts her; it is an intrusion from another world. She is uniquely alone. Her gift is to reproduce on stage the grievous idiocy with which people behave when they are on their own: humming and mumbling, grimacing at the looking glass, perhaps even singing into it, hopping, skipping, fiddling with their dress, starting and stopping a hundred trivial tasks – looking, in fact, definably batty. At these strange pursuits we, the customers, peep and marvel, but we are always eavesdroppers; we never 'get into the act'.

The theatre is Miss Lillie's hermitage. It is an empty room in which she has two hours to kill, and the audience, like Alice, is 'just a thing in her dream'. She is like a child dressing up in front of the mirror, amusing herself while the grown-ups are out. The fact that we are amused as well proves that she has conquered the rarest of all theatrical arts, the art of public solitude, which Stanislavsky said was the key to all great acting. To carry it off, as she does, requires a vast amount of sheer nerve and more than a whiff of genius, which is really another word for creative self-sufficiency. One might add that it probably helps to have had experience, at an early age, of pulling faces in church.

Her future, like her act, seldom looks the same from one day to the next. She would like to take her solo show to South America and Asia, with a split week in Tibet, where she feels she has many fans. A musical has been written for her, based on the life of Madame Tussaud. Its title, which she finds hauntingly seductive, is *The Works*. But wherever her choice falls, the queues will form. There is no substitute for this magnetic sprite. She alone can reassure us that from a theatre increasingly enslaved to logic the spirit of unreason, of anarchy and caprice, has not quite vanished.

(*1956*)

RUTH DRAPER

AT THE CRITERION, LONDON

I am sure that what happened to me at the Criterion Theatre on Tuesday night was happening to very few other people in the house. I was seeing Ruth Draper for the first time. The rest of her audience were annual loyalists, ancient friends of her art; for some of them, I afterwards discovered, she has all but ruined the pleasures of normal play-going, since her large supporting cast, which exists only at her mind's fingertips, is so much more satisfactory than any which makes the vulgar mistake of being visible.

I cannot content myself with a few perfunctory references to the familiar, inimitable etcetera with which she presents her well-loved gallery of etceteras: she must have enough notices of that kind to paper a palace. I want to declare Miss Draper open to the new generation of playgoers, and to trample on their suspicions, which I once shared, that she might turn out to be a museum-piece, ripe for the dust-sheet and oblivion. She is, on the contrary, about as old-fashioned and mummified as spring, and as I watched her perform her thronging monologues the other night, I could only conclude that this was the best and most modern group acting I had ever seen. It seems, in passing, absurd to use a singular verb in connexion with so plural a player. Let me put it that Ruth Draper are now at their height of their career, and add that you have only six weeks in which to see them.

She works her miracles benignly and unfussed; and do not be misled by her aquiline nose and razor-edged eyes into taking her for one of those prima donnas who prefer to give solo performances merely because their egos cannot abide competition. I have an idea that, at the back of her mind, Miss Draper is hoping still to find a company of actors skilful enough to stand up to comparison with the accuracy, tact, and wisdom of her technique. She is actually doing her contemporaries a great kindness by not exposing them to such a hazard. The riches of her style lie in its quietness; it is a peaceful spawning of microscopically observed details, each of which does the work of an explanatory paragraph in a novel. Within the space of a short story, she manages to sketch in enough background for an epic.

Her first and wittiest study is of a dowager opening a bazaar and pausing in her inspection of the stalls to inquire cautiously: 'Is that a rose or a tomato?' Next she is a fisherman's wife, wrinkled in granite, gossiping on the porch while her rheumatic husband ('an awful heavy man to rub') complains from within the house. Then follows the fabled procession of the women in Mr Clifford's life – tireless secretary, dry-hearted wife, and patient mistress. The patience of the last-named, by the by, seemed to me a little too monumental; we were almost, for a moment, in the swamps of sentimentalism, and I caught echoes of the almighty cooing of Dame Sybil Thorndike on an off day. With the finale, however, we are back on the peaks: the Parisian actress preparing for a world tour. During this exhibition the audience broke out into applause, amazingly when you consider that Miss Draper had just concluded a long tirade blazing with charm and avarice, but spoken entirely in Russian.

Watching her is like being present at a successful audition for the role of a theatrical immortal. I can pay her no higher compliment than to say that the best plays of Chekhov read as if they had been written at her express commission. To older playgoers I must apologize for dwelling on so much that they already knew. Younger ones will form an orderly queue outside the Criterion, and need not cross their fingers.

(*1952*)

THREE INDIVIDUALISTS
(1) GARBO

What, when drunk, one sees in other women, one sees in Garbo sober. She is woman apprehended with all the pulsating clarity of one of Aldous Huxley's mescalin jags. To watch her is to achieve direct, cleansed perception of something which, like a flower or a fold of silk, is raptly, unassertively, and beautifully itself. Nothing intrudes between her and the observer except the observer's neuroses: her contri-

bution is calm and receptiveness, an absorbent repose which normally, in women, coexists only with the utmost vanity. Tranced by
the ecstasy of existing, she gives to each onlooker what he needs: her
largesse is intarissable. Most actresses in action live only to look at
men, but Garbo looks at flowers, clouds, and furniture with the same
admiring compassion, like Eve on the morning of creation, and better
cast than Mr Huxley as Adam. Fame, by insulating her against a
multitude of experiences which we take for granted, has increased
rather than diminished her capacity for wonder. In England two
years ago she visited Westminster Abbey, early one morning when
no one was about, and in this most public of places found a source of
enormous private enchantment. A walk along a busy street is for her a
semi-mystical adventure. Like a Martian guest, she questions you
about your everyday life, infecting you with her eagerness, shaming
you into a heightened sensitivity. Conversing with her, you feel
like Ramon Novarro, blinded in *Mata Hari*, to whom she said:
'Here are your eyes,' and touched her own.

I half-believed, until I met her, the old hilarious slander which
whispered that she was a brilliant Swedish female impersonator who
had kept up the pretence too long; behind the dark glasses, it was
hinted, beneath the wild brown hair, there lurked the features of a
proud Scandinavian diplomat, now proclaiming their masculinity so
stridently that exposure to cameras was out of the question. This idle
fabrication was demolished within seconds of her entering the room;
sidelong, a little tentative, like an animal thrust under a searchlight,
she advanced, put out a hand in greeting, murmured something
muted and sibilant to express her pleasure, and then, gashing her
mouth into a grin, expunged all doubt. This was a girl, all right. It is
an indication of the mystery which surrounds her that I felt pleased
even to have ascertained her sex.

'Are you all things to all men?' someone asks her in *Two-Faced
Woman*; to which the honest reply (I forget the scripted one) would
be: 'To all men, women, and children.' Garbo, Hepburn, and
Dietrich are perhaps the only screen personalities for whom such a
claim could seriously be made. 'She has sex, but no particular gender,'
I once wrote of Dietrich, 'her masculinity appeals to women, and her
sexuality to men'; which is also true of Hepburn. Yet Garbo trans-
cends both of them. Neither Hepburn nor Dietrich could have

played Garbo's scenes with her son in *Anna Karenina*; something predatory in them would have forbidden such selfless maternal raptures. Garbo alone can be intoxicated by innocence. She turns her coevals into her children, taking them under her wing like a great, sailing swan. Her love is thus larger than Hepburn's or Dietrich's, which does not extend beyond the immediately desired object. It was Alistair Cooke who pointed out that in her films she seemed to see life in reverse and, because she was aware of the fate in store for them, offered the shelter of her sympathy to all around her. Through the cellophane *Kitsch* (how it dates!) of the Lubitsch touch she pierced, in *Ninotchka*, to affirm her pity for the human condition. The words were addressed to Melvyn Douglas, but we all knew for whom they were really intended, and glowed in the knowledge: 'Bomps will fall, civilizations will crumble – but *not yet. . . . Give us our moment!*' She seemed to be pleading the world's cause, and to be winning, too. Often, during the decade in which she talked to us, she gave signs that she was on the side of life against darkness: they seeped through a series of banal, barrel-scraping scripts like code messages borne through enemy lines. Sometimes, uttering sentences that were plainly designed to speed the end of literature, she could convey her universal charity only in glimpses, such as, for instance, a half-mocking, half-despairing catch in the wine-dark voice. Round the militant bluster of M-G-M dialogue she wrapped a Red Cross bandage of humanity.

It is likely that too many volumes have been read into and written about her, and that every additional adulatory word reinforces the terror I am sure she feels at the thought of having to face us again and measure up to the legend. Possibly we exaggerated her intelligence from the beginning; perhaps she was perfectly happy with the velvet-hung, musk-scented tin lizzies that Salka Viertel and S. N. Behrman (among others) turned out as vehicles for her. Perhaps association with Lewis Stone and Reginald Owen, a stout pair of uncle-substitutes who crop up, variously bewigged, in many of her films, was vitally necessary to inspire her. Recall, too, that Carl Brisson and John Gilbert are known to have been high on her list of ideal men; and that we have no evidence that she has ever read a book. Except physically, we know little more about Garbo than we know about Shakespeare. She looks, in fact, about thirty-four, but her date of birth is disputable; the textbooks oscillate between 1905 and 1906, and one biography ungallantly plumps for 1903, which may, of course, be a wound left by an embittered typesetter. Stockholm cradled her, and like Anna Christie, she was the daughter of an impoverished sailor. She had a brother and two sisters, left school at fourteen, entered the newly expanding Swedish film industry, and was discovered by Mauritz Stiller. After the completion of *Gösta Berling* in 1924, her life is a list of movies, twelve silent, fourteen talking, and a file of newspaper pictures catching her aghast and rain-coated, grey-faced and weirdly hatted, on the gangplanks of ships or the stairways to planes. We often know where she is going, but never why. Occasionally a man is with her, a sort of Kafkaesque guard, employed to escort her to her next inscrutable rendezvous. Baffled, we consult the astrologers, who tell us that those born, as she was, between the end of August and the end of September are almost bound to be perfectionists; but what, we are left sighing, is she perfecting?

She changed her name from Gustaffson to Garbo, the Swedish word for a sprite. I used to think the Spanish 'garbo' an insult to her, having heard it applied to matadors whose work seemed to me no more than pretty or neat. A Hispanophile friend has lately corrected me: 'garbo,' he writes, 'is animal grace sublimated – the flaunting of an assured natural charm, poise infected by *joie de vivre*, innate, high-spirited, controlled, the essentially female attribute (even in bull-fighters). . . .' In short, 'garbo' is Garbo without the melancholy, with no intimations of mortality. The word describes the embryo, the capital letter invests it with a soul. It is the difference between *Gösta Berling* and *Anna Karenina*.

But here again I am acquiescing in the myth of gloom. Long before the fit of hoarse hysterics that convulsed her when Melvyn Douglas fell off his chair, Garbo had laughed, even if it was only 'wild laughter in the throat of death', and made us laugh too. She was never wholly austere. Posing as a man in the tavern scene of *Queen Christina*, how blithely she made us smile at her awkwardness when asked to share a bedroom with the Spanish ambassador! A secret half-smile, with the lips drawn back as if bobbing for apples, was always her least resistible weapon. Her gaiety coalesced, to the dismay of academic distinctions, with plangency. Her retirement is unforgivable if only because it means that now we shall never see her as Masha in *The Three Sisters*, a part Chekhov might have written for her. It takes lesser actresses to express a single emotion, mirth or mirthlessness. Garbo's most radiant grins were belied always by the anxiety in the antennae-like eyebrows; and by the angle of her head she could effect a transition, not alone of mood, but of age. When it was tilted back, with the mouth sagging open, she was a child joyously anticipating a sweet; when it was tipped forward, the mouth still agape, she became a parent wide-eyed at her child's newest exploit.

Some of her impact, certainly, was derived from the exoticism of her accent; hers was probably the first Swedish voice that many a million filmgoers had ever heard. Anglo-Saxons are notoriously prone to ascribe messianic characteristics to any stranger with a Slavic, Teutonic, or Nordic intonation; Bergner and Bergman are examples that come to mind, and the history of the London stage is punctuated with shrieks of exultation over long-forgotten soubrettes with names like Marta Kling, Svenda Stellmar, or Ljuba Van Strusi. Garbo was unquestionably assisted by the fact that she had to be cast, more often than not, as an exile: how often, to go about her business of home-wrecking, she arrives by train from afar! The smoke clears, revealing the emissary of fate, hungrily licking her lips. The displaced person always inspires curiosity: who displaced her, what forces drove her from her native land? If it was Garbo's luck to provoke these inquiries, it was her gift which answered them. The impulse behind her voyages was romantic passion. Bergner might have left home to collect Pekes, Bergman to go on a hiking tour: Garbo could only have journeyed to escape or to seek a lover. Which is, as a line in *Ninotchka* has it, 'a netchul impulse common to all'.

Superficially, she changed very little in the course of her career; a certain solidity in her aspect suggested, at the very end, a spiritualized reworking of Irene Dunne, but that was all. She could still (and often did) fling her head flexibly back at right-angles to her spine, and she kissed as thirstily as ever, cupping her man's head in both hands and seeming very nearly to drink from it. And her appeal never lost its ambiguity. The after-dinner cooch-dance which drives Lionel Barrymore to hit the bottle in *Mata Hari* reveals an oddly androgynous physique, with strong-kneed legs as 'capable', in their way, as the spatulate fingers: nothing is here of Herrick's 'fleshie Principalities'. Pectorally, the eye notes a subsidence hardly distinguishable from concavity: the art that conceals art could scarcely go further. If this undenominational temple-dance is seductive (and, like the swimming-pool sequence in *Two-Faced Woman*, it is), the explanation lies in our awareness that we are watching a real, imperfectly shaped human being, and not a market-fattened glamour-symbol.

I dwell on Garbo's physical attributes because I think the sensual side of acting is too often under-rated: too much is written about how actors feel, too little about how they look. Garbo's looks, and especially her carriage, always set up a marvellous dissonance with what she was saying. The broad ivory yoke of her shoulders belonged to a javelin-thrower; she walked obliquely, seeming to sidle even when she strode, like a middle-weight boxer approaching an opponent: how could this athletic port enshrine so frail and suppliant a spirit? Queen Christina, reputedly her favourite character, is encased for several reels in masculine garb, and when besought by her counsellors to marry, she replies: 'I shall die a bachelor!' And think of: 'I am Mata Hari – I am my own master!' To lines like these Garbo could impart an enigmatic wit which nobody else could have carried off. Deficient in all the surface frills of femininity, she replaced them with a male directness. Her Marie Walewska was as lion-hearted as Napoleon himself, and I have heard her described as 'Charlemagne's Aunt'. Her independence (in the last analysis) of either sex is responsible for the cryptic amorality of her performances. In most of the characters she played the only discernible moral imperative is loyalty, an animal rather than a human virtue – that 'natural sense of honour' which, as Shaw says, 'is nowhere mentioned in the Bible'.

'Animal grace sublimated': I return to my correspondent's phrase. If it is true (as I think it is) that none of Garbo's clothes ever appear to be meant for her, much less to fit her, that is because her real state is not in clothes at all. Her costumes hamper her, whether they are stoles or redingotes or (as on one occasion) moiré, sequinned, principal-boy tights. She implies a nakedness which is bodily as well as spiritual. It is foolish to complain that, basically, she gave but one performance throughout her life. She has only one body, and in this incarnation that is all we can expect.

Through what hoops, when all is said and done, she has been put by Seastrom, Cukor, Clarence Brown, and the rest of her mentors! She has gone blonde for them, danced 'La Chica-Choca' for them, played a travesty of Sarah Bernhardt for them, stood straight-faced by for them as Lewis Stone warned her of 'a new weapon called The Tank'. Can we ask for more self-abnegation? A life of Duse was once mooted for her – what an *éducation sentimentale*, one guesses, she would have supplied for D'Annunzio! Later she hovered over, but did not settle on, a mimed role in Lifar's ballet version of *Phèdre*. And at the last moment, when all seemed fixed, she sidestepped the leading part in Balzac's *La Duchesse de Langeais*. The most recent, least plausible rumour of all insisted that she would film *La Folle de Chaillot*, with Chaplin as the Rag-Picker. . . .

So it looks as if we were never to know whether or not she was a great actress. Do I not find the death scene of *Camille* or the bedroom-stroking scene of *Queen Christina* commensurate with the demands of great acting? On balance, no. The great actress, as G. H. Lewes declared, must show her greatness in the highest reaches of her art; and it must strictly be counted against Garbo that she never attempted Hedda, or Masha, or St Joan, or Medea. We must acclaim a glorious woman who exhibited herself more profoundly to the camera than any of her contemporaries; but the final accolade must, if we are honest, be withheld.

(*1953*)

(2) W. C. FIELDS

If you had been visiting Philadelphia in the winter of 1892 and had wanted to buy a newspaper, you would have stood a good chance of having mild hysterics and a story to dine out on in after years. W. C. Fields, then a frowning urchin of thirteen, was spending a few halcyon months peddling papers; and his manner of vending contained already the germs of a technique which later made him one of the two or three funniest men in the world. While other lads piped about wars and football, Fields would pick on a five-line fill-in at the bottom of a page and, quite disenchantedly, hawk it at the top of his voice. 'Bronislaw Gimp acquires licence for two-year-old sheepdog!' he would bellow at passers-by, adding unnecessarily: 'Details on page

26!' And by the tone of his voice, his latest biographer* tells us, you would gather that Gimp was an arch-criminal, for Fields trusted no one. A flabby scowl sat squarely on his face – the same scowl that we see in the curious portrait with which John Decker celebrated the comedian's sixtieth birthday: with a doily on his head and a silver salt-cellar balanced on top of that he sits, squinting dyspeptically at the camera, perfectly well aware of the profanity of the caption: 'Sixty Years a Queen.' Fields disliked and suspected most of his fellow creatures to the end of his life: his face would work in convulsive tics as he spoke of them. For sixty-seven years he played duck's back to their water, until on Christmas Day, 1946, the 'fellow in the bright nightgown' (as he always referred to death) sneaked up on him and sapped him for good.

W. C. Fields: His Follies and Fortunes is certainly the best book we are likely to see about this droll and grandiose comic. Robert Lewis Taylor is a graduate of the *New Yorker*, and thus a master of the Harold Ross prose style – pungent and artless, innocently sly, superbly explicit: what one would call low-falutin'. Like all the *New Yorker*'s best profiles, this picture of Fields is composed with a sort of childish unsentimentality, the candour of a liquorous quiz kid. Taylor, having inscribed Fields's name glowingly on the roll of fame, beats him over the head with it. Except that he sometimes calls a mistress a 'friend', he spares us little. We learn of Fields's astonishing consumption of alcohol (two quarts of gin a day, apart from wines and whisky); of his quite sincere cruelty (his favourite sequence was one in which he took his small niece to a fun fair and parked her 'for safety' in the shooting gallery); of his never wholly cured habit of pilfering (on his first visit to England he strolled around stealing poultry hanging out in front of shops; it was his tribute to the salesmanship of the proprietors and, as he indignantly added: 'You don't think I'd have stolen chickens in the Balkans, do you?'); of his jovial callousness towards his friends, towards most women, and towards the clergy. One rainy night Fields, fairly far gone, was driving home waving a gin bottle in his free hand, and generously gave a lift to a hitch-hiker. The man was outraged when Fields offered him a drink, and, explaining that he was a clergyman, went on to deliver a free sermon to the comedian – 'I'll give you my number four,' he said, 'called

* *W. C. Fields: His Follies and Fortunes*, by Robert Lewis Taylor.

"The Evils of Alcohol".' He was well into his stride when Fields nonchalantly pulled up alongside a hedge, kicked the man out, dropped a bottle of gin after him, and roared: 'That's my number three – "How to keep warm in a ditch"!' Equally savage was his exchange with a bartender in *My Little Chickadee*. 'You remember the time I knocked down Waterfront Nell?' he said. The barman, pretty angrily, replied: 'Why, you didn't knock her down, I did.' 'Well,' Fields went on, unperturbed, 'I started kicking her first.' He once genially condescended to teach an acquaintance of his, against whom he bore some slight grudge, a simple juggling trick requiring two paring knives. 'I hope he worked at it,' said Fields afterwards, 'because if he did, he was almost certain to cut himself very painfully.' Some of the managements for whom he worked complained about such jests as these. Fields never lost his temper on such occasions. 'We must strive,' he would say thoughtfully, 'to instruct and uplift as well as entertain.' And, eyeing them carefully, he would light a cigar.

About all this Mr Taylor is quaintly frank; and he is even better at describing (for nobody could ever explain) the mysterious caverns of private humour in which Fields delighted. There was the two-reeler entitled *The Fatal Glass of Beer* which he did for Mack Sennett: it opened with Fields sitting on a campstool in a far Northern shack, wearing a coonskin coat and crooning to himself. From time to time he would get up, open the door, and cry: 'Tain't a fit night out for man nor beast!' whereupon an extra would pelt him in the face with a handful of snow. There was hardly any other dialogue in the film.

Fields nearly always wrote his own stories (under pen-names such as Mahatma Kane Jeeves), and would drive studio chiefs to despair by his failure to understand that the fact that he appeared in every shot did not necessarily ensure continuity of plot-line. Still, he continued to scrawl plots on the backs of old laundry bills and to get $25,000 a time for them. Often he would wander through the streets wearing a false beard, a repulsive clip-in moustache, and an opera cape, and amble into any party he saw in progress, introducing himself as 'Doctor Hugo Sternhammer, the Viennese anthropologist'. He first did this during the 1914–18 war. 'I remember telling one woman that the Kaiser was my third cousin,' he mused; 'she gave a little scream and ran like hell.' His treatment of women often bordered on the fantastic: finding strange, unaccountable depths of hilarity in the

Chinese, he made one of his mistresses dress in satin slippers and a split black skirt, and always called her 'The Chinaman'. Many of his letters to his last mistress and devoted nurse, Carlotta Monti, start out 'Dear Chinese People' and are signed, even more bewilderingly, 'Continental Person' or 'Ampico J. Steinway'. He liked ordering Chinese meals in his films: in *International House* (for Paramount in 1932) he called up room service and blandly asked for: 'A couple of hundred-year-old eggs, boiled in perfume.'

Fields enraged most people he worked with. Mae West still remembers how stunned she was when, in the middle of a take, he benignly ad-libbed: 'And how is my little brood mare?' He worked first for Mack Sennett and later for Universal and M-G-M (most notoriously in *David Copperfield*, in which he was narrowly restrained from doing his entire juggling routine); but after he left Ziegfeld's *Follies* in 1921 we are probably most indebted to Paramount, who suffered under him through twenty-one movies, including *Tilly and Gus, If I had a Million, Six of a Kind, Mrs Wiggs of the Cabbage Patch, Mississippi,* and *The Man on the Flying Trapeze.* Much of the time they had to fight to keep him from cursing during takes: in retaliation he devised two expressions – 'Godfrey Daniel!' and 'Mother of Pearl!' – with which he baffled the Hays Office for more than a decade. They granted him a salary so spectacular that even Bing Crosby raised his eyebrows, and, by their unearthly tolerance, they allowed him to turn out a series of films which must rank among the least money-making comedy classics in cinema history. At last he left them, his powers quite unimpaired, and went to Universal for his last four pictures, *You Can't Cheat an Honest Man, My Little Chickadee, The Bank Dick,* and the amazing *Never Give a Sucker an Even Break –* the last two of which probably represent the height of his achievement. They were made between 1938 and 1942, when Fields was moving reluctantly into his sixties. Some day they should be revived by the film societies, for in addition to being among the funniest films of a good period, they are splendid illustrations of the art of film-making without portfolio, or cinematic actor-management.

The function of a director in a Fields movie was clear right from the start. He either fought with or ignored them. He would reduce such men as Leo McCarey, Norman McLeod, George Marshall, and even George Cukor to impotent hysterics of rage by his incorrigible ad-libbing, his affectation of deafness whenever they suggested the slightest alteration in any of his lines or routines, and by his jubilant rudeness to anyone else who happened to be working in the neighbourhood. (Once, when it became known that Deanna Durbin was on a nearby lot and might be audible on clear days, Fields threatened 'to get a good bead from the upstairs balcony and shoot her'.) The only director to whose advice he ever paid attention was Gregory La Cava. 'Dago bastard!' he would growl as, fretfully, he listened to La Cava's analyses of his gifts: yet he admitted that the director was in the right when he implored Fields not to work too hard for his laughs. What La Cava said is worth quoting, for it is acute and provides some sort of key to Fields's later methods. 'You're not a natural comedian, Bill,' he said. 'You're a counter-puncher. You're the greatest straight man that ever lived. It's a mistake for you ever to do the leading. When you start to bawl out and ham around and trip over things, you're pushing. I hate to see it.' He said that in 1934.

La Cava was correct, as Fields's maturer films show. Fields quiescent and smouldering is funnier than Fields rampant and yelling. He played straight man to a malevolent universe which had singled him out for siege and destruction. He regarded the conspiracy of fate through a pair of frosty little blue eyes, an arm flung up to ward off an imminent blow, and his shoulders instinctively hunched in self-protection. It is hard to imagine him without the 'as I suspected' look with which he anticipates disaster. Always his face looked injured (as indeed it was: the nose was ruddy and misshapen not through drink, but from the beatings he received in his youth); he would talk like an old lag, watchfully, using his antic cigar almost as a cudgel. Puffy, gimlet-eyed, and magnificently alarmed, he would try to outwit the agents of calamity with sheer pomp, and invariably fail. Everything he says, even the most crushing insult, is uttered as if it were a closely guarded secret: he *admits* a line rather than speaks it. Only his alcoholic aplomb remains unpersecuted: that they cannot touch, these imps who plague him. Fields breakfasting with his screen family behaves with all the wariness of Micawber unexpectedly trapped in Fagin's thieves' kitchen. His face lights up only rarely, at the sight of something irresistibly and universally ludicrous, like a blind man. One remembers his efforts, in the general-store sequence of *It's a Gift*, to prevent a deaf and blind customer from knocking over things with his stick while Fields is attending to other clients. It was unforgettable, the mechanical enthusiasm of those brave, happy cries: 'Sit down, Mr Muckle, Mr Muckle, please sit down!' (A stack of electric light bulbs crashes to the floor.) 'Mr Muckle, honey, *please sit down*!'

His nose, resembling a doughnut pickled in vinegar or an eroded squash ball, was unique; so, too, was his voice. He both looked and sounded like a cement-mixer. He would screw up his lips to one side and purse his eyes before committing himself to speech; and then he would roll vowels around his palate as if it were a sieve with which he was prospecting for nuggets. The noise that finally emerged was something quietly raucous, like the crowing of a very lazy cock. (If you substitute 'Naw' for 'No, Sir' and cast Fields as Johnson, most of Boswell becomes wildly amusing, as well as curiously characteristic.) Fields's voice, nasal, tinny, and massively bored, is that of a prisoner who has been uselessly affirming his innocence in the same court for centuries: when, in *It's a Gift*, he drives a carload of people straight into a large reproduction of the Venus de Milo, his response as he surveys the fragments is unhesitating. 'Ran right in front of the car,' he murmurs, a little wearily.

The recent revival of *It's a Gift* (Norman McLeod for Paramount, 1934) was received gratefully by students of Fields's middle period. He does little heavy wooing in it, and robs surprisingly few people, but most of his other traits are well represented. The cigar is there; so is the straw hat, which nervously deserts him at moments of crisis and has to be retrieved and jammed back on to the large, round head which squats, Humpty-Dumpty-like, on the oddly boyish shoulders. There is Fields's old rival Baby LeRoy to spill a barrel of molasses, described by the comedian in a famous line as the 'spreadingest stuff I ever saw in m'life'. (To a friend who inquired the name of his new co-star, Fields replied: 'Fellow named LeRoy. Says he's a baby.') There is Kathleen Howard, the Fieldsian equivalent of Margaret Dumont, sneering with her wonderful baritone clarity at his 'scheme to revive the celluloid collar'. And there is the long and savoury sequence in which Fields, driven by Miss Howard's nocturnal scolding to seek sleep on the verandah, is kept awake by such things as a coconut rolling down a fire-escape, a squeaking clothes-line, an insurance salesman (who asks 'Are you Mr Karl LaFong, capital K small A small R small L capital L small A capital F small O small N small G?'), the whirr of bottles in a milk-crate, a 'vegetable gentle-man' selling calabashes, and, of course, by Master LeRoy, who drops grapes from above into the comedian's mouth. 'Shades of Bacchus!' mutters Fields, removing the eleventh.

In the same programme as *It's a Gift* was a revival of *Monkey Business*, which the Fields section of the audience took in glacial silence, because this is script-bound comedy, the comedy of quot-ability. Groucho owes much to Perelman: Fields owes nothing to anyone, except dubiously Harry Tate. Fields strolls out of the frame into the theatre, while the Brothers remain silhouettes. Fields's fantasy has its roots in the robust soil of drunken reverie: theirs are in the hothouse of nightmare. They will resort to razors and thumb-screws to get laughs that Fields would have got with a rolled-up newspaper. Their comic style is comparable with his only in that, as Mr Taylor notes, 'most people harbour a secret affection for anyone with a low opinion of humanity'. It is nowhere recorded what Fields thought of the Marx Brothers, but it is permissible to guess. Hearing them described: 'Possibly a squad of gipsies', he might have grunted, pronouncing the 'g' hard, as in gruesome.

Fields is pre-eminently a man's comedian. Women seldom become addicts of his pictures, and it is no coincidence that his closest friends (John Barrymore, Ben Hecht, Gene Fowler, Dave Chasen, Grantland Rice) were all men. He belongs inseparably to the pool-room and the bar-room – though rarely to the smoking-room; and while he looked like a brimming Toby Jug, it was always clear that no mantelpiece would hold him. Few wives drag their husbands to see his films, which may partly explain their persistently low profits. Like Sid Field, he rejected pathos to the last, even when working with child stars: he refused to tap the feminine audience by the means that Chaplin used in *The Kid*. It is appalling, indeed, to reflect what Fields might have done to Jackie Coogan, a less resilient youth than LeRoy. Perhaps it is a final judgement on him that no self-respecting mother will ever allow her children to read Mr Taylor's brilliant book – a chronicle of meanness, fraud, arrogance, and alcoholism.

We know, by the way, Fields's opinion of Chaplin. Late in life he was lured to a cinema where some of the little man's early two-reelers were being shown. The laughter inside was deafening, and halfway through Fields uneasily left. His companion found him outside in the car at the end of the show, and asked what he thought of Chaplin's work. 'The son of a bitch is a ballet dancer,' said Fields. 'He's pretty funny, don't you think?' his friend went on doggedly. 'He's the best ballet dancer that ever lived,' said Fields, 'and if I get a good chance I'll kill him with my bare hands.'

(1952)

(3) JAMES CAGNEY

Twenty-one years ago James Cagney, playing in his first film, invented a new kind of screen character. In more than fifty subsequent appearances he has polished and complicated it, but the type has remained substantially unchanged; and it may now be time to investigate its extraordinary influence. Morally and psychologically, it could be maintained that the Cagney code and manners have come to dominate a whole tradition of American melodrama.

Before Cagney boffed Mae Clark with a grapefruit in *Public Enemy*, Hollywood had adhered to what was, by general consent, a reasonable stringent set of moral principles. The film is no exception to the other popular narrative arts: in its infancy it clings to a broad and exaggerated ethical system, based on pure blacks and whites. In the theatre this period is represented by the morality play, and was superseded by Marlowe, whose heroes were noble and wicked, fraudulent and pious, cruel and idealistic, at the same time. In the novel the period of over-simplification ended with the Romantics; and in the film it ended with Cagney.

This is not to say that the American movie before 1930 was never immoral: the very urgency of the need for a Hays Office demonstrates the contrary. But its immorality, however blatant, was always incidental and subordinate: a sheikh might flay his wives with scorpions to enliven the curious, but he would be sure to be trampled on, baked, or impaled in the last reel. He was always transparently evil, and the flayee transparently innocent. In the early Westerns there is no doubt who is the villain; he is the man leaning against the bar in black frock-coat, ribbon bow-tie, and pencilled moustache. He is a killer, charmless and unfunny, and suffers dreadfully by comparison with the bronzed hero on the white horse; his part, too, is much shorter than the star's. In the twenties there was not only a rigid distinction between the good characters and bad; they were also evenly balanced in numbers and fame. Vice and virtue proclaimed themselves irrevocably within the first few hundred feet, or the director was failing at his job.

Cagney changed all this. In *Public Enemy* he presented, for the first time, a hero who was callous and evil, while being simultaneously equipped with charm, courage, and a sense of fun. Even more significantly, he was co-starred not with the grave young district attorney who would finally ensnare him, but with a bright, callow moll for him to slap. The result was that in one stroke Cagney abolished both the convention of the pure hero and that of approximate equipoise between vice and virtue. The full impact of this minor revolution was manifested in the 1942-7 period, when Ladd, Widmark, Duryea, and Bogart were able to cash in on Cagney's strenuous pioneering. It now becomes fascinating to trace the stages of development by which the Cagney villain (lover, brute, humorist, and killer) was translated into the Bogart hero (lover, brute, humorist, but non-killer). It is an involved story.

Probably it begins with the physical attributes of Cagney himself. One finds it hard to take such a small man seriously: how, after all, can a playful redhead of five feet eight inches really be a baron of vice? It is safe to say that if Cagney had been four inches taller, his popularity would be fathoms less than it is. Villains before him had tended to be huge; they loomed and slobbered, bellowed and shambled; you could see them coming. Cagney was and is spruce, dapper, and grinning. When he hits a friend over the ear with a revolver-butt, he does it as casually as he will presently press the elevator button on his way out. By retaining his brisk little smile throughout he makes one react warmly, with a grin, not coldly and aghast. Nobody in 1930, the year after Chicago's St Valentine's Day massacre, at which Capone's lieutenants slaughtered nine men in a disused garage, would have tolerated any romanticization of the gangster legend. When Muni played *Scarface* for Howard Hawks two years later, he presented the mob leader as an unhealthy, ungainly lout, a conception clearly in key with contemporary taste. Cagney unconsciously paved the way for the advent of the smooth, romantic gangster of the late thirties; he softened public opinion by sneaking up on it through a forgotten and unguarded loophole. He was never a romantic figure himself – at his height you can't be – nor was he sentimental – Cheshire cats never are – but he possessed, possibly in greater abundance than any other name star of the time, irresistible charm. It was a cocky, picaresque charm, the charm of pert urchins, the *gaminerie* of unlicked juvenile delinquents. Cagney, even with submachine-gun hot in hand and corpses piling at his ankles, can still persuade many people that it was not his fault. By such means he made gang law acceptable to the screen, and became by accident one of the most genuinely corrupting influences Hollywood has ever sent us. Cagney brought organized crime within the mental horizon of errand-boys, who saw him as a cavalier of the gutters – their stocky patron saint.

But before the actor comes the script. What literary circumstances were conspiring to produce a climate in which the brutal hero could flourish? It would be superficial to neglect Hemingway, who was beginning to project on to the American mind his own ideal of manhood – a noble savage, idly smoking, silhouetted against a background of dead illusions. Surveyed impartially, the Hemingway hero numbers among his principal characteristics that of extreme dumbness: he is the sincere fool who walks phlegmatically off the end of the pier. He is honourable, charmless, tough, and laconic; and he is always, in some sense, a pirate or an adventurer. What Cagney did was to extract the moral core from Hemingway's creation and put smartness in its place. The result was a character charmingly dishonourable, but saved from suavity or smugness by his brute energy and swift, impetuous speech. Perhaps the simplest point of departure is that, whereas the Hemingway man never hits a woman for fun, Cagney made a secure living out of doing just that.

The success of Cagney's methods made all sorts of variations possible, chief among them the *genre* popularized in the novels and films of Raymond Chandler. Here the central character is tough, cynically courageous, and predisposed towards brutality; he is in fact identical with the Cagney version in all vital respects save one – he is on the side of the law. The process is thus completed: the problem of how to retain the glamour of the killer without the moral obloquy of murder has been solved. Let your hero be a private eye, and he can slaughter just as insensitively in the name of self-defence.

Cagney himself has rarely compromised; at the height of his career he never lined up with the police or made any concessions to public morals beyond the token one of allowing himself to be killed at the end, as an indispensable but tiresome rubric. At his best (*Public Enemy*, *The Mayor of Hell*, *The G-Men*, *White Heat*) he flouts every standard of social behaviour with a disarming Irish pungency that makes murder look like an athletic exercise of high spirits and not a mean and easy transgression. He sweetened killing; and to have done this immediately after the Capone régime, during the era of the concentration camp and between two lacerating wars, is something of an achievement.

He was born in New York in 1904 and educated at Stuyvesant High School and Columbia University; his background was East Side, but not the slum and tenement area. He began his stage career, mysteriously, as a female impersonator in 1923, and thereafter for six years danced and understudied in vaudeville. He was mostly penniless. In 1929 William Keighley, then a Broadway director, saw Cagney and Joan Blondell in a romp called *Maggie the Magnificent* and starred them in *Penny Arcade*; the play was bought by First National, and all three went to Hollywood with it. Retitled *Sinners' Holiday*, it was released in 1930. Cagney made eight pictures with Joan Blondell in less than four years, and she proved a perfect punch-bag for his clenched, explosive talent; the best of the series, *Steel Highway*, started a revealing vogue for stories about men who work in dangerous proximity to death-dealing machines. These films invariably centred on a character who was happy only when close to sudden extinction, who enjoyed tight-roping along telegraph wires or lighting cigarettes around kegs of dynamite. For such parts Cagney was a natural, and Wellman, who directed *Steel Highway*, quickly exploited the new star's edgy gameness by putting him into *Public Enemy*, with Blondell and Mae Clark. When the film appeared in 1931, the age of the screen gangster had officially begun. Howard Hawks followed in 1932 with *Scarface*, which, though it had the advantage of one of Ben Hecht's best scripts, lacked Cagney's spearhead precision to hold it together. For ten years afterwards he led the gangster film to extraordinary box-office eminence, and four times appeared in the annual list of the ten top money-making stars. In 1932 Hawks made *The Crowd Roars* with Cagney and Blondell; in 1933 came *The Mayor of Hell*; in 1934 Michael Curtiz' *Jimmy the Gent*; in 1935 Keighley's expert and sombre *The G-Men*; and finally, feeling that things were becoming too easy for him, Warners teamed Cagney with Bogart in *Angels with Dirty Faces* (1938) and *The Roaring Twenties* (1939). At this point he had made thirty-two films in nine years; the association with Blondell had dissolved, and his most frequent sparring partner was Pat O'Brien.

Cagney was now maturely at his best. Even the most ascetic *cinéaste* will admit that it is impossible to forget how he looked and talked at the height of his popularity. The spring-heeled walk, poised forward on the toes; the fists clenched, the arms loosely swinging; the keen, roving eyes; the upper lip curling back in defiance and derision; the rich, high-pitched, hectoring voice; the stubby, stabbing index finger; the smug purr with which he accepts female attention – Cagney's women always had to duck under his guard before he would permit them to make love to him. He was practically unkillable; it would generally take a dozen Thompson guns and a bomb or two to bring him to his knees; and he would always die running at, not away from, his pursuers, in a spluttering, staggering zig-zag, ending with a solid and satisfying thump. He moved more gracefully than any other actor in Hollywood. And he had a beguiling capacity for reassuring while he murdered: he would wrinkle up his face into a chubby mask of sympathy and then let you have it in the stomach. His relaxation, even when springing, was absolute; he released his compact energy quite without effort. When circumstances forced him to shout, his face would register how distasteful he found it.

Cagney's first rival in the game of romantic murder appeared in 1936. Humphrey Bogart, five years Cagney's senior, had made half a dozen mediocre pictures since 1932, and had returned to the stage to play the escaping gangster, Duke Mantee, in *The Petrified Forest*. In 1936 the play was filmed and Bogart was established. It was a new style; speculative, sardonic, sourly lisping, he stood out in direct contrast to Cagney, who was agile, clean-cut, and totally unreflective. Bogart frequently appeared unshaven; Cagney, never; but the challenge was clear, for both men specialized in whimsical law-breaking and both commanded alarming sex-appeal. Cagney, who had captured several million infant hearts with pictures like *Here Comes the Navy*, *Devil Dogs of the Air*, and Howard Hawks's *Ceiling Zero*, had access to an audience to which Bogart never appealed; but Bogart split Cagney's female admirers, and was usually featured with bigger stars and better directors than Warners could offer Cagney. *Bullets or Ballots* (1936) followed *The Petrified Forest*; in 1937, after a brief and unsuccessful venture into legality as the D.A. in *Marked Woman*, Bogart made *San Quentin* and *Kid Galahad*; and he breasted the year with his superbly metallic playing of Baby-Face Morgan in Wyler's *Dead End*. He had added to the gangster film something which Cagney always avoided: the dimension of squalor. In Cagney's looting there had been an atmosphere, almost, of knight-errantry; Bogart, tired, creased, and gnarled, effectively debunked it. The two films they made together for Warners made an absorbing conflict of styles – with Cagney throwing his hard, twisting punches and Bogart lazily ducking them. Cagney's was the more accomplished exhibition of ring-craft, but Bogart's sewage snarl won him the decision. At times both men found themselves using the same tricks; each had perfected his own version of the fanged killer's smile, and a good deal of *The Roaring Twenties* developed into a sort of grinning contest.

The experience must have proved something to both Cagney and Warners, because he made no more gangster films for ten years. By then the war had begun, the mob was very small beer, and the echo of machine-guns across deserted lots had lost its fascination for movie audiences. Bogart graduated to the side of justice, and the second important change in the history of filmed mayhem had taken place. In 1941 he played Sam Spade for Huston in *The Maltese Falcon* – still the same wry brute, but more insidiously immoral, since now there was a righteous justification for his savagery. He repeated this performance in *Across the Pacific*, and when *The Big Sleep* appeared in 1945 it looked as if the pure gangster film was dead. In 1942 Paramount produced their answer to Bogart in *This Gun for Hire* – the soft and silky thuggishness of Alan Ladd; and Dick Powell entered what was by now a very competitive market with *Farewell, My Lovely* (1944) and *Cornered* (1945). Screen melodrama in this period was filled with ageing bandits, battering their way to glory under police protection. Meanwhile Cagney had not been idle, though films like *The Strawberry Blonde, Captains of the Clouds*, and *The Bride Came C.O.D.* (in which he daintily plucked cactus needles from Bette Davis's behind) were not materially helping his reputation. In 1942 Curtiz made *Yankee Doodle Dandy*, a masterpiece of heartfelt hokum, and Cagney won an Academy Award with his sturdy, chirpy pirouetting; but the shamelessness of his early days seemed to have vanished. The woman-slapping outlaws of the forties were performed by feature players, not by stars, and they were mostly in the hands of Dan Duryea, the impact of whose rancid and lascivious unpleasantness in *The Little Foxes* had been confirmed by his straw-hatted blackmailer in Lang's *Woman in the Window* (1944) and his raucous pimp in *Scarlet Street* (1945). The courage of nastiness had gone.

In 1942 Cagney formed his own production unit with his brother William, and in seven years made only four films – *Johnny Vagabond*, a philosophical failure; *Blood on the Sun*, a commonplace espionage thriller; *13 Rue Madeleine*, a documentary-style spy story; and *The Time of Your Life* – a shrug of a film, charmingly aimless and inexpensive, in which Cagney, as a talkative drinker, gave his best performance since *Yankee Doodle Dandy*. The critics were suggesting that Cagney had agreed to accept middle-age and abandoned the orgiastic killing of his youth. Then, in 1950, he suddenly returned to Warners and, with Raoul Walsh, made *White Heat*.

The style in that amazing film was the man himself: Cagney had never been more characteristic – flamboyant, serio-comic, and tricky as a menagerie. It is not easy to decide why he came back to straight gangster vehicles, though I have the impression that Twentieth Century–Fox had much to do with it; they had begun, in 1947, an ambitious campaign to sell Richard Widmark to the public. His weedy, snickering murderer in *Kiss of Death* gave an unexpected lease of life to the gangster film. Playing within the semi-documentary convention, he could not be permitted to dominate his films as Cagney had in the lawless thirties, but he had the same gimlet appeal and was tapping the same love of clever violence. By 1949 his popularity was such that it must have persuaded Warners to disturb the retirement of their senior hoodlum.

Walsh and Cagney reverted in *White Heat* to the frankly artificial framework of *Public Enemy*: there were a few location sequences, but the main burden fell on the star's personality. The scenario made a genuflection to contemporary demand by giving its hero a mother-complex, and Cagney staggered even his devotees by acting it up to the hilt with a blind conviction which was often terrifying: he never let up. The film dealt with the breakdown of a killer's mind and his slow, unwitting, unadmitting approach to the long tunnel of insanity. Cagney never indulged in self-pity for a moment: if the script called for a fit, he would throw one, outrageous and full-blooded; and by a miracle his integrity never gave out. The result was a lesson in neurosis which ranks, in recent Hollywood memory, only with Richard Basehart's in *Fourteen Hours*. One cannot unlearn the sequence in which Cagney, attempting to ward off a mutiny in the mob, succumbs to one of his recurring blackouts and drags himself to the cover of a bedroom, moaning in deep thick sighs like a wounded animal. And, above all, the scene in the prison refectory. Word is passed down the table to Cagney that his mother has been killed: he stops eating, grins spasmodically, murmuring to himself, and then goes berserk, letting out strange, bestial cries and punching, punching at everyone with a compulsive defiance as he scampers the length of the hall. No other actor in Hollywood could have got away with that.

The older, crisper Cagney was there too; even he has never outdone, for sheer casualness, the murder of the stool-pigeon, whom he has locked up in the luggage-trap of his car. 'Kinda stuffy in here,' the prisoner complains. 'Like some air?' says Cagney, cocking a wicked eyebrow; and, stopping only to pop a hot dog in his mouth, fires six shots into him through the body of the car. The climax was nerve-racking: cornered, he takes refuge in an explosives plant and is chased to the top of a huge circular vat of, presumably, T.N.T. Yelling: 'On top of the world, Ma, on top of the world!' he sends his last bullet into it and is blown sky-high. It was audacious and incredible in retrospect, but such was the intensity of Cagney's playing that one refused to laugh. It is seldom easy to deride perfect stylists, even if one disapproves of the ends to which the style is being put. There could be no question, in this sequence, that a very remarkable actor had hit his full stride and was carrying his audience with him.

I do not mean, by all this, to suggest that the crime film deserves over-serious analysis: it has always been openly unreal in structure, depending for its excitement on jazzed dialogue and overstated photography. But its influence on scripting and camera-work has been incalculable, involving many of the most expert and adult intelligences in Hollywood – Hecht, Hawks, Wyler, Toland, Huston, Wellman, Lang, Chandler, and Hellinger among them – and it has provided an incomparable outlet for at least one unique acting talent. If it has had a pernicious social influence, that is probably Cagney's fault, and there is no space here to balance the old scales between art and morality. For myself, I do not mind walking the Edgware Road in peril as long as there is a Cagney picture at Marble Arch. A great deal of desperate urgency and attack would have been lost to the cinema if the gang film had not arrived, making fantastic technical demands on cameraman and electrician and recording engineer, with Cagney, safe and exulting, at the wheel of a bullet-riddled Cadillac.

(1952)

Miscellany

SOME NOTES ON STAGE SEXUALITY

The most characteristic English play on the subject of physical love is Shakespeare's *Antony and Cleopatra*. It is characteristic because it has no love scenes. The English, as their drama represents them, are a nation endlessly communicative about love without ever enjoying it. Full-blooded physical relationships engaged in with mutual delight are theatrically tabu. Thwarted love is preferred, the kind Mr Coward wrote about in *Brief Encounter*, where two married people (married, of course, to two other people) form a sad and meagre attachment without being able to follow it through. At the end of a play on some quite different subject – religion, perhaps, or politics – it is customary for the hero to say, as he does in *Robert's Wife*: 'I was deeply in love with a fine woman,' and for the wife to reply: 'My dear, dear husband'; but there should be no hint elsewhere in the text that they have as much as brushed lips.

In comedies marriage is presented as the high road to divorce. Husband and wife begin the play at Daggers Drawn, their country house, and the whole point of the ensuing exercise is to lure them back into each other's arms. The reconciliation takes place in the last act. Left alone on stage, the two lovers exchange coy salutations:

HENRY: Hello, Sybil.
SYBIL: Hello, Henry.
    (*Curtain.*)

Among younger people the technique of courtship is even more rigorously codified. It is always practised on a *chaise-longue*. The girl sits down beside the boy and edges a few inches towards him, where-upon he edges a few inches away. This is repeated *ad lib* until the boy falls off. The purpose of the ritual is to show the English male's terror of sex and his instinctive tendency to yell for mother. He is always bashful and ashamed in the presence of women to whom he is not closely related. At first he addresses them as if they were new and disturbing nannies; later, as the relationship matures, he takes the giant step and treats the girl of his choice as a substitute mother. The plays of the twenties were full of scenes in which the hero, contorted with grief, confessed to his mother that he had transferred his affections to another woman.

A firmly established tenet of English drama is that love which is 'only physical' will not last, and is probably ghastly anyway. Englishmen who go to American plays such as *A Streetcar Named Desire* frequently say afterwards: 'Perhaps I'm naïve, but all this harping on sex strikes me as awfully boring.' (Or 'vulgar', or 'tasteless', the other key words of English criticism.) They *are* naïve: there is no perhaps about it. Graham Greene's *The Living Room* was one of the few modern plays whose hero admitted to having had and enjoyed an affair. The heroine of Terence Rattigan's *The Deep Blue Sea* made the same dreadful admission. In both cases the penalty for extra-marital pleasure was paid. Mr Rattigan's heroine tried to gas herself and Mr Greene's took poison. The idea that a man and a woman should fall head over hips in love and sensually exult in their mutual discovery is deeply offensive to English taste. Someone must suffer for it, and our playwrights see to it that someone does, harshly and irrevocably. *That*, it is felt, will teach them to flaunt themselves (the word is always 'flaunt'): why can't they be repressed like everybody else?

Proposals are regarded with more tolerance, though the approach to them is often extremely oblique. In country-house comedies it has been known to go like this:

DICK (*blushing*): I have something – rather important to ask you, Miss Godalming.

MISS G.: What is it, Tom? (*I should have explained that there is a mistaken-identity plot going on at the same time.*)

DICK: Well . . . Honestly, I don't know quite how to put it.

MISS G. (*softly*): Is it – so very difficult?

DICK: Well, dash it, Gloria – I mean Miss Godalming – we hardly know each other, and (*business of fiddling with tie*) a fellow feels such a fool. . . .

I leave the rest to your imagination, though it is a bequest I wouldn't want left to mine. It comes out, on this occasion, that all Dick wanted was to borrow her razor. The real proposal comes later. Dick trudges down to breakfast with a farcical cold, the result of having climbed a drain-pipe in a hailstorm, clad only in pyjamas, to steal the manuscript of Lady Godalming's scandalous autobiography from its place in the *escritoire*. The emotional climax is now at hand:

DICK: Would you bind passing the bustard?
MISS G. (*primly*): Not in the least, Richard.
DICK: Thag you. Atchoo. (*He munches dolefully, albeit with determination. All stage directions in English farce read like this, albeit worse.*) I say – Gloria!
MISS G.: Yes, Richard?
DICK: I dode suppose it batters a bit eddy more, but (*wildly*) I love you bost awfully, and – Gloria, will you let me use your razor for always?
MISS G. (*recklessly throwing her toast to the floor*): Of course I will, you darling chump!

Their embrace is interrupted by the French maid Marie, pronounced Murray, and the title of the piece, a miracle of catarrhal euphony, is *Barry Be Todight*.

English romantic drama is built around interrupted or frustrated embraces. Uninterrupted embraces only take place years before the curtain rises. Their purpose is purely functional – to provide illegitimate children who turn up later from nowhere, fully grown and ready to wreak all kinds of havoc. By this time their father has died; his widow has remarried and begun a new life in Wiltshire. The advent of the love-child is announced by the butler: 'There's a young person to see you, milady. A Mr Richard.' Milady goes out to prune some phlox, leaving the stage clear for the entrance of a shabby, gangling, ill-dressed youth. He surveys the room, nodding sagely to himself. As befits his station (he has travelled on the night train from Liverpool), he seems overawed and embarrassed.

Milady re-enters garlanded with phlox prunings. Then:

MILADY: Ah! You must be – let's see, what was it? – Mr Richard?
RICHARD: Yes, Lady Scarsley. I hope you don't mind my intruding?
MILADY: Not at all, not at all. (*Pause.*) Well now, how can I be of –
RICHARD: It's just as – *he* described it.

MILADY: What is?

RICHARD: This room. The mantelpiece, with all those funny china dogs on it. The picture of – Aunt Eliza, isn't it? And all his first editions – even the Ben Jonsons! And the photo of Uncle Roger at the siege of Srinegar! It's all – rather like a dream.

MILADY (*faintly*): How do you know all this?

RICHARD (*simply*): I'm – Richard, mother.

MILADY: You mean – ?

RICHARD: Richard. Richard's son.

MILADY: Richard's – ! *My dear boy . . .*

And so on. Richard is going to bring chaos to the quiet, secluded backwater of milady's life, but there is a play in him somewhere, and a fat part for a virginal young actor, which is the only kind of young actor the English stage adores.

Actresses, by an unjust dispensation, have far fewer chances. Prejudice forbids them any form of self-indulgence. Until she reaches the age of thirty, the English actress is allowed only to play ingenues, girls too young for love and scared of it. When she reaches fifty, she can begin to play sophisticated dowagers, women too old for love and disillusioned by it. Between thirty and fifty there is a total gap, covering the vital years in which women swap lovers and husbands, have affairs and divorces, and run the gamut from man to man. The erstwhile ingenue then returns to the stage, wheezing and thundering, as a dragon. Until some playwright arrives to reclaim those lost years, it must be assumed that no Englishwoman of mature intelligence engages in any kind of romantic activity at all.

And what conclusions can we draw? One, I think, is self-evident. Our dramatists do not hold the mirror up to nature; they hold it up to other mirrors. They ape the theatre of the past, instead of shaping the life of the present. They will wear gags and blinkers, spread half-truths and smoke-screens – anything rather than stare life in the face and set down the form and passion of what they see. To the exceptions, I apologize. At the rule, I shrug.

(1954)

SOME NOTES ON STAGE CHILDREN

On the whole, stage children come in four sizes – the Wide-Eyed Bouncers, the Bespectacled Swots, the Sensitive Types, and the Juvenile Delinquents. The Americans have lately added another to the list, the Tot Satanic, which reared both of its ugly heads in the heroine of *The Bad Seed*, a mass murderess on the right side of nine years old. If we English lag behind in the creation of really psychotic children, the reason may partly be that we lack the vocabulary for it. Psychiatry has not yet conquered our nurseries. The Manhattan mother, discussing her youngest, may say, not without a certain collector's pride: 'Raoul's developing what looks to us like a peach of an avoidance-syndrome.' And if daughter Kerry shows a tendency to throw lighted fireworks into the refrigerator, this is not mere devilment but 'a prototypal act of nuisance-aggression'. Children do not have memories, they have 'image-retentiveness', and instead of stealing the jam, they indulge in 'retaliatory pilfering'. In this way the average child can be made to seem interestingly abnormal, and the abnormal child downright insane. If cursed with a brat who does nothing all day but sit in the corner swatting flies, you whisper, 'His conative faculty's gone dead on us lately, but we're not worried – you know what Griebmann says about the destructiveness of activity for activity's sake'. These wonderful phrases have not yet passed into our language, and hence the lunatic child seldom appears on our stage.

Nor do we have the American habit, fast becoming a minor industry, of writing plays about fathers driven crazy by their failure to establish 'a good relationship' with their sons. If an English father were to grip his ten-year-old boy by the shoulders and say: 'Don't know how it is, son, but we never seem to – to *get through* to each other,' the child would assume that he was drunk. In an American play the child would burst into tears and take to drink himself.

The function of English stage children is usually to teach their elders the rudiments of good behaviour, on the out-of-the-mouths-of-babes-and-sucklings theory. If junior starts wearing a shoulder-holster and spitting in church, it is a hint to Mums and Dads that they had better set about patching up their marriage. If Sensitive Type spends her nights sulking in the rabbit-hutch, it is because she is being deprived of love. If a whole batch of sucklings flies off to a peace conference (as in Roger MacDougall's *Escapade*), it is to teach their parents the foolishness of war. Modern kid plays are always cautionary plays.

The smallest category is that devoted to Juvenile Delinquents. It takes as its text the words 'Society is the Real Criminal'. This quickly grows wearisome, not because it is not true, but because it tends to rob the child of any capacity for individual choice, which is the life-blood of drama. Whatever he does, it is never his doing: he is a pawn in a game of sociological chess. For recent examples, see *Cosh Boy* and *Murder Story*.

We next find, loitering in the toils of adolescence, a listless battalion of Sensitive Types. These are the direct descendants of the children in Victorian plays, who existed only for the purpose of dying young or being orphaned. The girls get tragic crushes, from which they are gently dissuaded: 'You must remember, darling, Robert is fifty years older than you. When you're twenty-five, he'll be seventy-nine. Had you thought of that?' The oldest inhabitants in this group are the Constant Nymph and Young Woodley. These two, by a sort of box-office mating, have bred dozens of equally tormented offspring. Before Mummy can announce in the last scene that 'Our little girl has become a woman,' her little girl must spend at least two acts hating Mummy's guts. Traumatic experiences are not uncommon. The heroine of *The Seventh Veil* was blighted as a concert pianist by a school caning, while *The Girl Who Couldn't Quite* was fixated by a wart on her nanny's nose. The latter, by the way, was the last ingenue on the English stage to utter the time-honoured line: 'I'm going to keep crying till there's no more cry left in me.'

Though a little short on cry, the dominant variety of child's play is undoubtedly school drama. It is always a public school; no other kind of education is known to the English theatre. Only three types of men need apply for jobs on the staff: breezy young half-wits (to teach Sports), thin-lipped sadists (to teach Latin or Science, according to the author's politics), and genial old bumblers (to teach a Broad

Understanding of Humanity). Sadists and bumblers alike address their charges in polysyllables: 'And what has the egregious Watson minor to say for himself? Come, come, boy, say not that the omniscience of yesternight has vanished with the snows of yesteryear!' Latin tags are also in evidence, a favourite being the one beginning '*Tempora mutantur. . . .*'

Every school has its Swot, who is named Crump or Pilkington and wears clothes that are slightly too small for him. Primitive Swots were always buffoons, but with the dawn of the liberal conscience they have become semi-sympathetic characters: 'Do they rag you,' the leading lady may inquire, 'for reading Swinburne in the dorm?' But the great majority of stage schoolboys, now as in the past, are Wide-Eyed Bouncers. These bounce like the kind of beach-ball one longs to throw out to sea. They begin every sentence with 'I say!' and their vocabulary of slang has survived unchanged from the era of Jack Harkaway and the horseless carriage. To them the Swot is 'a complete smear' who talks 'bilge', and they express derision in such terms as 'Three groans for the Beak!' Stool-pigeons are said to 'split', and no self-respecting Bouncer ever gets through a scene without using 'funk it', 'shirty', or 'lazy slacker'. Bouncers never leave a room: they 'cut along'. One of the finest recent snatches of Bouncer dialogue was contributed by Warren Chetham Strode: 'No decent chap mentions soccer at a rugger school' – though it is strongly challenged by someone else's masterly line: 'What rot, Sholto! Nobody sacks a man for blubbing!'

Every now and then our playwrights try their hand at the boy-born-to-be-king theme, in which the hero is a child with an aura of mystery surrounding him. J. M. Barrie's *The Boy David* is a fair example of this sort of thing. David tells Samuel that he has just had an important thought while minding the sheep. Invited to share it, he recites the opening verses of the Twenty-third Psalm. 'You must finish that some day,' says Samuel sagely. These chosen children, destined in later life to become prophets, poets, or inventors of the spinning-jenny, are regarded by their families – for the first act, at least – with resentment and hostility. They are the Cinderellas of the household, and represent the apotheosis of the Sensitive Type. Suddenly they perform a miracle or write a symphony. Their parents are appalled and beat them; but before long the mighty of the earth, having heard of the wonder, are besieging the little mud hut. The child is uncomfortably dressed in his best, and one of the visitors is sure to remark: 'Your son, my good woman, stands in no need of external finery. His power is within.' Emlyn Williams's *The Wind of Heaven* has all the earmarks of the breed, which has proved extremely prolific.

The classic, all-round English urchin is still, of course, Peter Pan. Pan is no Swot, but he combines the characteristics of all the other types. He is Wide-Eyed, he is Sensitive, and he is murderous enough at times to be classed as a Juvenile Delinquent. The only adult thing about Barrie's play is its unctuous sentimentality; the rest shows real insight into the cruelty and wantonness of childhood. It also gives a disquieting picture of the nanny-worship and mother-complexes which turn so many English children into interesting psychological wrecks. The 'Wendy bird' is first wounded and then deified as mother; the villain of the piece is Father, who ends up literally in the dog-house.

If someone were to undertake a full Freudian analysis of Pan, I have a feeling that it would teach us a great deal about all English dramatists who write about children. For they share with him one basic quality: a rooted aversion to growing up.

(*1954*)

PROSE AND THE PLAYWRIGHT

Where the modern poetic drama is concerned, I have always been for the man Bacon quotes who, when asked his opinion of poets, said he thought them the best writers, next to those that wrote prose. But lately, among my friends, I have been finding myself in a beleaguered minority; the post-war vogue of T. S. Eliot and Christopher Fry has brought back into play that ancient battering-ram of criticism, the assumption that the upper reaches of dramatic experience are the exclusive province of the poet. This kind of talk is probably giving the prose playwrights a brutal inferiority-complex, and I have a mind to contest it. For if Eliot is right in suggesting that there are certain subtle and rarefied states of being which can achieve theatrical expression only in verse, then a great battle has been lost, almost by default.

We tend to forget how long it took to make prose socially acceptable in the theatre. Up to the last quarter of the nineteenth century it remained a slightly dingy poor relation; the Greeks sniffed at it, Shakespeare reserved it mostly for persiflage, Molière shunned it whenever (as in *Tartuffe* or *Le Misanthrope*) he had anything ambitious in hand, and in the long eighteenth-century debates about the relative fitness of blank verse and heroic couplets for tragedy, prose seldom got more than a passing and perfunctory mention. The English romantics carried on the tradition of bardolatry: Shelley, Byron, Wordsworth, Keats, and Coleridge all wrote unactable verse tragedies, thus delivering what might easily have been the death-blow to serious drama in English. Nobody seemed to have noticed that ever since Shakespeare's death poetic tragedy had been languishing and prose comedy flourishing; and it occurred to no one that the latter's prosperity might be due not so much to its being comic as to its being prose. In the Elizabethan era, before drama had been clearly distinguished from other literary forms, it naturally contained a good deal of the epic, much of the lyric, and a strong flavour of what A. B. Walkley called 'that element of mixed philosophy and rhetoric which was soon afterwards to be diverted into other channels, in England by Sir Thomas Browne, in France by the great pulpit orators'. By the beginning of the last century the process of differentiation had taken place, and the drama stolidly ignored it.

The three gigantic musketeers of prose were, of course, Ibsen, Chekhov, and Shaw; they made it respectable, and Chekhov even went so far as to show that prose, by means of what it implied rather than what it stated, could reproduce the effect of poetry in purely theatrical terms. By 1900 it began to look as if prose had gained its point – and pretty tardily, too, since the novel had started to replace the verse epic two centuries earlier. It would have surprised the drama critics of the period to be told that within fifty years the old medium would once more be asserting its claim to dramatic supremacy. Yet that is what has happened. Just as prose has started to test its wings, we are asked to believe that it can never fly. The powers of the line that stops short of the margin are again being hymned and its mysteries celebrated.

This seems to me grossly unhistorical and based on an alarming number of unproven assumptions. For an irrevocable change has been overtaking language in the last three hundred years. Poetry and colloquial prose, which are now (in spite of Wordsworth) linguistically divorced, shared in the sixteenth century rich champaigns of vocabulary and image. Elizabethan pamphlets are as generous with metaphor as Elizabethan plays; and a dramatist could inject a shot of colloquialism into a tragic aria without courting bathos. Nobody titters when Hamlet, in mid-soliloquy, exclaims, 'Why, what an ass am I!'; but when Aaron, in Christopher Fry's tragedy *The Firstborn*, says of Moses that 'he took me by the scruff of my heart', it is comic in much the same way as Abe Burrows's parody of the 'sophisticated-type' love song: 'You put a piece of carbon-paper under your heart, and gave me just a copy of your love.' Everyone agrees that formal poetic diction is dead; yet if you spike a dramatic verse-form with the vernacular, the experiment invariably fails – unless a comic or ironic effect was what you had in mind. Auden, Isherwood, Eliot, and Fry have all exploited this trick of bathos; and it may be that the wheel has come full circle, that poetry in the theatre should be confined to comedy, where its potency still lingers.

The customary plea for verse is summed up in this extract from one of Dryden's essays: 'All the arguments which are formed against it, can amount to no more than this, that it is not so near conversation as prose, and therefore not so natural. But it is clear to all who understand poetry, that serious plays ought not to imitate conversation too nearly.' And once you admit that 'naturalness' is not enough, he continues, you are halfway to accepting poetry: 'You have lost that which you call natural, and have not acquired the last perfection of Art.' But Dryden's antithesis is a false one. The perfection of art in the theatre depends neither on naturalism nor on poetry. Drama has in its time borrowed tricks from both, but what it has built is a new and separate structure, whose foundation stones – the last acts of *The Master Builder* and *Three Sisters* – are architectural triumphs of prose over naturalism.

On naturalism I shrink from pronouncing, because I have never (has anyone?) seen a completely naturalistic play – I doubt if one exists. What bothers me is the way in which the higher criticism equates prose with poverty of dramatic expression. 'What is the prose for God?' cries one pundit, quoting from Granville Barker and forgetting that the answer to the question is on almost every page of the Bible. Nobody wants to banish luxury of language from the theatre; what needs banishing is the notion that it is incompatible with prose, the most flexible weapon the stage has ever had, and still shining new. Those playwrights who have followed the Ibsen-Chekhov lead are in the main stream of modern drama. Giraudoux for prime example; *La Folle de Chaillot* and *La Guerre de Troie* represent prose exulting in its own versatility, embracing slang and stateliness, gutter and glitter, in one enormous grasp. Synge and O'Casey stand beside Giraudoux in the great line; and when, earlier this year, Dylan Thomas's *Under Milk Wood* was published, nobody could doubt that only death had robbed us of another to join them. *Under Milk Wood* was commissioned by the BBC for sound broadcasting, but two Sunday-night stagings of it at the Old Vic proved that it could enmesh the watcher as well as the listener. Here, unfolding in the talk and thoughts of its inhabitants, was a day in the life of a Welsh coastal town, a devout and mischievous celebration of the sea, soil, wind, and wantonness of Wales. Prose went into battle rejoicing. Take, for instance, this exchange between Mrs Cherry Owen and her errant husband:

MRS CHERRY OWEN: Remember last night? In you reeled, my boy, as drunk as a deacon with a big wet bucket and a fish-frail full of stout and you looked at me and you said, 'God has come home!' you said, and then over the bucket you went, sprawling and bawling, and the floor was all flagons and eels.
CHERRY OWEN: Was I wounded?
MRS CHERRY OWEN: And then you took off your trousers and you said, 'Does anybody want to fight?' Oh, you old baboon.

Or the letter written by Mog Edwards, 'a draper mad with love', to his 'Beloved Myfanwy Price, my Bride in Heaven':

I love you until Death do us part and then we shall be together for ever and ever. A new parcel of ribbons has come from Carmarthen today, all the colours in the rainbow. I wish I could tie a ribbon in your hair a white one but it cannot be. I dreamed last night you were all dripping wet and you sat on my lap as the Reverend Jenkins went down the street. I see you got a mermaid in your lap he said and he lifted his hat. He is a proper Christian. Not like Cherry Owen who said you should have thrown her back he said. Business is very poorly . . . If this goes on I shall be in the workhouse. My heart is in your bosom and yours is in mine. God be with you always Myfanwy Price and keep you lovely for me in His Heavenly Mansion. I must stop now and remain, Your Eternal, Mog Edwards.

The whole play is a tumult of living, and its burden is compressed into the remark of Polly Garter, the town tart: 'Isn't life a terrible thing, thank God!' Philip Hope-Wallace, writing in the *Manchester Guardian*, sent his thoughts to the right place when he said: 'Not since *Juno and the Paycock* have we heard in a theatre words coming up thus, not chosen but compelled: a fountain from the heart.'

Thomas side-stepped the snare which besets the prose playwright who, though he abjures verse, secretly aspires to the condition of poetry. This fatal urge is responsible for the solemn, booming cadences, the sentences lying in comatose state, which one sometimes finds in the plays of Charles Morgan. *The Burning Glass* is a forest of prose on stilts, opulently teetering. Morgan's excuse, of course, is that Thomas had a head start on him, since (like O'Casey) he was putting words in the mouths of a people essentially imaginative. Morgan's characters are drawn from the English upper class, whose vocabulary is crippled by the restraints of social usage (no tears, no ecstasies), and about whom it is today practically impossible to write a great play. The spirit is not in them; or if it is, their tight lips firmly repress it. I doubt if even Arthur Miller or Tennessee Williams, the prose masters of the contemporary English-speaking theatre, could construct a tragedy around the country homes of Berks and Bucks. It is significant that the most successful passages of *The Cocktail Party* were those in which Eliot exposed the vacuity of *haut bourgeois* chatter:

JULIA: . . . The only man I ever met who could hear the cry of bats.
PETER: Hear the cry of bats?
JULIA: He could hear the cry of bats.
CELIA: But how do you know he could hear the cry of bats?
JULIA: Because he said so. And I believed him.

Eliot is here using verse to show how resolutely, how comically unpoetic his characters are; and, wryly but appropriately, it works.

One of the handicaps of poetry is that penumbra of holiness, the legacy of the nineteenth century, which still surrounds it, coaxing us into tolerating sentimental excesses we would never forgive in prose:

O God, O God, if I could return to yesterday, before I thought that I had made a decision. What devil left the door on the latch for these doubts to enter? And then you came back, you, the angel of destruction – just as I felt sure. In a moment, at your touch, there is nothing but ruin.

Exit, you might expect, into snowstorm; but you would be wrong. The lines come not from Victorian melodrama but from *The Cocktail Party*, printed as prose. Their lameness is particularly vexing because Eliot has shown himself capable of writing intensely muscular dramatic prose. So has Fry: one has only to read his lecture, 'An Experience of Critics', parts of which are as speakable as a Giraudoux tirade. Much of his latest play, *The Dark is Light Enough*, is infinitely less dramatic. Its construction rules out of court the old argument that poetic plays are deficient only in plot; *The Dark Is Light Enough* abounds in plot and incident, yet remains as static as a candle-lit tableau or darkling waxwork. It happens in a chateau on the Austro-Hungarian border. The Hungarian rebellion of 1848 has just begun, and a crisis is precipitated by the Countess Rosmarin, who decides to give shelter to Gettner, a deserter from the revolutionary army. The play's main action is the regeneration of Gettner, nihilist and traitor, by the Countess, who stands for divine charity, the justification of God's circuitous ways to man.

The first great drawback is the fact that Rosmarin, being by definition perfect, is incapable of development; in spite of Dame Edith Evans's vocal exertions, she can scarcely avoid resembling a benignly crinolined soup-kitchen. The second and greater drawback is, I am afraid, Fry's style, which – though it is noticeably less sportive than it used to be – seems now to have taken on the texture of diatomite, a substance used in the manufacture of pipestems which contains thousands of fossils to the cubic inch. The characters studiously express different attitudes towards life, but they use interchangeable rhythms and identical tricks of speech in which to do so. They *tell* us, with ruthless fluency, what kind of people they are, instead of letting us find out for ourselves. I needn't say that there are some fine set pieces of rhetoric; but the best of them – that in which Rosmarin

likens Gettner to a blue plucked goose shivering on the water's brink –
embodies in itself the germ of poetry's weakness: it describes in
repose rather than illustrates in action. And one regrets the readiness
with which Fry has succumbed to padding and jingle, in phrases
like 'for my sake, if my sake is worthy', 'a coward, if a coward is
what you are', 'splendidly sleeping', 'precariously promising', and
'inconsolable inclination'.

It is good to learn that he is at present making prose adaptations
of Anouilh's *L'Alouette* and Giraudoux's *La Guerre de Troie*; perhaps
the experience will lure him across the frontier into the large Gothic
landscapes of prose. The chance of converting Eliot is, I imagine,
much slimmer; but it may not be impertinent to suggest that even in
his best play, *Murder in the Cathedral*, the most impressive pages were
those which contained the speeches of self-exculpation by the four
knights and the sermon delivered by Beckett on Christmas Day. And
these were all prose:

I have spoken to you today, dear children of God, of the martyrs of
the past . . . because it is fitting, on Christ's birthday, to remember what
is that Peace which He brought; and because, dear children, I do not
think I shall ever preach to you again; and because it is possible that in a
short time you may have yet another martyr, and that one perhaps not
the last. . . .

In poetry, Fry gilds where Eliot anoints; in neither procedure are
there seeds of real dramatic vitality. If they, the foremost heretics, can
be persuaded off their crosses, away from their martyrdom in a lost
cause, the theatre would immediately benefit. Mallarmé once said, in
lapidary despair: '*Pour moi le cas d'un poète, en cette société qui ne le
permet de vivre, c'est le cas d'un homme qui s'isole pour sculpter son propre
tombeau.*' But he was slightly in error. It is not our society but our
theatre which rejects the poet; 'nowadays,' as Walkley said, 'we
expect a drama to be purely dramatic.' If poetic playwrights did not
exist, it might be an agreeable caprice to invent them; but it would no
longer be a necessity. And in a theatre starved by the cinema and
besieged by television, necessities must come first.

(*1954*)

A NOTE ON CRITICISM

Critics in the past have seen themselves variously as torch-bearers, pall-bearers, and lighthouses shining over unmapped seas; I see myself predominantly as a lock. If the key, which is the work of art, fits snugly into my mechanism of bias and preference, I click and rejoice; if not, I am helpless, and can only offer the artist the address of a better locksmith. Sometimes, unforeseen, a masterpiece seizes the knocker, batters down the door, and enters unopposed; and when that happens, I am a willing casualty. I cave in *con amore*. But mostly I am at a loss. It is a sombre truth that nowadays our intellectuals go to the cinema and shun the theatre. Their assistance is sadly missed; but their defection is my opportunity.

(*1954*)

ART FOR OUR SAKE

Riffling through my colleagues' comments on M. Sartre's *Nekrassov*, I see that, while most of them found it witty, nearly all of them deplored the way in which it 'resorted to propaganda' – as if the presence of propaganda in a play automatically condemned it. I used to share this assumption myself. None was readier than I to chide the proselytizing playwright, to mock at the zeal of the determined homilist. But now, in this arid theatrical season, I begin to wonder whether I was right. In demanding an end to propaganda, was I not depriving the drama of one of its most ancient sources of energy?

Nobody denies that there are bad propaganda plays, just as there are bad poetic plays. But to hold that all plays containing propaganda are by definition bad is to run counter to a theory of art on which much great drama is based and which nobody seriously challenged until the nineteenth century. I mean the notion that the purpose of art was 'to instruct through delight', the idea set forward in Sidney's

Defence of Poesie. Early playwrights would have been shocked by the suggestion that they were not propagandists. The whole of Greek tragedy (and all satire from Aristophanes through Ben Jonson to M. Sartre) is admonitory in intent, and admonition is nothing if not moral propaganda. *Everyman* is a propaganda play. So is *Henry V*; so are *An Enemy of the People*, *A Doll's House*, and *Ghosts*; so is the entire *oeuvre* of the greatest living European playwright, Bertolt Brecht.

At this point we had better define propaganda and distinguish between good and bad forms of it. A melodrama is a play whose author is more interested in the impact events are having on his audience than in their impact on his characters. A propaganda play is the same, with 'ideas' substituted for 'events'. Its aim is to start you thinking; and, though I agree that the effect of the greatest plays is to present an action so complete that only silence can succeed it in the mind, I cannot understand by what logic this rules out the theatre of parable, polemic, and pamphlet. Propaganda plays are admittedly distortions of life, but so are cartoon films, and they are all the better for it.

I know many good minor playwrights whose view of life is biased but clear, tendentious but honourable. Fear of being dubbed 'propagandist' prevents them from stating it. Instead, they give us feeble 'mood' plays with no point of view at all. This fear of commitment, of being thought *engagé*, accounts for the rash of pseudo-Chekhovs that has broken out all over the contemporary theatre. Don't comment, just record: kindly stick to the news. And this attitude is encouraged by the terminological vagueness which led one eminent British critic to dismiss Giraudoux's *La Folle de Chaillot* as 'a misty piece of Socialist propaganda'. Only a madman would wish that Chekhov had written didactically, yet it seems even madder to argue from this that the stage should never be used by lesser men as a political platform or as a pulpit. The logical end of that dispute is to exact from every playwright a guarantee that he holds no convictions strongly enough to let them influence his writing. And that is like demanding a certificate of intellectual impotence.

Bad propaganda plays occur when the idea being propagated is trite and too repetitively stressed, or when the author's tone is either embittered or sentimentally fulsome. But it is irrelevant to indict a propaganda play on the ground that it is 'unfair'. Morality plays are 'unfair' to the Devil; *Henry V* is 'unfair' to France. The self-indulgent hero of Mayakovsky's satire, *Klop*, is treated with formidable unfairness, yet the play prodded me, spurred me, irritated me into thought. Before calling him 'preacher' or 'sermonizer', remember the handicaps under which the propagandist works. He is a judge passing sentence on the strength of evidence which he has himself manufactured, and if the sentence is too harsh or too shrilly delivered, the audience will be quick to unmask him as a bigot. The finest and rarest sort of theatrical teacher is that defined in a dictum of Howard Lindsay's: 'If you are going to write a propaganda play, you had better not let any of your characters know what the propaganda is.' Brecht's *Mother Courage* falls into this category. Behind its every line, as behind every line of *Everyman*, there beats a passionate desire to improve the human condition. Honestly felt and truly expressed, this passion can generate a special and unique dramatic excitement, an irreplaceable theatrical heat. It brings us into contact not only with a man's power of narrative invention, but with the mind of the man himself.

There are many other kinds of theatrical excitement. All I seek to establish is that propaganda has a place in the hierarchy. Brecht once drew an analogy which I think worth quoting. Some surgeons, he said, are content to supply merely a diagnosis; others feel it their duty to recommend a cure. Most propaganda plays, admittedly, offer quack remedies. The danger is that our hatred of quacks may lead us to despise the true healers.

(*1956*)

PAUSING ON THE STAIRS

Would you know the shortest way to bad playwriting? I will tell you. It is to begin with a great theme, a Grand Purpose, in the hope that it will throw forth, of its own essential energy, such desirable by-products as character and dialogue. Woe to him who so far misunderstands the nature of drama as to suppose that abstractions can breed human beings! The diary of such a man might read: 'Really must decide on Theme tomorrow. Torn between Problems of Power, Loneliness, Colour, H-Bomb Threat, and Revolutionary Spirit in Eastern Europe. All major, surely? At least they can't say I'm ignoring the crisis of our time. Have worked out just what I feel about all five Themes, so the big creative effort is over. All that remains is the donkey-work of filling in dialogue and characters. But which Theme to choose? Went out for walk to clear head. Strange encounter with landlady on stairs: she said I looked like George III and tittered. Silly woman.'

Useless, of course, to point out that the genesis of good plays is hardly ever abstract; that it tends, on the contrary, to be something as concrete and casual as a glance intercepted, a remark overheard, or an insignificant news item buried at the bottom of page three. Yet it is by trivialities like these that the true playwright's blood is fired. They spur him to story-telling; they bring on the narrative fit that is his glory and his basic credential. Show me a congenital eavesdropper with the instincts of a peeping Tom, and I will show you the makings of a dramatist. Only the makings, of course: curiosity about people is merely the beginning of the road to the masterpiece: but if that curiosity is sustained you will find, when the rules have been mastered and the end has been reached, that a miracle has happened. Implicit in the play, surging between and beneath the lines, will be exactly what the author feels about the Major Issues of his Time.

To take off from a generality is an infertile exercise, as if a man should carry about with him the plan of some mighty edifice, hoping that if he stares at it long enough the human beings needed to build it will spring full-grown from the parchment. Vain hope, for the secret of life is not there. It hides where it has always hidden, in the most obvious and unguarded place. It lies somewhere within that staircase eccentric, my diarist's landlady, who likened him to George III and tittered. Study her, or your wife, or the grocer; probe them patiently; and you will find, to your resounding amazement, that you have written a play about power, loneliness, colour, bomb-fright, and revolution to boot. Would you know the shortest way to good playwriting? Pause on the stairs.

(1957)

HAZARDS OF PLAYGOING

There are a good many inconveniences attached to the simple act of going to a theatre. The greatest of these is usually the play itself, and on this most critics rightly concentrate. In an empty week, however, I have been pondering those minor irritations, peas under the mattress, that ought to be removed if playgoing is to take its proper place among life's softer options.

One such pea, in London at least, is the difficulty of finding out what theatre is housing the play you want to see. The list of attractions used by West End managers to advertise their wares in the newspapers is primarily a list of theatres, not of plays. If your choice is *Divorce Me, Darling*, you may have to run through the names of forty playhouses, before finding what you want. In New York you would simply look under 'D', and there, after *Dig My Gallows Deep* and before *Dreyfus and Son*, it would be, followed by the name and address of the theatre. The London system harks back to the days of the actor-managers, when you went to the Lyceum to see Irving without caring very much what you were going to see him in. Nowadays, when the play and not the playhouse is the thing, the New York arrangement is clearly more sensible.

Having identified the theatre, you next have to get there. Here London has the advantage of both Paris and New York, especially if you travel by taxi. Seen from the air round curtain-time, Broadway resembles a war of caterpillars; rows of cabs, minutely jerking forward, clog the whole area. In Paris, of course, all taxis vanish from the streets for half an hour before the curtain goes up. You occasionally catch sight of one roaring out to keep a date with destiny or dinner at Courbevoie, but the chance of its stopping is remote; the most you can expect is a tragic shrug from the driver as he flashes by the slave of fate or his stomach.

Assuming you arrive at the theatre, you must then dispose of your coat. You will almost certainly be wearing one. Indoor drama thrives only in cold weather; few people in hot climates would be foolish enough to spend a whole evening indoors with neither wine nor word on their lips. The cloakrooms of most London theatres are mere holes in the wall, wardrobes occupied by five hundred coats and one human being, and it is amazing that M. Ionesco has not yet written a play about them. Berlin and Moscow are the only cities known to me that have solved the garment-reclaiming problem. At the Schiller-Theater in Berlin there are two long walls of cloakrooms in the foyer, staffed by twenty attendants, and the same is true of the Moscow Art.

The scandal of London theatre programmes is notorious and seemingly incurable. Whenever I watch British audiences happily paying sixpence for eight pages of text, six of which are devoted to advertisements, a quotation from Brecht leaps to my mind: 'I can see their divine patience, but where is their divine fury?' In Paris, at the very least, you get a little booklet for your money; and in New York you get a rather larger booklet for nothing. *Playbill*, the Broadway programme, is published and edited by a private company; it is in fact a forty-page weekly magazine, with critical articles on international drama, and full biographies of the author, director, and actors. The only London theatre to have taken even a tentative step in this direction is the Westminster, where the programmes tell you not only who the actors are but where you last saw them. Unfortunately, in many of the plays produced at this theatre the information is not encouraging.

Interval amenities vary from capital to capital. In New York (as in Paris) I tend to doze, drugged by the heat: the reviving draughts that sweep across London theatres are unknown in these upholstered ovens. The New Yorkers themselves, forbidden liquor in theatres, obey laconic commands to 'get your orange drinks, get your refreshing orange drinks'. The French make unhurried bee-lines for the longest, best-stocked theatre bars on earth. Meanwhile the Englishman is barking his elbows in a tiny, thronged snuggery where warm gin is dispensed by surly, glaring, female teetotallers.

The final hazard of London playgoing is the playing of the National Anthem, during which we stand to attention, while gloves, scarves, and programmes fall unregarded to the floor. This compulsive display of patriotism (unknown outside Britain and the Commonwealth) is today almost classifiable as a game. People with at least one hand on the exit-door when the drum-roll begins are held to be exempt from standing through Dr Bull's little melody. The rest must stay rooted to the spot, staring vaingloriously at the curtain; if they move, some undefined forfeit is payable.

Only two British theatres have departed from this nightly habit of sending the Queen happy. One is Theatre Workshop, where (says the programme) 'the National Anthem will be played only in the presence of royalty or heads of States'. The other is the Royal Opera House, Covent Garden, where it is played once a year, at the beginning of the season. This seems a sane procedure. I might add that royalist hymns can be extremely irksome to foreigners. Some years ago the Americans in the London production of *Guys and Dolls* were requested to sing the anthem after the opening performance. All agreed except one, who shook his head and said: 'It ain't my toon.' Besought to change his mind, he declined. 'It's a matter of principle,' he said. 'I'm for the people. *They* oughta get sent.'

One thing about the London theatre, though: you can get into it. Contrast this with the Palais de Chaillot in Paris, the home of the Théâtre National Populaire and the most impenetrable playhouse on earth. You have, let us say, booked a seat and go to the *contrôle* to collect it. But no, this is the agency *contrôle*; you must go to the other, which handles private reservations. You sprint across, while a voice barks through a loudspeaker that unless you take your seat in three minutes you will be excluded from the performance.

You seize your ticket and dart ('*Deux minutes*') towards the escalator that leads to the vast subterranean auditorium. You scuttle, skidding, down two marble staircases ('*Une minute*'), whereupon the full Kafkaesque horror is unleashed on you: not a warning bell, but a deafening fanfare of hunting horns blares out of the wall at your ear. You run along echoing corridors, to cries of '*Au bout, monsieur, et puis à gauche*'. More trumpets shriek, and you fling yourself into your seat. Ten minutes pass, during which nothing happens. At length the curtain rises and you realize, too late, that you have no programme.

(*1958*)

PERORATION:
A SPEECH DELIVERED IN 1958 AT
THE NATIONAL FILM THEATRE,
LONDON

EVER since the Greeks we have been told that drama is a social art, a communal experience, and we still accept as fact what is nowadays mostly a fiction. For most people today the theatre is a place where *we* go – if we go at all – to see and hear *them*, the others, the glittering sealed-off people who provide what is called 'art' for us to wonder at. That 'they' belong to the same mundane world as 'us' and are subject to the same stresses and dismays is a notion that all too seldom bothers us. What we have lost, in the commercial theatre as a whole, with its talk of playgoing as 'an occasion', is the vital sense that we make drama: it is about us: and the moment it ceases to be about us, it ceases to be drama.

The opposition to this simple sentiment is deeply entrenched, even among comparatively literate people. I lately received a letter from a well-known Irish writer chastising me for my heresies. I had written somewhere that since art had a bearing on life, it was capable of influencing life, and that it was one of its functions to do so. Sadly, he rebuked me. To say that art could influence life, he asserted, was like saying that cricket could influence sport. Art, he went on, was as much a part of life as toad-in-the-hole or lipstick: it was something special and unique, a compartment of living rather than an interpretation of life. My correspondent is a sane and normally rational man, but on this subject he had fallen inadvertently into the dangerous midst of those who would segregate art from life, them from us. De Quincey was nearer to the truth when he defined art as *idem in alio* – the same thing in another form – by which he meant that art was parasitic on life. A statue is a man in clay or marble: a play is a human situation projected in theatrical terms. And the sculpture could no more exist without the man than the play could exist without the human situation. The *idem*, which art transmutes *in alio*, is reality –

our reality. What we have to decide is whether we want our drama to batten on the lipstick of life or the blood of it.

If drama is to play a part in human advancement, we must keep this in mind: are we studying the relevance of a text to philology or the relevance of a human experience to our lives? In most schools drama is taught as a suspiciously amusing branch of literature: we would gain much if it were taught as an offshoot of sociology. To study Shakespeare is not enough: to understand the sources of drama it would help if pupils were encouraged to improvise and write plays of their own based on current events in the world and their own lives. Shakespeare, as we all know, was not for an age but for all time; but the fact that he was so deeply of his own age is one of the reasons for his timelessness. The secret of theatrical longevity is neither to care about the past nor to worry over the future: it is to relate to the present.

I have to underline this platitude because the contemporary trend is to deny it. The idea of drama as an *alternative* to life is embedded in the modern psyche. The play that distracts is extolled at the expense of the play that focuses; and the play that supplies nourishment as well as entertainment will be lucky if the critics bestow on it no phrase more damning than 'strong meat' or 'not for the squeamish'. A *Daily Mail* editorial, entitled 'Cobblers and Lasts', appeared in March 1958 and stated in brisk, uncompromising terms the case for undernourished and undernourishing drama. The 'Let 'Em Eat Chips' school has rarely exposed itself so nakedly. The column began by quoting John Osborne, who had somewhere complained that London playgoers used the theatre 'as a sort of pleasant indigestion pill'. It continued:

Now we, in our ignorance, always imagined that that was what the theatre was for. It was something to do after dinner. It is a diversion It is a relaxation.

If the theatre is not that it is nothing. It should certainly not be a vehicle for propaganda, nor a lecture hall, nor a substitute for a revival meeting. Such things are better done elsewhere.

The stage is an ingenious device intended simply and solely to entertain. . . .

This vein, once embarked on, is almost unstoppable, and the writer went on to applaud the 'boisterous, bawdy and beautiful plays' of Shakespeare, who 'did not go to the theatre with a Message'; and ended with a smart pull-up-your-socks exhortation to Mr Osborne and the 'other members of the psycho-analytical school of literature' to put their talent to its proper use – i.e., to be resolutely trivial and lay off subjects they really feel strongly about. I am not aware that a 'psycho-analytical school' of playwrights exists, or that Mr Osborne would belong to it if it did; but if psycho-analysis means the un-ravelling of mental processes, it is certainly the stuff of drama, just as much as politics, sex, revivalism, or anything else. And I am perfectly sure that a playwright has as much right to sound off on politics as a political-leader writer has to sound off on drama. Yet this astounding editorial was not challenged by any of the *Mail*'s readers. Some of them must have been aware that the best plays, from Aeschylus to Arthur Miller, were more than diversions; that we read and see them not only for their turns of phrase but because they distil for us the living essence of societies and their problems; because they relate to us and speak, at their finest, to our whole souls, convincing us that what is happening on the stage, however far removed from us in time or geography, is not different in kind from what is happening in our hearts and habitual lives. Some *Mail* readers may have felt this to the extent of writing letters about it; if so, none was published. The editor clearly saw no need to print them. It is one of the tragedies of our culture that the cause of serious majority drama is supported only by a tiny minority. Many others, who might support it, are discouraged by being subjected night and day to the kind of propaganda for drivelling irresponsibility of which the editorial I have quoted is only one example.

I am not advocating a revolution: merely a return to the ancient idea that drama concerns all of us, that it is an extension and an illumination of our experience, not something different and 'artistic' and relaxingly apart. A French painter recently declared that, since nothing in nature precisely resembled anything else, he proposed to destroy all of his paintings which resembled anything that already existed. He became an abstractionist and is now immensely rich. Whether he is still, in any sense known to me, an artist, I cannot say. But I am sure that he was moving in the wrong direction, even for a painter; and even more for a playwright, since abstract, non-repre-sentational drama is, thanks to the stubborn physical reality of actors, almost impossible to achieve.

Stanislavsky talked once of the methods by which an actor's imagination could be kindled and excited. 'How can it be done?' he asked, and answered himself: 'By relating the subject of the play and its separate moments to real life as it unfolds today before our eyes. Learn to see and hear. Love life. Learn to bring it into art.' The advice applies not only to actors, but to playwrights and audiences as well; and that excludes none of us, even critics.

INDEX

*Some more books published by Penguins
are described on the following pages*

A Pelican Book

The Contemporary Cinema

Penelope Houston

The cinema is uniquely of the twentieth century – an art which has earned its place alongside the novel and the theatre, but which is also a great international industry, tied to the economic laws of supply and demand.

Of the total history of the cinema one quarter belongs to the years since the war. *The Contemporary Cinema* thus ranges from neo-realism to the new wave, from *On the Town* to five years of *South Pacific*, from the Gainsborough Lady to *This Sporting Life*; and the directors include not only Antonioni, Truffaut, and Anderson, but also Renoir, Buñuel, and de Sica, not only Ford, Hitchcock, and Hawks, but also Kubrick, Ray, and Cassavetes.

In a sustained, imaginative survey of the whole post-war scene, Penelope Houston shows how the cinema has adjusted itself to meet a new audience which approaches films more critically than before, but in doing so encourages new talent. At the same time she makes clear the industrial problems (in particular, the fight to co-exist with TV) which are inseparable from the business of making, distributing, and promoting a very expensive product to a highly unreliable market.

The individual talent, the business decision, the screen, and the audience are all placed firmly in perspective by the Editor of *Sight and Sound*. This is what the cinema since the war looks like in 1963. The book is illustrated with over 30 plates, and a check-list of films provides a guide to more than one hundred directors.

A Pelican Book

Anger and After
A Guide to the New British Drama

John Russell Taylor

The first explosive performance in May 1956 of John Osborne's bombshell, *Look Back in Anger*, shook the audience, delighted the critics, and let a lot of badly needed fresh air into the post-war British theatre. In this well-informed survey John Russell Taylor takes a calm look at what has been going on on the stage and television screen since that shattering first night.

Avoiding both woolly theorizing about the 'new wave' and neat categorizing of writers and plays, he distinguishes four streams of new drama: Osborne's various successors at the Royal Court; Joan Littlewood's achievement in Theatre Workshop; provincial playwrights such as Arnold Wesker, whose work first appeared at the Belgrade Theatre, Coventry; and the amazing success of television drama, notably A.B.C.'s 'Armchair Theatre'. Detailed analyses of the plays of more than a dozen writers and critical conclusions on them make this a knowledgeable, comprehensive book on an exciting subject.

'Writes clearly and persuasively, furnishing a most intelligent and well-balanced guide to the post-Osborne drama in Britain today' – *Guardian*

'An excellent book, indispensable to anyone genuinely interested in contemporary drama' – *Listener*

For a complete list of books available please write to Penguin Books whose address can be found on the back of the title page